Java™ & XML

Other Java™ Titles from O'Reilly

Creating Effective JavaHelp™

Database Programming with JDBC™ and Java™

Developing Java Beans™

Enterprise JavaBeans™

Java™ 2D Graphics

Java™ & XML

Java™ and XSLT

Java™ Cookbook

Java™ Cryptography

Java™ Distributed Computing

Java™ Enterprise in a Nutshell

The Java™ Enterprise CD Bookshelf

Java™ Examples in a Nutshell

Java™ Foundation Classes in a Nutshell

Java™ I/0

Java™ in a Nutshell

Java™ Internationalization

Java™ Message Service

Java™ Network Programming

Java™ Performance Tuning

Java™ Professional Library

Java™ Security

JavaServer™ Pages

Java™ Servlet Programming

Java™ Swing

Java™ Threads

Jini™ in a Nutshell

Learning Java™

Java™ & XML

Second Edition

Brett McLaughlin

O'REILLY®

Beijing · Cambridge · Farnham · Köln · Paris · Sebastopol · Taipei · Tokyo

Java™ & XML, Second Edition

by Brett McLaughlin

Copyright © 2001, 2000 O'Reilly & Associates, Inc. All rights reserved.
Printed in the United States of America.

Published by O'Reilly & Associates, Inc., 101 Morris Street, Sebastopol, CA 95472.

Editor: Mike Loukides

Production Editor: Colleen Gorman

Cover Designer: Ellie Volckhausen

Printing History:

June 2000:	First Edition.
August 2001:	Second Edition.

ISBN: 0-596-00197-5

Table of Contents

Preface

When I wrote the preface to the first edition of *Java & XML* just over a year ago, I had no idea what I was getting into. I made jokes about XML appearing on hats and t-shirts; yet as I sit writing this, I'm wearing a t-shirt with "XML" emblazoned across it, and yes, I have a hat with XML on it also (in fact, I have two!). So, the promise of XML has been recognized, without any doubt. And that's good.

However, it has meant that more development is occurring every day, and the XML landscape is growing at a pace I never anticipated, even in my wildest dreams. While that's great for XML, it has made looking back at the first edition of this book somewhat depressing; why is everything so out of date? I talked about SAX 2.0, and DOM Level 2 as twinklings in eyes. They are now industry standard. I introduced JDOM, and now it's in JSR (Sun's Java™ Specification Request process). I hadn't even looked at SOAP, UDDI, WSDL, and XML data binding. They take up three chapters in this edition! Things have changed, to say the least.

If you're even remotely suspicious that you may have to work with XML in the next few months, this book can help. And if you've got the first edition lying somewhere on your desk at work right now, I invite you to browse the new one; I think you'll see that this book is still important to you. I've thrown out all the excessive descriptions of basic concepts, condensed the basic XML material into a single chapter, and rewritten nearly every example; I've also added many new examples and chapters. In other words, I tried to make this an in-depth technical book with lots of grit. It will take you beginners a little longer, as I do less handholding, but you'll find the knowledge to be gained much greater.

Organization

This book is structured in a very particular way: the first half of the book, Chapters 1 through 9, focus on grounding you in XML and the core Java APIs for handling XML. For each of the three XML manipulation APIs (SAX, DOM, and JDOM), I'll give you a chapter on the basics, and then a chapter on more advanced concepts. Chapter 10 is a transition chapter, starting to move up the XML "stack" a bit. It covers JAXP, which is an abstraction layer over SAX and DOM. The remainder of the book, Chapters 11 through 15, focus on specific XML topics that continually are brought up at conferences and tutorials I am involved with, and seek to get you neck-deep in using XML in your applications. These topics include new chapters on SOAP, data binding, and an updated look at business-to-business. Finally, there are two appendixes to wrap up the book. The summary of this content is as follows:

Chapter 1, Introduction

> We will look at what all the hype is about, examine the XML alphabet soup, and spend time discussing why XML is so important to the present and future of enterprise development.

Chapter 2, Nuts and Bolts

> This is a crash course in XML basics, from XML 1.0 to DTDs and XML Schema to XSLT to Namespaces. For readers of the first edition, this is the sum total (and then some) of all the various chapters on working with XML.

Chapter 3, SAX

> The Simple API for XML (SAX), our first Java API for handling XML, is introduced and covered in this chapter. The parsing lifecycle is detailed, and the events that can be caught by SAX and used by developers are demonstrated.

Chapter 4, Advanced SAX

> We'll push further with SAX in this chapter, covering less-used but still powerful items in the API. You'll find out how to use XML filters to chain callback behavior, use XML writers to output XML with SAX, and look at some of the less commonly used SAX handlers like `LexicalHandler` and `DeclHandler`.

Chapter 5, DOM

> This chapter moves on through the XML landscape to the next Java and XML API, the DOM (Document Object Model). You'll learn DOM basics, find out what is in the current specification (DOM Level 2), and how to read and write DOM trees.

Chapter 6, Advanced DOM

> Moving on through DOM, you'll learn about the various DOM modules like Traversal, Range, Events, CSS, and HTML. We'll also look at what the new version, DOM Level 3, offers and how to use these new features.

Chapter 7, JDOM

This chapter introduces JDOM, and describes how it is similar to and different from DOM and SAX. It covers reading and writing XML using this API.

Chapter 8, Advanced JDOM

In a closer examination of JDOM, we'll look at practical applications of the API, how JDOM can use factories with your own JDOM subclasses, and JAXP integration. You'll also see XPath in action in tandem with JDOM.

Chapter 9, JAXP

Now a full-fledged API with support for parsing and transformations, JAXP merits its own chapter. Here, we'll look at both the 1.0 and 1.1 versions, and you'll learn how to use this API to its fullest.

Chapter 10, Web Publishing Frameworks

This chapter looks at what a web publishing framework is, why it matters to you, and how to choose a good one. We then cover the Apache Cocoon framework, taking an in-depth look at its feature set and how it can be used to serve highly dynamic content over the Web.

Chapter 11, XML-RPC

In this chapter, we'll cover Remote Procedure Calls (RPC), its relevance in distributed computing as compared to RMI, and how XML makes RPC a viable solution for some problems. We'll then look at using XML-RPC Java libraries and building XML-RPC clients and servers.

Chapter 12, SOAP

In this chapter, we'll look at using configuration data in an XML format, and see why that format is so important to cross-platform applications, particularly as it relates to distributed systems and web services.

Chapter 13, Web Services

Continuing the discussions of SOAP and web services, this chapter details two important technologies, UDDI and WSDL.

Chapter 14, Content Syndication

Continuing in the vein of business-to-business applications, this chapter introduces another way for businesses to interoperate, using content syndication. You'll learn about Rich Site Summary, building information channels, and even a little Perl.

Chapter 15, Data Binding

Moving up the XML "stack," this chapter covers one of the higher-level Java and XML APIs, XML data binding. You'll learn what data binding is, how it can make working with XML a piece of cake, and the current offerings. I'll look at three frameworks: Castor, Zeus, and Sun's early access release of JAXB, the Java Architecture for XML Data Binding.

Chapter 16, Looking Forward
> This chapter points out some of the interesting things coming up over the horizon, and lets you in on some extra knowledge on each. Some of these guesses may be completely off; others may be the next big thing.

Appendix A, API Reference
> This appendix details all the classes, interfaces, and methods available for use in the SAX, DOM, JAXP, and JDOM APIs.

Appendix B, SAX 2.0 Features and Properties
> This appendix details the features and properties available to SAX 2.0 parser implementations.

Who Should Read This Book?

This book is based on the premise that XML is quickly becoming (and to some extent has already become) an essential part of Java programming. The chapters instruct you in the use of XML and Java, and other than in Chapter 1, they do not focus on *if* you should use XML. If you are a Java developer, you should use XML, without question. For this reason, if you are a Java programmer, want to be a Java programmer, manage Java programmers, or are associated with a Java project, this book is for you. If you want to advance, become a better developer, write cleaner code, or have projects succeed on time and under budget; if you need to access legacy data, need to distribute system components, or just want to know what the XML hype is about, this book is for you.

I tried to make as few assumptions about you as possible; I don't believe in setting the entry point for XML so high that it is impossible to get started. However, I also believe that if you spent your money on this book, you want more than the basics. For this reason, I only assumed that you know the Java language and understand some server-side programming concepts (such as Java servlets and Enterprise Java-Beans). If you have never coded Java before or are just getting started with the language, you may want to read *Learning Java* by Pat Niemeyer and Jonathan Knudsen (O'Reilly) before starting this book. I do not assume that you know anything about XML, and start with the basics. However, I do assume that you are willing to work hard and learn quickly; for this reason we move rapidly through the basics so that the bulk of the book can deal with advanced concepts. Material is not repeated unless appropriate, so you may need to reread previous sections or flip back and forth as we use previously covered concepts in later chapters. If you know some Java, want to learn XML, and are prepared to enter some example code into your favorite editor, you should be able to get through this book without any real problem.

Software and Versions

This book covers XML 1.0 and the various XML vocabularies in their latest form as of July of 2001. Because various XML specifications covered are not final, there may be minor inconsistencies between printed publications of this book and the current version of the specification in question.

All the Java code used is based on the Java 1.2 platform. If you're not using Java 1.2 by now, start to work to get there; the collections classes alone are worth it. The Apache Xerces parser, Apache Xalan processor, Apache SOAP library, and Apache FOP libraries were the latest stable versions available as of June of 2000, and the Apache Cocoon web publishing framework used is Version 1.8.2. The XML-RPC Java libraries used are Version 1.0 beta 4. All software used is freely available and can be obtained online from *http://java.sun.com*, *http://xml.apache.org*, and *http://www.xml-rpc.com*.

The source for the examples in this book is contained completely within the book itself. Both source and binary forms of all examples (including extensive Javadoc not necessarily included in the text) are available online from *http://www.oreilly.com/catalog/javaxml2/* and *http://www.newInstance.com*. All of the examples that could run as servlets, or be converted to run as servlets, can be viewed and used online at *http://www.newInstance.com*.

Conventions Used in This Book

The following font conventions are used in this book.

Italic is used for:

- Unix pathnames, filenames, and program names

- Internet addresses, such as domain names and URLs

- New terms where they are defined

Boldface is used for:

- Names of GUI items: window names, buttons, menu choices, etc.

Constant Width is used for:

- Command lines and options that should be typed verbatim

- Names and keywords in Java programs, including method names, variable names, and class names

- XML element names and tags, attribute names, and other XML constructs that appear as they would within an XML document

Comments and Questions

Please address comments and questions concerning this book to the publisher:

> O'Reilly & Associates, Inc.
> 101 Morris Street
> Sebastopol, CA 95472
> (800) 998-9938 (in the U.S. or Canada)
> (707) 829-0515 (international or local)
> (707) 829-0104 (fax)

You can also send us messages electronically. To be put on the mailing list or request a catalog, send email to:

> *info@oreilly.com*

To ask technical questions or comment on the book, send email to:

> *bookquestions@oreilly.com*

We have a web site for the book, where we'll list examples, errata, and any plans for future editions. You can access this page at:

> *http://www.oreilly.com/catalog/javaxml2/*

For more information about this book and others, see the O'Reilly web site:

> *http://www.oreilly.com*

Acknowledgments

Well, here I am writing acknowledgments again. It's no easier to remember everybody this time than it was the first. My editor, Mike Loukides, keeps me up at night stressing out about getting things done, which is exactly what a good editor does! Kyle Hart, marketing superwoman, keeps things going and reminds me that there's light at the end of the tunnel. Tim O'Reilly and Frank Willison are patient, yet pushy, just what good bosses should be. And Bob Eckstein and Marc Loy were there for me for pesky Swing GUI problems. (Besides, Bob's just funny. Face it.) O'Reilly is as good as it gets, all around. I'm honored to be associated with them.

I also want to think the incredible team of reviewers for this book. Many times, these folks turned a chapter around in less than 24 hours, yet still managed to give honest technical feedback. These guys are a large part of why this book stayed technical. Robert Sese, Philip Nelson, and Victor Brilon, you guys are amazing. Of course, I've always got to thank my partner in crime, Jason Hunter, for being annoyingly dedicated to JDOM and other technical issues (take a night off, man!). Finally, my company, Lutris Technologies, is about as good a place as you could hope to work for. They let me work long hours on this book, with never a complaint. In particular, Yancy Lind, Paul Morgan, David Young, and Keith Bigelow are simply the best at what they do. Thanks, guys!

To my parents, Larry and Judy McLaughlin, thanks again. I love you both for putting up with your rather ambitious and driven son (you realize, of course, those characteristics also make for a terribly obnoxious child!). Sarah Jane, my aunt, and my grandparents, Dean and Gladys McLaughlin, don't ever think that because I don't see you often I don't think about you all the time. Granddad, I'm more thankful than you'll ever know that you're getting to see a second edition. I love you all.

To my second set of parents (my wife's folks), Gary and Shirley Greathouse, you're just the best. One day I'll learn to take these writing skills and explain what you both mean to me, but it might take a whole book on its own. I love you both, for your humor and your wisdom. To Quinn and Joni for providing such levity at Sunday lunches. To Lonnie and Laura, can't wait to see Baby J. To Bill and Terri for being friends, and very wise ones at that, and to Bill for being a pastor like no other.

The laughter in my life comes from several hilarious characters, and I just can't pass up mentioning them here: Kendra, Brittany, Lisette, Janay, Rocky, Dustin, Tony, Stephanie, Robbie, Erin, Angela, Mike, Matt, Carlos, and John. I'll see you all Sunday, and can we please stop going to Mazzio's? And to the nonhuman part of my life, my dogs: Seth, Charlie, Jake, Moses, Molly, and Daisy. You haven't lived until the cold tongue of a basset hound wakes you up in the morning.

Finally, to the two people that mean more to me than anyone; my grandfather, Robert Earl Burden, who one day I'll see again. I think about you every day, and my children will hear about you soon. Most of all, to my wife, Leigh. Words just don't cut it. One day all the songs and tears that have come to me because of what you mean to me will come out, and you'll finally understand how much you mean to me.

And to the Lord who got me this far. Even so, come Lord Jesus.

In this chapter:
- *XML Matters*
- *What's Important?*
- *The Essentials*
- *What's Next?*

1

Introduction

Introductory chapters are typically pretty easy to write. In most books, you give an overview of the technology covered, explain a few basics, and try and get the reader interested. However, for this second edition of *Java and XML*, things aren't so easy. In the first edition, there were still a lot of people coming to XML, or skeptics wanting to see if this new type of markup was really as good as the hype. Over a year later, everyone is using XML in hundreds of ways. In a sense, you probably don't need an introduction. But I'll give you an idea of what's going to be covered, why it matters, and what you'll need to get up and running.

XML Matters

First, let me simply say that XML matters. I know that sounds like the beginning of a self-help seminar, but it's worth starting with. There are still many developers, managers, and executives who are afraid of XML. They are afraid of the perception that XML is "cutting-edge," and of XML's high rate of change. (This is a second edition, a year later, right? Has that much changed?) They are afraid of the cost of hiring folks like you and me to work in XML. Most of all, they are afraid of adding yet another piece to their application puzzles.

To try and assuage these fears, let me quickly run down the major reasons that you should start working with XML, today. First, XML is portable. Second, it allows an unprecedented degree of interoperability. And finally, XML matters. . . because it doesn't matter! If that's completely confusing, read on and all will soon make sense.

Portability

XML is portable. If you've been around Java long, or have ever wandered through Moscone Center at JavaOne, you've heard the mantra of Java: "portable code."

1

Compile Java code, drop those *.class* or *.jar* files onto any operating system, and the code runs. All you need is a Java Runtime Environment (JRE) or Java Virtual Machine (JVM), and you're set. This has continually been one of Java's biggest draws, because developers can work on Linux or Windows workstations, develop and test code, and then deploy on Sparcs, E4000s, HP-UX, or anything else you could imagine.

As a result, XML is worth more than a passing look. Because XML is simply text, it can obviously be moved between various platforms. Even more importantly, XML must conform to a specification defined by the World Wide Web Consortium (W3C) at *http://www.w3.org*. This means that XML is a standard. When you send XML, it conforms to this standard; when some other application receives it, the XML still conforms to that standard. The receiving application can count on that. This is essentially what Java provides: any JVM knows what to expect, and as long as code conforms to those expectations, it will run. By using XML, you get portable data. In fact, recently you may have heard the phrase "portable code, portable data" in reference to the combination of Java and XML. It's a good saying, because it turns out (as not all marketing-type slogans do) to be true.

Interoperability

Second, XML allows interoperability above and beyond what we've ever seen in enterprise applications. Some of you probably think this is just another form of portability, but it's more than that. Remember that XML stands for the *Extensible Markup Language*. And it is extensibility that is so important in business interoperating. Consider HTML, the hypertext markup language, for example. HTML is a standard. It's all text. So, in those respects, it's just as portable as XML. In fact, clients using different browsers on different operating systems can all view HTML more or less identically. However, HTML is aimed specifically at presentation. You couldn't use HTML to represent a furniture manifest, or a billing invoice. That's because the standard tightly defines the allowed tags, the format, and everything else in HTML. This allows it to remain focused on presentation, which is both an advantage and a disadvantage.

However, XML says very little about the elements and content of a document. Instead, it focuses on the structure of the document; elements must begin and end, each attribute must have a single value, and so on. The content of the document and the elements and attributes used remain up to you. You can develop your own document formatting, content, and custom specifications for representing your data. And this allows interoperability. The various furniture chains can agree upon a certain set of constraints for XML, and then exchange data in those formats; they get all the advantages of XML (like portability), as well as the ability to apply their business knowledge to the data being exchanged to make it meaningful. A billing system can include a customized format appropriate for invoices, broadcast this format, and export and import invoices from other billing systems. XML's extensibility makes it perfect for cross-application operation.

Even more intriguing is the large number of vertical standards* being developed. Browse the ebXML project at *http://www.ebxml.org* and see what's going on. Here, businesses are working together to develop standards built upon XML that allow global electronic commerce. The telecommunications industry has undertaken similar efforts. Soon, vertical markets across the world will have agreed upon standards for exchanging data, all built on XML.

It Doesn't Matter

When all is said and done, XML matters because it doesn't matter. I said this earlier, and I want to say it again, because it's at the root of why XML is so important. Proprietary solutions for data, formats that are binary and must be decoded in certain ways, and other data solutions all matter in the final analysis. They involve communication with other companies, extensive documentation, coding efforts, and reinvention of tools for transmission. XML is so attractive because you don't need any special expertise and can spend your time doing other things. In Chapter 2, I describe in 25 or so pages most of what you'll ever need to author XML. It doesn't require documentation, because that documentation is already written. You don't need special encoders or decoders; there are APIs and parsers already written that handle all of this for you. And you don't have to incur risk; XML is now a proven technology, with millions of developers working, fixing, and extending it every day.

XML is important because it becomes such a reliable, unimportant part of your application. Write your constraints, encode your data in XML, and forget about it. Then go on to the important things; the complex business logic and presentation that involves weeks and months of thought and hard work. Meanwhile, XML will happily chug along representing your data with nary a whimper or whine (OK, I'm getting a bit dramatic, but you get the idea).

So if you've been afraid of XML, or even skeptical, jump on board now. It might be the most important decision, with the fewest side effects, that you'll ever make. The rest of this book will get you up and running with APIs, transport protocols, and more odds and ends than you can shake a stick at.

---

* A *vertical standard*, or *vertical market*, refers to a standard or market targeting a specific business. Instead of moving horizontally (where common functionality is preferred), the focus is on moving vertically, providing functionality for a specific audience, like shoe manufacturers or guitar makers.

What's Important?

Once you've accepted that XML can help you out, the next question is what *part* of it you need. As I mentioned earlier, there are literally hundreds of applications of XML, and trying to find the right one is not an easy task. I've got to pick out twelve or thirteen key topics from these hundreds, and manage to make them all applicable to you; not an easy task! Fortunately, I've had a year to gather feedback from the first edition of this book, and have been working with XML in production applications for well over two years now. That means that I've at least got an idea of what's interesting and useful. When you boil all the various XML machinery down, you end up with just a few categories.

Low-Level APIs

An API is an application programming interface, and a low-level API is one that lets you deal directly with an XML document's content. In other words, there is little to no preprocessing, and you get raw XML content to work with. It is the most efficient way to deal with XML, and also the most powerful. At the same time, it requires the most knowledge about XML, and generally involves the most work to turn document content into something useful.

The two most common low-level APIs today are SAX, the Simple API for XML, and DOM, the Document Object Model. Additionally, JDOM (which is not an acronym, nor is it an extension of DOM) has gained a lot of momentum lately. All three of these are in some form of standardization (SAX as a de facto, DOM by the W3C, and JDOM by Sun), and are good bets to be long-lasting technologies. All three offer you access to an XML document, in differing forms, and let you do pretty much anything you want with the document. I'll spend quite a bit of time on these APIs, as they are the basis for everything else you'll do in XML. I've also devoted a chapter to JAXP, Sun's Java API for XML Processing, which provides a thin abstraction layer over SAX and DOM.

High-Level APIs

High-level APIs are the next step up the ladder. Instead of offering direct access to a document, they rely on low-level APIs to do that work for them. Additionally, these APIs present the document in a different form, either more user-friendly, or modeled in a certain way, or in some form other than a basic XML document structure. While these APIs are often easier to use and quicker to develop with, you may pay an additional processing cost while your data is converted to a different format. Also, you'll need to spend some time learning the API, most likely in addition to some lower-level APIs.

In this book, the main example of a high-level API is XML data binding. Data binding allows for taking an XML document and providing that document as a Java object. Not a tree-based object, mind you, but a custom Java object. If you had elements named "person" and "firstName", you would get an object with methods like getPerson() and setFirstName(). Obviously, this is a simple way to quickly get going with XML; hardly any in-depth knowledge is required! However, you can't easily change the structure of the document (like making that "person" element become an "employee" element), so data binding is suited for only certain applications. You can find out all about data binding in Chapter 14.

XML-Based Applications

In addition to APIs built specifically for working with a document or its content, there are a number of applications built on XML. These applications use XML directly or indirectly, but are focused on a specific business process, like displaying stylized web content or communicating between applications. These are all examples of XML-based applications that use XML as a part of their core behavior. Some require extensive XML knowledge, some require none; but all belong in discussions about Java and XML. I've picked out the most popular and useful to discuss here.

First, I'll cover web publishing frameworks, which are used to take XML and format them as HTML, WML (Wireless Markup Language), or as binary formats like Adobe's PDF (Portable Document Format). These frameworks are typically used to serve clients complex, highly customized web applications. Next, I'll look at XML-RPC, which provides an XML variant on remote procedure calls. This is the beginning of a complete suite of tools for application communication. Building on XML-RPC, I'll describe SOAP, the Simple Object Access Protocol, and how it expands upon what XML-RPC provides. Then you'll get to see the emerging players in the web services field by examining UDDI (Universal Discovery, Description, and Integration) and WSDL (Web Services Descriptor Language) in a business-to-business chapter. Putting all these tools in your toolbox will make you formidable not only in XML, but in any enterprise application environment.

And finally, in the last chapter I'll gaze into my crystal ball and point out what appears to be gathering strength in the coming months and years, and try and give you a heads-up on what is worth monitoring. This should keep you ahead of the curve, which is where any good developer should be.

The Essentials

Now you're ready to learn how to use Java and XML to their best. What do you need? I will address that subject, give you some basics, and then let you get after it.

An Operating System and Java

I say this almost tongue in cheek; if you expect to get through this book with no OS (operating system) and no Java installation, you just might be in a bit over your head. Still, it's worth letting you know what I expect. I wrote the first half of this book and the examples for those chapters on a Windows 2000 machine, running both JDK 1.2 and JDK 1.3 (as well as 1.3.1). I did most of my compiling under Cygwin (from Cygnus), so I usually operate in a Unix-esque environment. The last half of the book was written on my (at the time) brand new Macintosh G4 running OS X. That system comes with JDK 1.3, and is a beauty, for those of you who are curious.

In any case, all the examples should work unchanged with Java 1.2 or above; I used no features of JDK 1.3. However, I did not write this code to compile under Java 1.1, as I felt using the Java 2 Collections classes was important. Additionally, if you're working with XML, you need to take a long hard look at updating your JDK if you're still on 1.1 (I know some of you have no choice). If you are stuck on a 1.1 JVM, you should be able to get the collections from Sun (*http://java.sun.com*), make some small modifications, and be up and running.

A Parser

You will need an XML parser. One of the most important layers to any XML-aware application is the XML parser. This component handles the important task of taking a raw XML document as input and making sense of the document; it will ensure that the document is well-formed, and if a DTD or schema is referenced, it may be able to ensure that the document is valid. What results from an XML document being parsed is typically a data structure that can be manipulated and handled by other XML tools or Java APIs. I'm going to leave the detailed discussions of these APIs for later chapters. For now, just be aware that the parser is one of the core building blocks to using XML data.

Selecting an XML parser is not an easy task. There are no hard and fast rules, but two main criteria are typically used. The first is the speed of the parser. As XML documents are used more often and their complexity grows, the speed of an XML parser becomes extremely important to the overall performance of an application. The second factor is conformity to the XML specification. Because performance is often more of a priority than some of the obscure features in XML, some parsers may not conform to finer points of the XML specification in order to squeeze out additional speed. You must decide on the proper balance between these factors based on your application's needs. In addition, most XML parsers are validating, which means they offer the option to validate your XML with a DTD or XML Schema, but some are not. Make sure you use a validating parser if that capability is needed in your applications.

Here's a list of the most commonly used XML parsers. The list does not show whether a parser validates or not, as there are current efforts to add validation to several of the parsers that do not yet offer it. No overall ranking is suggested here, but there is a wealth of information on the web pages for each parser:

- Apache Xerces: *http://xml.apache.org*

- IBM XML4J: *http://alphaworks.ibm.com/tech/xml4j*

- James Clark's XP: *http://www.jclark.com/xml/xp*

- Oracle XML Parser: *http://technet.oracle.com/tech/xml*

- Sun Microsystems Crimson: *http://xml.apache.org/crimson*

- Tim Bray's Lark and Larval: *http://www.textuality.com/Lark*

- The Mind Electric's Electric XML: *http://www.themindelectric.com/products/xml/xml.html*

- Microsoft's MXSML Parser: *http://msdn.microsoft.com/xml/default.asp*

WARNING   I've included Microsoft's MSXML parser in this list in deference to their efforts to address numerous compliance issues in their latest versions. However, their parser still tends to be "doing its own thing" and is not guaranteed to work with the examples in this book because of that. Use it if you need to, but be willing to do a little extra work if you make this decision.

Throughout this book, I tend to use Apache Xerces because it is open source. This is a huge plus to me, so I'd recommend you try out Xerces if you don't already have a parser selected.

APIs

Once you've gotten the parser part of the equation taken care of, you'll need the various APIs I'll be talking about (low-level and high-level). Some of these will be included with your parser download, while others need to be downloaded manually. I'll expect you to either have these on hand, or be able to get them from an Internet web site, so ensure you've got web access before getting too far into any of the chapters.

First, the low-level APIs: SAX, DOM, JDOM, and JAXP. SAX and DOM should be included with any parser you download, as those APIs are interface-based and will be implemented within the parser. You'll also get JAXP with most of these, although you may end up with an older version; hopefully by the time this book is out, most parsers will have full JAXP 1.1 (the latest production version) support.

JDOM is currently bundled as a separate download, and you can get it from the web site at *http://www.jdom.org.*

As for the high-level APIs, I cover a couple of alternatives in the data binding chapter. I'll look briefly at Castor and Quick, available online at *http://castor.exolab.org* and *http://sourceforge.net/projects/jxquick,* respectively. I'll also take some time to look at Zeus, available at *http://zeus.enhydra.org.* All of these packages contain any needed dependencies within the downloaded bundles.

Application Software

Last in this list is the myriad of specific technologies I'll talk about in the chapters. These technologies include things like SOAP toolkits, WSDL validators, the Cocoon web publishing framework, and so on. Rather than try and cover each of these here, I'll address the more specific applications in appropriate chapters, including where to get the packages, what versions are needed, installation issues, and anything else you'll need to get up and running. I can spare you all the ugly details here, and only bore those of you who choose to be bored (just kidding! I'll try to stay entertaining). In any case, you can follow along and learn everything you need to know.

In some cases, I do build on examples in previous chapters. For example, if you start reading Chapter 6 before going through Chapter 5, you'll probably get a bit lost. If this occurs, just back up a chapter and you'll see where the confusing code originated. As I already mentioned, you can skim Chapter 2 on XML basics, but I'd recommend you go through the rest of the book in order, as I try to logically build up concepts and knowledge.

What's Next?

Now you're probably ready to get on with it. In the next chapter, I'm going to give you a crash course in XML. If you're new to XML, or are shaky on the basics, this chapter will fill in the gaps. If you're an old hand to XML, I'd recommend you skim the chapter, and move on to the code in Chapter 3. In either case, get ready to dive into Java and XML; things get exciting from here on in.

In this chapter:
• *The Basics*
• *Constraints*
• *Transformations*
• *And More...*
• *What's Next?*

2

Nuts and Bolts

With the introductions behind us, let's get to it. Before heading straight into Java, though, some basic structures must be laid down. These address a fundamental understanding of the concepts in XML and how the extensible markup language works. In other words, you need an XML primer. If you are already an XML expert, skim through this chapter to make sure you're comfortable with the topics addressed. If you're completely new to XML, on the other hand, this chapter can get you ready for the rest of the book without hours, days, or weeks of study.

Where Did All the Chapters Go?

Readers of the first edition of *Java & XML* may be a little confused. In that edition, there were (count 'em!) three full chapters just on XML itself. When I worked on the first edition over a year ago, I was faced with writing a book that was part XML, part Java, and couldn't completely address either. There was no other reliable resource to direct you to for additional help. Today, books like *Learning XML* by Erik Ray (O'Reilly) and *XML in a Nutshell* by Elliotte Rusty Harold and W. Scott Means (O'Reilly) have rectified that problem. It's now enough to give you a whirlwind tour of XML in this chapter, and let you refer to one of those excellent books for more detail on "pure" XML. As a result, I was able to condense several chapters into this one, paving the way for new chapters on Java, which I'm sure is what you want! Be prepared for some radical departures from the first edition; now at least you know why.

You can use this chapter as a glossary while you read the rest of the book. I won't spend time in future chapters explaining XML concepts, in order to deal strictly with Java and get to some more advanced concepts. So if you hit something that completely befuddles you, check this chapter for information. And if you are still a little lost, I highly recommended that this book be read with a copy of Elliotte Harold and Scott Means' excellent book *XML in a Nutshell* (O'Reilly) open. That will give you all the information you need on XML concepts, and then I can focus on Java ones.

Finally, I'm big on examples. I'm going to load the rest of the chapters as full of them as possible. I'd rather give you too much information than barely engage you. To get started along those lines, I'll introduce several XML and related documents in this chapter to illustrate the concepts in this primer. You might want to take the time to either type these into your editor or download them from the book's web site (*http://www.newInstance.com*), as they will be used in this chapter and throughout the rest of the book. It will save you time later on.

The Basics

It all begins with the XML 1.0 Recommendation, which you can read in its entirety at *http://www.w3.org/TR/REC-xml*. Example 2-1 shows a simple XML document that conforms to this specification. It's a portion of the XML table of contents for this book (I've only included part of it because it's long!). The complete file is included with the samples for the book, available online at *http://www.oreilly.com/catalog/javaxml2* and *http://www.newInstance.com*. I'll use it to illustrate several important concepts.

Example 2-1. The contents.xml document

```
<?xml version="1.0"?>
<!DOCTYPE book SYSTEM "DTD/JavaXML.dtd">

<!-- Java and XML Contents -->
<book xmlns="http://www.oreilly.com/javaxml2"
      xmlns:ora="http://www.oreilly.com"
>
  <title ora:series="Java">Java and XML</title>

  <!-- Chapter List -->
  <contents>
    <chapter title="Introduction" number="1">
      <topic name="XML Matters" />
      <topic name="What's Important" />
      <topic name="The Essentials" />
      <topic name="What&apos;s Next?" />
    </chapter>
    <chapter title="Nuts and Bolts" number="2">
      <topic name="The Basics" />
      <topic name="Constraints" />
```

Example 2-1. The contents.xml document (continued)

```
      <topic name="Transformations" />
      <topic name="And More..." />
      <topic name="What&apos;s Next?" />
    </chapter>
    <chapter title="SAX" number="3">
      <topic name="Getting Prepared" />
      <topic name="SAX Readers" />
      <topic name="Content Handlers" />
      <topic name="Gotcha!" />
      <topic name="What&apos;s Next?" />
    </chapter>
    <chapter title="Advanced SAX" number="4">
      <topic name="Properties and Features" />
      <topic name="More Handlers" />
      <topic name="Filters and Writers" />
      <topic name="Even More Handlers" />
      <topic name="Gotcha!" />
      <topic name="What&apos;s Next?" />
    </chapter>
    <chapter title="DOM" number="5">
      <topic name="The Document Object Model" />
      <topic name="Serialization" />
      <topic name="Mutability" />
      <topic name="Gotcha!" />
      <topic name="What&apos;s Next?" />
    </chapter>

    <!-- And so on... -->

  </contents>

  <ora:copyright>&OReillyCopyright;</ora:copyright>
</book>
```

XML 1.0

A lot of this specification describes what is mostly intuitive. If you've done any HTML authoring, or SGML, you're already familiar with the concept of elements (such as contents and chapter in the example) and attributes (such as title and name). In XML, there's little more than definition of how to use these items, and how a document must be structured. XML spends more time defining tricky issues like whitespace than introducing any concepts that you're not at least somewhat familiar with.

An XML document can be broken into two basic pieces: the header, which gives an XML parser and XML applications information about how to handle the document;

and the content, which is the XML data itself. Although this is a fairly loose division, it helps us differentiate the instructions to applications within an XML document from the XML content itself, and is an important distinction to understand. The header is simply the XML declaration, in this format:

```
<?xml version="1.0"?>
```

The header can also include an encoding, and whether the document is a standalone document or requires other documents to be referenced for a complete understanding of its meaning:

```
<?xml version="1.0" encoding="UTF8" standalone="no"?>
```

The rest of the header is made up of items like the DOCTYPE declaration:

```
<!DOCTYPE Book SYSTEM "DTD/JavaXML.dtd">
```

In this case, I've referred to a file on my local system, in the directory *DTD/* called *JavaXML.dtd*. Any time you use a relative or absolute file path or a URL, you want to use the SYSTEM keyword. The other option is using the PUBLIC keyword, and following it with a public identifier. This means that the W3C or another consortium has defined a standard DTD that is associated with that public identifier. As an example, take the DTD statement for XHTML 1.0:

```
<!DOCTYPE html PUBLIC "-//W3C//DTD XHTML 1.0 Transitional//EN"
  "http://www.w3.org/TR/xhtml1/DTD/xhtml1-transitional.dtd">
```

Here, a public identifier is supplied (the funny little string starting with "-//"), followed by a system identifier (the URL). If the public identifier cannot be resolved, the system identifier is used instead.

You may also see processing instructions at the top of a file, and they are generally considered part of a document's header, rather than its content. They look like this:

```
<?xml-stylesheet href="XSL\JavaXML.html.xsl" type="text/xsl"?>
<?xml-stylesheet href="XSL\JavaXML.wml.xsl" type="text/xsl"
                 media="wap"?>
<?cocoon-process type="xslt"?>
```

Each is considered to have a *target* (the first word, like xml-stylesheet or cocoon-process), and *data* (the rest). More often than not, the data is in the form of name-value pairs, which can really help readability. This is only a good practice, though, and not required, so don't depend on it.

Other than that, the bulk of your XML document should be content; in other words, elements, attributes, and data that you have put into it.

The root element

The root element is the highest-level element in the XML document, and must be the first opening tag and the last closing tag within the document. It provides a reference point that enables an XML parser or XML-aware application to recognize a beginning and end to an XML document. In our example, the root element is book:

```
<book xmlns="http://www.oreilly.com/javaxml2"
      xmlns:ora="http://www.oreilly.com"
>
      <!-- Document content -->
</book>
```

This tag and its matching closing tag surround all other data content within the XML document. XML specifies that there may be only one root element in a document. In other words, the root element must enclose all other elements within the document. Aside from this requirement, a root element does not differ from any other XML element. It's important to understand this, because XML documents can reference and include other XML documents. In these cases, the root element of the referenced document becomes an enclosed element in the referring document, and must be handled normally by an XML parser. Defining root elements as standard XML elements without special properties or behavior allows document inclusion to work seamlessly.

Elements

So far I have glossed over defining an actual element. Let's take an in-depth look at elements, which are represented by arbitrary names and must be enclosed in angle brackets. There are several different variations of elements in the sample document, as shown here:

```
<!-- Standard element opening tag -->
<contents>

 <!-- Standard element with attribute -->
 <chapter title="Nuts and Bolts" number="2">

 <!-- Element with textual data -->
 <title ora:series="Java">Java and XML</title>

 <!-- Empty element -->
 <sectionBreak />

 <!-- Standard element closing tag -->
 </contents>
```

The first rule in creating elements is that their names must start with a letter or underscore, and then may contain any amount of letters, numbers, underscores, hyphens, or periods. They may not contain embedded spaces:

```
<!-- Embedded spaces are not allowed -->
<my element name>
```

XML element names are also case-sensitive. Generally, using the same rules that govern Java variable naming will result in sound XML element naming. Using an element named tcbo to represent *Telecommunications Business Object* is not a good idea because it is cryptic, while an overly verbose tag name like beginningOfNewChapter just clutters up a document. Keep in mind that your XML documents will probably be seen by other developers and content authors, so clear documentation through good naming is essential.

Every opened element must in turn be closed. There are no exceptions to this rule as there are in many other markup languages, like HTML. An ending element tag consists of the forward slash and then the element name: </content>. Between an opening and closing tag, there can be any number of additional elements or textual data. However, you cannot mix the order of nested tags: the first opened element must always be the last closed element. If any of the rules for XML syntax are not followed in an XML document, the document is not *well-formed*. A well-formed document is one in which all XML syntax rules are followed, and all elements and attributes are correctly positioned. However, a well-formed document is not necessarily *valid*, which means that it follows the constraints set upon a document by its DTD or schema. There is a significant difference between a well-formed document and a valid one; the rules I discuss in this section ensure that your document is well-formed, while the rules discussed in the constraints section allow your document to be valid.

As an example of a document that is not well-formed, consider this XML fragment:

```
<tag1>
 <tag2>
</tag1>
 </tag2>
```

The order of nesting of tags is incorrect, as the opened <tag2> is not followed by a closing </tag2> within the surrounding tag1 element. However, if these syntax errors are corrected, there is still no guarantee that the document will be valid.

While this example of a document that is not well-formed may seem trivial, remember that this would be acceptable HTML, and commonly occurs in large tables within an HTML document. In other words, HTML and many other markup languages do not require well-formed XML documents. XML's strict adherence to ordering and nesting rules allows data to be parsed and handled much more quickly than when using markup languages without these constraints.

The last rule I'll look at is the case of empty elements. I already said that XML tags must always be paired; an opening tag and a closing tag constitute a complete XML element. There are cases where an element is used purely by itself, like a flag stating a chapter is incomplete, or where an element has attributes but no textual data, like an image declaration in HTML. These would have to be represented as:

```
<chapterIncomplete></chapterIncomplete>
<img src="/images/xml.gif"></img>
```

This is obviously a bit silly, and adds clutter to what can often be very large XML documents. The XML specification provides a means to signify both an opening and closing element tag within one element:

```
<chapterIncomplete />
<img src="/images/xml.gif" />
```

What's with the Space Before Your End-Slash, Brett?

Well, let me tell you. I've had the unfortunate pleasure of working with Java and XML since late 1998, when things were rough, at best. And some web browsers at that time (and some today, to be honest) would only accept XHTML (HTML that is well-formed) in very specific formats. Most notably, tags like <br> that are never closed in HTML must be closed in XHTML, resulting in <br/>. Some of these browsers would completely ignore a tag like this; however, oddly enough, they would happily process
 (note the space before the end-slash). I got used to making my XML not only well-formed, but consumable by these browsers. I've never had a good reason to change these habits, so you get to see them in action here.

This nicely solves the problem of unnecessary clutter, and still follows the rule that every XML element must have a matching end tag; it simply consolidates both start and end tag into a single tag.

Attributes

In addition to text contained within an element's tags, an element can also have attributes. Attributes are included with their respective values within the element's opening declaration (which can also be its closing declaration!). For example, in the chapter tag, the title of the chapter was part of what was noted in an attribute:

```
<chapter title="Advanced SAX" number="4">
  <topic name="Properties and Features" />
```

```
    <topic name="More Handlers" />
    <topic name="Filters and Writers" />
    <topic name="Even More Handlers" />
    <topic name="Gotcha!" />
    <topic name="What&apos;s Next?" />
</chapter>
```

In this example, `title` is the attribute name; the value is the title of the chapter, "Advanced SAX." Attribute names must follow the same rules as XML element names, and attribute values must be within quotation marks. Although both single and double quotes are allowed, double quotes are a widely used standard and result in XML documents that model Java programming practices. Additionally, single and double quotation marks may be used in attribute values; surrounding the value in double quotes allows single quotes to be used as part of the value, and surrounding the value in single quotes allows double quotes to be used as part of the value. This is not good practice, though, as XML parsers and processors often uniformly convert the quotes around an attribute's value to all double (or all single) quotes, possibly introducing unexpected results.

In addition to learning how to use attributes, there is an issue of when to use attributes. Because XML allows such a variety of data formatting, it is rare that an attribute cannot be represented by an element, or that an element could not easily be converted to an attribute. Although there's no specification or widely accepted standard for determining when to use an attribute and when to use an element, there is a good rule of thumb: use elements for multiple-valued data and attributes for single-valued data. If data can have multiple values, or is very lengthy, the data most likely belongs in an element. It can then be treated primarily as textual data, and is easily searchable and usable. Examples are the description of a book's chapters, or URLs detailing related links from a site. However, if the data is primarily represented as a single value, it is best represented by an attribute. A good candidate for an attribute is the section of a chapter; while the section item itself might be an element and have its own title, the grouping of chapters within a section could be easily represented by a `section` attribute within the `chapter` element. This attribute would allow easy grouping and indexing of chapters, but would never be directly displayed to the user. Another good example of a piece of data that could be represented in XML as an attribute is if a particular table or chair is on layaway. This instruction could let an XML application used to generate a brochure or flier know not to include items on layaway in current stock; obviously this is a true or false value, and has only a singular value at any time. Again, the application client would never directly see this information, but the data would be used in processing and handling the XML document. If after all of this analysis you are still unsure, you can always play it safe and use an element.

You may have already come up with alternate ways to represent these various examples, using different approaches. For example, rather than using a `title` attribute, it might make sense to nest `title` elements within a `chapter` element. Perhaps an empty tag, `<layaway />`, might be more useful to mark furniture on layaway. In XML, there is rarely only one way to perform data representation, and often several good ways to accomplish the same task. Most often the application and use of the data dictates what makes the most sense. Rather than tell you how to write XML, which would be difficult, I show you how to use XML so you gain insight into how different data formats can be handled and used. This gives you the knowledge to make your own decisions about formatting XML documents.

Entity references and constants

One item I have not discussed is escaping characters, or referring to other constant type data values. For example, a common way to represent a path to an installation directory is `<path-to-Cocoon>`. Here, the user would replace the text with the appropriate choice of installation directory. In this example, the chapter that discusses web applications must give some details on installing and using Apache Cocoon, and might need to represent this data within an element:

```
<topic>
 <heading>Installing Cocoon</heading>
 <content>
  Locate the Cocoon.properties file in the <path-to-Cocoon>/bin
  directory.
 </content>
</topic>
```

The problem is that XML parsers attempt to handle this data as an XML tag, and then generate an error because there is no closing tag. This is a common problem, as any use of angle brackets results in this behavior. *Entity references* provide a way to overcome this problem. An entity reference is a special data type in XML used to refer to another piece of data. The entity reference consists of a unique name, preceded by an ampersand and followed by a semicolon: `&[entity name];`. When an XML parser sees an entity reference, the specified substitution value is inserted and no processing of that value occurs. XML defines five entities to address the problem discussed in the example: `&lt;` for the less-than bracket, `&gt;` for the greater-than bracket, `&amp;` for the ampersand sign itself, `&quot;` for a double quotation mark, and `&apos;` for a single quotation mark or apostrophe. Using these special references, you can accurately represent the installation directory reference as:

```
<topic>
 <heading>Installing Cocoon</heading>
 <content>
```

```
    Locate the Cocoon.properties file in the
    &lt;path-to-Cocoon&gt;/bin directory.
  </content>
</topic>
```

Once this document is parsed, the data is interpreted as "<path-to-Cocoon>" and the document is still considered well-formed.

Also be aware that entity references are user-definable. This allows a sort of short-cut markup; in the XML example I have been walking through, I reference an external shared copyright text. Because the copyright is used for multiple O'Reilly books, I don't want to include the text within this XML document; however, if the copyright is changed, the XML document should reflect the changes. You may notice that the syntax used in the XML document looks like the predefined XML entity references:

```
<ora:copyright>&OReillyCopyright;</ora:copyright>
```

Although you won't see how the XML parser is told what to reference when it sees &OReillyCopyright; until the section on DTDs, you should see that there are more uses for entity references than just representing difficult or unusual characters within data.

Unparsed data

The last XML construct to look at is the CDATA section marker. A CDATA section is used when a significant amount of data should be passed on to the calling application without any XML parsing. It is used when an unusually large number of characters would have to be escaped using entity references, or when spacing must be preserved. In an XML document, a CDATA section looks like this:

```
<unparsed-data>
  <![CDATA[Diagram:
      <Step 1>Install Cocoon to "/usr/lib/cocoon"
      <Step 2>Locate the correct properties file.
      <Step 3>Download Ant from "http://jakarta.apache.org"
                            -----> Use CVS for this <----
  ]]>
</unparsed-data>
```

In this example, the information within the CDATA section does not have to use entity references or other mechanisms to alert the parser that reserved characters are being used; instead, the XML parser passes them unchanged to the wrapping program or application.

At this point, you have seen the major components of XML documents. Although each has only been briefly described, this should give you enough information to recognize XML tags when you see them and know their general purpose. With

existing resources like O'Reilly's *XML in a Nutshell* by your side, you are ready to
look at some of the more advanced XML specifications.

Namespaces

Although I will not delve too deeply into XML namespaces here, note the use of a
namespace in the root element of Example 2-1. An *XML namespace* is a means of
associating one or more elements in an XML document with a particular URI.
This effectively means that the element is identified by both its name and its
namespace URI. In this XML example, it may be necessary later to include portions of other O'Reilly books. Because each of these books may also have Chapter,
Heading, or Topic elements, the document must be designed and constructed in
a way to avoid namespace collision problems with other documents. The XML
namespaces specification nicely solves this problem. Because the XML document
represents a specific book, and no other XML document should represent the
same book, using a namespace associated with a URI like *http://www.oreilly.com/
javaxml2* can create a unique namespace. The namespace specification requires
that a unique URI be associated with a prefix to distinguish the elements in the
namespace from elements in other namespaces. A URL is recommended, and supplied here:

```
<book xmlns="http://www.oreilly.com/javaxml2"
      xmlns:ora="http://www.oreilly.com"
>
```

In fact, I've defined two namespaces. The first is considered the default
namespace, because no prefix is supplied. Any element without a prefix is associated with this namespace. As a result, all of the elements in the XML document
except the copyright element, prefixed with ora, are in this default namespace.
The second defines a prefix, which allows the tag <ora:copyright> to be associated with this second namespace.

A final interesting (and somewhat confusing) point: XML Schema, which I will
talk about more in a later section, requires the schema of an XML document to be
specified in a manner that looks very similar to a set of namespace declarations;
see Example 2-2.

Example 2-2. Referencing an XML Schema

```
<?xml version="1.0"?>
<addressBook xmlns:xsi="http://www.w3.org/1999/XMLSchema/instance"
             xmlns="http://www.oreilly.com/catalog/javaxml"
             xsi:schemaLocation="http://www.oreilly.com/catalog/javaxml
                          mySchema.xsd"
>
```

Example 2-2. Referencing an XML Schema (continued)

```
  <person>
    <name>
      <firstName>Brett</firstName>
      <lastName>McLaughlin</lastName>
    </name>
    <email>brettmclaughlin@earthlink.net</email>
  </person>
  <person>
    <name>
      <firstName>Eddie</firstName>
      <lastName>Balucci</lastName>
    </name>
    <email>eddieb@freeworld.net</email>
  </person>
</addressBook>
```

Several things happen here, and it is important to understand them all. First, the XML Schema instance namespace is defined and associated with a URL. This namespace, abbreviated `xsi`, is used for specifying information in XML documents about a schema, exactly as is being done here. Thus, the first line makes the elements in the XML Schema instance available to the document for use. The next line defines the namespace for the XML document itself. Because the document does not use an explicit namespace, like the one associated with *http://www.oreilly.com/javaxml2* in earlier examples, the default namespace is declared. This means that all elements without an explicit namespace and associated prefix (all of them, in this example) will be associated with this default namespace.

With both the document and XML Schema instance namespaces defined like this, we can then actually do what we want, which is to associate a schema with this document. The `schemaLocation` attribute, which belongs to the XML Schema instance namespace, is used to accomplish this. I've prefaced this attribute with its namespace (`xsi`), which was just defined. The argument to this attribute is actually *two* URIs: the first specifies the namespace associated with a schema, and the second the URI of the schema to refer to. In the example, this results in the first URI being the default namespace just declared, and the second a file on the local filesystem called *mySchema.xsd*. Like any other XML attribute, the entire pair is enclosed in a single set of quotation marks. And as simple as that, you have referenced a schema in your XML document!

Seriously, it's not simple, and is to date one of the most misunderstood portions of using namespaces and XML Schema. I look more at the mechanics used here as we continue. For now, keep in mind how namespaces allow elements from various groupings to be used, yet remain identified as a part of them specific grouping.

Constraints

Next up to bat is dealing with constraining XML. If there's nothing you get out of this chapter other than the rationale behind constraining XML, then I'm a happy author. Because XML is extensible and can represent data in hundreds and even thousands of ways, constraints on a document provide meaning to those various formats. Without document constraints, it is impossible (in most cases) to tell what the data in a document means. In this section, I'm going to cover the two current standard means of constraining XML: DTDs (included in the XML 1.0 specification) and XML Schema (recently a standard put out by the W3C). Choose the one best suited for you.

DTDs

An XML document is not very usable without an accompanying DTD (or schema). Just as XML can effectively describe data, the DTD makes this data usable for many different programs in a variety of ways by defining the structure of the data. In this section, I show you the most common constructs used within a DTD. I use the XML representation of a portion of the table of contents for this book as an example again, and go through the process of constructing a DTD for the XML table of contents document.

The DTD defines how data is formatted. It must define each allowed element in an XML document, the allowed attributes and possibly the acceptable attribute values for each element, the nesting and occurrences of each element, and any external entities. DTDs can specify many other things about an XML document, but these basics are what we will focus on. You will learn the constructs that a DTD offers by applying them to and constraining the XML file from Example 2-1. The complete DTD is shown in Example 2-3, which I'll refer to in this section.

Example 2-3. DTD for Example 2-1

```
<!ELEMENT book (title, contents, ora:copyright)>
<!ATTLIST book
          xmlns       CDATA   #REQUIRED
          xmlns:ora   CDATA   #REQUIRED
>
<!ELEMENT title (#PCDATA)>
<!ATTLIST title
          ora:series  (C | Java | Linux | Oracle |
                       Perl | Web | Windows)
                       #REQUIRED
>
<!ELEMENT contents (chapter+)>
<!ELEMENT chapter (topic+)>
```

Example 2-3. DTD for Example 2-1 (continued)

```
<!ATTLIST chapter
          title       CDATA   #REQUIRED
          number      CDATA   #REQUIRED
>
<!ELEMENT topic EMPTY>
<!ATTLIST topic
          name        CDATA   #REQUIRED
>

<!-- Copyright Information -->
<!ELEMENT ora:copyright (copyright)>
<!ELEMENT copyright (year, content)>
<!ATTLIST copyright
          xmlns CDATA  #REQUIRED
>
<!ELEMENT year EMPTY>
<!ATTLIST year
          value  CDATA  #REQUIRED
>
<!ELEMENT content (#PCDATA)>
<!ENTITY OReillyCopyright SYSTEM
    "http://www.newInstance.com/javaxml2/copyright.xml"
>
```

Elements

The bulk of the DTD is composed of ELEMENT definitions (covered in this section) and ATTRIBUTE definitions (covered in the next). An element definition begins with the ELEMENT keyword, following the standard <! opening of a DTD tag, and then the name of the element. Following that name is the *content model* of the element. The content model is generally within parentheses, and specifies what content can be included within the element. Take the book element as an example:

```
<!ELEMENT book (title, contents, ora:copyright)>
```

This says that for any book element, there may be a title element, a contents element, and an ora:copyright element within it. The definitions for these elements are defined later with their content models, and so on. You should be aware that in this standard case, the order specified in the content model is the order that the elements *must* appear within the document. Additionally, each element *must* appear, once and only once, when no modifiers are used (which I'll cover momentarily). In this case, each book element must have a title element, a contents element, and then an ora:copyright element, without exception. If these rules are broken, the document is not considered valid (although it still could be well-formed).

Of course, in many cases you need to specify multiple occurrences of an element, or optional occurrences. You can do this using the recurrence modifiers listed in Table 2-1.

Table 2-1. DTD recurrence modifiers

Operator	Description
[Default]	Must appear once and only once (1)
?	May appear once or not at all (0..1)
+	Must appear at least once, up to an infinite number of times (1..N)
*	May appear any number of times, including not at all (0..N)

As an example, take a look at the `contents` element definition:

```
<!ELEMENT contents (chapter+)>
```

Here, the `contents` element must have at least one `chapter` element within it, but there can be an unlimited number of those chapters.

If an element has character data within it, the `#PCDATA` keyword is used as its content model:

```
<!ELEMENT title (#PCDATA)>
```

If an element should always be an empty element, the `EMPTY` keyword is used:

```
<!ELEMENT topic EMPTY>
```

Attributes

Once you've handled the element definition, you'll want to define attributes. These are defined through the `ATTLIST` keyword. The first value is the name of the element, and then you have various attributes defined. Those definitions involve giving the name of the attribute, the type of attribute, and then whether the attribute is required or implied (which means it is not required, essentially). Most attributes with textual values will simply be of the type `CDATA`, as shown here:

```
<!ATTLIST chapter
          title     CDATA  #REQUIRED
          number    CDATA  #REQUIRED
>
```

You can also specify a set of values that an attribute must take on for the document to be considered valid:

```
<!ATTLIST title
          ora:series  (C | Java | Linux | Oracle |
                       Perl | Web | Windows)
                       #REQUIRED
>
```

Entities

You can specify entity reference resolution in a DTD using the ENTITY keyword. This works a lot like the DOCTYPE reference I talked about earlier, where a public ID and/or system ID may be specified. In the example DTD, I've specified a system ID, a URL, for the OReillyCopyright entity reference to resolve to:

```
<!ENTITY OReillyCopyright SYSTEM
    "http://www.newInstance.com/javaxml2/copyright.xml"
>
```

This results in the *copyright.xml* file at the specified URL being loaded as the value of the O'Reilly copyright entity reference in the sample document. You'll see this in action in the next few chapters.

Now this is hardly an extensive reference on DTDs, but it should give you enough basic knowledge to get going. As I've suggested, have some additional resources specifically on XML available (like *XML in a Nutshell*) as you go through this book in case you run across something you're unsure about. By assuming that you have that or the online specifications from *http://www.w3.org* around, I can delve into Java topics more quickly.

XML Schema

XML Schema is a newly finalized candidate recommendation from the W3C. It seeks to improve upon DTDs by adding more typing and quite a few more constructs than DTDs, as well as following an XML format. I'm going to spend relatively little time here talking about schemas, because they are a "behind-the-scenes" detail for Java and XML. In the chapters where you'll be working with schemas (Chapter 14, for instance), I'll address specific points you need to be aware of. However, the specification for XML Schema is so enormous that it would take up an entire book of explanation on its own. Example 2-4 shows the XML Schema constraining Example 2-1.

Example 2-4. XML Schema constraining Example 2-1

```
<?xml version="1.0" encoding="UTF-8"?>

<xs:schema xmlns:xs="http://www.w3.org/2001/XMLSchema"
           xmlns="http://www.oreilly.com/javaxml2"
           xmlns:ora="http://www.oreilly.com"
           targetNamespace="http://www.oreilly.com/javaxml2"
           elementFormDefault="qualified"
>
  <xs:import namespace="http://www.oreilly.com"
             schemaLocation="contents-ora.xsd" />
```

Example 2-4. XML Schema constraining Example 2-1 (continued)

```
<xs:element name="book">
  <xs:complexType>
    <xs:sequence>
      <xs:element ref="title" />
      <xs:element ref="contents" />
      <xs:element ref="ora:copyright" />
    </xs:sequence>
  </xs:complexType>
</xs:element>

<xs:element name="title">
  <xs:complexType>
    <xs:simpleContent>
      <xs:restriction base="xs:string">
        <xs:attribute ref="ora:series" use="required" />
      </xs:restriction>
    </xs:simpleContent>
  </xs:complexType>
</xs:element>

<xs:element name="contents">
  <xs:complexType>
    <xs:sequence>
      <xs:element name="chapter" maxOccurs="unbounded">
        <xs:complexType>
          <xs:sequence>
            <xs:element name="topic" maxOccurs="unbounded">
              <xs:complexType>
                <xs:attribute name="name"
                              type="xs:string"
                              use="required" />
              </xs:complexType>
            </xs:element>
          </xs:sequence>
          <xs:attribute name="title" type="xs:string" use="required"/>
          <xs:attribute name="number" type="xs:byte" use="required"/>
        </xs:complexType>
      </xs:element>
    </xs:sequence>
  </xs:complexType>
</xs:element>

</xs:schema>
```

In addition, you'll need the schema in Example 2-5, for reasons you will soon understand.

Example 2-5. Additional XML Schema for Example 2-1

```
<?xml version="1.0" encoding="UTF-8"?>

<xs:schema xmlns="http://www.oreilly.com"
           xmlns:xs="http://www.w3.org/2001/XMLSchema"
           targetNamespace="http://www.oreilly.com"
           attributeFormDefault="qualified"
           elementFormDefault="qualified"
>
  <xs:attribute name="series" type="xs:string"/>
  <xs:element name="copyright" type="xs:string" />
</xs:schema>
```

Before diving into the specifics of these schemas, notice that various namespace declarations are made. First, the XML Schema namespace itself is attached to the xs prefix, allowing separation of XML Schema constructs from the elements and attributes being constrained. Next, the default namespace is attached to the namespace of the elements being defined; in Example 2-4 this is the Java and XML namespace, and in Example 2-5 it's the O'Reilly namespace. I've also assigned the targetNamespace attribute this same value. This attribute specifies to the schema the namespace of the elements and attributes being constrained. This is easy to forget, and can wreak a lot of havoc, so be careful to include it. At this point, namespaces are defined for the elements being constrained (the default namespace) and the constructs being used (the XML Schema namespace).

Last, I've specified the value of attributeFormDefault and elementForm-Default as "qualified." This indicates that I'll use fully qualified names for the elements and attributes, rather than just local names. I won't go into detail about this, but I highly recommend you use qualified names at all times. Trying to deal with multiple namespaces and unqualified names at the same time is a mess I wouldn't want to wander into.

Elements and attributes

Elements are defined with the element construct. You'll generally need to define your own data types by nesting a complexType tag within the element element, which defines the name of the element (through the name attribute). Take a look at this fragment of Example 2-4:

```
<xs:element name="book">
  <xs:complexType>
    <xs:sequence>
      <xs:element ref="title" />
      <xs:element ref="contents" />
      <xs:element ref="ora:copyright" />
```

```
      </xs:sequence>
    </xs:complexType>
  </xs:element>
```

Here, I've specified that the book element has complex content. Within it there should be three elements: title, contents, and ora:copyright. By using the sequence construct, I've ensured that they appear in the specified order; and with no modifiers, an element must appear once and only once. For each of these other elements, I've used the ref keyword to reference another element definition. This points to the definitions for each of these elements in another part of the schema, and keeps things organized and easy to follow.

Later in the file, the title element is defined:

```
<xs:element name="title">
  <xs:complexType>
    <xs:simpleContent>
      <xs:restriction base="xs:string">
        <xs:attribute ref="ora:series" use="required" />
      </xs:restriction>
    </xs:simpleContent>
  </xs:complexType>
</xs:element>
```

This element is really just a simple XML Schema string type; however, I've added an attribute to it, so I must define a complexType. Since I'm extending an existing type, I use the simpleContent and restriction keywords (as nested elements) to define this type. simpleContent informs the schema that this is a basic type, and restriction, with the base of "xs:string", lets the schema know I want to allow just what the XML Schema string type allows, plus the additional attribute defined here (with the attribute keyword). For the attribute itself, I reference the type defined elsewhere, and specify that it must appear for this element (through use="required"). I realize that this paragraph is a mouthful, and not completely obvious; however, take your time and you'll get it all.

One other thing you'll notice is the use of minOccurs and maxOccurs attributes on the element element; these attributes allow an element to appear a specified number of times other than the default, which is once and only once. For example, specifying minOccurs="0" and maxOccurs="1" allows an element to appear once, or not at all. To allow an element to appear an unlimited number of times, you can use the value of "unbounded" for the maxOccurs attribute, as in Example 2-4.

Multiple namespaces

You'll notice that I defined *two* schemas, though, which may have you puzzled. For each namespace in a document, one schema must be defined. Additionally, you can't use the same external schema for both namespaces, and simply point both at that external schema. As a result, using the ora prefix and namespace requires an additional schema, which I called `contents-ora.xsd`. You'll also need to use the `schemaLocation` attribute I talked about earlier to reference this schema; however, don't add another attribute. Instead, you can append another namespace and schema-location pair to the end of the value of the attribute, as shown here:

```
<book xmlns="http://www.oreilly.com/javaxml2"
      xmlns:ora="http://www.oreilly.com"
      xmlns:xsi="http://www.w3.org/2001/XMLSchema-instance"
      xsi:schemaLocation="http://www.oreilly.com/javaxml2 XSD/contents.xsd
                          http://www.oreilly.com XSD/contents-ora.xsd"
>
```

This essentially says for the namespace *http://www.oreilly.com/javaxml2*, look up definitions in the schema called *contents.xsd* in the *XSD/* directory. For the *http://www. oreilly.com* namespace, use the *contents-ora.xsd* schema in the same directory. You'll then need to define the two schemas I showed you in Examples 2-4 and 2-5. Finally, import the O'Reilly schema into the Java and XML one, since elements in the Java and XML schema refer to attributes in the O'Reilly one:

```
<xs:import namespace="http://www.oreilly.com"
           schemaLocation="contents-ora.xsd" />
```

This import is fairly self-explanatory, so I won't dwell on it. You should realize that dealing with multiple namespaces is about the most complex thing you can do in schemas, and can easily trip you up. (It tripped me up, until Eric van der Vlist saved the day.) I also recommend a good XML Schema–capable editor. While I'm generally slow to recommend commercial products, in this case XMLSpy 4.0 (*http: //www.xmlspy.com*) turned out to be wonderfully helpful.

I've barely scratched the surface of either DTDs or XML Schema, and there are even other constraint models not covered at all! For example, Relax (and Relax NG, which includes what used to be TREX) is gaining a lot of steam, as it's considered a lot easier and more lightweight than XML Schema. You can check out the activity online at *http://www.oasis-open.org/committees/relax-ng/*. No matter what technology you choose, though, you should be able to find something that helps you constrain your XML documents. With these constraints in place, validation and interoperability become a snap. Consider yourself educated on XML constraints, and get ready to move on to the next topic in this whirlwind tour: XML transformations.

Transformations

As useful as XML transformations can be, they are not simple to implement. In fact, rather than trying to specify the transformation of XML in the original XML 1.0

specification, three separate recommendations have come out to define how transformations should occur. Although one of these (XPath) is also used in several other XML specifications, by far the most common use of the components I outline here is to transform XML from one format into another.

Because these three specifications are tied together tightly and almost always used in concert, there is rarely a clear distinction between them. This can often make for a discussion that is easy to understand, but not necessarily technically correct. In other words, the term XSLT, which refers specifically to extensible stylesheet transformations, is often applied to both extensible stylesheets (XSL) and XPath. In the same fashion, XSL is often used as a grouping term for all three technologies. In this section, I distinguish among the three recommendations, and remain true to the letter of the specifications outlining these technologies. However, in the interest of clarity, I use XSL and XSLT interchangeably to refer to the complete transformation process throughout the rest of the book. Although this may not follow the letter of these specifications, it certainly follows their spirit, as well as avoiding lengthy definitions of simple concepts when you already understand what I mean.

XSL

XSL is the Extensible Stylesheet Language. It is defined as a language for expressing stylesheets. This broad definition is broken down into two parts:

- XSL is a language for transforming XML documents.

- XSL is an XML vocabulary for specifying the formatting of XML documents.

The definitions are similar, but one deals with moving from one XML document form to another, while the other focuses on the actual presentation of content within each document. Perhaps a clearer definition would be to say that XSL handles the specification of how to transform a document from format A to format B. The components of the language handle the processing and identification of the constructs used to do this.

XSL and trees

The most important concept to understand in XSL is that all data within XSL processing stages is in tree structures (see Figure 2-1). In fact, the rules you define using XSL are themselves held in a tree structure. This allows simple processing of the hierarchical structure of XML documents. Templates are used to match the root element of the XML document being processed. Then "leaf" rules are applied to "leaf" elements, filtering down to the most nested elements. At any point in this progression, elements can be processed, styled, ignored, copied, or have a variety of other things done to them.

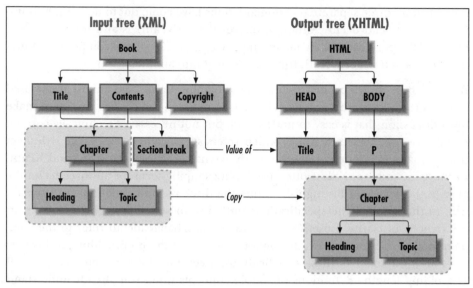

Figure 2-1. Tree operations within XSL

A nice advantage of this tree structure is that it allows the grouping of XML documents to be maintained. If element A contains elements B and C, and element A is moved or copied, the elements contained within it receive the same treatment.

This makes the handling of large data sections that need to receive the same treatment fast and easy to notate concisely in the XSL stylesheet. You will see more about how this tree is constructed when I talk specifically about XSLT in the next section.

Formatting objects

The XSL specification is almost entirely concerned with defining formatting objects. A formatting object is based on a large model, not surprisingly called the formatting model. This model is all about a set of objects that are fed as input into a formatter. The formatter applies the objects to the document, either in whole or in part, and what results is a new document that consists of all or part of the data from the original XML document in a format specific to the objects the formatter used. Because this is such a vague, shadowy concept, the XSL specification attempts to define a concrete model these objects should conform to. In other words, a large set of properties and vocabulary make up the set of features that formatting objects can use. These include the types of areas that may be visualized by the objects, the properties of lines, fonts, graphics, and other visual objects, inline and block formatting objects, and a wealth of other syntactical constructs.

Formatting objects are used heavily when converting textual XML data into binary formats such as PDF files, images, or document formats such as Microsoft Word.

For transforming XML data to another textual format, these objects are seldom used explicitly. Although an underlying part of the stylesheet logic, formatting objects are rarely invoked directly, since the resulting textual data often conforms to another predefined markup language such as HTML. Because most enterprise applications today are based at least in part on web architecture and use a browser as a client, I spend the most time looking at transformations to HTML and XHTML. While formatting objects are covered only lightly, the topic is broad enough to merit its own coverage in a separate book. For further information, consult the XSL specification at *http://www.w3.org/TR/WD-xsl.*

XSLT

The second component of XML transformations is XSL Transformations. XSLT is the language that *specifies* the conversion of a document from one format to another (where XSL defined the means of that specification). The syntax used within XSLT is generally concerned with textual transformations that do not result in binary data output. For example, XSLT is instrumental is generating HTML or WML (Wireless Markup Language) from an XML document. In fact, the XSLT specification outlines the syntax of an XSL stylesheet more explicitly than the XSL specification itself!

Just as in the case of XSL, XSLT is always well-formed, valid XML. A DTD is defined for XSL and XSLT that delineates the allowed constructs. For this reason, you should only have to learn new syntax to use XSLT as opposed to the entirely new structures that had to be digested to use DTDs themselves. Just as in XSL, XSLT is based on a hierarchical tree structure of data, where nested elements are leaves, or children, of their parents. XSLT provides a mechanism for matching patterns within the original XML document (using an XPath expression, which I'll discuss next), and applying formatting to that data. This results in simply outputting the data without the unwanted XML element names, or inserting the data into a complex HTML table and displaying it to the user with highlighting and coloring. XSLT also provides syntax for many common operators, such as conditionals, copying of document tree fragments, advanced pattern matching, and the ability to access elements within the input XML data in an absolute and relative path structure. All these constructs are designed to ease the process of transforming an XML document into a new format. For a thorough treatment of the XSLT language, see *Java and XSLT* by Eric Burke (O'Reilly), which has an excellent discussion of how to put XSLT to work with Java.

XPath

The final piece of the XML transformations puzzle, XPath provides a mechanism for referring to the wide variety of element and attribute names and values in an

XML document. As I mentioned earlier, many XML specifications are now using XPath, but this discussion is concerned only with its use in XSLT. With the complex structure that an XML document can have, locating one specific element or set of elements can be difficult. It is made more difficult because access to a DTD or other set of constraints that outlines the document's structure cannot be assumed; documents that are not validated must be able to be transformed just as valid documents can. To accomplish this addressing of elements, XPath defines syntax in line with the tree structure of XML, and the XSLT processes and constructs that use it.

Referencing any element or attribute within an XML document is most easily accomplished by specifying the path to the element relative to the current element being processed. In other words, if element B is the current element and element C and element D are nested within it, a relative path most easily locates them. This is similar to the relative paths used in operating system directory structures. At the same time, XPath also defines addressing for elements relative to the root of a document. This covers the common case of needing to reference an element not within the current element's scope; in other words, an element that is not nested within the element being processed. Finally, XPath defines syntax for actual pattern matching: find an element whose parent is element E and which has a sibling element F. This fills in the gaps left between the absolute and relative paths. In all these expressions, attributes can be used as well, with similar matching abilities. Several examples are shown in Example 2-6.

Example 2-6. XPath expressions

```
<!-- Match the element named Book relative to the current element -->
<xsl:value-of select="Book" />

<!-- Match the element named Contents nested within the Book element -->
<xsl:value-of select="Book/Contents" />

<!-- Match the Contents element using an absolute path -->
<xsl:value-of select="/Book/Contents" />

<!-- Match the name attribute of the current element -->
<xsl:value-of select="@name" />

<!-- Match the title attribute of the Chapter element -->
<xsl:value-of select="Chapter/@title" />
```

Because the input document is often not fixed, an XPath expression can result in the evaluation of no input data, one input element or attribute, or multiple input elements and attributes. This ability makes XPath very useful and handy; it also causes the introduction of some additional terms. The result of evaluating an

XPath expression is generally referred to as a *node set*. This name shouldn't be surprising, as it is in line with the idea of a hierarchical or tree structure, often dealt with in terms of its *leaves* or *nodes*. The resultant node set can then be transformed, copied, or ignored, or have any other legal operation performed on it. In addition to expressions to select node sets, XPath also defines several node set functions, such as not() and count(). These functions take in a node set as input (typically in the form of an XPath expression) and then further pare the results. All of these expressions and functions are collectively part of the XPath specification and XPath implementations; however, XPath is also often used to signify any expression that conforms to the specification itself. As with XSL and XSLT, this makes it easier to talk about XSL and XPath, though it is not always technically correct.

With all that in mind, you're at least somewhat prepared to take a look at a simple XSL stylesheet, shown in Example 2-7. Although you may not understand all of this now, let's briefly look at some key aspects of the stylesheet.

Example 2-7. XSL stylesheet for Example 2-1

```
<?xml version="1.0"?>

<xsl:stylesheet xmlns:javaxml2="http://www.oreilly.com/javaxml2"
                xmlns:xsl="http://www.w3.org/1999/XSL/Transform"
                xmlns:ora="http://www.oreilly.com"
                version="1.0"
>

  <xsl:template match="javaxml2:book">
    <html>
      <head>
        <title><xsl:value-of select="javaxml2:title" /></title>
      </head>
      <body>
        <xsl:apply-templates select="*[not(self::javaxml2:title)]" />
      </body>
    </html>
  </xsl:template>

  <xsl:template match="javaxml2:contents">
    <center>
     <h2>Table of Contents</h2>
    </center>
    <hr />
    <ul>
     <xsl:for-each select="javaxml2:chapter">
      <b>
       Chapter <xsl:value-of select="@number" />.
```

Example 2-7. XSL stylesheet for Example 2-1 (continued)

```
            <xsl:text> </xsl:text>
            <xsl:value-of select="@title" />
          </b>
          <xsl:for-each select="javaxml2:topic">
           <ul>
            <li><xsl:value-of select="@name" /></li>
           </ul>
          </xsl:for-each>
        </xsl:for-each>
      </ul>
    </xsl:template>

  <xsl:template match="ora:copyright">
    <p align="center"><font size="-1">
     <xsl:copy-of select="*" />
    </font></p>
  </xsl:template>

</xsl:stylesheet>
```

Template matching

The basis of all XSL work is template matching. For any element you want some
sort of output to occur on, you generally provide a template that matches the element. You signify a template with the **template** keyword, and provide the name of
the element to match in its **match** attribute:

```
    <xsl:template match="javaxml2:book">
      <html>
        <head>
          <title><xsl:value-of select="javaxml2:title" /></title>
        </head>
        <body>
          <xsl:apply-templates select="*[not(self::javaxml2:title)]" />
        </body>
      </html>
    </xsl:template>
```

Here, the **book** element (in the **javaxml2**-associated namespace) is being
matched. When an XSL processor encounters the **book** element, the instructions
within this template are carried out. In the example, several HTML formatting
tags are output (the **html**, **head**, **title**, and **body** tags). Be sure to distinguish
your XSL elements from other elements (such as HTML elements) with proper
use of namespaces.

Instead of applying a template, you can use the **value-of** construct to obtain the
value of an element, and provide the element name to match through the **select**

attribute. In the example, the character data within the `title` element is extracted and used as the title of the HTML form to output.

On the other hand, when you want to cause the templates associated with an element's children to be applied, use `apply-templates`. Be sure to do this, or nested elements can be ignored! You can specify the elements to apply templates to using the `select` attribute; by specifying a value of "*" to that attribute, all templates left will be applied to all nested elements. In the example, though, I want to exclude the `title` element (since I already used it in the document heading). To accomplish this, I've used the `not` keyword, and specified the `title` element on the `self` axis, which basically means "everything (*), except (not) the `title` element in this document (`self::javaxml2:title`). That's a quick overview, but I'm just trying to give you enough information to move on to the Java code.

Looping

You'll also often find a need for looping in XSL. Look at this fragment from Example 2-7:

```
<xsl:template match="javaxml2:contents">
  <center>
   <h2>Table of Contents</h2>
  </center>
  <hr />
  <ul>
   <xsl:for-each select="javaxml2:chapter">
    <b>
     Chapter <xsl:value-of select="@number" />.
     <xsl:text> </xsl:text>
     <xsl:value-of select="@title" />
    </b>
    <xsl:for-each select="javaxml2:topic">
     <ul>
      <li><xsl:value-of select="@name" /></li>
     </ul>
    </xsl:for-each>
   </xsl:for-each>
  </ul>
</xsl:template>
```

Here, I'm looping through each element named `chapter` using the `for-each` construct. In Java, this would be:

```
for (Iterator i = chapters.iterator(); i.hasNext(); ) {
    // take action on each chapter
}
```

Within the loop, the "current" element becomes the next `chapter` element encountered. For each, I output the chapter number; this is accomplished by getting the value (through `value-of`) of the number attribute. To indicate that I want an attribute (not the default, an element), I prefix the attribute name with the "@" sign. I do the same thing to get the `title` attribute's value, and then in a subloop I move through the topics for each chapter.

Notice the rather odd code fragment `<xsl:text> <xsl:text>`. The `text` construct provides a way to directly output characters to the result tree. This construct generates a space between the word "Chapter" and the chapter number (there is a single space between the opening and closing `text` tags).

Copying

You will also find times when all the template matching in the world isn't as useful as simply passing on the content, unchanged, to the output tree. This is the case with the copyright element:

```
<xsl:template match="ora:copyright">
  <p align="center"><font size="-1">
   <xsl:copy-of select="*" />
  </font></p>
</xsl:template>
```

In addition to a little bit of HTML formatting, this template instructs all the content of the `copyright` element to be copied to the output tree, using the `copy-of` construct. Simple enough.

You'll learn how to use a publishing framework like Cocoon to render the result of this transformation to HTML, a PDF, or more in Chapter 10. Rather than keeping you waiting, though, Figure 2-2 shows the transformed output from Example 2-1 and the stylesheet in Example 2-6.

I realize that I've virtually flown through this material, but again, I'm just trying to get you past the basics and to the good stuff, the Java and XML. Have a reference handy, and don't sweat it too much.

And More...

Lest I mislead you into thinking that's all that there is to XML, I want to make sure that you realize there are a multitude of other XML-related technologies. I can't possibly get into them all here. You should take a quick glance at things like CSS (Cascading Style Sheets) and XHTML if you are working on web design. Document authors will want to find out more about XLink and XPointer (both of which I cover in Chapter 16). XQL (XML Query Language) will be of interest to

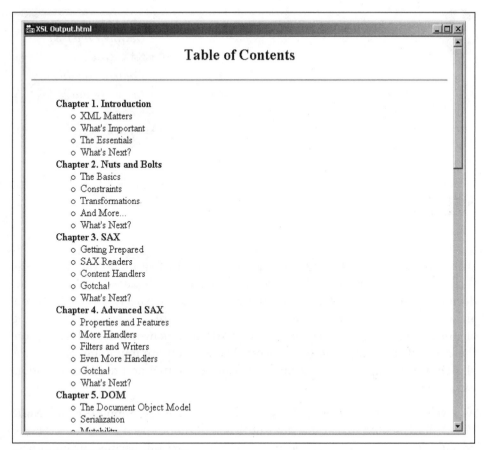

Figure 2-2. Result of XSL transformation

database programmers. In other words, there's something XML for pretty much every technology space right now. Take a look at the W3C XML activity page at *http://www.w3.org/XML* and see what looks interesting.

What's Next?

With some baseline knowledge of XML, you're ready to dive into the Java side of things. In the next chapter, I'll introduce you to SAX, the Simple API for XML. This is ground zero of the Java and XML APIs, and will get you started on seeing how you can use XML in your own Java applications. You'll learn how to read documents, set various options for DTD and schema validation, use namespace processing, and more, and understand when SAX is the right tool for a particular job. Fire up your editor and turn the page.

3

In this chapter:
• *Getting Prepared*
• *SAX Readers*
• *Content Handlers*
• *Error Handlers*
• *Gotcha!*
• *What's Next?*

SAX

When dealing with XML programmatically, one of the first things you have to do is take an XML document and parse it. As the document is parsed, the data in the document becomes available to the application using the parser, and suddenly you are within an XML-aware application! If this sounds a little too simple to be true, it almost is. This chapter describes how an XML document is parsed, focusing on the events that occur within this process. These events are important, as they are all points where application-specific code can be inserted and data manipulation can occur.

As a vehicle for this chapter, I'm going to introduce the Simple API for XML (SAX). SAX is what makes insertion of this application-specific code into events possible. The interfaces provided in the SAX package will become an important part of any programmer's toolkit for handling XML. Even though the SAX classes are small and few in number, they provide a critical framework for Java and XML to operate within. Solid understanding of how they help in accessing XML data is critical to effectively leveraging XML in your Java programs. In later chapters, we'll add to this toolkit other Java and XML APIs like DOM, JDOM, JAXP, and data binding. But, enough fluff; it's time to talk SAX.

Getting Prepared

There are a few items that you must have before beginning to code. They are:

• An XML parser
• The SAX classes
• An XML document

First, you must obtain an XML parser. Writing a parser for XML is a serious task, and there are several efforts going on to provide excellent XML parsers, especially in the open source arena. I am not going to detail the process of actually writing an XML parser here; rather, I will discuss the applications that wrap this parsing behavior, focusing on using existing tools to manipulate XML data. This results in better and faster programs, as neither you nor I spend time trying to reinvent what is already available. After selecting a parser, you must ensure that a copy of the SAX classes is on hand. These are easy to locate, and are key to Java code's ability to process XML. Finally, you need an XML document to parse. Then, on to the code!

Obtaining a Parser

The first step to coding Java that uses XML is locating and obtaining the parser you want to use. I briefly talked about this process in Chapter 1, and listed various XML parsers that could be used. To ensure that your parser works with all the examples in the book, you should verify your parser's compliance with the XML specification. Because of the variety of parsers available and the rapid pace of change within the XML community, all of the details about which parsers have what compliance levels are beyond the scope of this book. Consult the parser's vendor and visit the web sites previously given for this information.

In the spirit of the open source community, all of the examples in this book use the Apache Xerces parser. Freely available in binary and source form at *http://xml. apache.org*, this C- and Java-based parser is already one of the most widely contributed-to parsers available (not that hardcore Java developers like us care about C, though, right?). In addition, using an open source parser such as Xerces allows you to send questions or bug reports to the parser's authors, resulting in a better product, as well as helping you use the software quickly and correctly. To subscribe to the general list and request help on the Xerces parser, send a blank email to *xerces-j-dev-subscribe@xml.apache.org*. The members of this list can help if you have questions or problems with a parser not specifically covered in this book. Of course, the examples in this book all run normally on any parser that uses the SAX implementation covered here.

Once you have selected and downloaded an XML parser, make sure that your Java environment, whether it be an IDE (Integrated Development Environment) or a command line, has the XML parser classes in its classpath. This will be a basic requirement for all further examples.

NOTE   If you don't know how to deal with CLASSPATH issues, you may be in
            a bit over your head. However, assuming you are comfortable with
            your system CLASSPATH, set it to include your parser's *jar* file, as
            shown here:

```
c: set CLASSPATH=.;c:\javaxml2\lib\xerces.jar;%CLASSPATH%

c: echo %CLASSPATH%
.;c:\javaxml2\lib\xerces.jar;c:\java\jdk1.3\lib\tools.jar
```

            Of course, your path will be different from mine, but you get the
            idea.

Getting the SAX Classes and Interfaces

Once you have your parser, you need to locate the SAX classes. These classes are
almost always included with a parser when downloaded, and Xerces is no exception. If this is the case with your parser, you should be sure not to download the
SAX classes explicitly, as your parser is probably packaged with the latest version of
SAX that is supported by the parser. At this time, SAX 2.0 has long been final, so
expect the examples detailed here (which are all using SAX 2) to work as shown,
with no modifications.

If you are not sure whether you have the SAX classes, look at the *jar* file or class
structure used by your parser. The SAX classes are packaged in the org.xml.sax
structure. Ensure, at a minimum, that you see the class org.xml.sax.XMLReader.
This will indicate that you are (almost certainly) using a parser with SAX 2 support, as the XMLReader class is core to SAX 2.

Finally, you may want to either download or bookmark the SAX API Javadocs on
the Web. This documentation is extremely helpful in using the SAX classes, and the
Javadoc structure provides a standard, simple way to find out additional information about the classes and what they do. This documentation is located at *http://
www.megginson.com/SAX.* You may also generate Javadoc from the SAX source if you
wish, by using the source included with your parser, or by downloading the complete source from *http://www.megginson.com/SAX.* Finally, many parsers include documentation with a download, and this documentation may have the SAX API
documentation packaged with it (Xerces being an example of this case).

Have an XML Document on Hand

You should also make sure that you have an XML document to parse. The output
shown in the examples is based on parsing the XML document discussed in

Chapter 2. Save this file as *contents.xml* somewhere on your local hard drive. I highly recommend that you follow what I'm demonstrating by using this document; it contains various XML constructs for demonstration purposes. You can simply type the file in from the book, or you may download the XML file from the book's web site, *http://www.newInstance.com.*

SAX Readers

Without spending any further time on the preliminaries, it's time to code. As a sample to familiarize you with SAX, this chapter details the `SAXTreeViewer` class. This class uses SAX to parse an XML document supplied on the command line, and displays the document visually as a Swing `JTree`. If you don't know anything about Swing, don't worry; I don't focus on that, but just use it for visual purposes. The focus will remain on SAX, and how events within parsing can be used to perform customized action. All that really happens is that a `JTree` is used, which provides a nice simple tree model, to display the XML input document. The key to this tree is the `DefaultMutableTreeNode` class, which you'll get quite used to in using this example, as well as the `DefaultTreeModel` that takes care of the layout.

The first thing you need to do in any SAX-based application is get an instance of a class that conforms to the SAX `org.xml.sax.XMLReader` interface. This interface defines parsing behavior and allows us to set features and properties (which I'll cover later in this chapter). For those of you familiar with SAX 1.0, this interface replaces the `org.xml.sax.Parser` interface.

WARNING   This is a good time to point out that SAX 1.0 is not covered in this book. While there is a very small section at the end of this chapter explaining how to convert SAX 1.0 code to SAX 2.0, you really are not in a good situation if you are using SAX 1.0. While the first edition of this book came out on the heels of SAX 2.0, it's now been well over a year since the API was released in a 2.0 final form. I strongly urge you to move on to Version 2 if you haven't already.

Instantiating a Reader

SAX provides an interface all SAX-compliant XML parsers should implement. This allows SAX to know exactly what methods are available for callback and use within an application. For example, the Xerces main SAX parser class, `org.apache.xerces.parsers.SAXParser`, implements the `org.xml.sax.XMLReader` interface. If you have access to the source of your parser, you should see the same interface implemented in your parser's main SAX parser class. Each XML parser must have one class (and sometimes has more than one) that implements this interface, and that is the class you need to instantiate to allow for parsing XML:

```
// Instantiate a Reader
XMLReader reader =
  new org.xml.sax.SAXParser();

// Do something with the parser
reader.parse(uri);
```

With that in mind, it's worth looking at a more realistic example. Example 3-1 is the skeleton for the SAXTreeViewer class I was just referring to, which allows viewing of an XML document as a graphical tree. This also gives you a chance to look at each of the SAX events and associated callback methods that can be used to perform action within the parsing of an XML document.

Example 3-1. The SAXTreeViewer skeleton

```
package javaxml2;

import java.io.IOException;
import java.util.HashMap;
import java.util.Iterator;
import java.util.Map;
import org.xml.sax.Attributes;
import org.xml.sax.ContentHandler;
import org.xml.sax.ErrorHandler;
import org.xml.sax.InputSource;
import org.xml.sax.Locator;
import org.xml.sax.SAXException;
import org.xml.sax.SAXParseException;
import org.xml.sax.XMLReader;
import org.xml.sax.helpers.XMLReaderFactory;

// This is an XML book - no need for explicit Swing imports
import java.awt.*;
import javax.swing.*;
import javax.swing.tree.*;

public class SAXTreeViewer extends JFrame {

    /** Default parser to use */
    private String vendorParserClass =
        "org.apache.xerces.parsers.SAXParser";

    /** The base tree to render */
    private JTree jTree;

    /** Tree model to use */
```

Example 3-1. The SAXTreeViewer skeleton (continued)

```
    DefaultTreeModel defaultTreeModel;

    public SAXTreeViewer() {
        // Handle Swing setup
        super("SAX Tree Viewer");
        setSize(600, 450);
    }

    public void init(String xmlURI) throws IOException, SAXException {
        DefaultMutableTreeNode base =
            new DefaultMutableTreeNode("XML Document: " +
                xmlURI);

        // Build the tree model
        defaultTreeModel = new DefaultTreeModel(base);
        jTree = new JTree(defaultTreeModel);

        // Construct the tree hierarchy
        buildTree(defaultTreeModel, base, xmlURI);

        // Display the results
        getContentPane().add(new JScrollPane(jTree),
            BorderLayout.CENTER);
    }

    public void buildTree(DefaultTreeModel treeModel,
                          DefaultMutableTreeNode base, String xmlURI)
        throws IOException, SAXException {

        // Create instances needed for parsing
        XMLReader reader =
            XMLReaderFactory.createXMLReader(vendorParserClass);

        // Register content handler

        // Register error handler

        // Parse
    }

    public static void main(String[] args) {
        try {
            if (args.length != 1) {
                System.out.println(
                    "Usage: java javaxml2.SAXTreeViewer " +
                    "[XML Document URI]");
                System.exit(0);
            }
```

Example 3-1. The SAXTreeViewer skeleton (continued)

```
        SAXTreeViewer viewer = new SAXTreeViewer();
        viewer.init(args[0]);
        viewer.setVisible(true);
    } catch (Exception e) {
        e.printStackTrace();
    }
  }
}
```

This should all be fairly straightforward.* Other than setting up the visual proper-ties for Swing, this code takes in the URI of an XML document (our *contents.xml* from the last chapter). In the `init()` method, a `JTree` is created for displaying the contents of the URI. These objects (the tree and URI) are then passed to the method that is worth focusing on, the `buildTree()` method. This is where pars-ing will take place, and the visual representation of the XML document supplied will be created. Additionally, the skeleton takes care of creating a base node for the graphical tree, with the path to the supplied XML document as that node's text.

U-R-What?

I've just breezed by what URIs are both here and in the last chapter. In short, a URI is a *uniform resource indicator*. As the name suggests, it provides a standard means of identifying (and thereby locating, in most cases) a specific resource; this resource is almost always some sort of XML document, for the purposes of this book. URIs are related to URLs, *uniform resource locators*. In fact, a URL is always a URI (although the reverse is not true). So in the examples in this and other chapters, you could specify a filename or a URL, like *http://www.newInstance.com/javaxml2/copyright.xml*, and either would be accepted.

You should be able to load and compile this program if you made the preparations talked about earlier to ensure that an XML parser and the SAX classes are in your class path. If you have a parser other than Apache Xerces, you can replace the value of the `vendorParserClass` variable to match your parser's `XMLReader` implemen-tation class, and leave the rest of the code as is. This simple program doesn't do much yet; in fact, if you run it and supply a legitimate filename as an argument, it should happily grind away and show you an empty tree, with the document's

---

* Don't be concerned if you are not familiar with the Swing concepts involved here; to be honest, I had to look most of them up myself! For a good reference on Swing, pick up a copy of *Java Swing* by Robert Eckstein, Marc Loy, and Dave Wood (O'Reilly).

filename as the base node. That's because you have only instantiated a reader, not requested that the XML document be parsed.

WARNING   If you have trouble compiling this source file, you most likely have problems with your IDE or system's class path. First, make sure you obtained the Apache Xerces parser (or your vendor's parser). For Xerces, this involves downloading a zipped or gzipped file. This archive can then be extracted, and will contain a *xerces.jar* file; it is this *jar* file that contains the compiled class files for the program. Add this archive to your class path. You should then be able to compile the source file listing.

Parsing the Document

Once a reader is loaded and ready for use, you can instruct it to parse an XML document. This is conveniently handled by the `parse()` method of `org.xml.sax.XMLReader` class, and this method can accept either an `org.xml.sax.InputSource` or a simple string URI. It's a much better idea to use the SAX `InputSource` class, as that can provide more information than a simple location. I'll talk more about that later, but suffice it to say that an `InputSource` can be constructed from an I/O `InputStream`, `Reader`, or a string URI.

You can now add construction of an `InputSource` from the provided URI, as well as the invocation of the `parse()` method to the example. Because the document must be loaded, either locally or remotely, a `java.io.IOException` may result, and must be caught. In addition, the `org.xml.sax.SAXException` will be thrown if problems occur while parsing the document. Notice that the `buildTree` method can throw both of these exceptions:

```
public void buildTree(DefaultTreeModel treeModel,
                      DefaultMutableTreeNode base, File file)
    throws IOException, SAXException {

    // Create instances needed for parsing
    XMLReader reader =
        XMLReaderFactory.createXMLReader(vendorParserClass);

    // Register content handler

    // Register error handler

    // Parse
    InputSource inputSource =
        new InputSource(xmlURI);
    reader.parse(inputSource);
}
```

Compile these changes and you are ready to execute the parsing example. You should specify the path to your file as the first argument to the program:

```
c:\javaxml2\build>java javaxml2.SAXTreeViewer ..\Ch03\xml\contents.xml
```

WARNING   Supplying an XML URI can be a rather strange task. In versions of Xerces before 1.1, a normal filename could be supplied (for example, on Windows, *..\xml\contents.xml*). However, this behavior changed in Xerces 1.1 and 1.2, and the URI had to be in this form: *file:///c:/javaxml2/xml/contents.xml*. However, in the latest versions of Xerces (from 1.3 up, as well as 2.0), this behavior has moved back to accepting normal filenames. Be aware of these issues if you are using Xerces 1.1 through 1.2.

The rather boring output shown in Figure 3-1 may make you doubt that anything has happened. However, if you lean nice and close, you may hear your hard drive spin briefly (or you can just have faith in the bytecode). In fact, the XML document is parsed. However, no callbacks have been implemented to tell SAX to take action during the parsing; without these callbacks, a document is parsed quietly and without application intervention. Of course, we want to intervene in that process, so it's now time to look at creating some parser *callback methods*. A callback method is a method that is not directly invoked by you or your application code. Instead, as the parser begins to work, it calls these methods at certain events, without any intervention. In other words, instead of your code calling *into* the parser, the parser calls *back* to yours. That allows you to programmatically insert behavior into the parsing process. This intervention is the most important part of using SAX. Parser callbacks let you insert action into the program flow, and turn the rather boring, quiet parsing of an XML document into an application that can react to the data, elements, attributes, and structure of the document being parsed, as well as interact with other programs and clients along the way.

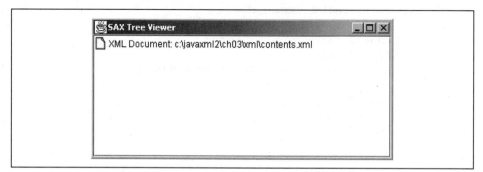

Figure 3-1. An uninteresting JTree

Using an InputSource

I mentioned earlier that I would touch on using a SAX InputSource again, albeit briefly. The advantage to using an InputSource instead of directly supplying a URI is simple: it can provide more information to the parser. An InputSource encapsulates information about a single object, the document to parse. In situations where a system identifier, public identifier, or stream may all be tied to one URI, using an InputSource for encapsulation can become very handy. The class has accessor and mutator methods for its system ID and public ID, a character encoding, a byte stream (java.io.InputStream), and a character stream (java. io.Reader). Passed as an argument to the parse() method, SAX also guarantees that the parser will never modify the InputSource. The original input to a parser is still available unchanged after its use by a parser or XML-aware application. In our example, it's important because the XML document uses a relative path to the DTD in it:

```
<!DOCTYPE Book SYSTEM "DTD/JavaXML.dtd">
```

By using an InputSource and wrapping the supplied XML URI, you have set the system ID of the document. This effectively sets up the path to the document for the parser and allows it to resolve all relative paths within that document, like the *JavaXML.dtd* file. If instead of setting this ID, you parsed an I/O stream, the DTD wouldn't be located (as it has no frame of reference); you could simulate this by changing the code in the buildTree() method as shown here:

```
// Parse
InputSource inputSource =
    new InputSource(new java.io.FileInputStream(
        new java.io.File(xmlURI)));
reader.parse(inputSource);
```

As a result, you would get the following exception when running the viewer:

```
C:\javaxml2\build>java javaxml2.SAXTreeViewer ..\ch03\xml\contents.xml
org.xml.sax.SAXParseException: File
   "file:///C:/javaxml2/build/DTD/JavaXML.dtd" not found.
```

While this seems a little silly (wrapping a URI in a file and I/O stream), it's actually quite common to see people using I/O streams as input to parsers. Just be sure that you don't reference any other files in the XML and that you set a system ID for the XML stream (using the setSystemID() method on InputSource). So the above code sample could be "fixed" by changing it to the following:

```
// Parse
InputSource inputSource =
    new InputSource(new java.io.FileInputStream(
        new java.io.File(xmlURI)));
```

```
inputSource.setSystemID(xmlURI);
reader.parse(inputSource);
```

Always set a system ID. Sorry for the excessive detail; now you can bore coworkers with your knowledge about SAX InputSources.

Content Handlers

In order to let an application do something useful with XML data as it is being parsed, you must register *handlers* with the SAX parser. A handler is nothing more than a set of callbacks that SAX defines to let programmers insert application code at important events within a document's parsing. These events take place as the document is parsed, not after the parsing has occurred. This is one of the reasons that SAX is such a powerful interface: it allows a document to be handled sequentially, without having to first read the entire document into memory. Later, we will look at the Document Object Model (DOM), which has this limitation.[*]

There are four core handler interfaces defined by SAX 2.0: org.xml.sax.ContentHandler, org.xml.sax.ErrorHandler, org.xml.sax.DTDHandler, and org.xml.sax.EntityResolver. In this chapter, I will discuss ContentHandler and ErrorHandler. I'll leave discussion of DTDHandler and EntityResolver for the next chapter; it is enough for now to understand that EntityResolver works just like the other handlers, and is built specifically for resolving external entities specified within an XML document. Custom application classes that perform specific actions within the parsing process can implement each of these interfaces. These implementation classes can be registered with the reader using the methods setContentHandler(), setErrorHandler(), setDTDHandler(), and setEntityResolver(). Then the reader invokes the callback methods on the appropriate handlers during parsing.

For the SAXTreeViewer example, a good start is to implement the ContentHandler interface. This interface defines several important methods within the parsing lifecycle that our application can react to. Since all the necessary import statements are in place (I cheated and put them in already), all that is needed is to code an implementation of the ContentHandler interface. For simplicity, I'll do this as a nonpublic class, still within the *SAXTreeViewer.java* source file. Add in the JTreeContentHandler class, as shown here:

```
class JTreeContentHandler implements ContentHandler {

    /** Tree Model to add nodes to */
    private DefaultTreeModel treeModel;
```

---

[*] Of course, this limitation is also an advantage; having the entire document in memory allows for random access. In other words, it's a double-edged sword, which I'll look at more in Chapter 5.

```
    /** Current node to add sub-nodes to */
    private DefaultMutableTreeNode current;

    public JTreeContentHandler(DefaultTreeModel treeModel,
                               DefaultMutableTreeNode base) {
        this.treeModel = treeModel;
        this.current = base;
    }


    // ContentHandler method implementations
}
```

Don't bother trying to compile the source file at this point; you'll get a ton of errors about methods defined in `ContentHandler` not being implemented. The rest of this section walks through each of these methods, adding as we go. In this basic class, it's enough to pass in the `TreeModel` implementation, which is used to add new nodes to the `JTree`, and the base node (created in the `buildTree()` method, earlier). The base node is set to a member variable called `current`; this variable always points to the node being worked with, and the code needs to move that node down the tree hierarchy (when nested elements are found), as well as back up the tree (when elements end and the parent becomes current again). With that in place, it's time to look at the various `ContentHandler` callbacks and implement each. First take a quick glance at the `ContentHandler` interface, which shows the callbacks that need to be implemented:

```
public interface ContentHandler {
    public void setDocumentLocator(Locator locator);
    public void startDocument() throws SAXException;
    public void endDocument() throws SAXException;
    public void startPrefixMapping(String prefix, String uri)
        throws SAXException;
    public void endPrefixMapping(String prefix)
        throws SAXException;
    public void startElement(String namespaceURI, String localName,
                    String qName, Attributes atts)
        throws SAXException;
    public void endElement(String namespaceURI, String localName,
                    String qName)
        throws SAXException;
    public void characters(char ch[], int start, int length)
        throws SAXException;
    public void ignorableWhitespace(char ch[], int start, int length)
        throws SAXException;
    public void processingInstruction(String target, String data)
        throws SAXException;
    public void skippedEntity(String name)
        throws SAXException;
}
```

The Document Locator

The first method you need to define is one that sets an `org.xml.sax.Locator` for use within any other SAX events. When a callback event occurs, the class implementing a handler often needs access to the location of the SAX parser within an XML file. This is used to help the application make decisions about the event and its location within the XML document, such as determining the line on which an error occurred. The `Locator` class has several useful methods such as `getLineNumber()` and `getColumnNumber()` that return the current location of the parsing process within an XML file when invoked. Because this location is only valid for the current parsing lifecycle, the `Locator` should be used only within the scope of the `ContentHandler` implementation. Since this might be handy to use later, the code shown here saves the provided `Locator` instance to a member variable:

```
class JTreeContentHandler implements ContentHandler {

    /** Hold onto the locator for location information */
    private Locator locator;

    // Constructor

    public void setDocumentLocator(Locator locator) {
        // Save this for later use
        this.locator = locator;
    }
}
```

The Beginning and the End of a Document

In any lifecycle process, there must always be a beginning and an end. These important events should each occur once, the former before all other events, and the latter after all other events. This rather obvious fact is critical to applications, as it allows them to know exactly when parsing begins and ends. SAX provides callback methods for each of these events, `startDocument()` and `endDocument()`.

The first method, `startDocument()`, is called before any other callbacks, including the callback methods within other SAX handlers, such as `DTDHandler`. In other words, `startDocument()` is not only the first method called within `Content-Handler`, but also within the entire parsing process, aside from the `setDocument-Locator()` method just discussed. This ensures a finite beginning to parsing, and lets the application perform any tasks it needs to before parsing takes place.

The second method, `endDocument()`, is always the last method called, again across all handlers. This includes situations in which errors occur that cause parsing to halt. I will discuss errors later, but there are both recoverable errors and unrecoverable errors. If an unrecoverable error occurs, the `ErrorHandler`'s callback method is invoked, and then a final call to `endDocument()` completes the attempted parsing.

In the example code, no visual event should occur with these methods; however, as with implementing any interface, the methods must still be present:

```
public void startDocument() throws SAXException {
    // No visual events occur here
}

public void endDocument() throws SAXException {
    // No visual events occur here
}
```

Both of these callback methods can throw `SAXExceptions`. The only types of exceptions that SAX events ever throw, they provide another standard interface to the parsing behavior. However, these exceptions often wrap other exceptions that indicate what problems have occurred. For example, if an XML file was parsed over the network via a URL, and the connection suddenly became invalid, a `java.net.SocketException` might occur. However, an application using the SAX classes should not have to catch this exception, because it should not have to know where the XML resource is located (it might be a local file, as opposed to a network resource). Instead, the application can catch the single `SAXException`. Within the SAX reader, the original exception is caught and rethrown as a `SAXException`, with the originating exception stuffed inside the new one. This allows applications to have one standard exception to trap for, while allowing specific details of what errors occurred within the parsing process to be wrapped and made available to the calling program through this standard exception. The `SAXException` class provides a method, `getException()`, which returns the underlying `Exception` (if one exists).

Processing Instructions

I talked about processing instructions (PIs) within XML as a bit of a special case. They were not considered XML elements, and were handled differently by being made available to the calling application. Because of these special characteristics, SAX defines a specific callback for handling processing instructions. This method receives the target of the processing instruction and any data sent to the PI. For this chapter's example, the PI can be converted to a new node and displayed in the tree viewer:

```
public void processingInstruction(String target, String data)
    throws SAXException {
```

```
DefaultMutableTreeNode pi =
    new DefaultMutableTreeNode("PI (target = '" + target +
                                "', data = '" + data + "')");
current.add(pi);
}
```

In a real application using XML data, this is where an application could receive instructions and set variable values or execute methods to perform application-specific processing. For example, the Apache Cocoon publishing framework might set flags to perform transformations on the data once it is parsed, or to display the XML as a specific content type. This method, like the other SAX callbacks, throws a SAXException when errors occur.

NOTE   It's worth pointing out that this method will not receive notification of the XML declaration:

```
<?xml version="1.0" standalone="yes"?>
```

In fact, SAX provides no means of getting at this information (and you'll find out that it's not currently part of DOM or JDOM, either!). The general underlying principle is that this information is for the XML parser or reader, not the consumer of the document's data. For that reason, it's not exposed to the developer.

Namespace Callbacks

From the discussion of namespaces in Chapter 2, you should be starting to realize their importance and impact on parsing and handling XML. Alongside XML Schema, XML Namespaces is easily the most significant concept added to XML since the original XML 1.0 Recommendation. With SAX 2.0, support for namespaces was introduced at the element level. This allows a distinction to be made between the namespace of an element, signified by an element prefix and an associated namespace URI, and the local name of an element. In this case, the term *local name* refers to the unprefixed name of an element. For example, the local name of the ora:copyright element is simply copyright. The namespace prefix is ora, and the namespace URI is declared as *http://www.oreilly.com.*

There are two SAX callbacks specifically dealing with namespaces. These callbacks are invoked when the parser reaches the beginning and end of a *prefix mapping.* Although this is a new term, it is not a new concept; a prefix mapping is simply an element that uses the xmlns attribute to declare a namespace. This is often the root element (which may have multiple mappings), but can be any element within an XML document that declares an explicit namespace. For example:

```
<catalog>
  <books>
```

```
    <book title="XML in a Nutshell"
          xmlns:xlink="http://www.w3.org/1999/xlink">
      <cover xlink:type="simple" xlink:show="onLoad"
              xlink:href="xmlnutCover.jpg" ALT="XML in a Nutshell"
              width="125" height="350" />
    </book>
  </books>
</catalog>
```

In this case, an explicit namespace is declared several element nestings deep within the document. That prefix and URI mapping (in this case, xlink and *http://www.w3.org/1999/xlink*, respectively) are then available to elements and attributes within the declaring element.

The startPrefixMapping() callback is given the namespace prefix as well as the URI associated with that prefix. The mapping is considered "closed" or "ended" when the element that declared the mapping is closed, which triggers the endPrefixMapping() callback. The only twist to these callbacks is that they don't quite behave in the sequential manner in which SAX usually is structured; the prefix mapping callback occurs directly *before* the callback for the element that declares the namespace, and the ending of the mapping results in an event just *after* the close of the declaring element. However, it actually makes a lot of sense: for the declaring element to be able to use the declared namespace mapping, the mapping must be available before the element's callback. It works in just the opposite way for ending a mapping: the element must close (as it may use the namespace), and then the namespace mapping can be removed from the list of available mappings.

In the JTreeContentHandler, there aren't any visual events that should occur within these two callbacks. However, a common practice is to store the prefix and URI mappings in a data structure. You will see in a moment that the element callbacks report the namespace URI, but not the namespace prefix. If you don't store these prefixes (reported through startPrefixMapping()), they won't be available in your element callback code. The easiest way to do this is to use a Map, add the reported prefix and URI to this Map in startPrefixMapping(), and then remove them in endPrefixMapping(). This can be accomplished with the following code additions:

```
class JTreeContentHandler implements ContentHandler {

    /** Hold onto the locator for location information */
    private Locator locator;

    /** Store URI to prefix mappings */
    private Map namespaceMappings;
```

```
/** Tree Model to add nodes to */
private DefaultTreeModel treeModel;

/** Current node to add sub-nodes to */
private DefaultMutableTreeNode current;

public JTreeContentHandler(DefaultTreeModel treeModel,
                           DefaultMutableTreeNode base) {
    this.treeModel = treeModel;
    this.current = base;
    this.namespaceMappings = new HashMap();
}

// Existing methods

public void startPrefixMapping(String prefix, String uri) {
    // No visual events occur here.
    namespaceMappings.put(uri, prefix);
}

public void endPrefixMapping(String prefix) {
    // No visual events occur here.
    for (Iterator i = namespaceMappings.keySet().iterator();
        i.hasNext(); ) {

        String uri = (String)i.next();
        String thisPrefix = (String)namespaceMappings.get(uri);
        if (prefix.equals(thisPrefix)) {
            namespaceMappings.remove(uri);
            break;
        }
    }
}
}
```

One thing of note: I used the URI as a key to the mappings, rather than the prefix. As I mentioned a moment ago, the startElement() callback reports the namespace URI for the element, not the prefix. So keying on URIs makes those lookups faster. However, as you see in endPrefixMapping(), it does add a little bit of work to removing the mapping when it is no longer available. In any case, storing namespace mappings in this fashion is a fairly typical SAX trick, so store it away in your toolkit for XML programming.

WARNING   The solution shown here is far from a complete one in terms of dealing with more complex namespace issues. It's perfectly legal to reassign prefixes to new URIs for an element's scope, or to assign multiple prefixes to the same URI. In the example, this would result in widely scoped namespace mappings being overwritten by narrowly scoped ones in the case where identical URIs were mapped to different prefixes. In a more robust application, you would want to store prefixes and URIs separately, and have a method of relating the two without causing overwriting. However, you get the idea in the example of how to handle namespaces in the general sense.

Element Callbacks

By now you are probably ready to get to the data in the XML document. It is true that over half of the SAX callbacks have nothing to do with XML elements, attributes, and data. This is because the process of parsing XML is intended to do more than simply provide your application with the XML data; it should give the application instructions from XML PIs so your application knows what actions to take, let the application know when parsing begins and when it ends, and even tell it when there is whitespace that can be ignored! If some of these callbacks don't make much sense yet, keep reading.

Of course, there certainly are SAX callbacks intended to give you access to the XML data within your documents. The three primary events involved in getting that data are the start and end of elements and the `characters()` callback. These tell you when an element is parsed, the data within that element, and when the closing tag for that element is reached. The first of these, `startElement()`, gives an application information about an XML element and any attributes it may have. The parameters to this callback are the name of the element (in various forms) and an `org.xml.sax.Attributes` instance. This helper class holds references to all of the attributes within an element. It allows easy iteration through the element's attributes in a form similar to a `Vector`. In addition to being able to reference an attribute by its index (used when iterating through all attributes), it is possible to reference an attribute by its name. Of course, by now you should be a bit cautious when you see the word "name" referring to an XML element or attribute, as it can mean various things. In this case, either the complete name of the attribute (with a namespace prefix, if any), called its *Q name*, can be used, or the combination of its local name and namespace URI if a namespace is used.

There are also helper methods such as getURI(int index) and getLocal-Name(int index) that help give additional namespace information about an attribute. Used as a whole, the Attributes interface provides a comprehensive set of information about an element's attributes.

In addition to the element attributes, you get several forms of the element's name. This again is in deference to XML namespaces. The namespace URI of the element is supplied first. This places the element in its correct context across the document's complete set of namespaces. Then the local name of the element is supplied, which is the unprefixed element name. In addition (and for backwards compatibility), the Q name of the element is supplied. This is the unmodified, unchanged name of the element, which includes a namespace prefix if present; in other words, exactly what was in the XML document: ora:copyright for the copyright element. With these three types of names supplied, you should be able to describe an element with or without respect to its namespace.

In the example, several things occur that illustrate this capability. First, a new node is created and added to the tree with the local name of the element. Then, that node becomes the current node, so all nested elements and attributes are added as leaves. Next, the namespace is determined, using the supplied namespace URI and the namespaceMappings object (to get the prefix) that you just added to the code from the last section. This is added as a node, as well. Finally, the code iterates through the Attributes interface, adding each (with local name and namespace information) as a child node. The code to accomplish all this is shown here:

```
public void startElement(String namespaceURI, String localName,
                         String qName, Attributes atts)
    throws SAXException {

    DefaultMutableTreeNode element =
        new DefaultMutableTreeNode("Element: " + localName);
    current.add(element);
    current = element;

    // Determine namespace
    if (namespaceURI.length() > 0) {
        String prefix =
            (String)namespaceMappings.get(namespaceURI);
        if (prefix.equals("")) {
            prefix = "[None]";
        }
        DefaultMutableTreeNode namespace =
            new DefaultMutableTreeNode("Namespace: prefix = '" +
                prefix + "', URI = '" + namespaceURI + "'");
        current.add(namespace);
    }
```

```
        // Process attributes
        for (int i=0; i<atts.getLength(); i++) {
            DefaultMutableTreeNode attribute =
                new DefaultMutableTreeNode("Attribute (name = '" +
                                            atts.getLocalName(i) +
                                            "', value = '" +
                                            atts.getValue(i) + "')");
            String attURI = atts.getURI(i);
            if (attURI.length() > 0) {
                String attPrefix =
                    (String)namespaceMappings.get(namespaceURI);
                if (attPrefix.equals("")) {
                    attPrefix = "[None]";
                }
                DefaultMutableTreeNode attNamespace =
                    new DefaultMutableTreeNode("Namespace: prefix = '" +
                        attPrefix + "', URI = '" + attURI + "'");
                attribute.add(attNamespace);
            }
            current.add(attribute);
        }
    }
```

The end of an element is much easier to code. Since there is no need to give any visual information, all that must be done is to walk back up the tree one node, leaving the element's parent as the new current node:

```
    public void endElement(String namespaceURI, String localName,
                           String qName)
        throws SAXException {

        // Walk back up the tree
        current = (DefaultMutableTreeNode)current.getParent();
    }
```

One final note before moving on to element data: you may have noticed that with a namespace URI and an element's Q name, it would be possible to figure out the prefix as well as the URI from the information supplied to the `startElement()` callback, without having to use a map of namespace associations. That's absolutely true, and would serve the example code well. However, most applications have hundreds and even thousands of lines of code in these callbacks (or, better yet, in methods invoked from code within these callbacks). In those cases, relying on parsing of the element's Q name is not nearly as robust a solution as storing the data in a custom structure. In other words, splitting the Q name on a colon is great for simple applications, but isn't so wonderful for complex (and therefore more realistic) ones.

Element Data

Once the beginning and end of an element block are identified and the element's attributes are enumerated for an application, the next piece of important information is the actual data contained within the element itself. This generally consists of additional elements, textual data, or a combination of the two. When other elements appear, the callbacks for those elements are initiated, and a type of pseudo-recursion happens: elements nested within elements result in callbacks "nested" within callbacks. At some point, though, textual data will be encountered. Typically the most important information to an XML client, this data is usually either what is shown to the client or what is processed to generate a client response.

In XML, textual data within elements is sent to a wrapping application via the `characters()` callback. This method provides the wrapping application with an array of characters as well as a starting index and the length of the characters to read. Generating a `String` from this array and applying the data is a piece of cake:

```
public void characters(char[] ch, int start, int length)
    throws SAXException {

    String s = new String(ch, start, length);
    DefaultMutableTreeNode data =
        new DefaultMutableTreeNode("Character Data: '" + s + "'");
    current.add(data);
}
```

Seemingly a simple callback, this method often results in a significant amount of confusion because the SAX interface and standards do not strictly define how this callback must be used for lengthy pieces of character data. In other words, a parser may choose to return all contiguous character data in one invocation, or split this data up into multiple method invocations. For any given element, this method will be called not at all (if no character data is present within the element) or one or more times. Parsers implement this behavior differently, often using algorithms designed to increase parsing speed. Never count on having all the textual data for an element within one callback method; conversely, never assume that multiple callbacks would result from one element's contiguous character data.

As you write SAX event handlers, be sure to keep your mind in a hierarchical mode. In other words, you should not get in the habit of thinking that an element *owns* its data and child elements, but only that it serves as a parent. Also keep in mind that the parser is moving along, handling elements, attributes, and data as it comes across them. This can make for some surprising results. Consider the following XML document fragment:

```
<parent>This element has <child>embedded text</child> within it.</parent>
```

Forgetting that SAX parses sequentially, making callbacks as it sees elements and data, and forgetting that the XML is viewed as hierarchical, you might make the assumption that the output here would be something like Figure 3-2.

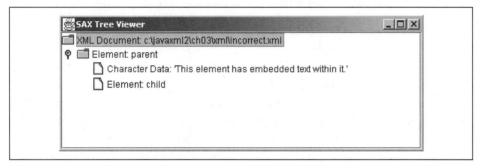

Figure 3-2. Expected, and incorrect, graphical tree

This seems logical, as the **parent** element completely "owns" the **child** element. But what actually occurs is that a callback is made at each SAX event-point, resulting in the tree shown in Figure 3-3.

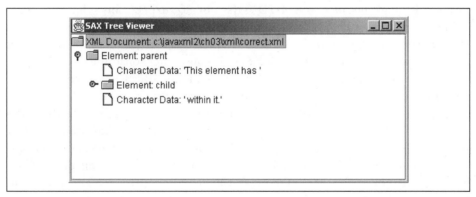

Figure 3-3. Actual generated tree

SAX does not read ahead, so the result is exactly what you would expect if you viewed the XML document as sequential data, without all the human assumptions that we tend to make. This is an important point to remember.

Finally, whitespace is often reported by the characters() method. This introduces additional confusion, as another SAX callback, ignorableWhitespace(),
also reports whitespace. Unfortunately, a lot of books (including, I'm embar-
rassed to admit, my first edition of *Java and XML*) got the details of whitespace
either partially or completely wrong. So, let me take this opportunity to set the
record straight. First, if no DTD or XML Schema is referenced, the ignorable-
Whitespace() method should never be invoked. Period.

The reason is that a DTD (or schema) details the content model for an element.
In other words, in the *JavaXML.dtd* file, the contents element can only have
chapter elements within it. Any whitespace between the start of the contents
element and the start of a chapter element is (by logic) ignorable. It doesn't
mean anything, because the DTD says not to expect any character data
(whitespace or otherwise). The same thing applies for whitespace between the end
of a chapter element and the start of another chapter element, or between it
and the end of the contents element. Because the constraints (in DTD or
schema form) specify that no character data is allowed, this whitespace cannot be
meaningful. However, *without* a constraint specifying that information to a parser,
that whitespace *cannot* be interpreted as meaningless. So by removing the reference to a DTD, these various whitespaces would trigger the characters() callback, where previously they triggered the ignorableWhitespace() callback.
Thus whitespace is never simply ignorable, or nonignorable; it all depends on
what (if any) constraints are referenced. Change the constraints, and you might
change the meaning of the whitespace.

Let's dive even deeper. In the case where an element can only have other elements within it, things are reasonably clear. Whitespace in between elements is
ignorable. However, consider a mixed content model:

```
<!ELEMENT p (b* | i* | a* | #PCDATA)>
```

If this looks like gibberish, think of HTML; it represents (in part) the constraints
for the p element, or paragraph tag. Of course, text within this tag can exist, and

also bold (b), italics (i), and links (a) elements as well. In this model, there is no whitespace between the starting and ending p tags that will ever be reported as ignorable (with or without a DTD or schema reference). That's because it's impossible to distinguish between whitespace used for readability and whitespace that is supposed to be in the document. For example:

```
<p>
  <i>Java and XML</i>, 2nd edition, is now available at bookstores, as
    well as through O'Reilly at
    <a href="http://www.oreilly.com">http://www.oreilly.com</a>.
</p>
```

In this XHTML fragment, the whitespace between the opening p element and the opening i element is not ignorable, and therefore reported through the **characters()** callback. If you aren't completely confused (and I don't think you are), be prepared to closely monitor both of the character-related callbacks. That will make explaining the last SAX callback related to this issue a snap.

Ignorable Whitespace

With all that whitespace discussion done, adding an implementation for the **ignorableWhitespace()** method is a piece of cake. Since the whitespace reported is ignorable, the code does just that—ignore it:

```
public void ignorableWhitespace(char[] ch, int start, int length)
    throws SAXException {

    // This is ignorable, so don't display it
}
```

Whitespace is reported in the same manner as character data; it can be reported with one callback, or a SAX parser may break up the whitespace and report it over several method invocations. In either case, adhere closely to the precautions about not making assumptions or counting on whitespace as textual data in order to avoid troublesome bugs in your applications.

Entities

As you recall, there is only one entity reference in the *contents.xml* document, **OReillyCopyright**. When parsed and resolved, this results in another file being loaded, either from the local filesystem or some other URI. However, validation is not turned on in the reader implementation being used.* An often overlooked

---

* I'm assuming that even if you aren't using Apache Xerces, your parser does not leave validation on by default. If you get different results than shown in this chapter, consult your documentation and see if validation is on. If it is, sneak a peek at Chapter 4 and see how to turn it off.

facet of nonvalidating parsers is that they are not required to resolve entity references, and instead may skip them. This has caused some headaches before, as
parser results may simply not include entity references that were expected to be
included. SAX 2.0 nicely accounts for this with a callback that is issued when an
entity is skipped by a nonvalidating parser. The callback gives the name of the
entity, which can be included in the viewer's output:

```
public void skippedEntity(String name) throws SAXException {
    DefaultMutableTreeNode skipped =
        new DefaultMutableTreeNode("Skipped Entity: '" + name + "'");
    current.add(skipped);
}
```

Before you go looking for the OReillyCopyright node, though, you should be
aware that most established parsers will not skip entities, even if they are not validating. Apache Xerces, for example, never invokes this callback; instead, the entity
reference is expanded and the result included in the data available after parsing.
In other words, it's there for parsers to use, but you will be hard-pressed to find a
case where it crops up! If you do have a parser that exhibits this behavior, note
that the parameter passed to the callback does not include the leading ampersand
and trailing semicolon in the entity reference. For &OReillyCopyright;, only
the name of the entity reference, OReillyCopyright, is passed to
skippedEntity().

The Results

Finally, you need to register the content handler implementation with the
XMLReader you've instantiated. This is done with setContentHandler(). Add
the following lines to the buildTree() method:

```
public void buildTree(DefaultTreeModel treeModel,
                      DefaultMutableTreeNode base, String xmlURI)
    throws IOException, SAXException {

    // Create instances needed for parsing
    XMLReader reader =
        XMLReaderFactory.createXMLReader(vendorParserClass);
    ContentHandler jTreeContentHandler =
        new JTreeContentHandler(treeModel, base);

    // Register content handler
    reader.setContentHandler(jTreeContentHandler);

    // Register error handler

    // Parse
```

```
    InputSource inputSource =
        new InputSource(xmlURI);
    reader.parse(inputSource);
}
```

If you have entered all of these document callbacks, you should be able to compile the `SAXTreeViewer` source file. Once done, you may run the SAX viewer demonstration on the XML sample file created earlier. Also, make sure that you have added your working directory to the classpath. The complete Java command should read:

```
C:\javaxml2\build>java javaxml2.SAXTreeViewer ..\ch03\xml\contents.xml
```

This should result in a Swing window firing up, loaded with the XML document's content. If you experience a slight pause in startup, you are probably waiting on your machine to connect to the Internet and resolve the `OReillyCopyright` entity reference. If you aren't online, refer to Chapter 2 for instructions on replacing the reference in the DTD with a local copyright file. In any case, your output should look similar to Figure 3-4, depending on what nodes you have expanded.

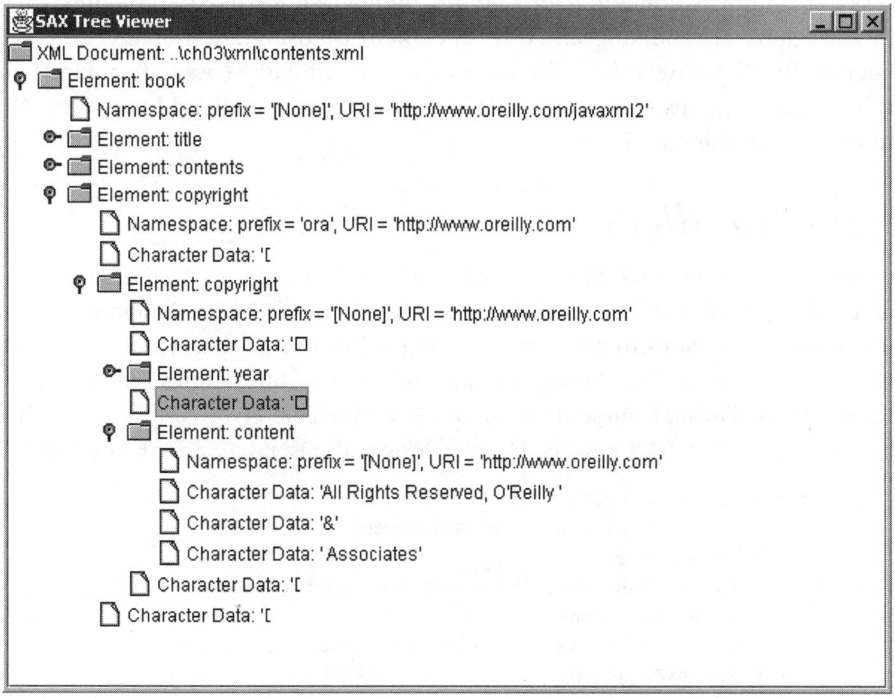

Figure 3-4. SAXTreeViewer in action

A couple of things to notice: first, the surrounding whitespace of elements is not present, since the presence of a DTD and strict content model forces that whitespace to be ignored (as it is reported to the ignorableWhitespace() callback). Second, the entity reference is resolved, and you see the contents of the *copyright.xml* file nested within the larger tree structure. Also, because this file has no DTD, whitespace that might be considered ignorable is reported as character data through the characters() callback. That results in the odd little control characters in the tree's text value (these are most often carriage returns in the underlying document). Finally, notice how the text "O'Reilly & Associates" within *copyright.xml* is actually reported through three invocations of the characters() callback. This is a perfect illustration of textual data not being reported as one block of text. In this case, the parser split the text on the entity reference (&), which is a common behavior. In any case, you should try running the viewer on different XML documents and see how the output changes.

You have now seen how a SAX-compliant parser handles a well-formed XML document. You should also be getting an understanding of the document callbacks that occur within the parsing process and of how an application can use these callbacks to get information about an XML document as it is parsed. In the next chapter, I will look at validating an XML document by using additional SAX classes designed for handling DTDs. Before moving on, though, I want to address the issue of what happens when your XML document is not valid, and the errors that can result from this condition.

Error Handlers

In addition to providing the ContentHandler interface for handling parsing events, SAX provides an ErrorHandler interface that can be implemented to treat various error conditions that may arise during parsing. This class works in the same manner as the document handler already constructed, but defines only three callback methods. Through these three methods, all possible error conditions are handled and reported by SAX parsers. Here's a look at the ErrorHandler interface:

```
public interface ErrorHandler {
    public abstract void warning (SAXParseException exception)
        throws SAXException;
    public abstract void error (SAXParseException exception)
        throws SAXException;
    public abstract void fatalError (SAXParseException exception)
        throws SAXException;
}
```

Each method receives information about the error or warning that has occurred through a SAXParseException. This object holds the line number where the trouble was encountered, the URI of the document being treated (which could be the parsed document or an external reference within that document), and normal exception details such as a message and a printable stack trace. In addition, each method can throw a SAXException. This may seem a bit odd at first; an exception handler that throws an exception? Keep in mind that each handler receives a parsing exception. This can be a warning that should not cause the parsing process to stop or an error that needs to be resolved for parsing to continue; however, the callback may need to perform system I/O or another operation that can throw an exception, and it needs to be able to send any problems resulting from these actions up the application chain. It can do this through the SAXException the error handler callback is allowed to throw.

As an example, consider an error handler that receives error notifications and writes those errors to an error log. This callback method needs to be able to either append to or create an error log on the local filesystem. If a warning were to occur within the process of parsing an XML document, the warning would be reported to this method. The intent of the warning is to give information to the callback and then continue parsing the document. However, if the error handler could not write to the log file, it might need to notify the parser and application that all parsing should stop. This can be done by catching any I/O exceptions and rethrowing these to the calling application, thus causing any further document parsing to stop. This common scenario is why error handlers must be able to throw exceptions (see Example 3-2).

Example 3-2. Error handler that may throw a SAXException

```
public void warning(SAXParseException exception)
    throws SAXException {

    try {
        FileWriter fw = new FileWriter("error.log");
        BufferedWriter bw = new BufferedWriter(fw);
        bw.write("Warning: " + exception.getMessage() + "\n");
        bw.flush();
        bw.close();
        fw.close();
    } catch (IOException e) {
        throw new SAXException("Could not write to log file", e);
    }
}
```

With this in mind, it's possible to define the skeleton of an ErrorHandler implementation and register it with the reader implementation in the same way that the content handler was registered. In the interests of keeping this book from becoming a treatise on Swing, these methods will just stop parsing and report warnings and errors through the command line. First, add another nonpublic class to the end of the *SAXTreeViewer.java* source file:

```
class JTreeErrorHandler implements ErrorHandler {

    // Method implementations

}
```

Next, in order to actually use the custom error handler, you need to register this error handler with your SAX reader. This is done with the `setErrorHandler()` method on the `XMLReader` instance, and needs to occur in the example's `buildTree()` method:

```
public void buildTree(DefaultTreeModel treeModel,
                      DefaultMutableTreeNode base, String xmlURI)
    throws IOException, SAXException {

    // Create instances needed for parsing
    XMLReader reader =
        XMLReaderFactory.createXMLReader(vendorParserClass);
    ContentHandler jTreeContentHandler =
        new JTreeContentHandler(treeModel, base);
    ErrorHandler jTreeErrorHandler = new JTreeErrorHandler();

    // Register content handler
    reader.setContentHandler(jTreeContentHandler);

    // Register error handler
    reader.setErrorHandler(jTreeErrorHandler);

    // Parse
    InputSource inputSource =
        new InputSource(xmlURI);
    reader.parse(inputSource);
}
```

Finally, let's take a look at coding the three methods required by the `ErrorHandler` interface.

Warnings

Any time a warning (as defined by the XML 1.0 specification) occurs, this method is invoked in the registered error handler. There are several conditions that can generate a warning; however, all of them are related to the DTD and validity of a document, and I will discuss them in the next chapter. For now, you just need to define a simple method that prints out the line number, URI, and warning message when a warning occurs. Because (for demonstration purposes) I want any warnings to stop parsing, this code throws a SAXException and lets the wrapping application exit gracefully, cleaning up any used resources:

```
public void warning(SAXParseException exception)
    throws SAXException {

    System.out.println("**Parsing Warning**\n" +
                       " Line:    " +
                       exception.getLineNumber() + "\n" +
                       " URI:     " +
                       exception.getSystemId() + "\n" +
                       " Message: " +
                       exception.getMessage());
    throw new SAXException("Warning encountered");
}
```

Nonfatal Errors

Errors that occur within parsing that can be recovered from, but constitute a violation of some portion of the XML specification, are considered nonfatal errors. An error handler should always at least log these, as they are typically serious enough to merit informing the user or administrator of the application, if not so critical as to cause parsing to cease. Like warnings, most nonfatal errors are concerned with validation, and will be covered in the next chapter in more detail. Also like warnings, in the example this error handler just reports the information sent to the callback method and exits the parsing process:

```
public void error(SAXParseException exception)
    throws SAXException {

    System.out.println("**Parsing Error**\n" +
                       " Line:    " +
                       exception.getLineNumber() + "\n" +
                       " URI:     " +
                       exception.getSystemId() + "\n" +
                       " Message: " +
                       exception.getMessage());
    throw new SAXException("Error encountered");
}
```

Fatal Errors

Fatal errors are those that necessitate stopping the parser. These are typically related to a document not being well-formed, and make further parsing either a complete waste of time or technically impossible. An error handler should almost always notify the user or application administrator when a fatal error occurs; without intervention, these can bring an application to a shuddering halt. For the example, I'll just emulate the behavior of the other two callback methods, stopping the parsing and writing an error message to the screen when a fatal error is encountered:

```
public void fatalError(SAXParseException exception)
    throws SAXException {

    System.out.println("**Parsing Fatal Error**\n" +
                     " Line:     " +
                     exception.getLineNumber() + "\n" +
                     " URI:      " +
                     exception.getSystemId() + "\n" +
                     " Message: " +
                     exception.getMessage());
    throw new SAXException("Fatal Error encountered");
}
```

With this third error handler coded, you should be able to compile the example source file successfully and run it on the XML document again. Your output should not be any different than it was earlier, as there are no reportable errors in the XML. Next, I'll show you how to make some of these errors occur (for testing purposes, of course!).

Breaking the Data

Now that some error handlers are in place, it is worthwhile to generate some problems and see these handlers in action. Most warnings and nonfatal errors are associated with document validity issues, which I will address in the next chapter (when turning on validation is covered in detail). However, there is one nonfatal error that results from a nonvalidated XML document, involving the version of XML that a document reports. To view this error, make the following change to the first line of the XML table of contents example:

```
<?xml version="1.2"?>
```

Now run the Java SAX viewer program on the modified XML document. Your output should be similar to that shown here:

```
C:\javaxml2\build>java javaxml2.SAXTreeViewer ..\ch03\xml\contents.xml
**Parsing Error**
  Line:    1
  URI:     file:///C:/javaxml2/ch03/xml/contents.xml
  Message: XML version "1.2" is not supported.
org.xml.sax.SAXException: Error encountered
```

When an XML parser is operating upon a document that reports a version of XML greater than that supported by the parser, a nonfatal error is reported, in accordance with the XML 1.0 specification. This tells an application that newer features expected to be utilized by the document may not be available within the parser and the version that it supports. Because parsing continues, this is a nonfatal error. However, because it signifies a major impact on the document (such as newer syntax possibly generating subsequent errors), it is considered more important than a warning. This is why the `error()` method is invoked and triggers the error message and parsing halt in the example program.

All other meaningful warnings and nonfatal errors will be discussed in the next chapter; still, there is a variety of fatal errors that a nonvalidated XML document may have. These are related to an XML document not being well-formed. There is no logic built into XML parsers to try to resolve or estimate fixes to malformed XML, so an error in syntax results in the parsing process halting. The easiest way to demonstrate one of these errors is to introduce problems within your XML document. Reset the XML declaration to specify an XML version of 1.0, and make the following change to the XML document:

```
<?xml version="1.0"?>
<!DOCTYPE Book SYSTEM "DTD/JavaXML.dtd">

<!-- Java and XML Contents -->
<book xmlns="http://www.oreilly.com/javaxml2"
      xmlns:ora="http://www.oreilly.com"
>
  <!-- Note the missing end slash on the title element -->
  <title ora:series="Java">Java and XML<title>

  <!-- Rest of content -->
</book>
```

This is no longer a well-formed document. To see the fatal error that parsing this document generates, run the SAXVTreeViewer program on this modified file to get the following the output:

```
C:\javaxml2\build>java javaxml2.SAXTreeViewer ..\ch03\xml\contents.xml
**Parsing Fatal Error**
  Line:    23
  URI:     file:///C:/javaxml2/ch03/xml/contents.xml
  Message: The element type "title" must be terminated by the matching
           end-tag "</title>".
org.xml.sax.SAXException: Fatal Error encountered
```

The parser reports an incorrect ending to the `title` element. This fatal error is exactly as expected; parsing could not continue beyond this error. With this error handler, you begin to see what can go wrong within the parsing process, as well as how to handle those events. In Chapter 4 I will revisit the error handler and its methods and look at the problems that can be reported by a validating parser.

Gotcha!

Before leaving this introduction to parsing XML documents with SAX, there are a few pitfalls to make you aware of. These "gotchas" will help you avoid common programming mistakes when using SAX, and I will discuss more of these for other APIs in the appropriate sections.

My Parser Doesn't Support SAX 2.0

For those of you who are forced to use a SAX 1.0 parser, perhaps in an existing application, don't despair. First, you always have the option of changing parsers; keeping current on SAX standards is an important part of an XML parser's responsibility, and if your vendor is not doing this, you may have other concerns to address with them as well. However, there are certainly cases where you are forced to use a parser because of legacy code or applications; in these situations, you are still not left out in the cold.

SAX 2.0 includes a helper class, `org.xml.sax.helpers.ParserAdapter`, which can actually cause a SAX 1.0 `Parser` implementation to behave like a SAX 2.0 `XMLReader` implementation. This handy class takes in a 1.0 `Parser` implementation as an argument and then can be used instead of that implementation. It allows a `ContentHandler` to be set (which is a SAX 2.0 construct), and handles all namespace callbacks properly (also a feature of SAX 2.0). The only functionality loss you will see is that skipped entities will not be reported, as this capability was not available in a 1.0 implementation in any form, and cannot be emulated by a 2.0 adapter class. Example 3-3 shows this behavior in action.

Example 3-3. Using SAX 1.0 with SAX 2.0 code constructs

```
try {
    // Register a parser with SAX
    Parser parser =
        ParserFactory.makeParser(
            "org.apache.xerces.parsers.SAXParser");

    ParserAdapter myParser = new ParserAdapter(parser);

    // Register the document handler
    myParser.setContentHandler(contentHandler);

    // Register the error handler
    myParser.setErrorHandler(errHandler);

    // Parse the document
    myParser.parse(uri);
```

Example 3-3. Using SAX 1.0 with SAX 2.0 code constructs (continued)

```
} catch (ClassNotFoundException e) {
    System.out.println(
        "The parser class could not be found.");
} catch (IllegalAccessException e) {
    System.out.println(
        "Insufficient privileges to load the parser class.");
} catch (InstantiationException e) {
    System.out.println(
        "The parser class could not be instantiated.");
} catch (ClassCastException e) {
    System.out.println(
        "The parser does not implement org.xml.sax.Parser");
} catch (IOException e) {
    System.out.println("Error reaading URI: " + e.getMessage());
} catch (SAXException e) {
    System.out.println("Error in parsing: " + e.getMessage());
}
```

If SAX is new to you and this example doesn't make much sense, don't worry about it; you are using the latest and greatest version of SAX (2.0) and probably won't ever have to write code like this. This code is helpful only in cases where a 1.0 parser must be used.

The SAX XMLReader: Reused and Reentrant

One of Java's nicest features is the easy reuse of objects, and the memory advantages of this reuse. SAX parsers are no different. Once an XMLReader has been instantiated, it is possible to continue using that reader, parsing several or even hundreds of XML documents. Different documents or InputSources may be continually passed to a reader, allowing it to be used for a variety of different tasks. However, readers are not *reentrant*. That means that once the parsing process has started, a reader may not be used until the parsing of the requested document or input has completed. In other words, the process cannot be reentered. For those prone to coding recursive methods, this is definitely a gotcha! The first time that you attempt to use a reader that is in the middle of processing another document, you will receive a rather nasty SAXException and all parsing will stop. What is the lesson learned? Parse one document at a time, or pay the price of instantiating multiple reader instances.

The Misplaced Locator

Another dangerous but seemingly innocuous feature of SAX events is the Locator instance that is made available through the setDocumentLocator() callback method. This gives the application the origin of a SAX event, and is useful for making decisions about the progress of parsing and reaction to events. However, this origin point is valid only for the duration of the life of the `ContentHandler` instance; once parsing is complete, the `Locator` is no longer valid, including the case when another parse begins. A "gotcha" that many XML newcomers make is to hold a reference to the `Locator` object within a class member variable *outside* of the callback method:

```
public void setDocumentLocator(Locator locator) {
    // Saving the Locator to a class outside the ContentHandler
    myOtherClass.setLocator(locator);
}
...

public myOtherClassMethod() {
    // Trying to use this outside of the ContentHandler
    System.out.println(locator.getLineNumber());
}
```

This is an extremely bad idea, as this `Locator` instance becomes meaningless as soon as the scope of the `ContentHandler` implementation is left. Often, using the member variable resulting from this operation results in not only erroneous information being supplied to an application, but exceptions being generated in the running code. In other words, use this object locally, and not globally. In the `JTreeContentHandler` implementation class, the supplied `Locator` instance is saved to a member variable. It could then correctly be used (for example) to give you the line number of each element as it was encountered:

```
public void startElement(String namespaceURI, String localName,
                         String rawName, Attributes atts)
    throws SAXException {

    DefaultMutableTreeNode element =
        new DefaultMutableTreeNode("Element: " + localName +
            " at line " + locator.getLineNumber());
    current.add(element);
    // Rest of existing code...
}
```

Getting Ahead of the Data

The `characters()` callback method accepts a character array, as well as start and length parameters, to signify which index to start at and how far to read into the array. This can cause some confusion; a common mistake is to include code like this example to read from the character array:

```
public void characters(char[] ch, int start, int length)
    throws SAXException {
```

```
      for (int i=0; i<ch.length; i++)
          System.out.print(i);
  }
```

The mistake here is in reading from the beginning to the end of the character array. This natural "gotcha" results from years of iterating through arrays, either in Java, C, or another language. However, in the case of a SAX event, this can cause quite a bug. SAX parsers are required to pass starting and length values on the character array that any loop constructs should use to read from the array. This allows lower-level manipulation of textual data to occur in order to optimize parser performance, such as reading data ahead of the current location as well as array reuse. This is all legal behavior within SAX, as the expectation is that a wrapping application will not try to "read past" the length parameter sent to the callback.

Mistakes as in the example shown can result in gibberish data being output to the screen or used within the wrapping application, and are almost always problematic for applications. The loop construct looks very normal and compiles without a hitch, so this gotcha can be a very tricky problem to track down. Instead, you can simply convert this data to a `String`, use it, and never worry:

```
  public void characters(char[] ch, int start, int length)
      throws SAXException {

      String data = new String(ch, start, length);
      // Use the string
  }
```

What's Next?

Now that you have a taste of SAX, you are ready for some of the more advanced features of the API. These include setting properties and features, using validation and namespace processing, and the `EntityResolver` and `DTDHandler` interfaces. Additionally, you'll take a look at many less used (but still valuable) features of the Simple API for XML, as well as the optional add-ons to SAX, such as filters and the `org.xml.sax.ext` package. This should get those of you who are using SAX in applications up, running, and even flying past developers around you. That's always good. Keep that editor humming, and turn the page.

4

Advanced SAX

The last chapter was a good introduction to SAX. However, there are several more topics that will round out your knowledge of SAX. While I've called this chapter "Advanced SAX," don't be intimidated. It could just as easily be called "Less-Used Portions of SAX that are Still Important." In writing these two chapters, I followed the 80/20 principle. 80% of you will probably never need to use the material in this chapter, and Chapter 3 will completely cover your needs. However, for those power users out there working in XML day in and day out, this chapter covers some of the finer points of SAX that you'll need.

I'll start with a look at setting parser properties and features, and discuss configuring your parser to do whatever you need it to. From there, I'll move on to some more handlers: the `EntityResolver` and `DTDHandler` left over from the last chapter. At that point, you should have a comprehensive understanding of the standard SAX 2.0 distribution. However, we'll push on to look at some SAX extensions, beginning with the writers that can be coupled with SAX, as well as some filtering mechanisms. Finally, I'll introduce some new handlers to you, the `LexicalHandler` and `DeclHandler`, and show you how they are used. When all is said and done (including another "Gotcha!" section), you should be ready to take on the world with just your parser and the SAX classes. So slip into your shiny spacesuit and grab the flightstick—ahem. Well, I got carried away with the taking on the world. In any case, let's get down to it.

Properties and Features

With the wealth of XML-related specifications and technologies emerging from the World Wide Web Consortium (W3C), adding support for any new feature or property of an XML parser has become difficult. Many parser implementations have added proprietary extensions or methods at the cost of code portability. While these software packages may implement the SAX XMLReader interface, the methods for setting document and schema validation, namespace support, and other core features are not standard across parser implementations. To address this, SAX 2.0 defines a standard mechanism for setting important properties and features of a parser that allows the addition of new properties and features as they are accepted by the W3C without the use of proprietary extensions or methods.

Setting Properties and Features

Lucky for you and me, SAX 2.0 includes the methods needed for setting properties and features in the XMLReader interface. This means you have to change little of your existing code to request validation, set the namespace separator, and handle other feature and property requests. The methods used for these purposes are outlined in Table 4-1.

Table 4-1. Property and feature methods

Method	Returns	Parameters	Syntax
setProperty()	void	String propertyID, Object value	parser.setProperty("[Property URI]", propertyValue);
setFeature()	void	String featureID, boolean state	parser.setFeature("[Feature URI]", featureState);
getProperty()	Object	String propertyID	Object propertyValue = parser.getProperty("[Property URI]");
getFeature()	boolean	String featureID	boolean featureState = parser.getFeature("[Feature URI]");

For these methods, the ID of a specific property or feature is a URI. The core set of features and properties is listed in Appendix B. Additional documentation on features and properties supported by your vendor's XML parser should also be available. These URIs are similar to namespace URIs; they are only used as *associations* for particular features. Good parsers ensure that you do not need network access to resolve these features; think of them as simple constants that happen to be in URI form. These methods are simply invoked and the URI is dereferenced locally, often to constantly represent what action in the parser needs to be taken.

WARNING Don't type these property and feature URIs into a browser to "check for their existence." Often, this results in a *404 Not Found* error. I've had many browsers report this to me, insisting that the URIs are invalid. However, this is not the case; the URI is just an identifier, and as I pointed out, usually resolved locally. Trust me: just use the URI, and trust the parser to do the right thing.

In the parser configuration context, a *property* requires some object value to be usable. For example, for lexical handling, a DOM Node implementation would be supplied as the value for the appropriate property. In contrast, a *feature* is a flag used by the parser to indicate whether a certain type of processing should occur. Common features are validation, namespace support, and including external parameter entities.

The most convenient aspect of these methods is that they allow simple addition and modification of features. Although new or updated features will require a parser implementation to add supporting code, the method by which features and properties are accessed remains standard and simple; only a new URI need be defined. Regardless of the complexity (or obscurity) of new XML-related ideas, this robust set of four methods should be sufficient to allow parsers to implement the new ideas.

SAX Properties and Features

More often than not, the features and properties you deal with are the standard SAX-defined ones. These are features and properties that should be available with any SAX distribution, and that any SAX-compliant parser should support. Additionally, this preserves vendor-independence in your code, so I recommend that you use SAX-defined properties and features whenever possible.

Validation

The most common feature you'll use is the validation feature. The URI for this guy is *http://xml.org/sax/features/validation,* and not surprisingly, it turns validation on or off in the parser. For example, if you want to turn on validation in the parsing example from the last chapter (remember the Swing viewer?), make this change in the *SAXTreeViewer.java* source file:

```
public void buildTree(DefaultTreeModel treeModel,
                      DefaultMutableTreeNode base, String xmlURI)
    throws IOException, SAXException {

    // Create instances needed for parsing
    XMLReader reader =
        XMLReaderFactory.createXMLReader(vendorParserClass);
    ContentHandler jTreeContentHandler =
        new JTreeContentHandler(treeModel, base);
    ErrorHandler jTreeErrorHandler = new JTreeErrorHandler();

    // Register content handler
    reader.setContentHandler(jTreeContentHandler);
```

```
        // Register error handler
        reader.setErrorHandler(jTreeErrorHandler);

        // Request validation
        reader.setFeature("http://xml.org/sax/features/validation", true);

        // Parse
        InputSource inputSource =
            new InputSource(xmlURI);
        reader.parse(inputSource);
    }
```

Compile these changes, and run the example program. Nothing happens, right? Not surprising; the XML we've looked at so far is all valid with respect to the DTD supplied. However, it's easy enough to fix that. Make the following change to your XML file (notice that the element in the DOCTYPE declaration no longer matches the actual root element, since XML is case-sensitive):

```
<?xml version="1.0"?>
<!DOCTYPE Book SYSTEM "DTD/JavaXML.dtd">

<!-- Java and XML Contents -->
<book xmlns="http://www.oreilly.com/javaxml2"
      xmlns:ora="http://www.oreilly.com"
>
```

Now run your program on this modified document. Because validation is turned on, you should get an ugly stack trace reporting the error. Of course, because that's all that our error handler methods do, this is precisely what we want:

```
C:\javaxml2\build>java javaxml2.SAXTreeViewer
    c:\javaxml2\ch04\xml\contents.xml
**Parsing Error**
  Line:   7
  URI:    file:///c:/javaxml2/ch04/xml/contents.xml
  Message: Document root element "book", must match DOCTYPE root "Book".
org.xml.sax.SAXException: Error encountered
        at javaxml2.JTreeErrorHandler.error(SAXTreeViewer.java:445)
[Nasty Stack Trace to Follow...]
```

Remember, turning validation on or off does not affect DTD processing; I talked about this in the last chapter, and wanted to remind you of this subtle fact. To get a better sense of this, turn off validation (comment out the feature setting, or supply it the "false" value), and run the program on the modified XML. Even though the DTD is processed, as seen by the resolved OReillyCopyright entity reference, no errors occur. That's the difference between *processing* a DTD and *validating* an XML document against that DTD. Memorize, understand, and recite this to yourself; it will save you hours of confusion in the long run.

Namespaces

Next to validation, you'll most commonly deal with namespaces. There are two features related to namespaces: one that turns namespace processing on or off, and one that indicates whether namespace prefixes should be reported as attributes. The two are essentially tied together, and you should always "toggle" both, as shown in Table 4-2.

Table 4-2. Toggle values for namespace-related features

Value for namespace processing	Value for namespace prefix reporting
True	False
False	True

This should make sense: if namespace processing is on, the xmlns-style declarations on elements should not be exposed to your application as attributes, as they are only useful for namespace handling. However, if you do not want namespace processing to occur (or want to handle it on your own), you will want these xmlns declarations reported as attributes so you can use them just as you would use other attributes. However, if these two fall out of sync (both are true, or both are false), you can end up with quite a mess!

Consider writing a small utility method to ensure these two features stay in sync with each other. I often use the method shown here for this purpose:

```
private void setNamespaceProcessing(XMLReader reader, boolean state)
    throws SAXNotSupportedException, SAXNotRecognizedException {

    reader.setFeature(
        "http://xml.org/sax/features/namespaces", state);
    reader.setFeature(
        "http://xml.org/sax/features/namespace-prefixes", !state);
}
```

This maintains the correct setting for both features, and you can now simply call this method instead of two setFeature() invocations in your own code. Personally, I've used this feature less than ten times in about two years; the default values (processing namespaces as well as not reporting prefixes as attributes) almost always work for me. Unless you are writing low-level applications that either don't need namespaces or can use the speed increase obtained from not processing namespaces, or you need to handle namespaces on your own, I wouldn't worry too much about either of these features.

This code brings up a rather important aspect of features and properties, though: invoking the feature and property methods can result in SAXNotSupported-Exceptions and SAXNotRecognizedExceptions. These are both in the org.xml.sax package, and need to be imported in any SAX code that uses them. The first indicates that the parser knows about the feature or property but doesn't support it. You won't run into this much in even average quality parsers, but it is commonly used when a standard property or feature is not yet coded in. So invoking `setFeature()` on the namespace processing feature on a parser in development might result in a `SAXNotSupportedException`. The parser recognizes the feature, but doesn't have the ability to perform the requested processing. The second exception most commonly occurs when using vendor-specific features and properties (covered in the next section), and then switching parser implementations. The new implementation won't know anything about the other vendor's features or properties, and will throw a `SAXNotRecognizedException`.

You should always explicitly catch these exceptions so you can deal with them. Otherwise, you end up losing valuable information about what happened in your code. For example, let me show you a modified version of the code from the last chapter that tries to set up various features, and how that changes the exception-handling architecture:

```
public void buildTree(DefaultTreeModel treeModel,
                          DefaultMutableTreeNode base, String xmlURI)
    throws IOException, SAXException {

    String featureURI = "";

    try {
        // Create instances needed for parsing
        XMLReader reader =
            XMLReaderFactory.createXMLReader(vendorParserClass);
        ContentHandler jTreeContentHandler =
            new JTreeContentHandler(treeModel, base);
        ErrorHandler jTreeErrorHandler = new JTreeErrorHandler();

        // Register content handler
        reader.setContentHandler(jTreeContentHandler);

        // Register error handler
        reader.setErrorHandler(jTreeErrorHandler);

        /** Deal with features **/
        featureURI = "http://xml.org/sax/features/validation";

        // Request validation
        reader.setFeature(featureURI, true);

        // Namespace processing - on
        featureURI = "http://xml.org/sax/features/namespaces";
        setNamespaceProcessing(reader, true);
```

```
// Turn on String interning
featureURI = "http://xml.org/sax/features/string-interning";
reader.setFeature(featureURI, true);

// Turn off schema processing
featureURI =
    "http://apache.org/xml/features/validation/schema";
reader.setFeature(featureURI, false);

// Parse
InputSource inputSource =
    new InputSource(xmlURI);
reader.parse(inputSource);
} catch (SAXNotRecognizedException e) {
    System.out.println("The parser class " + vendorParserClass +
        " does not recognize the feature URI " + featureURI);
    System.exit(0);
} catch (SAXNotSupportedException e) {
    System.out.println("The parser class " + vendorParserClass +
        " does not support the feature URI " + featureURI);
    System.exit(0);
}
}
```

By dealing with these exceptions as well as other special cases, you give the user better information and improve the quality of your code.

Interning and entities

The three remaining SAX-defined features are fairly obscure. The first, *http://xml. org/sax/features/string-interning*, turns string interning on or off. By default this is false (off) in most parsers. Setting it to true means that every element name, attribute name, namespace URI and prefix, and other strings have java.lang. String.intern() invoked on them. I'm not going to get into great detail about interning here; if you don't know what it is, check out Sun's Javadoc on the method at *http://java.sun.com/j2se/1.3/docs/api/index.html*. In a nutshell, every time a string is encountered, Java attempts to return an existing reference for the string in the current string pool, instead of (possibly) creating a new String object. Sounds like a good thing, right? Well, the reason it's off by default is most parsers have their own optimizations in place that can outperform string interning. My advice is to leave this setting alone; many people have spent weeks tuning things like this so you don't have to mess with them.

The other two features determine whether textual entities are expanded and resolved (*http://xml.org/sax/features/external-general-entities*), and whether parameter entities are included (*http://xml.org/sax/features/external-parameter-entities*) when parsing occurs. These are set to true for most parsers, as they deal with all the entities that XML has to offer. Again, I recommend you leave these settings as is, unless you have a specific reason for disabling entity handling.

DOM nodes and literal strings

The two standard SAX properties are a little less clear in their usage. In both cases, the properties are more useful for *obtaining* values, whereas with features the common use is to *set* values. Additionally, both properties are more helpful in error handling than in any general usage. And finally, both properties provide access to what is being parsed at a given time. The first, identified by the URI *http://xml.org/ sax/properties/dom-node*, returns the current DOM node being processed, or the root DOM node if parsing isn't occurring. Of course, I haven't really talked about DOM yet, but this will make more sense in the next two chapters. The second property, identified by the URI *http://xml.org/sax/properties/xml-string*, returns the literal string of characters being processed. You'll find varying support for these properties in various parsers, showing that many parser implementers find these properties of arguable use as well. For example, Xerces does not support the `xml-string` property, to avoid having to buffer the input document (at least in that specific way). On the other hand, it does support the `dom-node` property so that you can turn a SAX parser into (essentially) a DOM tree iterator.

Proprietary Properties and Features

In addition to the standard, SAX-defined features and properties, most parsers define several features and properties of their own. For example, Apache Xerces has a page of features it supports at *http://xml.apache.org/xerces-j/properties.html*, and properties it supports at *http://xml.apache.org/xerces-j/properties.html*. I'm not going to cover these in great detail, and you should steer clear of them whenever possible; it locks your code into a specific vendor. However, there are times when using a vendor's specific functionality will save you some work. In those cases, exercise caution, but don't be foolish; use what your parser gives you!

As an example, take the Xerces feature that enables and disables XML schema processing: *http://apache.org/xml/features/validation/schema*. Because there is no standard support for XML schemas across parsers or in SAX, use this specific feature (it's set to true by default) to avoid spending parsing time to deal with any referenced XML schemas in your documents, for example. You save time in production if you don't use this processing, and it needs a vendor-specific feature. Check out your vendor documentation for options available in addition to SAX's.

More Handlers

In the last chapter, I showed you the `ContentHandler` and `ErrorHandler` interfaces and briefly mentioned the `EntityResolver` and `DTDHandler` interfaces as well. Now that you've got a good understanding of SAX basics, you're ready to look at these two other handlers.* You'll find that you use `EntityResolver` every now and then (more if you're writing applications to be resold), and that the `DTDHandler` is something rarely ever pulled out of your bag of tricks.

Using an EntityResolver

The first of these new handlers is `org.xml.sax.EntityResolver`. This interface does exactly what it says: resolves entities (or at least declares a method that resolves entities, but you get the idea). The interface defines only a single method, and it looks like this:

```
public InputSource resolveEntity(String publicID, String systemID)
    throws SAXException, IOException;
```

You can create an implementation of this interface, and register it with your `XMLReader` instance (through `setEntityResolver()`, not surprisingly). Once that's done, every time the reader comes across an entity reference, it passes the public ID and system ID for that entity to the `resolveEntity()` method of your implementation. Now you can change the normal process of entity resolution.

Typically, the XML reader resolves the entity through the specified public or system ID, whether it be a file, URL, or other resource. And if the return value from the `resolveEntity()` method is `null`, this process executes unchanged. As a result, you should always make sure that whatever code you add to your `resolveEntity()` implementation, it returns `null` in the default case. In other words, start with an implementation class that looks like Example 4-1.

Example 4-1. Simple implementation of EntityResolver

```
package javaxml2;

import java.io.IOException;

import org.xml.sax.EntityResolver;
import org.xml.sax.InputSource;
import org.xml.sax.SAXException;

public class SimpleEntityResolver implements EntityResolver {

    public InputSource resolveEntity(String publicID, String systemID)
        throws IOException, SAXException {
```

---

* For the picky reader, I know that technically `EntityResolver` isn't a "handler," per se. Of course, I could easily argue that the interface might be named `EntityHandler`, so it's close enough for me!

Example 4-1. Simple implementation of EntityResolver (continued)

```
    // In the default case, return null
    return null;
  }
}
```

You can compile this class with no problems, and register it with the reader implementation used in the SAXTreeViewer class within the buildTree() method:

```
// Create instances needed for parsing
XMLReader reader =
    XMLReaderFactory.createXMLReader(vendorParserClass);
ContentHandler jTreeContentHandler =
    new JTreeContentHandler(treeModel, base, reader);
ErrorHandler jTreeErrorHandler = new JTreeErrorHandler();

// Register content handler
reader.setContentHandler(jTreeContentHandler);

// Register error handler
reader.setErrorHandler(jTreeErrorHandler);

// Register entity resolver
reader.setEntityResolver(new SimpleEntityResolver());

// Other instructions and parsing...
```

Recompiling and rerunning the example class creates no change. Of course, that's exactly what was predicted, so don't be too surprised. By always returning a null value, the process of entity resolution proceeds normally. If you don't believe that anything is happening, though, you can make this small change to echo what's going on to the system output:

```
public InputSource resolveEntity(String publicID, String systemID)
    throws IOException, SAXException {

    System.out.println("Found entity with public ID " + publicID +
        " and system ID " + systemID);

    // In the default case, return null
    return null;
  }
```

Recompile this class and run the sample tree viewer. Once the Swing GUI comes up, move it out of the way and check out the shell or command prompt output; it should look similar to Example 4-2.

Example 4-2. Output from SAXTreeViewer with verbose output

```
C:\javaxml2\build>java javaxml2.SAXTreeViewer
    c:\javaxml2\ch04\xml\contents.xml
Found entity with public ID null and
    system ID file:///c:/javaxml2/ch04/xml/DTD/JavaXML.dtd
Found entity with public ID null and
    system ID http://www.newInstance.com/javaxml2/copyright.xml
```

As always, the line breaks are purely for display purposes. In any case, you can see that both references in the XML document, for the DTD and the `OReillyCopyright` entity reference, are passed to the `resolveEntity()` method.

At this point, you might be scratching your head; a DTD is an entity? The term "entity" is a bit vague as it is used in `EntityResolver`. Perhaps a better name would have been `ExternalReferenceResolver`, but that wouldn't be very fun to type. In any case, keep in mind that any external reference in your XML is going to be passed on to this method. So what's the point, you may be asking yourself. Remember the reference for `OReillyCopyright`, and how it accesses an Internet URL (*http://www.newInstance.com/javaxml2/copyright.xml*)? What if you don't have Internet access? What if you have a local copy you already downloaded, and want to save time by using that copy? What if you simply want to put your own copyright in place? All of these are viable questions, and real-world problems that you may have to solve in your applications. The answer, of course, is the `resolveEntity()` method I've been talking about.

If you return a valid `InputSource` (instead of `null`) from this method, that `InputSource` is used as the value for the entity reference, rather than the public or system ID specified. In other words, you can specify your own data instead of letting the reader handle resolution on its own. As an example, create a *copyright. xml* file on your local machine, as shown in Example 4-3.

Example 4-3. Local copy of copyright.xml

```
<copyright xmlns="http://www.oreilly.com">
  <year value="2001" />
  <content>This is my local version of the copyright.</content>
</copyright>
```

Save this in a directory you can access from your Java code (I used the same directory as my *contents.xml* file), and make the following change to the `resolveEntity()` method:

```
public InputSource resolveEntity(String publicID, String systemID)
    throws IOException, SAXException {
```

```
    // Handle references to online version of copyright.xml
    if (systemID.equals(
        "http://www.newInstance.com/javaxml2/copyright.xml")) {
        return new InputSource(
            "file:///c:/javaxml2/ch04/xml/copyright.xml");
    }

    // In the default case, return null
    return null;
}
```

You can see that instead of allowing resolution to the online resource, an InputSource that provides access to the local version of *copyright.xml* is returned. If you recompile your source file and run the tree viewer, you can visually verify that this local copy is used. Figure 4-1 shows the ora:copyright element expanded, including the local copyright document's content.

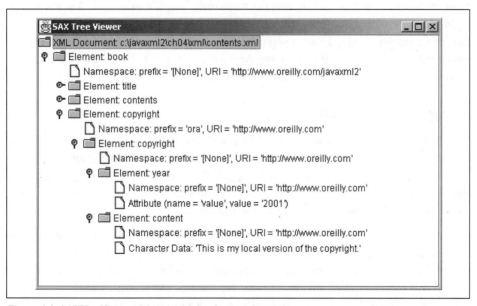

Figure 4-1. SAXTreeViewer running with local copyrights.xml

In real-world applications, this method tends to become a lengthy laundry list of if/then/else blocks, each one handling a specific system or public ID. And this brings up an important point: try to avoid this class and method becoming a kitchen sink for IDs. If you no longer need a specific resolution to occur, remove the if clause for it. Additionally, try to use different EntityResolver implementations for different applications, rather than trying to use one generic implementation for all your applications. Doing this avoids code bloat, and more importantly, speeds up entity resolution. If you have to wait for your reader to run through fifty or a hundred `String.equals()` comparisons, you can really bog down an application. Be sure to put references accessed often at the top of the `if/else` stack, so they are encountered first and result in quicker entity resolution.

Finally, I want to make one more recommendation concerning your `EntityResolver` implementations. You'll notice that I defined my implementation in a separate class file, while the `ErrorHandler`, `ContentHandler`, and (in the next section) `DTDHandler` implementations were in the same source file as parsing occurred in. That wasn't an accident! You'll find that the way you deal with content, errors, and DTDs is fairly static. You write your program, and that's it. When you make changes, you're making a larger rewrite, and need to make big changes anyway. However, you'll make many changes to the way you want your application to resolve entities. Depending on the machine you're on, the type of client you're deploying to, and what and where documents are available, you'll need different versions of an `EntityResolver` implementation. To allow for rapid changes to this implementation without causing editing or recompilation of your core parsing code, I use a separate source file for `EntityResolver` implementations; I suggest you do the same. And with that, you should know all that you need to know about resolving entities in your applications using SAX.

Using a DTDHandler

After a rather extensive look at `EntityResolver`, I'm going to cruise through `DTDHandler` pretty quickly. In two years of extensive XML programming, I've used this interface only once, in writing JDOM, and even then it was a rather obscure case. More often than not, you won't work with it much unless you have lots of unparsed entities in your XML documents.

The `DTDHandler` interface allows you to receive notification when a reader encounters an unparsed entity or notation declaration. Of course, both of these events occur in DTDs, not XML documents, which is why this is called `DTDHandler`. Rather than go on and on, let me just show you what the interface looks like. It's right here for you to check out in Example 4-4.

Example 4-4. The DTDHandler interface

```
package org.xml.sax;

public interface DTDHandler {

    public void notationDecl(String name, String publicID,
                             String systemID)
        throws SAXException;
```

Example 4-4. The DTDHandler interface (continued)

```
    public void unparsedEntityDecl(String name, String publicId,
                                    String systemId, String notationName)
        throws SAXException;
}
```

These two methods do exactly what you would expect. The first reports a notation declaration, including its name, public ID, and system ID. Remember the NOTATION structure in DTDs?

```
    <!NOTATION jpeg SYSTEM "images/jpeg">
```

The second method provides information about an unparsed entity declaration, which looks as follows:

```
    <!ENTITY stars_logo SYSTEM "http://www.nhl.com/img/team/dal38.gif"
                    NDATA jpeg>
```

In both cases, you can take action at these occurrences if you create an implementation of DTDHandler and register it with your reader through the XMLReader's setDTDHandler() method. This is generally useful when writing low-level applications that must either reproduce XML content (such as an XML editor), or when you want to build up some Java representation of a DTD's constraints (such as for data binding, covered in Chapter 15). In most other situations, it isn't something you will need very often.

The DefaultHandler Class

Before finishing up with handlers (for now, at least), there's one other important handler-related class you should know about. This class is org.xml.sax. helpers.DefaultHandler, and can be a very good friend to you SAX developers out there. Remember that so far, implementing the various handler interfaces required a class to implement ContentHandler, one to implement ErrorHandler, one to implement EntityResolver (this one is OK for all the reasons I discussed about keeping that implementation in a separate source file), and one to implement DTDHandler, if needed. Additionally, you get the joy of implementing the numerous methods in ContentHandler, even if you don't need them all to do anything.

And here comes DefaultHandler to the rescue. This class doesn't define any behavior of its own; however, it does implement ContentHandler, ErrorHandler, EntityResolver, and DTDHandler, and provides empty implementations of each method of each interface. So you can have a single class (call it, for example, MyHandlerClass) that extends DefaultHandler. This class only needs to override methods it needs to perform action in. You might implement startElement(), characters(), endElement(), and fatalError(), for example. In any combination of implemented methods, though, you'll save tons of lines of code for methods you don't need to provide action for, and make your code a lot clearer too. Then, the argument to `setErrorHandler()`, `setContentHandler()`, and `setDTDHandler()` would be the same instance of this `MyHandlerClass`. Theoretically, you could pass the instance to `setEntityResolver()` as well, although (for about the fourth time!) I discourage mixing the `resolveEntity()` method in with these other interface methods.

Filters and Writers

At this point, I want to diverge from the beaten path. So far, I've detailed everything that's in a "standard" SAX application, from the reader to the callbacks to the handlers. However, there are a lot of additional features in SAX that can really turn you into a power developer, and take you beyond the confines of "standard" SAX. In this section, I'll introduce you to two of these: SAX filters and writers. Using classes both in the standard SAX distribution and available separately from the SAX web site (*http://www.megginson.com/SAX*), you can add some fairly advanced behavior to your SAX applications. This will also get you in the mindset of using SAX as a pipeline of events, rather than a single layer of processing. I'll explain this concept in more detail, but suffice it to say that it really is the key to writing efficient and modular SAX code.

XMLFilters

First on the list is a class that comes in the basic SAX download from David Megginson's site, and should be included with any parser distribution supporting SAX 2.0. The class in question here is `org.xml.sax.XMLFilter`. This class extends the `XMLReader` interface, and adds two new methods to that class:

```
public void setParent(XMLReader parent);

public XMLReader getParent();
```

It might not seem like there is much to say here; what's the big deal, right? Well, by allowing a hierarchy of `XMLReaders` through this filtering mechanism, you can build up a processing chain, or *pipeline*, of events. To understand what I mean by a pipeline, here's the normal flow of a SAX parse:

- Events in an XML document are passed to the SAX reader.

- The SAX reader and registered handlers pass events and data to an application.

What developers started realizing, though, is that it is simple to insert one or more additional links into this chain:

- Events in an XML document are passed to the SAX reader.

- The SAX reader performs some processing and passes information to another SAX reader.

- Repeat until all SAX processing is done.

- Finally, the SAX reader and registered handlers pass events and data to an application.

It's the middle steps that introduce a pipeline, where one reader that performed specific processing passes its information on to another reader, repeatedly, instead of having to lump all code into one reader. When this pipeline is set up with multiple readers, modular and efficient programming results. And that's what the XMLFilter class allows for: chaining of XMLReader implementations through filtering. Enhancing this even further is the class org.xml.sax.helpers. XMLFilterImpl, which provides a helpful implementation of XMLFilter. It is the convergence of an XMLFilter and the DefaultHandler class I showed you in the last section; the XMLFilterImpl class implements XMLFilter, ContentHandler, ErrorHandler, EntityResolver, and DTDHandler, providing pass-through versions of each method of each handler. In other words, it sets up a pipeline for all SAX events, allowing your code to override any methods that need to insert processing into the pipeline.

Let's use one of these filters. Example 4-5 is a working, ready-to-use filter. You're past the basics, so we will move through this rapidly.

Example 4-5. NamespaceFilter class

```
package javaxml2;

import org.xml.sax.Attributes;
import org.xml.sax.SAXException;
import org.xml.sax.XMLReader;
import org.xml.sax.helpers.XMLFilterImpl;

public class NamespaceFilter extends XMLFilterImpl {

    /** The old URI, to replace */
    private String oldURI;

    /** The new URI, to replace the old URI with */
    private String newURI;

    public NamespaceFilter(XMLReader reader,
                           String oldURI, String newURI) {
        super(reader);
        this.oldURI = oldURI;
        this.newURI = newURI;
    }

    public void startPrefixMapping(String prefix, String uri)
```

Example 4-5. NamespaceFilter class (continued)

```
        throws SAXException {

        // Change URI, if needed
        if (uri.equals(oldURI)) {
            super.startPrefixMapping(prefix, newURI);
        } else {
            super.startPrefixMapping(prefix, uri);
        }
    }

    public void startElement(String uri, String localName,
                            String qName, Attributes attributes)
        throws SAXException {

        // Change URI, if needed
        if (uri.equals(oldURI)) {
            super.startElement(newURI, localName, qName, attributes);
        } else {
            super.startElement(uri, localName, qName, attributes);
        }
    }

    public void endElement(String uri, String localName, String qName)
        throws SAXException {

        // Change URI, if needed
        if (uri.equals(oldURI)) {
            super.endElement(newURI, localName, qName);
        } else {
            super.endElement(uri, localName, qName);
        }
    }
}
```

I start out by extending XMLFilterImpl, so I don't have to worry about any events
that I don't explicitly need to change; the XMLFilterImpl class takes care of them
by passing on all events unchanged unless a method is overridden. I can get down
to the business of what I want the filter to do; in this case, that's changing a
namespace URI from one to another. If this task seems trivial, don't underesti-
mate its usefulness. Many times in the last several years, the URI of a namespace
for a specification (such as XML Schema or XSLT) has changed. Rather than having to hand-edit all of my XML documents or write code for XML that I receive,
this NamespaceFilter takes care of the problem for me.

Passing an XMLReader instance to the constructor sets that reader as its parent, so
the parent reader receives any events passed on from the filter (which is all events,

by virtue of the XMLFilterImpl class, unless the NamespaceFilter class over-rides that behavior). By supplying two URIs, the original and the URI to replace it with, you set this filter up. The three overridden methods handle any needed interchanging of that URI. Once you have a filter like this in place, you supply a reader to it, and then operate upon the *filter*, not the *reader*. Going back to *contents. xml* and SAXTreeViewer, suppose that O'Reilly has informed me that my book's online URL is no longer *http://www.oreilly.com/javaxml2*, but *http://www.oreilly.com/ catalog/javaxml2*. Rather than editing all my XML samples and uploading them, I can just use the NamespaceFilter class:

```
public void buildTree(DefaultTreeModel treeModel,
                      DefaultMutableTreeNode base, String xmlURI)
    throws IOException, SAXException {

    // Create instances needed for parsing
    XMLReader reader =
        XMLReaderFactory.createXMLReader(vendorParserClass);
    NamespaceFilter filter =
        new NamespaceFilter(reader,
            "http://www.oreilly.com/javaxml2",
            "http://www.oreilly.com/catalog/javaxml2");
    ContentHandler jTreeContentHandler =
        new JTreeContentHandler(treeModel, base, reader);
    ErrorHandler jTreeErrorHandler = new JTreeErrorHandler();

    // Register content handler
    filter.setContentHandler(jTreeContentHandler);

    // Register error handler
    filter.setErrorHandler(jTreeErrorHandler);

    // Register entity resolver
    filter.setEntityResolver(new SimpleEntityResolver());

    // Parse
    InputSource inputSource =
        new InputSource(xmlURI);
    filter.parse(inputSource);
}
```

Notice, as I said, that all operation occurs upon the filter, not the reader instance. With this filtering in place, you can compile both source files (*NamespaceFilter.java* and *SAXTreeViewer.java*), and run the viewer on the *contents.xml* file. You'll see that the O'Reilly namespace URI for my book is changed in every occurrence, shown in Figure 4-2.

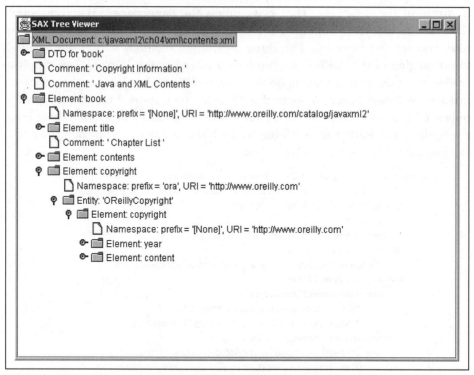

Figure 4-2. SAXTreeViewer on contents.xml with NamespaceFilter in place

Of course, you can chain these filters together as well, and use them as standard libraries. When I'm dealing with older XML documents, I often create several of these with old XSL and XML Schema URIs and put them in place so I don't have to worry about incorrect URIs:

```
XMLReader reader =
    XMLReaderFactory.createXMLReader(vendorParserClass);
NamespaceFilter xslFilter =
    new NamespaceFilter(reader,
        "http://www.w3.org/TR/XSL",
        "http://www.w3.org/1999/XSL/Transform");
NamespaceFilter xsdFilter =
    new NamespaceFilter(xslFilter,
        "http://www.w3.org/TR/XMLSchema",
        "http://www.w3.org/2001/XMLSchema");
```

Here, I'm building a longer pipeline to ensure that no old namespace URIs sneak by and cause my applications any trouble. Be careful not to build too long a pipeline; each new link in the chain adds some processing time. All the same, this is a great way to build reusable components for SAX.

XMLWriter

Now that you understand how filters work in SAX, I want to introduce you to a specific filter, XMLWriter. This class, as well as a subclass of it, DataWriter, can be downloaded from David Megginson's SAX site at *http://www.megginson.com/SAX*. XMLWriter extends XMLFilterImpl, and DataWriter extends XMLWriter. Both of these filter classes are used to output XML, which may seem a bit at odds with what you've learned so far about SAX. However, just as you could insert statements that output to Java Writers in SAX callbacks, so can this class. I'm not going to spend a lot of time on this class, because it's not really the way you want to be outputting XML in the general sense; it's much better to use DOM, JDOM, or another XML API if you want mutability. However, the XMLWriter class offers a valuable way to inspect what's going on in a SAX pipeline. By inserting it between other filters and readers in your pipeline, it can be used to output a snapshot of your data at whatever point it resides in your processing chain. For example, in the case where I'm changing namespace URIs, it might be that you want to actually store the XML document with the new namespace URI (be it a modified O'Reilly URI, a updated XSL one, or the XML Schema one) for later use. This becomes a piece of cake by using the XMLWriter class. Since you've already got SAXTreeViewer using the NamespaceFilter, I'll use that as an example. First, add import statements for java.io.Writer (for output), and the com. megginson.sax.XMLWriter class. Once that's in place, you'll need to insert an instance of XMLWriter between the NamespaceFilter and the XMLReader instances; this means output will occur after namespaces have been changed but before the visual events occur. Change your code as shown here:

```
public void buildTree(DefaultTreeModel treeModel,
                      DefaultMutableTreeNode base, String xmlURI)
    throws IOException, SAXException {

    // Create instances needed for parsing
    XMLReader reader =
        XMLReaderFactory.createXMLReader(vendorParserClass);
    XMLWriter writer =
        new XMLWriter(reader, new FileWriter("snapshot.xml"));
    NamespaceFilter filter =
        new NamespaceFilter(writer,
            "http://www.oreilly.com/javaxml2",
            "http://www.oreilly.com/catalog/javaxml2");
    ContentHandler jTreeContentHandler =
        new JTreeContentHandler(treeModel, base, reader);
    ErrorHandler jTreeErrorHandler = new JTreeErrorHandler();

    // Register content handler
    filter.setContentHandler(jTreeContentHandler);
```

```
            // Register error handler
            filter.setErrorHandler(jTreeErrorHandler);

            // Register entity resolver
            filter.setEntityResolver(new SimpleEntityResolver());

            // Parse
            InputSource inputSource =
                new InputSource(xmlURI);
            filter.parse(inputSource);
        }
```

Be sure you set the parent of the `NamespaceFilter` instance to be the `XMLWriter`, not the `XMLReader`. Otherwise, no output will actually occur. Once you've got these changes compiled in, run the example. You should get a *snapshot. xml* file created in the directory you're running the example from; an excerpt from that document is shown here:

```
<?xml version="1.0" standalone="yes"?>

<book xmlns="http://www.oreilly.com/catalog/javaxml2">
  <title ora:series="Java"
         xmlns:ora="http://www.oreilly.com">Java and XML</title>



  <contents>
    <chapter title="Introduction" number="1">
      <topic name="XML Matters"></topic>
      <topic name="What's Important"></topic>
      <topic name="The Essentials"></topic>
      <topic name="What's Next?"></topic>
    </chapter>
    <chapter title="Nuts and Bolts" number="2">
      <topic name="The Basics"></topic>
      <topic name="Constraints"></topic>
      <topic name="Transformations"></topic>
      <topic name="And More..."></topic>
      <topic name="What's Next?"></topic>
    </chapter>
    <!-- Other content... -->

  </contents>
</book>
```

Notice that the namespace, as changed by `NamespaceFilter`, is modified here. Snapshots like this, created by `XMLWriter` instances, can be great tools for debugging and logging of SAX events.

Both XMLWriter and DataWriter offer a lot more in terms of methods to output XML, both in full and in part, and you should check out the Javadoc included with the downloaded package. I do not encourage you to use these classes for general output. In my experience, they are most useful in the case demonstrated here.

Even More Handlers

Now I want to show you two more handler classes that SAX offers. Both of these interfaces are no longer part of the core SAX distribution, and are located in the org.xml.sax.ext package to indicate they are extensions to SAX. However, most parsers (such as Apache Xerces) include these two classes for use. Check your vendor documentation, and if you don't have these classes, you can download them from the SAX web site. I warn you that not all SAX drivers support these extensions, so if your vendor doesn't include them, you may want to find out why, and see if an upcoming version of the vendor's software will support the SAX extensions.

LexicalHandler

The first of these two handlers is the most useful: org.xml.sax.ext. LexicalHandler. This handler provides methods that can receive notification of several lexical events such as comments, entity declarations, DTD declarations, and CDATA sections. In ContentHandler, these lexical events are essentially ignored, and you just get the data and declarations without notification of when or how they were provided.

This is not really a general-use handler, as most applications don't need to know if text was in a CDATA section or not. However, if you are working with an XML editor, serializer, or other component that must know the exact *format* of the input document, not just its contents, the LexicalHandler can really help you out. To see this guy in action, you first need to add an import statement for org.xml. sax.ext.LexicalHandler to your *SAXTreeViewer.java* source file. Once that's done, you can add LexicalHandler to the implements clause in the nonpublic class JTreeContentHandler in that source file:

```
class JTreeContentHandler implements ContentHandler, LexicalHandler {
    // Callback implementations
}
```

By reusing the content handler already in this class, our lexical callbacks can operate upon the JTree for visual display of these lexical callbacks. So now you need to add implementations for all the methods defined in LexicalHandler. Those methods are as follows:

```
public void startDTD(String name, String publicID, String systemID)
        throws SAXException;
public void endDTD() throws SAXException;
```

```
public void startEntity(String name) throws SAXException;
public void endEntity(String name) throws SAXException;
public void startCDATA() throws SAXException;
public void endCDATA() throws SAXException;
public void comment(char[] ch, int start, int length)
        throws SAXException;
```

To get started, let's look at the first lexical event that might happen in processing an XML document: the start and end of a DTD reference or declaration. That triggers the startDTD() and endDTD() callbacks, shown here:

```
public void startDTD(String name, String publicID,
                     String systemID)
    throws SAXException {

    DefaultMutableTreeNode dtdReference =
        new DefaultMutableTreeNode("DTD for '" + name + "'");
    if (publicID != null) {
        DefaultMutableTreeNode publicIDNode =
            new DefaultMutableTreeNode("Public ID: '" +
                publicID + "'");
        dtdReference.add(publicIDNode);
    }
    if (systemID != null) {
        DefaultMutableTreeNode systemIDNode =
            new DefaultMutableTreeNode("System ID: '" +
                systemID + "'");
        dtdReference.add(systemIDNode);
    }
    current.add(dtdReference);
}

public void endDTD() throws SAXException {
    // No action needed here
}
```

This adds a visual cue when a DTD is encountered, and a system ID and public ID if present. Continuing on, there are a pair of similar methods for entity references, startEntity() and endEntity(). These are triggered before and after (respectively) processing entity references. You can add a visual cue for this event as well, using the code shown here:

```
public void startEntity(String name) throws SAXException {
    DefaultMutableTreeNode entity =
        new DefaultMutableTreeNode("Entity: '" + name + "'");
    current.add(entity);
    current = entity;
}
```

```
    public void endEntity(String name) throws SAXException {
        // Walk back up the tree
        current = (DefaultMutableTreeNode)current.getParent();
    }
```

This ensures that the content of, for example, the `OReillyCopyright` entity reference is included within an "Entity" tree node. Simple enough.

Because the next lexical event is a `CDATA` section, and there aren't any currently in the *contents.xml* document, you may want to make the following change to that document (the `CDATA` allows the ampersand in the `title` element's content):

```
<?xml version="1.0"?>
<!DOCTYPE book SYSTEM "DTD/JavaXML.dtd">

<!-- Java and XML Contents -->
<book xmlns="http://www.oreilly.com/javaxml2"
      xmlns:ora="http://www.oreilly.com"
>
  <title ora:series="Java"><![CDATA[Java & XML]]></title>

  <!-- Other content -->
</book>
```

With this change, you are ready to add code for the `CDATA` callbacks. Add in the following methods to the `JTreeContentHandler` class:

```
    public void startCDATA() throws SAXException {
        DefaultMutableTreeNode cdata =
            new DefaultMutableTreeNode("CDATA Section");
        current.add(cdata);
        current = cdata;
    }

    public void endCDATA() throws SAXException {
        // Walk back up the tree
        current = (DefaultMutableTreeNode)current.getParent();
    }
```

This is old hat by now; the title element's content now appears as the child of a `CDATA` node. And with that, only one method is left, that which receives comment notification:

```
    public void comment(char[] ch, int start, int length)
        throws SAXException {

        String comment = new String(ch, start, length);
        DefaultMutableTreeNode commentNode =
            new DefaultMutableTreeNode("Comment: '" + comment + "'");
        current.add(commentNode);
    }
```

This method behaves just like the `characters()` and `ignorableWhitespace()` methods. Keep in mind that only the text of the comment is reported to this method, not the surrounding <!– and –> delimiters. With these changes in place, you can compile the example program and run it. You should get output similar to that shown in Figure 4-3.

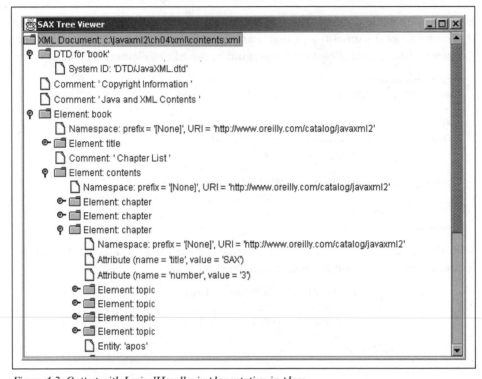

Figure 4-3. Output with LexicalHandler implementation in place

You'll notice one oddity, though: an entity named `[dtd]`. This occurs anytime a `DOCTYPE` declaration is in place, and can be removed (you probably don't want it present) with a simple clause in the `startEntity()` and `endEntity()` methods:

```
public void startEntity(String name) throws SAXException {
    if (!name.equals("[dtd]")) {
        DefaultMutableTreeNode entity =
            new DefaultMutableTreeNode("Entity: '" + name + "'");
        current.add(entity);
        current = entity;
    }
}


public void endEntity(String name) throws SAXException {
    if (!name.equals("[dtd]")) {
```

```
                        // Walk back up the tree
                        current = (DefaultMutableTreeNode)current.getParent();
            }
        }
```

This clause removes the offending entity. That's really about all that there is to say about LexicalHandler. Although I've filed it under advanced SAX, it's pretty straightforward.

DeclHandler

The last handler to deal with is the DeclHandler. This interface defines methods that receive notification of specific events within a DTD, such as element and attribute declarations. This is another item only good for very specific cases; again, XML editors and components that must know the exact lexical structure of documents and their DTDs come to mind. I'm not going to show you an example of using the DeclHandler; at this point you know more than you'll probably ever need to about handling callback methods. Instead, I'll just give you a look at the interface, shown in Example 4-6.

Example 4-6. The DeclHandler interface

```
package org.xml.sax.ext;

import org.xml.sax.SAXException;

public interface DeclHandler {

    public void attributeDecl(String eltName, String attName,
                              String type, String defaultValue,
                              String value)
        throws SAXException;

    public void elementDecl(String name, String model)
        throws SAXException;

    public void externalEntityDecl(String name, String publicID,
                                   String systemID)
        throws SAXException;

    public void internalEntityDecl(String name, String value)
        throws SAXException;
}
```

This example is fairly self-explanatory. The first two methods handle the <!ELEMENT> and <!ATTLIST> constructs. The third, externalEntityDecl(), reports entity declarations (through <!ENTITY>) that refer to external resources.

The final method, `internalEntityDecl()`, reports entities defined inline. That's all there is to it.

And with that, I've given you everything that there is to know about SAX. Well, that's probably an exaggeration, but you certainly have plenty of tools to start you on your way. Now you just need to get coding to build up your own set of tools and tricks. Before closing the book on SAX, though, I want to cover a few common mistakes in dealing with SAX.

Gotcha!

As you get into the more advanced features of SAX, you certainly don't reduce the number of problems you can get yourself into. However, these problems often become more subtle, which makes for some tricky bugs to track down. I'll point out a few of these common problems.

Return Values from an EntityResolver

As I mentioned in the section on `EntityResolvers`, you should always ensure that you return `null` as a starting point for `resolveEntity()` method implementations. Luckily, Java ensures that you return something from the method, but I've often seen code like this:

```
public InputSource resolveEntity(String publicID, String systemID)
    throws IOException, SAXException {

    InputSource inputSource = new InputSource();

    // Handle references to online version of copyright.xml
    if (systemID.equals(
        "http://www.newInstance.com/javaxml2/copyright.xml")) {
        inputSource.setSystemId(
            "file:///c:/javaxml2/ch04/xml/copyright.xml");
    }

    // In the default case, return null
    return inputSource;
}
```

As you can see, an `InputSource` is created initially and then the system ID is set on that source. The problem here is that if no `if` blocks are entered, an `InputSource` with no system or public ID, as well as no specified `Reader` or `InputStream`, is returned. This can lead to unpredictable results; in some parsers, things continue with no problems. In other parsers, though, returning an empty `InputSource` results in entities being ignored, or in exceptions being thrown. In other words, return `null` at the end of every `resolveEntity()` implementation, and you won't have to worry about these details.

DTDHandler and Validation

I've described setting properties and features in this chapter, their affect on validation, and also the `DTDHandler` interface. In all that discussion of DTDs and validation, it's possible you got a few things mixed up; I want to be clear that the `DTDHandler` interface has nothing at all to do with validation. I've seen many developers register a `DTDHandler` and wonder why validation isn't occurring. However, `DTDHandler` doesn't do anything but provide notification of notation and unparsed entity declarations! Probably not what the developer expected. Remember that it's a *property* that sets validation, not a handler instance:

```
reader.setFeature("http://xml.org/sax/features/validation", true);
```

Anything less than this (short of a parser validating by default) won't get you validation, and probably won't make you very happy.

Parsing on the Reader Instead of the Filter

I've talked about pipelines in SAX in this chapter, and hopefully you got an idea of how useful they could be. However, there's an error I see among filter beginners time and time again, and it's a frustrating one to deal with. The problem is setting up the pipeline chain incorrectly: this occurs when each filter does not set the preceding filter as its parent, ending in an `XMLReader` instance. Check out this code fragment:

```
public void buildTree(DefaultTreeModel treeModel,
                      DefaultMutableTreeNode base, String xmlURI)
    throws IOException, SAXException {

    // Create instances needed for parsing
    XMLReader reader =
        XMLReaderFactory.createXMLReader(vendorParserClass);
    XMLWriter writer =
        new XMLWriter(reader, new FileWriter("snapshot.xml"));
    NamespaceFilter filter =
        new NamespaceFilter(reader,
            "http://www.oreilly.com/javaxml2",
            "http://www.oreilly.com/catalog/javaxml2");
    ContentHandler jTreeContentHandler =
        new JTreeContentHandler(treeModel, base, reader);
    ErrorHandler jTreeErrorHandler = new JTreeErrorHandler();

    // Register content handler
    reader.setContentHandler(jTreeContentHandler);
```

```
    // Register error handler
    reader.setErrorHandler(jTreeErrorHandler);

    // Register entity resolver
    reader.setEntityResolver(new SimpleEntityResolver());

    // Parse
    InputSource inputSource =
        new InputSource(xmlURI);
    reader.parse(inputSource);
}
```

See anything wrong? Parsing is occurring on the XMLReader instance, not at the
end of the pipeline chain. In addition, the NamespaceFilter instance sets its parent to the XMLReader, instead of the XMLWriter instance that should precede it in
the chain. These errors are not obvious, and will throw your intended pipeline
into chaos. In this example, no filtering will occur at all, because parsing occurs on
the reader, not the filters. If you correct that error, you still won't get output, as
the writer is left out of the pipeline through improper setting of the
NamespaceFilter's parent. Setting the parent properly sets you up, though, and
you'll finally get the behavior you expected in the first place. Be very careful with
parentage and parsing when handling SAX pipelines.

What's Next?

That's plenty of information on the Simple API for SAX. Although there is certainly more to dig into, the information in this chapter and the last should have
you ready for almost anything you'll run into. Of course, SAX isn't the only API
for working with XML; to be a true XML expert you'll need to master DOM,
JDOM, JAXP, and more. I'll start you on the next API in this laundry list, the Document Object Model (DOM), in the next chapter.

To introduce DOM, I'll start with the basics, much as the last chapter gave you a
solid start on SAX. You'll find out about tree APIs and how DOM is significantly
different from SAX, and see the DOM core classes. I'll show you a sample application that serializes DOM trees, and soon you'll be writing your own DOM code.

5

DOM

In the previous chapters, I've talked about Java and XML in the general sense, but I have described only SAX in depth. As you may be aware, SAX is just one of several APIs that allow XML work to be done within Java. This chapter and the next will widen your API knowledge as I introduce the Document Object Model, commonly called the DOM. This API is quite a bit different from SAX, and complements the Simple API for XML in many ways. You'll need both, as well as the other APIs and tools in the rest of this book, to be a competent XML developer.

Because DOM is fundamentally different from SAX, I'll spend a good bit of time discussing the concepts behind DOM, and why it might be used instead of SAX for certain applications. Selecting any XML API involves tradeoffs, and choosing between DOM and SAX is certainly no exception. I'll move on to possibly the most important topic: code. I'll introduce you to a utility class that serializes DOM trees, something that the DOM API itself doesn't currently supply. This will provide a pretty good look at the DOM structure and related classes, and get you ready for some more advanced DOM work. Finally, I'll show you some problem areas and important aspects of DOM in the "Gotcha!" section.

The Document Object Model

The Document Object Model, unlike SAX, has its origins in the World Wide Web Consortium (W3C). Whereas SAX is public-domain software, developed through long discussions on the XML-dev mailing list, DOM is a standard just like the actual XML specification. The DOM is not designed specifically for Java, but to represent the content and model of documents across all programming languages and tools. Bindings exist for JavaScript, Java, CORBA, and other languages, allowing the DOM to be a cross-platform and cross-language specification.

In addition to being different from SAX in regard to standardization and language bindings, the DOM is organized into "levels" instead of versions. DOM Level One is an accepted recommendation, and you can view the completed specification at *http://www.w3.org/TR/REC-DOM-Level-1/*. Level 1 details the functionality and navigation of content within a document. A document in the DOM is not just limited to XML, but can be HTML or other content models as well! Level Two, which was finalized in November of 2000, adds upon Level 1 by supplying modules and options aimed at specific content models, such as XML, HTML, and Cascading Style Sheets (CSS). These less-generic modules begin to "fill in the blanks" left by the more general tools provided in DOM Level 1. You can view the current Level 2 Recommendation at *http://www.w3.org/TR/DOM-Level-2/*. Level Three is already being worked on, and should add even more facilities for specific types of documents, such as validation handlers for XML, and other features that I'll discuss in Chapter 6.

Language Bindings

Using the DOM for a specific programming language requires a set of interfaces and classes that define and implement the DOM itself. Because the methods involved are not outlined specifically in the DOM specification, and instead focus on the model of a document, *language bindings* must be developed to represent the conceptual structure of the DOM for its use in Java or any other language. These language bindings then serve as APIs for you to manipulate documents in the fashion outlined in the DOM specification.

I am obviously concerned with the Java language binding in this book. The latest Java bindings, the DOM Level 2 Java bindings, can be downloaded from *http://www.w3.org/TR/DOM-Level-2/java-binding.html*. The classes you should be able to add to your classpath are all in the `org.w3c.dom` package (and its subpackages). However, before downloading these yourself, you should check the XML parser and XSLT processor you purchased or downloaded; like the SAX packages, the DOM packages are often included with these products. This also ensures a correct match between your parser, processor, and the version of DOM that is supported.

Most XSLT processors do not handle the task of generating a DOM input themselves, but instead rely on an XML parser that is capable of generating a DOM tree. This maintains the loose coupling between parser and processor, letting one or the other be substituted with comparable products. As Apache Xalan, by default, uses Apache Xerces for XML parsing and DOM generation, it is the level of support for DOM that Xerces provides that is of interest. The same would be true if you were using Oracle's XSLT and XML processor and parser.[*]

---

[*] I don't want to imply that you cannot use one vendor's parser and another vendor's processor. In most of these cases, it's possible to specify a different parser for use. However, the default is always going to be the use of the vendor's software across the board.

The Basics

In addition to fundamentals about the DOM specification, I want to give you a bit of information about the DOM programming structure itself. At the core of DOM is a tree model. Remember that SAX gave you a piece-by-piece view of an XML document, reporting each event in the parsing lifecycle as it happened. DOM is in many ways the converse of this, supplying a complete in-memory representation of the document. The document is supplied to you in a tree format, and all of this is built upon the DOM `org.w3c.dom.Node` interface. Deriving from this interface, DOM provides several XML-specific interfaces, like `Element`, `Document`, `Attr`, and `Text`. So, in a typical XML document, you might get a structure that looks like Figure 5-1.

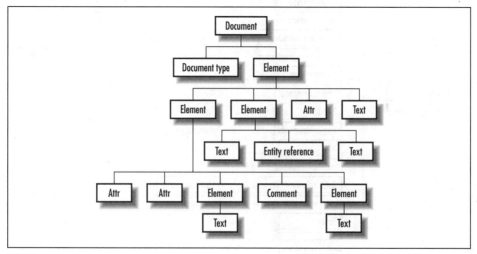

Figure 5-1. DOM structure representing XML

A tree model is followed in every sense. This is particularly notable in the case of the `Element` nodes that have textual values (as in the `Title` element). Instead of the textual value of the node being available through the `Element` node (through, for example, a `getText()` method), there is a child node of type `Text`. So you would get the child (or children) and the value of the element from the `Text` node itself. While this might seem a little odd, it does preserve a very strict tree model in DOM, and allows tasks like walking the tree to be very simple algorithms, without a lot of special cases. Because of this model, all DOM structures can be treated either as their generic type, `Node`, or as their specific type (`Element`, `Attr`, etc.). Many of the navigation methods, like `getParent()` and `getChildren()`, are on that basic `Node` interface, so you can walk up and down the tree without worrying about the specific structure type.

Another facet of DOM to be aware of is that, like SAX, it defines its own list structures. You'll need to use the NodeList and NamedNodeMap classes when working
with DOM, rather than Java collections. Depending on your point of view, this
isn't a positive or negative, just a fact of life. Figure 5-2 shows a simple UML-style
model of the DOM core interfaces and classes, which you can refer to throughout
the rest of the chapter.

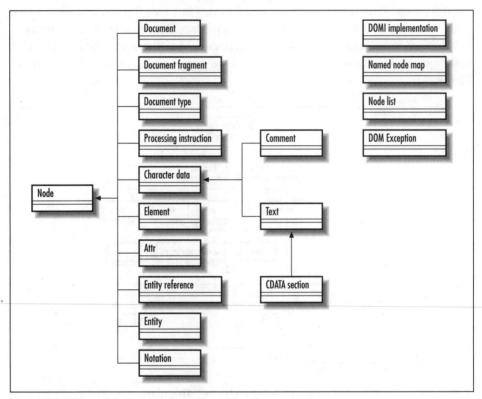

Figure 5-2. UML model of core DOM classes and interfaces

Why Not SAX?

As a final conceptual note before getting into the code, newbies to XML may be
wondering why they can't just use SAX for dealing with XML. But sometimes using
SAX is like taking a hammer to a scratch on a wall; it's just not the right tool for the
job. I discuss a few issues with SAX that make it less than ideal in certain situations.

SAX is sequential

The sequential model that SAX provides does not allow for random access to an
XML document. In other words, in SAX you get information about the XML

document as the parser does, and lose that information when the parser does. When the second element in a document comes along, it cannot access information in the fourth element, because that fourth element hasn't been parsed yet. When the fourth element *does* comes along, it can't "look back" on that second element. Certainly, you have every right to save the information encountered as the process moves along; coding all these special cases can be very tricky, though. The other, more extreme option is to build an in-memory representation of the XML document. We will see in a moment that a DOM parser does exactly that, so performing the same task in SAX would be pointless, and probably slower and more difficult.

SAX siblings

Moving laterally between elements is also difficult with the SAX model. The access provided in SAX is largely hierarchical, as well as sequential. You are going to reach leaf nodes of the first element, then move back up the tree, then down again to leaf nodes of the second element, and so on. At no point is there any clear indication of what "level" of the hierarchy you are at. Although this can be implemented with some clever counters, it is not what SAX is designed for. There is no concept of a sibling element, or of the next element at the same level, or of which elements are nested within which other elements.

The problem with this lack of information is that an XSLT processor (refer to Chapter 2) must be able to determine the siblings of an element, and more importantly, the children of an element. Consider the following code snippet in an XSL template:

```
<xsl:template match="parentElement">
  <!-- Add content to the output tree -->
  <xsl:apply-templates select="childElementOne|childElementTwo" />
</xsl:template>
```

Here, templates are applied via the `xsl:apply-templates` construct, but they are being applied to a specific node set that matches the given XPath expression. In this example, the template should be applied only to the elements `childElementOne` or `childElementTwo` (separated by the XPath OR operator, the pipe). In addition, because a relative path is used, these must be direct children of the element `parentElement`. Determining and locating these nodes with a SAX representation of an XML document would be extremely difficult. With an in-memory, hierarchical representation of the XML document, locating these nodes is trivial, a primary reason why the DOM approach is heavily used for input into XSLT processors.

Why use SAX at all?

All these discussions about the "shortcomings" of SAX may have you wondering why one would ever choose to use SAX at all. But these shortcomings are all in regard to a specific application of XML data, in this case processing it through XSL, or using random access for any other purpose. In fact, all of these "problems" with using SAX are the exact reason you would choose to use SAX.

Imagine parsing a table of contents represented in XML for an issue of National Geographic. This document could easily be 500 lines in length, more if there is a lot of content within the issue. Imagine an XML index for an O'Reilly book: hundreds of words, with page numbers, cross-references, and more. And these are all fairly small, concise applications of XML. As an XML document grows in size, so does the in-memory representation when represented by a DOM tree. Imagine (yes, keep imagining) an XML document so large and with so many nestings that the representation of it using the DOM begins to affect the performance of your application. And now imagine that the same results could be obtained by parsing the input document sequentially using SAX, and would only require one-tenth, or one-hundredth, of your system's resources to accomplish the task.

Just as in Java there are many ways to do the same job, there are many ways to obtain the data in an XML document. In some scenarios, SAX is easily the better choice for quick, less-intensive parsing and processing. In others, the DOM provides an easy-to-use, clean interface to data in a desirable format. You, the developer, must always analyze your application and its purpose to make the correct decision as to which method to use, or how to use both in concert. As always, the power to make good or bad decisions lies in your knowledge of the alternatives. Keeping that in mind, it's time to look at the DOM in action.

Serialization

One of the most common questions about using DOM is, "I have a DOM tree; how do I write it out to a file?" This question is asked so often because DOM Levels 1 and 2 do not provide a standard means of serialization for DOM trees. While this is a bit of a shortcoming of the API, it provides a great example in using DOM (and as you'll see in the next chapter, DOM Level 3 seeks to correct this problem). In this section, to familiarize you with the DOM, I'm going to walk you through a class that takes a DOM tree as input, and serializes that tree to a supplied output.

Getting a DOM Parser

Before I talk about outputting a DOM tree, I will give you information on getting a DOM tree in the first place. For the sake of example, all that the code in this chapter does is read in a file, create a DOM tree, and then write that DOM tree back out to another file. However, this still gives you a good start on DOM and prepares you for some more advanced topics in the next chapter.

As a result, there are two Java source files of interest in this chapter. The first is the serializer itself, which is called (not surprisingly) *DOMSerializer.java*. The second, which I'll start on now, is *SerializerTest.java*. This class takes in a filename for the XML document to read and a filename for the document to serialize out to. Additionally, it demonstrates how to take in a file, parse it, and obtain the resultant DOM tree object, represented by the `org.w3c.dom.Document` class. Go ahead and download this class from the book's web site, or enter in the code as shown in Example 5-1, for the `SerializerTest` class.

Example 5-1. The SerializerTest class

```java
package javaxml2;

import java.io.File;
import org.w3c.dom.Document;

// Parser import
import org.apache.xerces.parsers.DOMParser;

public class SerializerTest {

    public void test(String xmlDocument, String outputFilename)
        throws Exception {

        File outputFile = new File(outputFilename);
        DOMParser parser = new DOMParser();

        // Get the DOM tree as a Document object

        // Serialize
    }

    public static void main(String[] args) {
        if (args.length != 2) {
            System.out.println(
                "Usage: java javaxml2.SerializerTest " +
                "[XML document to read] " +
                "[filename to write out to]");
            System.exit(0);
        }

        try {
            SerializerTest tester = new SerializerTest();
            tester.test(args[0], args[1]);
        } catch (Exception e) {
```

Example 5-1. The SerializerTest class (continued)

```
            e.printStackTrace();
        }
    }
}
```

This example obviously has a couple of pieces missing, represented by the two comments in the `test()` method. I'll supply those in the next two sections, first explaining how to get a DOM tree object, and then detailing the `DOMSerializer` class itself.

DOM Parser Output

Remember that in SAX, the focus of interest in the parser was the lifecycle of the process, as all the callback methods provided us "hooks" into the data as it was being parsed. In the DOM, the focus of interest lies in the output from the parsing process. Until the entire document is parsed and added into the output tree structure, the data is not in a usable state. The output of a parse intended for use with the DOM interface is an `org.w3c.dom.Document` object. This object acts as a "handle" to the tree your XML data is in, and in terms of the element hierarchy I've discussed, it is equivalent to one level above the root element in your XML document. In other words, it "owns" each and every element in the XML document input.

Because the DOM standard focuses on manipulating data, there is a variety of mechanisms used to obtain the `Document` object after a parse. In many implementations, such as older versions of the IBM XML4J parser, the `parse()` method returned the `Document` object. The code to use such an implementation of a DOM parser would look like this:

```
    File outputFile = new File(outputFilename);
    DOMParser parser = new DOMParser();
    Document doc = parser.parse(xmlDocument);
```

Most newer parsers, such as Apache Xerces, do not follow this methodology. In order to maintain a standard interface across both SAX and DOM parsers, the `parse()` method in these parsers returns `void`, as the SAX example of using the `parse()` method did. This change allows an application to use a DOM parser class and a SAX parser class interchangeably; however, it requires an additional method to obtain the `Document` object result from the XML parsing. In Apache Xerces, this method is named `getDocument()`. Using this type of parser (as I do in the example), you can add the following example to your `test()` method to obtain the resulting DOM tree from parsing the supplied input file:

```
        public void test(String xmlDocument, String outputFilename)
            throws Exception {

            File outputFile = new File(outputFilename);
            DOMParser parser = new DOMParser();

            // Get the DOM tree as a Document object
            parser.parse(xmlDocument);
            Document doc = parser.getDocument();

            // Serialize
        }
```

This of course assumes you are using Xerces, as the import statement at the beginning of the source file indicates:

```
    import org.apache.xerces.parsers.DOMParser;
```

If you are using a different parser, you'll need to change this import to your vendor's DOM parser class. Then consult your vendor's documentation to determine which of the parse() mechanisms you need to employ to get the DOM result of your parse. In Chapter 7, I'll look at Sun's JAXP API and other ways to standardize a means of accessing a DOM tree from any parser implementation. Although there is some variance in getting this result, all the uses of this result that we look at are standard across the DOM specification, so you should not have to worry about any other implementation curveballs in the rest of this chapter.

DOMSerializer

I've been throwing the term *serialization* around quite a bit, and should probably make sure you know what I mean. When I say serialization, I simply mean outputting the XML. This could be a file (using a Java File), an OutputStream, or a Writer. There are certainly more output forms available in Java, but these three cover most of the bases (in fact, the latter two do, as a File can be easily converted to a Writer, but accepting a File is a nice convenience feature). In this case, the serialization taking place is in an XML format; the DOM tree is converted back to a well-formed XML document in a textual format. It's important to note that the XML format is used, as you could easily code serializers to write HTML, WML, XHTML, or any other format. In fact, Apache Xerces provides these various classes, and I'll touch on them briefly at the end of this chapter.

Getting started

To get you past the preliminaries, Example 5-2 is the skeleton for the DOMSerializer class. It imports all the needed classes to get the code going, and defines the different entry points (for a File, OutputStream, and Writer) to the class. Two of these three methods simply defer to the third (with a little I/O magic). The example also sets up some member variables for the indentation to use, the line separator, and methods to modify those properties.

Example 5-2. The DOMSerializer skeleton

```
package javaxml2;

import java.io.File;
import java.io.FileWriter;
import java.io.IOException;
import java.io.OutputStream;
import java.io.OutputStreamWriter;
import java.io.Writer;
import org.w3c.dom.Document;
import org.w3c.dom.DocumentType;
import org.w3c.dom.NamedNodeMap;
import org.w3c.dom.Node;
import org.w3c.dom.NodeList;

public class DOMSerializer {

    /** Indentation to use */
    private String indent;

    /** Line separator to use */
    private String lineSeparator;

    public DOMSerializer() {
        indent = "";
        lineSeparator = "\n";
    }

    public void setLineSeparator(String lineSeparator) {
        this.lineSeparator = lineSeparator;
    }

    public void serialize(Document doc, OutputStream out)
        throws IOException {

        Writer writer = new OutputStreamWriter(out);
        serialize(doc, writer);
    }

    public void serialize(Document doc, File file)
        throws IOException {

        Writer writer = new FileWriter(file);
        serialize(doc, writer);
    }
```

Example 5-2. The DOMSerializer skeleton (continued)

```
    public void serialize(Document doc, Writer writer)
        throws IOException {

        // Serialize document

    }
}
```

Once this code is saved into a *DOMSerializer.java* source file, everything ends up in the version of the `serialize()` method that takes a `Writer`. Nice and tidy.

Launching serialization

With the setup in place for starting serialization, it's time to define the process of working through the DOM tree. One nice facet of DOM already mentioned is that all of the specific DOM structures that represent XML (including the `Document` object) extend the DOM `Node` interface. This enables the coding of a single method that handles serialization of all DOM node types. Within that method, you can differentiate between node types, but by accepting a `Node` as input, it enables a very simple way of handling all DOM types. Additionally, it sets up a methodology that allows for recursion, any programmer's best friend. Add the `serializeNode()` method shown here, as well as the initial invocation of that method in the `serialize()` method (the common code point just discussed):

```
    public void serialize(Document doc, Writer writer)
        throws IOException {

        // Start serialization recursion with no indenting
        serializeNode(doc, writer, "");
        writer.flush();
    }

    public void serializeNode(Node node, Writer writer,
                              String indentLevel)
        throws IOException {
    }
```

Additionally, an `indentLevel` variable is put in place; this sets us up for recursion. In other words, the `serializeNode()` method can indicate how much the node being worked with should be indented, and when recursion takes place, can add another level of indentation (using the `indent` member variable). Starting out (within the `serialize()` method), there is an empty `String` for indentation; at the next level, the default is two spaces for indentation, then four spaces at the next level, and so on. Of course, as recursive calls unravel, things head back up to no indentation. All that's left now is to handle the various node types.

Working with nodes

Once within the `serializeNode()` method, the first task is to determine what type of node has been passed in. Although you could approach this with a Java methodology, using the `instanceof` keyword and Java reflection, the DOM language bindings for Java make this task much simpler. The `Node` interface defines a helper method, `getNodeType()`, which returns an integer value. This value can be compared against a set of constants (also defined within the `Node` interface), and the type of `Node` being examined can be quickly and easily determined. This also fits very naturally into the Java `switch` construct, which can be used to break up serialization into logical sections. The code here covers almost all DOM node types; although there are some additional node types defined (see Figure 5-2), these are the most common, and the concepts here can be applied to the less common node types as well:

```java
public void serializeNode(Node node, Writer writer,
                          String indentLevel)
    throws IOException {

    // Determine action based on node type
    switch (node.getNodeType()) {
        case Node.DOCUMENT_NODE:
            break;

        case Node.ELEMENT_NODE:
            break;

        case Node.TEXT_NODE:
            break;

        case Node.CDATA_SECTION_NODE:
            break;

        case Node.COMMENT_NODE:
            break;

        case Node.PROCESSING_INSTRUCTION_NODE:
            break;

        case Node.ENTITY_REFERENCE_NODE:
            break;

        case Node.DOCUMENT_TYPE_NODE:
            break;
    }
}
```

This code is fairly useless; however, it helps to see all of the DOM node types laid out here in a line, rather than mixed in with all of the code needed to perform actual serialization. I want to get to that now, though, starting with the first node passed into this method, an instance of the Document interface.

Because the Document interface is an extension of the Node interface, it can be used interchangeably with the other node types. However, it is a special case, as it contains the root element as well as the XML document's DTD and some other special information not within the XML element hierarchy. As a result, you need to extract the root element and pass that back to the serialization method (starting recursion). Additionally, the XML declaration itself is printed out:

```
case Node.DOCUMENT_NODE:
    writer.write("<?xml version=\"1.0\"?>");
    writer.write(lineSeparator);

    Document doc = (Document)node;
    serializeNode(doc.getDocumentElement(), writer, "");
    break;
```

WARNING   DOM Level 2 (as well as SAX 2.0) does not expose the XML declaration. This may not seem like a big deal, until you consider that the encoding of the document is included in this declaration. DOM Level 3 is expected to address this deficiency, and I'll cover that in the next chapter. Be careful not to write DOM applications that depend on this information until this feature is in place.

Since the code needs to access a Document-specific method (as opposed to one defined in the generic Node interface), the Node implementation must be cast to the Document interface. Then invoke the object's getDocumentElement() method to obtain the root element of the XML input document, and in turn pass that on to the serializeNode() method, starting the recursion and traversal of the DOM tree.

Of course, the most common task in serialization is to take a DOM Element and print out its name, attributes, and value, and then print its children. As you would suspect, all of these can be easily accomplished with DOM method calls. First you need to get the name of the XML element, which is available through the getNodeName() method within the Node interface. The code then needs to get the children of the current element and serialize these as well. A Node's children can be accessed through the getChildNodes() method, which returns an instance of a DOM NodeList. It is trivial to obtain the length of this list, and then iterate through the children calling the serialization method on each, continuing the recursion. There's also quite a bit of logic that ensures correct indentation and line feeds; these are really just formatting issues, and I won't spend time on them here. Finally, the closing bracket of the element can be output:

```
case Node.ELEMENT_NODE:
    String name = node.getNodeName();
    writer.write(indentLevel +."<" + name);
    writer.write(">");

    // recurse on each child
    NodeList children = node.getChildNodes();
    if (children != null) {
        if ((children.item(0) != null) &&
            (children.item(0).getNodeType() ==
            Node.ELEMENT_NODE)) {

            writer.write(lineSeparator);
        }
      for (int i=0; i<children.getLength(); i++) {
            serializeNode(children.item(i), writer,
                indentLevel + indent);
        }
        if ((children.item(0) != null) &&
            (children.item(children.getLength()-1)
                .getNodeType() ==
            Node.ELEMENT_NODE)) {

            writer.write(indentLevel);
        }
    }

    writer.write("</" + name + ">");
    writer.write(lineSeparator);
    break;
```

Of course, astute readers (or DOM experts) will notice that I left out something important: the element's attributes! These are the only pseudo-exception to the strict tree that DOM builds. They should be an exception, though, since an attribute is not really a child of an element; it's (sort of) lateral to it. Basically the relationship is a little muddy. In any case, the attributes of an element are available through the getAttributes() method on the Node interface. This method returns a NamedNodeMap, and that too can be iterated through. Each Node within this list can be polled for its name and value, and suddenly the attributes are handled! Enter the code as shown here to take care of this:

```
case Node.ELEMENT_NODE:
    String name = node.getNodeName();
    writer.write(indentLevel + "<" + name);
    NamedNodeMap attributes = node.getAttributes();
    for (int i=0; i<attributes.getLength(); i++) {
```

```
        Node current = attributes.item(i);
        writer.write(" " + current.getNodeName() +
                    "=\"" + current.getNodeValue() +
                    "\"");
    }
    writer.write(">");

    // recurse on each child
    NodeList children = node.getChildNodes();
    if (children != null) {
        if ((children.item(0) != null) &&
            (children.item(0).getNodeType() ==
            Node.ELEMENT_NODE)) {

            writer.write(lineSeparator);
        }
      for (int i=0; i<children.getLength(); i++) {
            serializeNode(children.item(i), writer,
                indentLevel + indent);
        }
        if ((children.item(0) != null) &&
            (children.item(children.getLength()-1)
                    .getNodeType() ==
            Node.ELEMENT_NODE)) {

            writer.write(indentLevel);
        }
    }

    writer.write("</" + name + ">");
    writer.write(lineSeparator);
    break;
```

Next on the list of node types is Text nodes. Output is quite simple, as you only need to use the now-familiar getNodeValue() method of the DOM Node interface to get the textual data and print it out; the same is true for CDATA nodes, except that the data within a CDATA section should be enclosed within the CDATA XML semantics (surrounded by <![CDATA[and]]>). You can add the logic within those two cases now:

```
case Node.TEXT_NODE:
    writer.write(node.getNodeValue());
    break;

case Node.CDATA_SECTION_NODE:
    writer.write("<![CDATA[" +
            node.getNodeValue() + "]]>");
    break;
```

Dealing with comments in DOM is about as simple as it gets. The `getNodeValue()` method returns the text within the `<!--` and `-->` XML constructs. That's really all there is to it; see this code addition:

```
case Node.COMMENT_NODE:
    writer.write(indentLevel + "<!-- " +
                    node.getNodeValue() + " -->");
    writer.write(lineSeparator);
    break;
```

Moving on to the next DOM node type: the DOM bindings for Java define an interface to handle processing instructions that are within the input XML document, rather obviously called `ProcessingInstruction`. This is useful, as these instructions do not follow the same markup model as XML elements and attributes, but are still important for applications to know about. In the table of contents XML document, there aren't any PIs present (although you could easily add some for testing).

The PI node in the DOM is a little bit of a break from what you have seen so far: to fit the syntax into the `Node` interface model, the `getNodeValue()` method returns all data instructions within a PI in one `String`. This allows quick output of the PI; however, you still need to use `getNodeName()` to get the name of the PI. If you were writing an application that received PIs from an XML document, you might prefer to use the actual `ProcessingInstruction` interface; although it exposes the same data, the method names (`getTarget()` and `getData()`) are more in line with a PI's format. With this understanding, you can add in the code to print out any PIs in supplied XML documents:

```
case Node.PROCESSING_INSTRUCTION_NODE:
    writer.write("<?" + node.getNodeName() +
                    " " + node.getNodeValue() +
                    "?>");
    writer.write(lineSeparator);
    break;
```

While the code to deal with PIs is perfectly workable, there is a problem. In the case that handled document nodes, all the serializer did was pull out the document element and recurse. The problem is that this approach ignores any other child nodes of the `Document` object, such as top-level PIs and any `DOCTYPE` declarations. Those node types are actually *lateral* to the document element (root element), and are ignored. Instead of just pulling out the document element, then, the following code serializes *all* child nodes on the supplied `Document` object:

```
case Node.DOCUMENT_NODE:
    writer.write("<xml version=\"1.0\">");
    writer.write(lineSeparator);
```

```
        // recurse on each child
        NodeList nodes = node.getChildNodes();
        if (nodes != null) {
            for (int i=0; i<nodes.getLength(); i++) {
                serializeNode(nodes.item(i), writer, "");
            }
        }
        /*
        Document doc = (Document)node;
        serializeNode(doc.getDocumentElement(), writer, "");
        */
        break;
```

With this in place, the code can deal with DocumentType nodes, which represent a
DOCTYPE declaration. Like PIs, a DTD declaration can be helpful in exposing
external information that might be needed in processing an XML document.
However, since there can be public and system IDs as well as other DTD-specific
data, the code needs to cast the Node instance to the DocumentType interface to
access this additional data. Then, use the helper methods to get the name of the
Node, which returns the name of the element in the document that is being constrained, the public ID (if it exists), and the system ID of the DTD referenced.
Using this information, the original DTD can be serialized:

```
    case Node.DOCUMENT_TYPE_NODE:
        DocumentType docType = (DocumentType)node;
        writer.write("<!DOCTYPE " + docType.getName());
        if (docType.getPublicId() != null)  {
            System.out.print(" PUBLIC \"" +
                docType.getPublicId() + "\" ");
        } else {
            writer.write(" SYSTEM ");
        }
writer.write("\"" + docType.getSystemId() + "\">");
        writer.write(lineSeparator);
        break;
```

All that's left at this point is handling entities and entity references. In this chapter, I will skim over entities and focus on entity references; more details on entities and notations are in the next chapter. For now, a reference can simply be
output with the & and ; characters surrounding it:

```
    case Node.ENTITY_REFERENCE_NODE:
        writer.write("&" + node.getNodeName() + ";");
        break;
```

There are a few surprises that may trip you up when it comes to the output from a
node such as this. The definition of how entity references should be processed
within DOM allows a lot of latitude, and also relies heavily on the underlying

parser's behavior. In fact, most XML parsers have expanded and processed entity references before the XML document's data ever makes its way into the DOM tree. Often, when expecting to see an entity reference within your DOM structure, you will find the text or values *referenced* rather than the entity reference itself. To test this for your parser, you'll want to run the `SerializerTest` class on the *contents.xml* document (which I'll cover in the next section) and see what it does with the `OReillyCopyright` entity reference. In Apache, this comes across as an entity reference, by the way.

And that's it! As I mentioned, there are a few other node types, but covering them isn't worth the trouble at this point; you get the idea about how DOM works. In the next chapter, I'll take you deeper than you probably ever wanted to go. For now, let's put the pieces together and see some results.

The Results

With the `DOMSerializer` class complete, all that's left is to invoke the serializer's `serialize()` method in the test class. To do this, add the following lines to the `SerializerTest` class:

```
public void test(String xmlDocument, String outputFilename)
    throws Exception {

    File outputFile = new File(outputFilename);
    DOMParser parser = new DOMParser();

    // Get the DOM tree as a Document object
    parser.parse(xmlDocument);
    Document doc = parser.getDocument();

    // Serialize
    DOMSerializer serializer = new DOMSerializer();
    serializer.serialize(doc, new File(outputFilename));
}
```

This fairly simple addition completes the classes, and you can run the example on Chapter 2's *contents.xml* file, as shown:

```
C:\javaxml2\build>java javaxml2.SerializerTest
    c:\javaxml2\ch05\xml\contents.xml
    output.xml
```

While you don't get any exciting output here, you can open up the newly created *output.xml* file and check it over for accuracy. It should contain all the information in the original XML document, with only the differences already discussed in previous sections. A portion of my *output.xml* is shown in Example 5-3.

Example 5-3. A portion of the output.xml serialized DOM tree

```
<?xml version="1.0"?>
<!DOCTYPE book SYSTEM "DTD/JavaXML.dtd">
<!-- Java and XML Contents  -->
<book xmlns="http://www.oreilly.com/javaxml2"
      xmlns:ora="http://www.oreilly.com">
  <title ora:series="Java">Java and XML</title>


  <!-- Chapter List  -->

  <contents>
    <chapter number="2" title="Nuts and Bolts">
      <topic name="The Basics"></topic>

      <topic name="Constraints"></topic>

      <topic name="Transformations"></topic>

      <topic name="And More..."></topic>

      <topic name="What's Next?"></topic>

    </chapter>
```

You may notice that there is quite a bit of extra whitespace in the output; that's because the serializer adds some line feeds every time `writer.write(lineSeparator)` appears in the code. Of course, the underlying DOM tree has some line feeds in it as well, which are reported as `Text` nodes. The end result in many of these cases is the double line breaks, as seen in the output.

WARNING   Let me be very clear that the `DOMSerializer` class shown in this chapter is for example purposes, and is not a good production solution. While you are welcome to use the class in your own applications, realize that several important options are left out, like encoding and setting advanced options for indentation, line feeds, and line wrapping. Additionally, entities are handled only in passing (complete treatment would be twice as long as this chapter already is!). Your parser probably has its own serializer class, if not multiple classes, that perform this task at least as well, if not better, than the example in this chapter. However, you now should understand what's going on under the hood in those classes. As a matter of reference, if you are using Apache Xerces, the classes to look at are in the `org.apache.xml.serialize`. Some particularly useful ones are the `XMLSerializer`, `XHTMLSerializer`, and `HTMLSerializer`. Check them out—they offer a good solution, until DOM Level 3 comes out with a standardized one.

Mutability

One glaring omission in this chapter is the topic of modifying a DOM tree. That's not an accident; working with DOM is a lot more complex than working with SAX. Rather than drowning you in information, I wanted to give a clear picture of the various node types and structures used in DOM. In the next chapter, in addition to looking at some of the finer points of DOM Levels 2 and 3, I'll address the mutability of DOM trees, and in particular how to create DOM trees. So don't panic—help is on the way!

Gotcha!

As in previous chapters, I want to revisit some of the common pitfalls for new XML Java developers. In this chapter, I have focused on the Document Object Model, and this section continues that emphasis. Although some of the points made here are more informational than directly affective on your programming, they can be helpful in making design decisions about when to use DOM, and instrumental in understanding what is going on under the hood of your XML applications.

Memory, Performance, and Deferred DOMs

Earlier, I described the reasons to use DOM or SAX. Although I emphasized that using the DOM requires that the entire XML document be read into memory and stored in a tree structure, enough cannot be said on the subject. All too common is the scenario where a developer loads up his extensive collection of complex XML documents into an XSLT processor and begins a series of offline transformations, leaving the process to grab a bite to eat. Upon returning, he finds that his Windows machine is showing the dreaded "blue screen of death" and his Linux box is screaming about memory problems. For this developer and the hundreds like him, beware the DOM for excessively large data!

Using the DOM requires an amount of memory proportional to the size and complexity of an XML document. However, you should dig a bit further into your parser's documentation. Often, today's parsers contain a feature modeled on what it typically called a *deferred DOM*. A deferred DOM tries to lower the memory cost of using DOM by not reading and allocating all information needed by a DOM node until that node is requested. Until that time, the nodes in existence, but not in use, are simply nulled out. This reduces the memory overhead for large documents when only a specific portion of the document must be processed. However, realize that with this decrease in memory, there is an increase in processing. Since nodes are not in memory, and must be filled with data when requested, there is generally more lag time when a node not previously accessed is requested. It's a tradeoff. However, a deferred DOM can often help save the day when dealing with large documents.

Polymorphism and the Node Interface

Previously in this chapter I stressed the tree model that DOM is built upon. I also told you that the key to this was a common interface, org.w3c.dom.Node. This class provides common functionality for all DOM classes, but sometimes it provides more. For example, this class defines a method called getNodeValue(), which returns a String. Sounds like a good idea, right? Without having to cast the Node to a specific type, you can quickly get its value. However, things get a little sticky when you consider types like Element. Remember that an Element has no textual content, but instead has children of type Text. So an Element in DOM has no value that has any meaning; the result is that you get something like #ELEMENT#. The exact value is parser-dependent, but you get the idea.

The same situation applies to other methods on the Node interface, like getNodeName(). For Text nodes, you get #TEXT#, which doesn't help too much. So what exactly is the gotcha here? You simply need to be careful when working with different DOM types through the Node interface. You may get some unexpected results along with the convenience of the common interface.

DOM Parsers Throwing SAX Exceptions

In this chapter's example of using DOM, I did not explicitly list the exceptions that could result from a document parse; instead a higher-level exception was caught. This was because, as I mentioned, the process of generating a DOM tree is left up to the parser implementation, and is not always the same. However, it is typically good practice to catch the specific exceptions that can occur and react to them differently, as the type of exception gives information about the problem that occurred. Rewriting the SerializerTest class's parser invocation this way might make a surprising facet of this process surface. For Apache Xerces this could be done as follows:

```
public void test(String xmlDocument, String outputFilename)
    throws Exception {

    try {
        File outputFile = new File(outputFilename);
        DOMParser parser = new DOMParser();
        parser.parse(xmlDocument);
        Document doc = parser.getDocument();
    } catch (IOException e) {
        System.out.println("Error reading URI: " + e.getMessage());
```

```
    } catch (SAXException e) {
        System.out.println("Error in parsing: " + e.getMessage());
    }

    // Serialize
    DOMSerializer serializer = new DOMSerializer();
    serializer.serialize(doc, new File(outputFilename));
}
```

The IOException seen here should not come as a surprise, as it signifies an error
in locating the specified filename as it did in the earlier SAX examples. Something else from the SAX section might make you think something was amiss; did
you notice the SAXException that can be thrown? The DOM parser throws a SAX
exception? Surely I have imported the wrong set of classes! Not so; these are the
right classes. Remember that it would be possible to build a tree structure of the
data in an XML document yourself, using SAX, but the DOM provides an alternative. However, this does not preclude SAX from being *used* in that alternative! In
fact, SAX provides a lightweight, fast way to parse a document; in this case, it just
happens that as it is parsed, it is inserted into a DOM tree. Because no standard
for the DOM creation exists, this is acceptable and not even uncommon. So don't
be surprised or taken aback when you find yourself importing and catching org.
xml.sax.SAXException in your DOM applications.

What's Next?

In Chapter 6, I'll continue being tour guide through the world of DOM, as we
look at some of DOM's more advanced (and less known) features. To get rolling,
I'll show you how to modify DOM trees, as well as create them. Then, it's on to the
less common functionality in the DOM. For starters, the additions included in
DOM Level 2 will be examined (some you've already used, and some you haven't).
Next, I'll cover using the DOM HTML bindings, which will help you when dealing
with DOM and web pages. Finally, I'll give you some information about changes
expected in the upcoming DOM Level 3 specification. That should give you plenty
of ammo to take over the world using DOM!

In this chapter:
- *Changes*
- *Namespaces*
- *DOM Level 2 Modules*
- *DOM Level 3*
- *Gotcha!*
- *What's Next?*

6

Advanced DOM

Just like in Chapter 4, there's nothing mystical about anything I'll cover in this chapter. The topics build upon a foundation that I set in the DOM basics from the last chapter. However, with the exception of the first section on mutation, many of these features are rarely used. While almost everything you've seen in SAX (except, perhaps, the DTDHandler and DeclHandler) will be handy, I've found many of the fringe features of DOM useful only in specific applications. For example, if you aren't doing any presentation logic, you'll probably never touch the DOM HTML bindings. The same goes for many of DOM Level 2's features; if you need them, you need them *badly*, and if you don't, you *really* don't.

In this chapter, I'll present some specific DOM topics that will be useful in your own DOM programming. I've tried to organize the chapter more like a reference than the previous chapters; if you want to find out more about the DOM Level 2 Traversal module, for example, you can simply thumb to that section. However, the code examples in this chapter do build upon each other, so you may still want to work through each section in order to get a complete picture of the current DOM model. This results in more practical code samples, rather than useless contrived ones that won't get you anywhere. So buckle up, and let's dive a little deeper into the world of DOM.

Changes

First and foremost, I want to talk about the mutability of a DOM tree. The biggest limitation when using SAX for dealing with XML is that you cannot change any of the XML structure you encounter, at least not without using filters and writers. Those aren't intended to be used for wholesale document changes anyway, so you'll need to use another API when you want to modify XML. DOM fits the bill nicely, as it provides XML creation and modification facilities.

In working with DOM, the process of creating an XML document is quite different from changing an existing one, so I'll take them one at a time. This section gives you a fairly realistic example to mull over. If you've ever been to an online auction site like eBay, you know that the most important aspects of the auction are the ability to *find* items, and the ability to find *out* about items. These functions depend on a user entering in a description of an item, and the auction using that information. The better auction sites allow users to enter in some basic information as well as actual HTML descriptions, which means the savvy user can bold, italicize, link, and add other formatting to their items' descriptions. This provides a good case for using DOM.

Creating a New DOM Tree

To get started, a little bit of groundwork is needed. Example 6-1 shows a simple HTML form that takes basic information about an item to be listed on an auction site. This would obviously be dressed up more for a real site, but you get the idea.

Example 6-1. HTML input form for item listing

```
<html>
 <head><title>Input/Update Item Listing</title></head>
 <body>
  <h1 align="center">Input/Update Item Listing</h1>
  <p align="center">
   <form method="POST" action="/javaxml2/servlet/javaxml2.UpdateItemServlet">
    Item ID (Unique Identifier): <br />
    <input name="id" type="text" maxLength="10" /><br /><br />
    Item Name: <br />
    <input name="name" type="text" maxLength="50" /><br /><br />
    Item Description: <br />
    <textarea name="description" rows="10" cols="30" wrap="wrap" ></textarea>
    <br /><br />
    <input type="reset" value="Reset Form" />  
    <input type="submit" value="Add/Update Item" />
   </form>
  </p>
 </body>
</html>
```

Notice that the target of this form submission is a servlet. That servlet is shown in Example 6-2. The doPost() method reads in these input parameters and puts their values into temporary variables. At that point, the servlet checks the filesystem for a specific file that has this information stored within it.

WARNING   For the sake of clarity, I'm dealing directly with the filesystem in this
             servlet. However, this is generally not a good idea. Consider using
             the ServletContext to get access to local resources, allowing your
             servlet to be distributed and modified easily depending on the server
             and servlet engine hosting it. That sort of detail tends to muddy
             examples up, so I'm keeping it simple here.

If the file doesn't exist (for a new listing, it wouldn't), it creates a new DOM tree
and builds up the tree structure using the values supplied. Once that's complete,
the servlet uses the DOMSerializer class (from Chapter 5) to write the DOM tree
out to the file, making it available the next time this servlet is invoked. Additionally, I've coded up a doGet() method; this method just displays the HTML shown
in Example 6-1. I'll use this later to allow modification of item listings. For now,
don't worry too much about it.

Example 6-2. The UpdateItemServlet class

```java
package javaxml2;

import java.io.File;
import java.io.IOException;
import java.io.PrintWriter;
import javax.servlet.ServletException;
import javax.servlet.http.HttpServlet;
import javax.servlet.http.HttpServletRequest;
import javax.servlet.http.HttpServletResponse;

// DOM imports
import org.w3c.dom.Attr;
import org.w3c.dom.Document;
import org.w3c.dom.DOMImplementation;
import org.w3c.dom.Element;
import org.w3c.dom.Text;

// Parser import
import org.apache.xerces.dom.DOMImplementationImpl;

public class UpdateItemServlet extends HttpServlet {

    private static final String ITEMS_DIRECTORY = "/javaxml2/ch06/xml/";

    public void doGet(HttpServletRequest req, HttpServletResponse res)
        throws ServletException, IOException {

        // Get output
        PrintWriter out = res.getWriter();
        res.setContentType("text/html");
```

Example 6-2. The UpdateItemServlet class (continued)

```java
            // Output HTML
            out.println("<html>");
            out.println(" <head><title>Input/Update Item Listing</title></head>");
            out.println(" <body>");
            out.println("   <h1 align='center'>Input/Update Item Listing</h1>");
            out.println("   <p align='center'>");
            out.println("     <form method='POST' " +
                "action='/javaxml2/servlet/javaxml2.UpdateItemServlet'>");
            out.println("       Item ID (Unique Identifier): <br />");
            out.println("       <input name='id' type='text' maxLength='10' />" +
                "<br /><br />");
            out.println("       Item Name: <br />");
            out.println("       <input name='name' type='text' maxLength='50' />" +
                "<br /><br />");
            out.println("       Item Description: <br />");
            out.println("       <textarea name='description' rows='10' cols='30' " +
                "wrap='wrap' ></textarea><br /><br />");
            out.println("       <input type='reset' value='Reset Form' />  ");
            out.println("       <input type='submit' value='Add/Update Item' />");
            out.println("     </form>");
            out.println("   </p>");
            out.println(" </body>");
            out.println("</html>");

            out.close();
    }

    public void doPost(HttpServletRequest req, HttpServletResponse res)
        throws ServletException, IOException {

        // Get parameter values
        String id = req.getParameterValues("id")[0];
        String name = req.getParameterValues("name")[0];
        String description = req.getParameterValues("description")[0];

        // Create new DOM tree
        DOMImplementation domImpl = new DOMImplementationImpl();
        Document doc = domImpl.createDocument(null, "item", null);
        Element root = doc.getDocumentElement();

        // ID of item (as attribute)
        root.setAttribute("id", id);

        // Name of item
        Element nameElement = doc.createElement("name");
        Text nameText = doc.createTextNode(name);
        nameElement.appendChild(nameText);
```

Example 6-2. The UpdateItemServlet class (continued)

```
    root.appendChild(nameElement);

    // Description of item
    Element descriptionElement = doc.createElement("description");
    Text descriptionText = doc.createTextNode(description);
    descriptionElement.appendChild(descriptionText);
    root.appendChild(descriptionElement);

    // Serialize DOM tree
    DOMSerializer serializer = new DOMSerializer();
    serializer.serialize(doc, new File(ITEMS_DIRECTORY + "item-" + name +
        ".xml"));

    // Print confirmation
    PrintWriter out = res.getWriter();
    res.setContentType("text/html");
    out.println("<HTML><BODY>Thank you for your submission. " +
        "Your item has been processed.</BODY></HTML>");
    out.close();
  }

}
```

Go ahead and compile this class. I'll walk you through it in just a moment, but
ensure that you have your environment set up to include the needed classes.

NOTE   Make sure the DOMSerializer class from the last chapter is in your
              classpath when compiling the UpdateItemServlet class. You'll also
              want to add this to the classes in your servlet engine's context. In my
              setup, using Tomcat, my context is called *javaxml2*, in a directory
              named *javaxml2* under the *webapps* directory. In my *WEB-INF/classes*
              directory, there is a *javaxml2* directory (for the package), and then
              the *DOMSerializer.class* and *UpdateItemServlet.class* files are within that
              directory. You should also ensure that a copy of your parser's *jar* file
              (*xerces.jar* in my case) is in the classpath of your engine. In Tomcat,
              you can simply drop a copy in Tomcat's *lib* directory. Finally, you'll
              need to ensure that Xerces, and the DOM Level 2 implementation
              within it, is loaded before the DOM Level 1 implementation in Tom-
              cat's *parser.jar* archive. Do this by renaming *parser.jar* to *z_parser.jar*.
              I'll explain more about this in Chapter 10, but for now just trust me
              and make the change. Then restart Tomcat and everything should
              work.

Once you've got your servlet in place and the servlet engine started, browse to the
servlet and let the GET request your browser generates load the HTML input
form. Fill this form out, as I have in Figure 6-1.

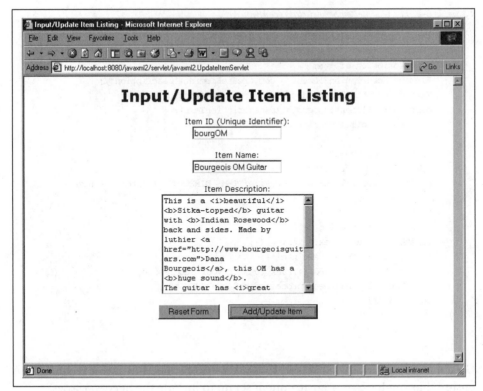

Figure 6-1. Filling out the items form

Since I'll talk in depth about the description field later, I want to show you the complete content I typed into that field. I know there's lots of markup (I went crazy on the bolding and italics!), but this will be important later on:

```
This is a <i>beautiful</i> <b>Sitka-topped</b> guitar with <b>Indian Rosewood</b>
back and sides. Made by luthier <a href="http://www.bourgeoisguitars.com">Dana
Bourgeois</a>, this OM has a <b>huge sound</b>.
The guitar has <i>great action</i>, a 1 3/4" nut, and all
<i>fossilized ivory</i> nut and saddle, with <i>ebony</i> end pins.
New condition, this is a <b>great guitar</b>!
```

Submitting this form posts its data (via a POST request) to the servlet, and the doPost() method takes effect. As for the actual DOM creation, it turns out to be pretty simple. First, you'll need to instantiate an instance of the org.w3c.dom. DOMImplementation class. This will be the base for all your DOM creation work. While you could certainly directly instantiate a DOM Document implementation, you would not be able to create a DocType class from it as you could from a DOMImplementation; using DOMImplementation is a better practice. Additionally, the DOMImplementation class has one more useful method, hasFeature().

I'll cover this method in detail later, so don't worry about it for now. In the example code, I've used Xerces' implementation, `org.apache.xerces.dom.DOMImplementationImpl` (sort of a confusing name, isn't it?). There is currently no vendor-neutral way to handle this, although DOM Level 3 (covered at the end of this chapter) provides some possibilities for the future. JAXP, detailed in Chapter 9, offers some solutions, but I'll get to those later.

Once you've got an instance of `DOMImplementation`, though, things are pretty simple. Take a look at the relevant code again:

```
// Create new DOM tree
DOMImplementation domImpl = new DOMImplementationImpl();
Document doc = domImpl.createDocument(null, "item", null);
Element root = doc.getDocumentElement();

// ID of item (as attribute)
root.setAttribute("id", id);

// Name of item
Element nameElement = doc.createElement("name");
Text nameText = doc.createTextNode(name);
nameElement.appendChild(nameText);
root.appendChild(nameElement);

// Description of item
Element descriptionElement = doc.createElement("description");
Text descriptionText = doc.createTextNode(description);
descriptionElement.appendChild(descriptionText);
root.appendChild(descriptionElement);

// Serialize DOM tree
DOMSerializer serializer = new DOMSerializer();
serializer.serialize(doc, new File(ITEMS_DIRECTORY + "item-" + id +
    ".xml"));
```

First, the `createDocument()` method is used to get a new `Document` instance. The first argument to this method is the namespace for the document's root element. I haven't gotten to the namespace yet, so I omit one by passing in a null value. The second argument is the name of the root element itself, which is simply `"item"`. The last argument is an instance of a `DocType` class, and I again pass in a null value since I have none for this document. If I did want a `DocType`, I could create one with the `createDocType()` method on the same class, `DOMImplementation`. If you're interested in that method, check out the complete DOM API coverage in Appendix A.

With a DOM tree to operate upon, I can retrieve the root element to work with (using `getDocumentElement()`, covered in the last chapter). Once I've got that, I add an attribute with the ID of the item using `setAttribute()`. I pass in the attribute name and value, and the root element is ready to go. Things begin to get simple now; each type of DOM construct can be created using the `Document` object as a factory. To create the "name" and "description" elements, I use the `createElement()` method, simply passing in the element name in each case. The same approach is used to create textual content for each; since an element has no content but instead has children that are `Text` nodes (remember this from the last chapter?), the `createTextNode()` method is the right selection. This method takes in the text for the node, which works out to be the description and item name. You might be tempted to use the `createCDATASection()` method, and wrap this text in `CDATA` tags. There is HTML within this element. However, that would prevent the content from being read in as a set of elements, and provide the content as a big blob of text. Later on, we'll want to deal with this as elements, so leave this as a `Text` node instead, using `createTextNode()` again. Once you've gotten all of these nodes created, all that's left is to link them together. Your best bet is to use `appendChild()` on each, appending the elements to the root, and the textual content of the elements to the correct parent. This is pretty self-explanatory. And finally, the whole document is passed into the `DOMSerializer` class from the last chapter and written out to an XML file on disk.

WARNING   I have assumed that the user is entering well-formed HTML; in other words, XHTML. In a production application you would probably run this input through JTidy (*http://www.sourceforge.net/projects/jtidy*) to ensure this; for this example, I'll just assume the input is XHTML.

I've provided a constant in the servlet, `ITEMS_DIRECTORY`, where you can specify what directory to use. The example code uses a Windows directory, and notice that the backslashes are all escaped. Don't forget this! Simply change this to the directory you want to use on your system. You can view the XML generated from the servlet by browsing to the directory you specified in this constant, and open up the XML file that should be located there. Mine looked as shown in Example 6-3.

Example 6-3. The XML generated from the UpdateItemServlet

```
<?xml version="1.0"?>
<item id="bourgOM">
<name>Bourgeois OM Guitar</name>
<description>This is a <i>beautiful</i> <b>Sitka-topped</b> guitar with
<b>Indian Rosewood</b> back and sides. Made by luthier
<a href="http://www.bourgeoisguitars.com">Dana Bourgeois</a>, this OM has a
<b>huge sound</b>.
```

Example 6-3. The XML generated from the UpdateItemServlet (continued)

```
The guitar has <i>great action</i>, a 1 3/4" nut, and all
<i>fossilized ivory</i> nut and saddle, with <i>ebony</i> end pins.
New condition, this is a <b>great guitar</b>!</description>
</item>
```

I've moved fairly quickly through this, but you should be starting to really catch your stride with DOM. Next, I want to discuss actually modifying a DOM tree that is already in existence.

Modifying a DOM Tree

The process of changing an existing DOM tree is slightly different from the process of creating one; in general, it involves loading the DOM from some source, traversing the tree, and then making changes. These changes are usually either to *structure* or *content*. If the change is to structure, it becomes a matter of creation again:

```
// Add a copyright element to the root
Element root = doc.getDocumentElement();
Element copyright = doc.createElement("copyright");
copyright.appendChild(doc.createTextNode("Copyright O'Reilly 2001"));
root.appendChild(copyright);
```

This is what I just described. The process of changing existing content is a little different, although not overly complex. As an example, I will show you a modified version of the `UpdateItemServlet`. This version reads the supplied ID and tries to load an existing file if it exists. If so, it doesn't create a new DOM tree, but instead modifies the existing one. Since there are so many additions, I'll reprint the entire class and highlight the changes:

```
package javaxml2;

import java.io.File;
import java.io.IOException;
import java.io.PrintWriter;
import javax.servlet.ServletException;
import javax.servlet.http.HttpServlet;
import javax.servlet.http.HttpServletRequest;
import javax.servlet.http.HttpServletResponse;

import org.xml.sax.SAXException;

// DOM imports
import org.w3c.dom.Attr;
import org.w3c.dom.Document;
```

```java
import org.w3c.dom.DOMImplementation;
import org.w3c.dom.Element;
import org.w3c.dom.NodeList;
import org.w3c.dom.Text;

// Parser import
import org.apache.xerces.dom.DOMImplementationImpl;
import org.apache.xerces.parsers.DOMParser;

public class UpdateItemServlet extends HttpServlet {

    private static final String ITEMS_DIRECTORY = "/javaxml2/ch06/xml/";

    // doGet() method is unchanged

    public void doPost(HttpServletRequest req, HttpServletResponse res)
        throws ServletException, IOException {

        // Get parameter values
        String id = req.getParameterValues("id")[0];
        String name = req.getParameterValues("name")[0];
        String description = req.getParameterValues("description")[0];

        // See if this file exists
        Document doc = null;
        File xmlFile = new File(ITEMS_DIRECTORY + "item-" + id + ".xml");

        if (!xmlFile.exists()) {
            // Create new DOM tree
            DOMImplementation domImpl = new DOMImplementationImpl();
            doc = domImpl.createDocument(null, "item", null);
            Element root = doc.getDocumentElement();

            // ID of item (as attribute)
            root.setAttribute("id", id);

            // Name of item
            Element nameElement = doc.createElement("name");
            Text nameText = doc.createTextNode(name);
            nameElement.appendChild(nameText);
            root.appendChild(nameElement);

            // Description of item
            Element descriptionElement = doc.createElement("description");
            Text descriptionText = doc.createText(description);
            descriptionElement.appendChild(descriptionText);
            root.appendChild(descriptionElement);
        } else {
```

```
                    // Load document
                    try {
                        DOMParser parser = new DOMParser();
                        parser.parse(xmlFile.toURL().toString());
                        doc = parser.getDocument();

                        Element root = doc.getDocumentElement();

                        // Name of item
                        NodeList nameElements =
                            root.getElementsByTagNameNS(docNS, "name");
                        Element nameElement = (Element)nameElements.item(0);
                        Text nameText = (Text)nameElement.getFirstChild();
                        nameText.setData(name);

                        // Description of item
                        NodeList descriptionElements =
                            root.getElementsByTagNameNS(docNS, "description");
                        Element descriptionElement = (Element)descriptionElements.item(0);

                        // Remove and recreate description
                        root.removeChild(descriptionElement);
                        descriptionElement = doc.createElement("description");
                        Text descriptionText = doc.createTextNode(description);
                        descriptionElement.appendChild(descriptionText);
                        root.appendChild(descriptionElement);
                    } catch (SAXException e) {
                        // Print error
                        PrintWriter out = res.getWriter();
                        res.setContentType("text/html");
                        out.println("<HTML><BODY>Error in reading XML: " +
                            e.getMessage() + ".</BODY></HTML>");
                        out.close();
                        return;
                    }
                }

            // Serialize DOM tree
            DOMSerializer serializer = new DOMSerializer();
            serializer.serialize(doc, xmlFile);

            // Print confirmation
            PrintWriter out = res.getWriter();
            res.setContentType("text/html");
            out.println("<HTML><BODY>Thank you for your submission. " +
                "Your item has been processed.</BODY></HTML>");
            out.close();
        }
    }
```

The changes are fairly simple, nothing to throw you for a loop. I create the `File` instance for the named file (using the ID supplied), and check for its existence. This tells the servlet whether the XML file representing the submitted item already exists. If not, it does everything discussed in the last section, with no changes. If the XML already exists (indicating the item has already been submitted), it is loaded and read into a DOM tree using techniques covered in the last chapter. At that point, some basic tree traversal begins.

The code grabs the root element, and then uses the `getElementsByTagName()` method to locate all elements named "name" and then all named "description." In each case, I know that only one will be found within the returned `NodeList`. I can access this using the `item()` method on the `NodeList`, and supplying "0" as the argument (the indexes are all zero-based). This effectively gives me the element desired. I could have simply gotten the children of the root through `getChildren()`, and peeled off the first and second. However, using the element names is easier to document and clearer. I get the "name" element's textual content by invoking `getFirstChild()`. Since I know that the "name" element has a single `Text` node, I can directly cast this to the appropriate type. Finally, the `setData()` method allows the code to change the existing value for a new name, which is the information the user supplied through the form.

You'll notice that I used a slightly different approach for the description of the item. Since there could conceivably be a complete document fragment within the element (remember the user could enter HTML, allowing for nested elements like "b", "a", and "img"), it's easier to just remove the existing "description" element and replace it with a new one. This avoids having to recurse through the tree and remove each child node, a time-consuming task. Once I've removed the node using the `removeChild()` method, it's simple to recreate and reappend it to the document's root element.

It's no accident that this code is hardwired to the format the XML was written out to. In fact, most DOM modification code relies on at least some understanding of the content to be dealt with. For cases when the structure or format is unknown, the DOM Level 2 traversal model is a better fit; I'll cover that a little later on in this chapter. For now, accept that knowing how the XML is structured (since this servlet created it earlier on!) is a tremendous advantage. Methods like `getFirstChild()` can be used and the result cast to a specific type, rather than needing lengthy type checking and switch blocks.

Once the creation or modification is complete, the resulting DOM tree is serialized back to XML, and the process can repeat itself. I've also had to add some error handling for SAX problems resulting from the DOM parsing, but this is also nothing new after the last chapter. As an exercise, update the doGet() method to read in a parameter from the URL and load the XML preferences, letting the user change them on the form. For example, the URL *http://localhost:8080/javaxml2/ servlet/javaxml2.UpdateItemServlet?id=bourgOM* would indicate that the item with the ID "bourgOM" should be loaded for editing. This is a simple change, and one you should be ready to knock out on your own by now.

Namespaces

An important addition to DOM Level 2 not yet discussed is DOM's support for XML namespaces. You'll remember from Chapters 3 and 4, that SAX 2.0 added namespace support, and the same is true for the second iteration of DOM. The key here is two new methods on the Node interface: getPrefix() and getNamespaceURI(). Additionally, all of the creation methods have namespace-aware versions available. So, instead of calling createElement(), you call createElementNS().

Overloaded?

To all of the Java programmers out there, createElementNS() looks pretty odd. Why not just overload createElement() to take in additional parameters? Well, you could if DOM was used only in Java or in languages that supported overloading. However, it's not; it's a cross-language specification, and that results in limitations with method names and backwards compatiblity when it comes to changing existing method signatures. So, DOM defined new methods with the NS suffix to identify them as namespace-aware versions. It's bad for straight Java, but good for DOM as a cross-language standard.

In each of these new namespace-aware methods, the first argument is the namespace URI, and the second is the *qualified* name of the element, attribute, etc. Note that I said qualified; this means that if you want to use a namespace URI of "http://www.oreilly.com" and a prefix of "ora" on an element called "copyright", you would call createElementNS("http://www.oreilly.com", "ora: copyright"). This is very important, and remembering to use that prefix will save you a lot of time down the road. Calling getPrefix() on that new element will correctly return "ora", though, as it should. If you want the element in the default namespace (with no prefix), just pass in the element name (the local name, in this case), and you're all set. Calling getPrefix() on a default-namespaced element returns null, by the way, as it does on an element not in any namespace.

WARNING   The prefix tells you very little about whether an element is a namespace. Elements with a default namespace (and no prefix) have the same return value from getPrefix() as elements not in *any* namespace. I'm hoping the next version of the specification modifies this to return an empty string ("") when the element is in the default namespace.

Rather than simply list all the new namespace-aware methods (you can find that list in Appendix A), I'd rather show you some real code. In fact, converting the UpdateItemServlet's doPost() method to use namespaces is a perfect example:

```
public void doPost(HttpServletRequest req, HttpServletResponse res)
    throws ServletException, IOException {

    // Get parameter values
    String id = req.getParameterValues("id")[0];
    String name = req.getParameterValues("name")[0];
    String description = req.getParameterValues("description")[0];

    // See if this file exists
    Document doc = null;
    File xmlFile = new File(ITEMS_DIRECTORY + "item-" + id + ".xml");
    String docNS = "http://www.oreilly.com/javaxml2";

    if (!xmlFile.exists()) {
        // Create new DOM tree
        DOMImplementation domImpl = new DOMImplementationImpl();
        doc = domImpl.createDocument(docNS, "item", null);
        Element root = doc.getDocumentElement();

        // ID of item (as attribute)
        root.setAttribute("id", id);

        // Name of item
        Element nameElement = doc.createElementNS(docNS, "name");
        Text nameText = doc.createTextNode(name);
        nameElement.appendChild(nameText);
        root.appendChild(nameElement);

        // Description of item
        Element descriptionElement =
            doc.createElementNS(docNS, "description");
        Text descriptionText = doc.createText(description);
        descriptionElement.appendChild(descriptionText);
        root.appendChild(descriptionElement);
    } else {
```

```
                        // Load document
                        try {
                            DOMParser parser = new DOMParser();
                            parser.parse(xmlFile.toURL().toString());
                            doc = parser.getDocument();

                            Element root = doc.getDocumentElement();

                            // Name of item
                            NodeList nameElements =
                                root.getElementsByTagNameNS(docNS, "name");
                            Element nameElement = (Element)nameElements.item(0);
                            Text nameText = (Text)nameElement.getFirstChild();
                            nameText.setData(name);

                            // Description of item
                            NodeList descriptionElements =
                                root.getElementsByTagNameNS(docNS, "description");
                            Element descriptionElement = (Element)descriptionElements.item(0);

                            // Remove and recreate description
                            root.removeChild(descriptionElement);
                            descriptionElement = doc.createElementNS(docNS, "description");
                            Text descriptionText = doc.createTextNode(description);
                            descriptionElement.appendChild(descriptionText);
                            root.appendChild(descriptionElement);
                        } catch (SAXException e) {
                            // Print error
                            PrintWriter out = res.getWriter();
                            res.setContentType("text/html");
                            out.println("<HTML><BODY>Error in reading XML: " +
                                e.getMessage() + ".</BODY></HTML>");
                            out.close();
                            return;
                        }
                    }

                    // Serialize DOM tree
                    DOMSerializer serializer = new DOMSerializer();
                    serializer.serialize(doc, xmlFile);

                    // Print confirmation
                    PrintWriter out = res.getWriter();
                    res.setContentType("text/html");
                    out.println("<HTML><BODY>Thank you for your submission. " +
                        "Your item has been processed.</BODY></HTML>");
                    out.close();
                }
```

Using the `createElementNS()` method to create namespaced elements and searching for them with `getElementsByTagNameNS()` seems to be perfect. The `createDocument()` method even has a handy place to insert the namespace URI for the root element. These elements are all put into the default namespace, and everything looks fine. However, there is a big problem here. Look at the output from running this servlet with no existing XML (this is generated XML, rather than modified XML):

```
<?xml version="1.0"?>
<item id="bourgOM">
<name>Bourgeois OM Guitar</name>
<description>This is a <i>beautiful</i> <b>Sitka-topped</b> guitar with
<b>Indian Rosewood</b> back and sides. Made by luthier
<a href="http://www.bourgeoisguitars.com">Dana Bourgeois</a>, this OM has a
<b>huge sound</b>.
The guitar has <i>great action</i>, a 1 3/4" nut, and all
<i>fossilized ivory</i> nut and saddle, with <i>ebony</i> end pins.
New condition, this is a <b>great guitar</b>!</description>
</item>
```

Does this look familiar? It is the XML from earlier, with *no change*! The one thing that DOM does not do is add namespace declarations. Instead, you'll need to manually add the `xmlns` attribute to your DOM tree; otherwise, when reading in the document, the elements won't be placed into a namespace and you will have some problems. One small change takes care of this, though:

```
// Create new DOM tree
DOMImplementation domImpl = new DOMImplementationImpl();
doc = domImpl.createDocument(docNS, "item", null);
Element root = doc.getDocumentElement();
root.setAttribute("xmlns", docNS);
```

Now you'll get the namespace declaration that you were probably expecting to show up the first go round. You can compile these changes, and try things out. You won't notice any difference; changes are made just as they were before. However, your documents should now have namespaces, both in the reading and writing portion of the servlet application.

A final word on this namespace detail: keep in mind that you could certainly modify the `DOMSerializer` class to look for namespaces on elements, and print out the appropriate `xmlns` declarations as it walks the tree. This is a perfectly legal change, and would be sort of valuable; in fact, it's what many solutions, like those found within Xerces, already do. In any case, as long as you are aware of this behavior, you are protected from being the victim of it.

DOM Level 2 Modules

Now that you've seen what the DOM and the Level 2 core offering provide, I will talk about some additions to DOM Level 2. These are the various modules that add functionality to the core. They are useful from time to time, in certain DOM applications.

First, though, you must have a DOM Level 2 parser available. If you are using a parser that you have purchased or downloaded on your own, this is pretty easy. For example, you can go to the Apache XML web site at *http://xml.apache.org*, download the latest version of Xerces, and you've got DOM Level 2. However, if you're using a parser bundled with another technology, things can get a little trickier. For example, if you've got Jakarta's Tomcat servlet engine, you will find *xml.jar* and *parser.jar* in the *lib/* directory and in the Tomcat classpath. This isn't so good, as these are DOM Level 1 implementations and won't support many of the features I talk about in this section; in that case, download a DOM Level 2 parser manually and ensure that it is loaded *before* any DOM Level 1 parsers.

WARNING   Beware of the newer versions of Tomcat. They do something ostensibly handy: load all *jar* files in the *lib/* directory at startup. Unfortunately, because this is done alphabetically, putting *xerces.jar* in the *lib/* directory means that *parser.jar*, a DOM Level 1 parser, will still be loaded first and you won't get DOM Level 2 support. A common trick to solve this problem is to rename the files: *parser.jar* becomes *z_parser.jar*, and *xml.jar* becomes *z_xml.jar*. This causes them to be loaded after Xerces, and then you will get DOM Level 2 support. This is the problem I mentioned earlier in the servlet example.

Once you've got a capable parser, you're ready to go. Before diving into the new modules, though, I want to show you a high-level overview of what these modules are all about.

Branching Out

When the DOM Level 1 specification came out, it was a single specification. It was defined basically as you read in Chapter 5, with a few minor exceptions. However, when activity began on DOM Level 2, a whole slew of specifications resulted, each called a *module*. If you take a look at the complete set of DOM Level 2 specifications, you'll see six different modules listed. Seems like a lot, doesn't it? I'm not going to cover all of these modules; you'd be reading about DOM for the next four or five chapters. However, I will give you the rundown on the purpose of each module, summarized in Table 6-1. I've included the module's specification, name, and purpose, which you'll need to use shortly.

Table 6-1. DOM specifications and purpose

Specification	Module name	Summary of purpose
DOM Level 2 Core	XML	Extends the DOM Level 1 specification; deals with basic DOM structures like `Element`, `Attr`, `Document`, etc.
DOM Level 2 Views	Views	Provides a model for scripts to dynamically update a DOM structure.
DOM Level 2 Events	Events	Defines an event model for programs and scripts to use in working with DOM.
DOM Level 2 Style	CSS	Provides a model for CSS (Cascading Style Sheets) based on the DOM Core and DOM Views specifications.
DOM Level 2 Traversal and Range	Traversal/ Range	Defines extensions to the DOM for traversing a document and identifying the range of content within that document.
DOM Level 2 HTML	HTML	Extends the DOM to provide interfaces for dealing with HTML structures in a DOM format.

If views, events, CSS, HTML, and traversal were all in a single specification, nothing would ever get done at the W3C! To facilitate all of this moving along, and yet not hamstringing the DOM in the process, the different concepts were broken up into separate specifications.

Once you figure out which specifications to use, you're almost ready to roll. A DOM Level 2 parser is not required to support each of these specifications; as a result, you need to verify that the features you want to use are present in your XML parser. Happily, this is fairly simple to accomplish. Remember the `hasFeature()` method I showed you on the `DOMImplementation` class? Well, if you supply it a module name and version, it will let you know if the module and feature requested are supported. Example 6-4 is a small program that queries an XML parser's support for the DOM modules listed in Table 6-1. You will need to change the name of your vendor's `DOMImplementation` implementation class, but other than that adjustment, it should work for any parser.

Example 6-4. Checking features on a DOM implementation

```
package javaxml2;

import org.w3c.dom.DOMImplementation;

public class DOMModuleChecker {

    /** Vendor DOMImplementation impl class */
    private String vendorImplementationClass =
        "org.apache.xerces.dom.DOMImplementationImpl";
```

Example 6-4. Checking features on a DOM implementation (continued)

```
/** Modules to check */
private String[] moduleNames =
    {"XML", "Views", "Events", "CSS", "Traversal", "Range", "HTML"};

public DOMModuleChecker() {
}

public DOMModuleChecker(String vendorImplementationClass) {
    this.vendorImplementationClass = vendorImplementationClass;
}

public void check() throws Exception {
    DOMImplementation impl =
        (DOMImplementation)Class.forName(vendorImplementationClass)
                                .newInstance();
    for (int i=0; i<moduleNames.length; i++) {
        if (impl.hasFeature(moduleNames[i], "2.0")) {
            System.out.println("Support for " + moduleNames[i] +
                " is included in this DOM implementation.");
        } else {
            System.out.println("Support for " + moduleNames[i] +
                " is not included in this DOM implementation.");
        }
    }
}

public static void main(String[] args) {
    if ((args.length != 0) && (args.length != 1)) {
        System.out.println("Usage: java javaxml2.DOMModuleChecker " +
            "[DOMImplementation impl class to query]");
        System.exit(-1);
    }

    try {
        DOMModuleChecker checker = null;
        if (args.length == 1) {
            checker = new DOMModuleChecker(args[1]);
        } else {
            checker = new DOMModuleChecker();
        }
        checker.check();
    } catch (Exception e) {
        e.printStackTrace();
    }
}
```

Running this program with *xerces.jar* in my classpath, I got the following output:

```
C:\javaxml2\build>java javaxml2.DOMModuleChecker
Support for XML is included in this DOM implementation.
Support for Views is not included in this DOM implementation.
Support for Events is included in this DOM implementation.
Support for CSS is not included in this DOM implementation.
Support for Traversal is included in this DOM implementation.
Support for Range is not included in this DOM implementation.
Support for HTML is not included in this DOM implementation.
```

By specifying the `DOMImplementation` implementation class for your vendor, you can check the supported modules in your own DOM parser. In the next few subsections, I will address a few of the modules that I've found useful, and that you will want to know about as well.

Traversal

First up on the list is the DOM Level 2 Traversal module. This is intended to provide tree-walking capability, but also to allow you to refine the nature of that behavior. In the earlier section on DOM mutation, I mentioned that most of your DOM code will know something about the structure of a DOM tree being worked with; this allows for quick traversal and modification of both structure and content. However, for those times when you do not know the structure of the document, the traversal module comes into play.

Consider the auction site again, and the items input by the user. Most critical are the item name and the description. Since most popular auction sites provide some sort of search, you would want to provide the same in this fictional example. Just searching item titles isn't going to cut it in the real world; instead, a set of key words should be extracted from the item descriptions. I say key words because you don't want a search on "adirondack top" (which to a guitar lover obviously applies to the wood on the top of a guitar) to return toys ("top") from a particular mountain range ("Adirondack"). The best way to do this in the format discussed so far is to extract words that are formatted in a certain way. So the words in the description that are bolded, or in italics, are perfect candidates. Of course, you could grab all the nontextual child elements of the `description` element. However, you'd have to weed through links (the `a` element), image references (`img`), and so forth. What you really want is to specify a custom traversal. Good news; you're in the right place.

The whole of the traversal module is contained within the `org.w3c.dom.traversal` package. Just as everything within core DOM begins with a `Document` interface, everything in DOM Traversal begins with the `org.w3c.dom.traversal.DocumentTraversal` interface. This interface provides two methods:

```
NodeIterator createNodeIterator(Node root, int whatToShow, NodeFilter filter,
                                boolean expandEntityReferences);
TreeWalker createTreeWalker(Node root, int whatToShow, NodeFilter filter,
                            boolean expandEntityReferences);
```

Most DOM implementations that support traversal choose to have their `org.w3c.dom.Document` implementation class implement the `DocumentTraversal` interface as well; this is how it works in Xerces. In a nutshell, using a `NodeIterator` provides a list view of the elements it iterates over; the closest analogy is a standard Java `List` (in the `java.util` package). `TreeWalker` provides a tree view, which you may be more used to in working with XML by now.

NodeIterator

I want to get past all the conceptualization and into the code sample I referred to earlier. I want access to all content within the description of an item from the auction site that is within a specific set of formatting tags. To do this, I first need access to the DOM tree itself. Since this doesn't fit into the servlet approach (you probably wouldn't have a servlet building the search phrases, you'd have some standalone class), I need a new class, `ItemSearcher` (Example 6-5). This class takes any number of item files to search through as arguments.

Example 6-5. The ItemSearcher class

```
package javaxml2;

import java.io.File;

// DOM imports
import org.w3c.dom.Document;
import org.w3c.dom.Element;
import org.w3c.dom.Node;
import org.w3c.dom.NodeList;
import org.w3c.dom.traversal.DocumentTraversal;
import org.w3c.dom.traversal.NodeFilter;
import org.w3c.dom.traversal.NodeIterator;

// Vendor parser
import org.apache.xerces.parsers.DOMParser;

public class ItemSearcher {

    private String docNS = "http://www.oreilly.com/javaxml2";

    public void search(String filename) throws Exception {
        // Parse into a DOM tree
        File file = new File(filename);
        DOMParser parser = new DOMParser();
```

Example 6-5. The ItemSearcher class (continued)

```
    parser.parse(file.toURL().toString());
    Document doc = parser.getDocument();

    // Get node to start iterating with
    Element root = doc.getDocumentElement();
    NodeList descriptionElements =
        root.getElementsByTagNameNS(docNS, "description");
    Element description = (Element)descriptionElements.item(0);

    // Get a NodeIterator
    NodeIterator i = ((DocumentTraversal)doc)
        .createNodeIterator(description, NodeFilter.SHOW_ALL, null, true);

    Node n;
    while ((n = i.nextNode()) != null) {
        if (n.getNodeType() == Node.ELEMENT_NODE) {
            System.out.println("Encountered Element: '" +
                n.getNodeName() + "'");
        } else if (n.getNodeType() == Node.TEXT_NODE) {
            System.out.println("Encountered Text: '" +
                n.getNodeValue() + "'");
        }
    }
}

public static void main(String[] args) {
    if (args.length == 0) {
        System.out.println("No item files to search through specified.");
        return;
    }

    try {
        ItemSearcher searcher = new ItemSearcher();
        for (int i=0; i<args.length; i++) {
            System.out.println("Processing file: " + args[i]);
            searcher.search(args[i]);
        }
    } catch (Exception e) {
        e.printStackTrace();
    }
}
}
```

As you can see, I've created a `NodeIterator`, and supplied it the `description` element to start with for iteration. The constant value passed as the filter instructs the iterator to show all nodes. You could just as easily provide values like `Node.SHOW_ELEMENT` and `Node.SHOW_TEXT`, which would show only elements or textual nodes, respectively. I haven't yet provided a `NodeFilter` implementation (I'll get to that next), and I allowed for entity reference expansion. What is nice about all this is that the iterator, once created, doesn't have just the child nodes of `description`. Instead, it actually has *all* nodes under `description`, even when nested multiple levels deep. This is extremely handy for dealing with unknown XML structure!

At this point, you still have all the nodes, which is not what you want. I added some code (the last `while` loop) to show you how to print out the element and text node results. You can run the code as is, but it's not going to help much. Instead, the code needs to provide a filter, so it only picks up elements with the formatting desired: the text within an `i` or `b` block. You can provide this customized behavior by supplying a custom implementation of the `NodeFilter` interface, which defines only a single method:

```
public short acceptNode(Node n);
```

This method should return `NodeFilter.FILTER_SKIP`, `NodeFilter.FILTER_REJECT`, or `NodeFilter.FILTER_ACCEPT`. The first skips the examined node, but continues to iterate over its children; the second rejects the examined node and its children (only applicable in `TreeWalker`); and the third accepts and passes on the examined node. It behaves a lot like SAX, in that you can intercept nodes as they are being iterated and decide if they should be passed on to the calling method. Add the following nonpublic class to the *ItemSearcher.java* source file:

```java
class FormattingNodeFilter implements NodeFilter {

    public short acceptNode(Node n) {
        if (n.getNodeType() == Node.TEXT_NODE) {
            Node parent = n.getParentNode();
            if ((parent.getNodeName().equalsIgnoreCase("b")) ||
                (parent.getNodeName().equalsIgnoreCase("i"))) {
                return FILTER_ACCEPT;
            }
        }
        // If we got here, not interested
        return FILTER_SKIP;
    }
}
```

This is just plain old DOM code, and shouldn't pose any difficulty to you. First, the code only wants text nodes; the text of the formatted elements is desired, not the elements themselves. Next, the parent is determined, and since it's safe to assume that `Text` nodes have `Element` node parents, the code immediately invokes `getNodeName()`. If the element name is either "b" or "i", the code has found search text, and returns `FILTER_ACCEPT`. Otherwise, `FILTER_SKIP` is returned.

All that's left now is a change to the iterator creation call instructing it to use the new filter implementation, and to the output, both in the existing search() method of the ItemSearcher class:

```
// Get a NodeIterator
NodeIterator i = ((DocumentTraversal)doc)
    .createNodeIterator(description, NodeFilter.SHOW_ALL,
        new FormattingNodeFilter(), true);


Node n;
while ((n = i.nextNode()) != null) {
    System.out.println("Search phrase found: '" + n.getNodeValue() + "'");
}
```

NOTE   Some astute readers will wonder what happens when a NodeFilter implementation conflicts with the constant supplied to the createNodeIterator() method (in this case that constant is NodeFilter.SHOW_ALL). Actually, the short constant filter is applied first, and then the resulting list of nodes is passed to the filter implementation. If I had supplied the constant NodeFilter. SHOW_ELEMENT, I would not have gotten any search phrases, because my filter would not have received any Text nodes to examine; just Element nodes. Be careful to use the two together in a way that makes sense. In the example, I could have safely used NodeFilter. SHOW_TEXT also.

Now, the class is useful and ready to run. Executing it on the *bourgOM.xml* file I explained in the first section, I get the following results:

```
bmclaugh@GANDALF ~/javaxml2/build
$ java javaxml2.ItemSearcher ../ch06/xml/item-bourgOM.xml
Processing file: ../ch06/xml/item-bourgOM.xml
Search phrase found: 'beautiful'
Search phrase found: 'Sitka-topped'
Search phrase found: 'Indian Rosewood'
Search phrase found: 'huge sound'
Search phrase found: 'great action'
Search phrase found: 'fossilized ivory'
Search phrase found: 'ebony'
Search phrase found: 'great guitar'
```

This is perfect: all of the bolded and italicized phrases are now ready to be added to a search facility. (Sorry; you'll have to write that yourself!)

TreeWalker

The TreeWalker interface is almost exactly the same as the NodeIterator interface; the only difference is that you get a tree view instead of a list view. This is primarily useful if you want to deal with only a certain type of node within a tree; for instance, the tree with only elements or without any comments. By using the constant filter value (such as `NodeFilter.SHOW_ELEMENT`) and a filter implementation (like one that passes on `FILTER_SKIP` for all comments), you can essentially get a view of a DOM tree without extraneous information. The `TreeWalker` interface provides all the basic node operations, such as `firstChild()`, `parentNode()`, `nextSibling()`, and of course `getCurrentNode()`, which tells you where you are currently walking.

I'm not going to give an example here. By now, you should see that this is identical to dealing with a standard DOM tree, except that you can filter out unwanted items by using the `NodeFilter` constants. This is a great, simple way to limit your view of XML documents to only information you are interested in seeing. Use it well; it's a real asset, as is `NodeIterator`! You can also check out the complete specification online at *http://www.w3.org/TR/DOM-Level-2-Traversal-Range/*.

Range

The DOM Level 2 Range module is one of the least commonly used modules, probably due to a lack of understanding of DOM Range rather than any lack of usefulness. This module provides a way to deal with a set of content within a document. Once you've defined that range of content, you can insert into it, copy it, delete parts of it, and manipulate it in various ways. The most important thing to start with is realizing that "range" in this sense refers to a number of pieces of a DOM tree grouped together. It does *not* refer to a set of allowed values, where a high and low or start and end are defined. Therefore, DOM Range has nothing at all to do with validation of data values. Get that, and you're already ahead of the pack.

Like traversal, working with `Range` involves a new DOM package: `org.w3c.dom.ranges`. There are actually only two interfaces and one exception within this class, so it won't take you long to get your bearings. First is the analog to `Document` (and `DocumentTraversal`): that's `org.w3c.dom.ranges.DocumentRange`. Like the `DocumentTraversal` class, Xerces' `Document` implementation class implements `Range`. And also like `DocumentTraversal`, it has very few interesting methods; in fact, only one:

```
public Range createRange();
```

All other range operations operate upon the `Range` class (rather, an implementation of the interface; but you get the idea). Once you've got an instance of the `Range` interface, you can set the starting and ending points, and edit away. As an example, let's go back to the `UpdateItemServlet`. I mentioned that it's a bit of a hassle to try and remove all the children of the `description` element and then set the new description text; that's because there is no way to tell if a single `Text` node is within the description, or if many elements and text nodes, as well as nested nodes, exist within a description that is primarily HTML. I showed you how to simply remove the old description element and create a new one. However, DOM Range makes this unnecessary. Take a look at this modification to the doPost() method of that servlet:

```
// Load document
try {
    DOMParser parser = new DOMParser();
    parser.parse(xmlFile.toURL().toString());
    doc = parser.getDocument();

    Element root = doc.getDocumentElement();

    // Name of item
    NodeList nameElements =
        root.getElementsByTagNameNS(docNS, "name");
    Element nameElement = (Element)nameElements.item(0);
    Text nameText = (Text)nameElement.getFirstChild();
    nameText.setData(name);

    // Description of item
    NodeList descriptionElements =
        root.getElementsByTagNameNS(docNS, "description");
    Element descriptionElement = (Element)descriptionElements.item(0);

    // Remove and recreate description
    Range range = ((DocumentRange)doc).createRange();
    range.setStartBefore(descriptionElement.getFirstChild());
    range.setEndAfter(descriptionElement.getLastChild());
    range.deleteContents();
    Text descriptionText = doc.createTextNode(description);
    descriptionElement.appendChild(descriptionText);

    range.detach();
} catch (SAXException e) {
    // Print error
    PrintWriter out = res.getWriter();
    res.setContentType("text/html");
    out.println("<HTML><BODY>Error in reading XML: " +
        e.getMessage() + ".</BODY></HTML>");
    out.close();
    return;
}
```

To remove all the content, I first create a new Range, using the DocumentRange cast. You'll need to add import statements for the DocumentRange and Range classes to your servlet, too (they are both in the org.w3c.dom.ranges package).

NOTE   In the first part of the DOM Level 2 Modules section, I showed you how to check which modules a parser implementation supports. I realize that Xerces reported that it did not support Range. However, running this code with Xerces 1.3.0, 1.3.1, and 1.4 all worked without a hitch. Strange, isn't it?

Once the range is ready, set the starting and ending points. Since I want all content within the `description` element, I start before the first child of that `Element` node (using `setStartBefore()`), and end after its last child (using `setEndAfter()`). There are other, similar methods for this task, `setStartAfter()` and `setEndBefore()`. Once that's done, it's simple to call `deleteContents()`. Just like that, not a bit of content is left. Then the servlet creates the new textual description and appends it. Finally, I let the JVM know that it can release any resources associated with the `Range` by calling `detach()`. While this step is commonly overlooked, it can really help with lengthy bits of code that use the extra resources.

Another option is to use `extractContents()` instead of `deleteContents()`. This method removes the content, then returns the content that has been removed. You could insert this as an archived element, for example:

```
// Remove and recreate description
Range range = ((DocumentRange)doc).createRange();
range.setStartBefore(descriptionElement.getFirstChild());
range.setEndAfter(descriptionElement.getLastChild());
Node oldContents = range.extractContents();
Text descriptionText = doc.createTextNode(description);
descriptionElement.appendChild(descriptionText);

// Set this as content to some other, archival, element
archivalElement.appendChild(oldContents);
```

Don't try this in your servlet; there is no `archivalElement` in this code, and it is just for demonstration purposes. However, it should be starting to sink in that the DOM Level 2 Range module can really help you in editing documents' contents. It also provides yet another way to get a handle on content when you aren't sure of the structure of that content ahead of time.

There's a lot more to ranges in DOM; check this out on your own, along with all of the DOM modules covered in this chapter. However, you should now have enough of an understanding of the basics to get you going. Most importantly, realize that at any point in an active `Range` instance, you can simply invoke `range.insertNode(Node newNode)` and add new content, wherever you are in a document! It is this robust editing quality of ranges that make them so attractive. The next time you need to delete, copy, extract, or add content to a structure that you know little about, think about using ranges. The specification gives you information on all this and more, and is located online at *http://www.w3.org/TR/DOM-Level-2-Traversal-Range/*.

Events, Views, and Style

Aside from the HTML module, which I'll talk about next, there are three other DOM Level 2 modules: Events, Views, and Style. I'm not going to cover these three in depth in this book, largely because I believe that they are more useful for client programming. So far, I've focused on server-side programming, and I'm going to keep in that vein throughout the rest of the book. These three modules are most often used on client software such as IDEs, web pages, and the like. Still, I want to briefly touch on each so you'll still be on top of the DOM heap at the next alpha-geek soirée.

Events

The Events module provides just what you are probably expecting: a means of "listening" to a DOM document. The relevant classes are in the `org.w3c.dom.events` package, and the class that gets things going is `DocumentEvent`. No surprise here; compliant parsers (like Xerces) implement this interface in the same class that implements `org.w3c.dom.Document`. The interface defines only one method:

```
public Event createEvent(String eventType);
```

The string passed in is the type of event; valid values in DOM Level 2 are "UIEvent", "MutationEvent", and "MouseEvent". Each of these has a corresponding class: `UIEvent`, `MutationEvent`, and `MouseEvent`. You'll note, in looking at the Xerces Javadoc, that they provide only the `MutationEvent` interface, which is the only event type Xerces supports. When an event is "fired" off, it can be handled (or "caught") by an `EventListener`.

This is where the DOM core support comes in; a parser supporting DOM events should have the `org.w3c.dom.Node` interface implementing the `org.w3c.dom.events.EventTarget` interface. So every node can be the target of an event. This means that you have the following method available on those nodes:

```
public void addEventListener(String type, EventListener listener,
                             boolean capture);
```

Here's the process. You create a new `EventListener` (which is a custom class you would write) implementation. You need to implement only a single method:

```
public void handleEvent(Event event);
```

Register that listener on any and all nodes you want to work with. Code in here typically does some useful task, like emailing users that their information has been changed (in some XML file), revalidating the XML (think XML editors), or asking users if they are sure they want to perform the action.

At the same time, you'll want your code to trigger a new Event on certain actions, like the user clicking on a node in an IDE and entering new text, or deleting a selected element. When the Event is triggered, it is passed to the available EventListener instances, starting with the active node and moving up. This is where your listener's code executes, *if the event types are the same.* Additionally, you can have the event stop propagating at that point (once you've handled it), or bubble up the event chain and possibly be handled by other registered listeners.

So there you have it; events in only a page! And you thought specifications were hard to read. Seriously, this is some useful stuff, and if you are working with client-side code, or software that will be deployed standalone on user's desktops (like that XML editor I keep talking about), this should be a part of your DOM toolkit. Check out the full specification online at *http://www.w3.org/TR/DOM-Level-2-Events/*.

Views

Next on the list is DOM Level 2 Views. The reason I don't cover views in much detail is that, really, there is very little to be said. From every reading I can make of the (one-page!) specification, it's simply a basis for future work, perhaps in vertical markets. The specification defines only two interfaces, both in the org.w3c. dom.views package. Here's the first:

```
package org.w3c.dom.views;

public interface AbstractView {
    public DocumentView getDocument();

}
```

And here's the second:

```
package org.w3c.dom.views;

public interface DocumentView {
    public AbstractView getDefaultView();

}
```

Seems a bit cyclical, doesn't it? A single *source document* (a DOM tree) can have multiple *views* associated with it. In this case, view refers to a presentation, like a styled document (after XSL or CSS has been applied), or perhaps a version with Shockwave and one without. By implementing the AbstractView interface, you can define your own customized versions of displaying a DOM tree. For example, consider this example subinterface:

```
package javaxml2;

import org.w3c.dom.views.AbstractView;

public interface StyledView implements AbstractView {

    public void setStylesheet(String stylesheetURI);

    public String getStylesheetURI();
}
```

I've left out the method implementations, but you can see how this could be used to provide stylized views of a DOM tree. Additionally, a compliant parser implementation would have the `org.w3c.dom.Document` implementation implement `DocumentView`, which allows you to query a document for its default view. It's expected that in a later version of the specification you will be able to register multiple views for a document, and more closely tie a view or views to a document.

Look for this to be fleshed out more as browsers like Netscape, Mozilla, and Internet Explorer provide these sorts of views of XML. Additionally, you can read the short specification and know as much as I do by checking it out online at *http:// www.w3.org/TR/DOM-Level-2-Views/*.

Style

Finally, there is the Style module, also referred to as simply CSS (Cascading Style Sheets). You can check this specification out at *http://www.w3.org/TR/DOM-Level-2-Style/*. This provides a binding for CSS stylesheets to be represented by DOM constructs. Everything of interest is in the `org.w3c.dom.stylesheets` and `org.w3c.dom.css` packages. The former contains generic base classes, and the latter provides specific applications to Cascading Style Sheets. Both are primarily used for showing a client a styled document.

You use this module exactly like you use the core DOM interfaces: you get a Style-compliant parser, parse a stylesheet, and use the CSS language bindings. This is particularly handy when you want to parse a CSS stylesheet and apply it to a DOM document. You're working from the same basic set of concepts, if that makes sense to you (and it should; when you can do two things with an API instead of one, that's generally good!). Again, I only briefly touch on the Style module, because it's accessible with the Javadoc in its entirety. The classes are aptly named (`CSSValueList`, `Rect`, `CSSDOMImplementation`), and are close enough to their XML DOM counterparts that I'm confident you'll have no problem using them if you need to.

HTML

For HTML, DOM provides a set of interfaces that model the various HTML elements. For example, you can use the `HTMLDocument` class, the `HTMLAnchorElement`, and the `HTMLSelectElement` (all in the `org.w3c.dom.html` package) to represent their analogs in HTML (`<HTML>`, `<A>`, and `<SELECT>` in this case). All of these provide convenience methods like `setTitle()` (on `HTMLDocument`), `setHref()` (on `HTMLAnchorElement`), and `getOptions()` (on `HTMLSelectElement`). All of these extend core DOM structures like `Document` and `Element`, and so can be used as any other DOM `Node` could.

However, it turns out that the HTML bindings are rarely used (at least directly). It's not because they aren't useful; instead, many tools have already been written to provide this sort of access through even more user-friendly tools. XMLC, a project within the Enhydra application server framework, is one such example (located online at *http://xmlc.enhydra.org*), and Cocoon, covered in Chapter 10, is another. These allow developers to work with HTML and web pages in a way that does not necessarily require even basic DOM knowledge, making it more accessible to web designers and newer Java developers. The end result of using these tools is that the HTML DOM bindings are rarely needed. But if you know about them, you can use them if you need to. Additionally, you can use standard DOM functionality on well-formed HTML documents (XHTML), treating elements as `Element` nodes and attributes as `Attr` nodes. Even without the HTML bindings, you can use DOM to work with HTML. Piece of cake.

Odds and Ends

What's left in DOM Level 2 besides these modules and namespace-awareness? Very little, and you've probably already used most of it. The `createDocument()` and `createDocumentType()` methods are new to the `DOMImplementation` class, and you've used both of them. Additionally, the `getSystemId()` and `getPublicId()` methods used in the `DOMSerializer` class on the `DocumentType` interface are also DOM Level 2 additions. Other than that, there isn't much; a few new `DOMException` error code constants, and that's about it. You can see the complete list of changes online at *http://www.w3.org/TR/2000/REC-DOM-Level-2-Core-20001113/changes.html*. The rest of the changes are the additional modules, one of which I'll cover next.

DOM Level 3

Before closing the book on DOM and looking at common gotchas, I will spend a little time letting you know what's coming in DOM Level 3, which is underway right now. In fact, I expect this specification to be finalized early in 2002, not long from the time you are probably reading this book. The items I point out here aren't all of the changes and additions in DOM Level 3, but they are the ones that I think are of general interest to most DOM developers (that's you now, if you were wondering). Many of these are things that DOM programmers have been requesting for several years, so now you can look forward to them as well.

The XML Declaration

The first change in the DOM that I want to point out seems pretty trivial at first glance: exposure of the XML declaration. Remember those? Here's an example:

```
<?xml version="1.0" standalone="yes" encoding="UTF-8"?>
```

There are three important pieces of information here that are not currently available in DOM: the version, the state of the standalone attribute, and the specified encoding. Additionally, the DOM tree itself has an encoding; this may or may not match up to the XML encoding attribute. For example, the associated encoding for "UTF-8" in Java turns out to be "UTF8", and there should be a way to distinguish between the two. All of these problems are solved in DOM Level 3 by the addition of four attributes to the Document interface. These are version (a String), standalone (a boolean), encoding (another String), and actualEncoding (String again). The accessor and mutator methods to modify these attributes are pretty straightforward:

```
public String getVersion();
public void setVersion(String version);

public boolean getStandalone();
public void setStandalone(boolean standalone);

public String getEncoding();
public void setEncoding(String encoding);

public String getActualEncoding();
public void setActualEncoding(String actualEncoding);
```

Most importantly, you'll finally be able to access the information in the XML declaration. This is a real boon to those writing XML editors and the like that need this information. It also helps developers working with internationalization and XML, as they can ascertain a document's encoding (encoding), create a DOM tree with its encoding (actualEncoding), and then translate as needed.

Node Comparisons

In Levels 1 and 2 of DOM, the only way to compare two nodes is to do it manually. Developers end up writing utility methods that use instanceof to determine the type of Node, and then compare all the available method values to each other. In

other words, it's a pain. DOM Level 3 offers several comparison methods that allevi-
ate this pain. I'll give you the proposed signatures, and then tell you about each.
They are all additions to the `org.w3c.dom.Node` interface, and look like this:

```
// See if the input Node is the same object as this Node
public boolean isSameNode(Node input);

// Tests for equality in structure (not object equality)
public boolean equalsNode(Node input, boolean deep);

/** Constants for document order */
public static final int DOCUMENT_ORDER_PRECEDING = 1;
public static final int DOCUMENT_ORDER_FOLLOWING = 2;
public static final int DOCUMENT_ORDER_SAME      = 3;
public static final int DOCUMENT_ORDER_UNORDERED = 4;

// Determine the document order of input in relation to this Node
public int compareDocumentOrder(Node input) throws DOMException;

/** Constants for tree position */
public static final int TREE_POSITION_PRECEDING  = 1;
public static final int TREE_POSITION_FOLLOWING  = 2;
public static final int TREE_POSITION_ANCESTOR   = 3;
public static final int TREE_POSITION_DESCENDANT = 4;
public static final int TREE_POSITION_SAME       = 5;
public static final int TREE_POSITION_UNORDERED  = 6;

// Determine the tree position of input in relation to this Node
public int compareTreePosition(Node input) throws DOMException;
```

The first method, `isSameNode()`, allows for object comparison. This doesn't
determine whether the two nodes have the same structure or data, but whether
they are the same object in the JVM. The second method, `equalsNode()`, is probably going to be more commonly used in your applications. It tests for `Node` equal-
ity in terms of data and type (obviously, an `Attr` will never be equal to a
`DocumentType`). It provides a parameter, `deep`, to allow comparison of just the
`Node` itself or of all its child `Node`s as well.

The next two methods, `compareDocumentOrder()` and `compareTreePosition()`,
allow for relational positioning of the current `Node` and an input `Node`. For both,
there are several constants defined to be used as return values. A node can be
before the current one in the document, after it, in the same position, or unordered. The unordered value occurs when comparing an attribute to an element,
or in any other case where the term "document order" has no contextual meaning. And finally, a `DOMException` occurs when the two nodes being queried are
not in the same DOM `Document` object. The final new method,
`compareTreePosition()`, provides the same sort of comparison, but adds the

ability to determine ancestry. Two additional constants, TREE_POSITION_ANCESTOR and TREE_POSITION_DESCENDANT, allow for this. The first denotes that the input Node is up the hierarchy from the reference Node (the one the method is invoked upon); the second indicates that the input Node is down the hierarchy from the reference Node.

With these four methods, you can isolate any DOM structure and determine how it relates to another. This addition to DOM Level 3 should serve you well, and you can count on using all of the comparison methods in your coding. Keep an eye on both the constant names and values, though, as they may change over the evolution of the specification.

Bootstrapping

The last addition in DOM Level 3 I want to cover is arguably the most important: the ability to bootstrap. I mentioned earlier that in creating DOM structures, you are forced to use vendor-specific code (unless you're using JAXP, which I'll cover in Chapter 9). This is a bad thing, of course, as it knocks out vendor-independence. For the sake of discussion, I'll repeat a code fragment that creates a DOM Document object using a DOMImplementation here:

```
import org.w3c.dom.Document;
import org.w3c.dom.DOMImplementation;

import org.apache.xerces.dom.DOMImplementationImpl;

// Class declaration and other Java constructs

DOMImplementation domImpl = DOMImplementationImpl.getDOMImplementation();
Document doc = domImpl.createDocument();
// And so on...
```

The problem is that there is no way to get a DOMImplementation without importing and using a vendor's implementation class. The solution is to use a factory that provides DOMImplementation instances. Of course, the factory is actually providing a vendor's *implementation* of DOMImplementation (I know, I know, it's a bit confusing). Vendors can set system properties or provide their own versions of this factory so that it returns the implementation class they want. The resulting code to create DOM trees then looks like this:

```
import org.w3c.dom.Document;
import org.w3c.dom.DOMImplementation;
import org.w3c.dom.DOMImplementationFactory;

// Class declaration and other Java constructs

DOMImplementation domImpl =
```

```
            DOMImplementationFactory.getDOMImplementation();
    Document doc = domImpl.createDocument();
    // And so on...
```

The class being added is `DOMImplementationFactory`, and should solve most of your vendor-independence issues once it's in place. Look for this as the flagship of DOM Level 3, as it's one of the most requested features for current levels of DOM.

Gotcha!

DOM has a set of troublesome spots just like SAX, and just like the APIs we'll cover in the next few chapters. I will point some of those out to you, and hopefully save you a few hours of debugging time along the way. Enjoy; these happen to be problems that I've run into and struggled against for quite a while before getting things figured out.

The Dreaded WRONG DOCUMENT Exception

The number one problem that I see among DOM developers is what I refer to as "the dreaded WRONG DOCUMENT exception." This exception occurs when you try to mix nodes from different documents. It most often shows up when you try to move a node from one document to another, which turns out to be a common task.

The problem arises because of the factory approach I mentioned earlier. Because each element, attribute, processing instruction, and so on is created from a `Document` instance, it is not safe to assume that those nodes are compatible with other `Document` instances; two instances of `Document` may be from different vendors with different supported features, and trying to mix and match nodes from one with nodes from the other can result in implementation-dependent problems. As a result, to use a node from a different document requires passing that node into the target document's `insertNode()` method. The result of this method is a new `Node`, which is compatible with the target document. In other words, this code is going to cause problems:

```
Element otherDocElement = otherDoc.getDocumentElement();
Element thisDocElement = thisDoc.getDocumentElement();

// Here's the problem - mixing nodes from different documents
thisDocElement.appendChild(otherDocElement);
```

This exception will result:

```
org.apache.xerces.dom.DOMExceptionImpl: DOM005 Wrong document
  at org.apache.xerces.dom.ChildAndParentNode.internalInsertBefore(
     ChildAndParentNode.java:314)
  at org.apache.xerces.dom.ChildAndParentNode.insertBefore(
     ChildAndParentNode.java:296)
```

```
    at org.apache.xerces.dom.NodeImpl.appendChild(NodeImpl.java:213)
    at MoveNode.main(MoveNode.java:30)
```

To avoid this, you must first import the desired node into the new document:

```
Element otherDocElement = otherDoc.getDocumentElement();
Element thisDocElement = thisDoc.getDocumentElement();

// Import the node into the right document
Element readyToUseElement = (Element)thisDoc.importNode(otherDocElement);

// Now this works
thisDocElement.appendChild(readyToUseElement);
```

Note that the result of importNode() is a Node, so it must be cast to the correct interface (Element in this case). Save yourself some time and effort and commit this to memory; write it on a notecard and tuck it under your pillow. Trust me, this is about the most annoying exception known to man!

Creating, Appending, and Inserting

Fixing the problem I just described often leads to another problem. A common error I've seen is when developers remember to import a node, and then forget to append it! In other words, code crops up looking like this:

```
Element otherDocElement = otherDoc.getDocumentElement();
Element thisDocElement = thisDoc.getDocumentElement();

// Import the node into the right document
Element readyToUseElement = (Element)thisDoc.importNode(otherDocElement);

// The node never gets appended!!
```

In this case, you have an element that belongs to the target document, but that never gets appended, or prepended, to anything within the document. The result is another tough-to-find bug, in that the document owns the element but the element is not in the actual DOM tree. Output ends up being completely devoid of the imported node, which can be quite frustrating. Watch out!

What's Next?

Well, you should be starting to feel like you're getting the hang of this XML thing. In the next chapter, I'll continue on the API trail by introducing you to JDOM, another API for accessing XML from Java. JDOM is similar to DOM (but is not DOM) in that it provides you a tree model of XML. I'll show you how it works, highlight when to use it, and cover the differences between the various XML APIs we've looked at so far. Don't get cocky yet; there's plenty more to learn!

7

JDOM

JDOM provides a means of accessing an XML document within Java through a tree structure, and in that respect is somewhat similar to the DOM. However, it was built specifically for Java (remember the discussion on language bindings for the DOM?), so is in many ways more intuitive to a Java developer than DOM. I'll describe these aspects of JDOM throughout the chapter, as well as talk about specific cases to use SAX, DOM, or JDOM. And for the complete set of details on JDOM, you should check out the web site at *http://www.jdom.org*.

Additionally, and importantly, JDOM is an open source API. And because the API is still finalizing on a 1.0 version, it also remains flexible.* You have the ability to suggest and implement changes yourself. If you find that you like JDOM, except for one little annoying thing, you can help us investigate solutions to your problem. In this chapter, I'll cover JDOM's current status, particularly with regard to standardization, and the basics on using the API, and I'll give you some working examples.

The Basics

Chapters 5 and 6 should have given you a pretty good understanding of dealing with XML tree representations. So when I say that JDOM also provides a tree-based representation of an XML document, that gives you a starting point for understanding how JDOM behaves. To help you see how the classes in JDOM match up to XML structures, take a look at Figure 7-1, which shows a UML model of JDOM's core classes.

---

* Because JDOM 1.0 is not final, some things may change between the publication of this book and your download. I'll try and keep a running list of changes on the JDOM web site (*http://www.jdom.org*) and work with O'Reilly to get these changes and updates available as quickly as possible.

Full Disclosure

In the interests of full disclosure, I should say that I am one of the co-creators of JDOM; my partner in crime on this particular endeavor is Jason Hunter, the noted author of *Java Servlet Programming* (O'Reilly). Jason and I had some issues with DOM, and during a long discussion at the 2000 O'Reilly Enterprise Java Conference, came up with JDOM. I also owe a great deal of credit to James Davidson (Sun Microsystems, servlet 2.2 specification lead, Ant author, etc.) and Pier Fumagalli (Apache/Jakarta/Cocoon superhero). Plus, the hundreds of good friends on the JDOM mailing lists.

All that to say that I'm partial to JDOM. So, if you sense some favoritism creeping through this chapter, I apologize; I use SAX, DOM, and JDOM often, but I happen to like one more than the others, because in my personal development, it has helped me out. Anyway, consider yourself forewarned!

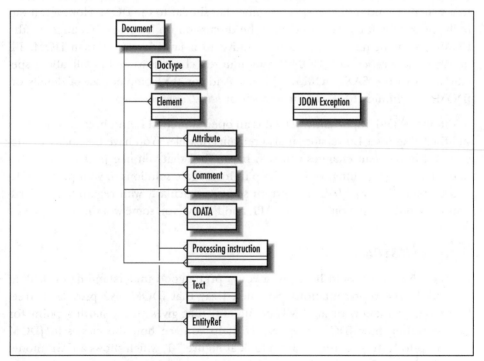

Figure 7-1. UML model of core JDOM classes

As you can see, the names of the classes tell the story. At the core of the JDOM structure is the Document object; it is both the representation of an XML document, and a container for all the other JDOM structures. Element represents an

XML element, Attribute an attribute, and so on down the line. If you've immersed yourself in DOM, though, you might think there are some things missing from JDOM. For example, where's the Text class? As you recall, DOM follows a very strict tree model, and element content is actually considered a child node (or nodes) of an element node itself. In JDOM, this was seen as inconvenient in many cases, and the API provides getText() methods on the Element class. This allows the content of an element to be obtained from the element itself, and therefore there is no Text class. This was felt to provide a more intuitive approach for Java developers unfamiliar with XML, DOM, or some of the vagaries of trees.

Java Collections Support

Another important item to take note of is that you don't see any list classes like SAX's Attributes class or DOM's NodeList and NamedNodeMap classes. This is a nod to Java developers; it was felt that using Java Collections (java.util.List, java.util.Map, etc.) would provide a familiar and simple API for XML usage. DOM must serve across languages (remember Java language bindings in Chapter 5?), and can't take advantage of language-specific things like Java Collections. For example, when invoking the getAttributes() method on the Element class, you get back a List; you can of course operate upon this List just as you would any other Java List, without looking up new methods or syntax.

Concrete Classes and Factories

Another basic tenet of JDOM that is different from DOM, and not so visible, is that JDOM is an API of concrete classes. In other words, Element, Attribute, ProcessingInstruction, Comment, and the rest are all classes that can be directly instantiated using the new keyword. The advantage here is that factories are not needed, as factories can oftentimes be intrusive into code. Creating a new JDOM document would be done like this:

```
Element rootElement = new Element("root");
Document document = new Document(rootElement);
```

That simple. On the other hand, not using factories can also be seen as a disadvantage. While you can subclass JDOM classes, you would have to explicitly use those subclasses in your code:

```
element.addContent(new FooterElement("Copyright 2001"));
```

Here, FooterElement is a subclass of org.jdom.Element, and does some custom processing (it could, for example, build up several elements that display a page footer). Because it subclasses Element, it can be added to the element variable through the normal means, the addContent() method. However, there is no means to define an element subclass and specify that it should always be used for element instantiation, like this:

```
// This code does not work!!
JDOMFactory factory = new JDOMFactory();
factory.setDocumentClass("javaxml2.BrettsDocumentClass");
factory.setElementClass("javaxml2.BrettsElementClass");


Element rootElement = JDOMFactory.createElement("root");
Document document = JDOMFactory.createDocument(rootElement);
```

The idea is that once the factory has been created, specific subclasses of JDOM structures can be specified as the class to use for those structures. Then, every time (for example) an `Element` is created through the factory, the `javaxml2.BrettsElementClass` is used instead of the default `org.jdom.Element` class.

Support for this as an option is growing, if not as a standard means of working with JDOM. That means that in the open source world, it's possible this functionality might be in place by the time you read this, or by the time JDOM is finalized in a 1.0 form. Stay tuned to *http://www.jdom.org* for the latest on these developments.

Input and Output

A final important aspect of JDOM is its input and output model. First, you should realize that JDOM is not a parser; it is an XML document representation in Java. In other words, like DOM and SAX, it is simply a set of classes that can be used to manipulate the data that a parser provides. As a result, JDOM must rely on a parser for reading raw XML.* It can also accept SAX events or a DOM tree as input, as well as JDBC `ResultSet` instances and more. To facilitate this, JDOM provides a package specifically for input, `org.jdom.input`. This package provides *builder* classes; the two you'll use most often are `SAXBuilder` and `DOMBuilder`. These build the core JDOM structure, a JDOM `Document`, from a set of SAX events or a DOM tree. As JDOM standardizes (see the section "Is JDOM a Standard?" at the end of this chapter), it's also expected that direct support for JDOM will materialize in parser efforts like Apache Xerces and Sun's Crimson.

For dealing with input streams, files or documents on disk, or building from existing XML not in a DOM tree, `SAXBuilder` is the best solution. It's fast and efficient, just like SAX. Using the builder is a piece of cake:

```
SAXBuilder builder = new SAXBuilder();
Document doc = builder.build(new FileInputStream("contents.xml"));
```

---

* By default, this parser is Xerces, which is included with JDOM. However, you can use any other XML parser with JDOM.

I'll detail this further in the code in the chapter, but you can see that it doesn't take much to get access to XML. If you already have your document in a DOM structure, you'll want to use DOMBuilder, which performs a fast conversion from one API to the other:

```
DOMBuilder builder = new DOMBuilder();
Document doc = builder.build(myDomDocumentObject);
```

It's fairly self-explanatory. This essentially converts from an org.w3c.dom. Document to an org.jdom.Document. The process of converting from a JDOM document back to one of these structures is essentially the same, in reverse; the org.jdom.output package is used for these tasks. To move from JDOM structures to DOM ones, DOMOutputter is used:

```
DOMOutputter outputter = new DOMOutputter();
org.w3c.dom.Document domDoc = outputter.output(myJDOMDocumentObject);
```

Taking a JDOM Document and firing off SAX events works in the same way:

```
SAXOutputter outputter = new SAXOutputter();
outputter.setContentHandler(myContentHandler);
outputter.setErrorHandler(myErrorHandler);
outputter.output(myJDOMDocumentObject);
```

This works just like dealing with normal SAX events, where you register content handlers, error handlers, and the rest, and then fire events to those handlers from the JDOM Document object supplied to the output() method.

The final outputter, and the one you'll probably work with more than any other, is org.jdom.output.XMLOutputter. This outputs XML to a stream or writer, which wraps a network connection, a file, or any other structure you want to push XML to. This also is effectively a production-ready version of the DOMSerializer class from Chapter 5, except of course it works with JDOM, not DOM. Using the XMLOutputter works like this:

```
XMLOutputter outputter = new XMLOutputter();
outputter.output(jdomDocumentObject, new FileOutputStream("results.xml"));
```

So there you have it; the input and output of JDOM all in a few paragraphs. One last thing to note, as illustrated in Figure 7-2: it is very easy to "loop" things because all the input and output of JDOM is actually part of the API. In other words, you can use a file as input, work with it in JDOM, output it to SAX, DOM, or a file, and then consume that as input, restarting the loop. This is particularly helpful in messaging-based applications, or in cases where JDOM is used as a component between other XML supplying and consuming components.

This isn't a comprehensive look at JDOM, but it gives you enough information to get started, and I'd rather show you things within the context of working code anyway! So, let's take a look at a utility program that can convert Java properties files to XML.

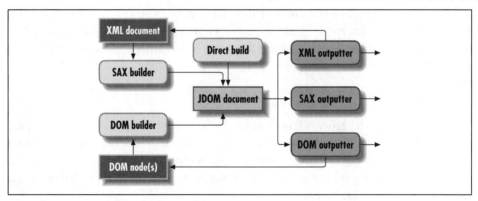

Figure 7-2. Input and output loops in JDOM

PropsToXML

To put some real code to the task of learning JDOM, let me introduce the PropsToXML class. This class is a utility that takes a standard Java properties file and converts it to an XML equivalent. Many developers out there have requested a means of doing exactly this; it often allows legacy applications using properties files to easily convert to using XML without the overhead of manually converting the configuration files.

Java Properties Files

If you have never worked with Java properties files, they are essentially files with name-value pairs that can be read easily with some Java classes (for instance, the java.util.Properties class). These files often look similar to Example 7-1, and in fact I'll use this example properties file throughout the rest of the chapter. Incidentally, it's from the Enhydra application server.

Example 7-1. A typical Java properties file

```
#
# Properties added to System properties
#

# sax parser implementing class
org.xml.sax.parser="org.apache.xerces.parsers.SAXParser"

#
# Properties used to start the server
#

# Class used to start the server
org.enhydra.initialclass=org.enhydra.multiServer.bootstrap.Bootstrap
```

Example 7-1. A typical Java properties file (continued)

```
# initial arguments passed to the server (replace command line args)
org.enhydra.initialargs="./bootstrap.conf"

# Classpath for the parent top enhydra classloader
org.enhydra.classpath="."

# separator for the classpath above
org.enhydra.classpath.separator=":"
```

No big deal here, right? Well, using an instance of the Java `Properties` class, you can load these properties into the object (using the `load(InputStream inputStream)` method) and then deal with them like a `Hashtable`. In fact, the `Properties` class extends the `Hashtable` class in Java; nice, huh? The problem is that many people write these files like the example with names separated by a period (.) to form a sort of hierarchical structure. In the example, you would have a top level (the properties file itself), then the `org` node, and under it the `xml` and `enhydra` nodes, and under the `enhydra` node several nodes, some with values. You'd expect a structure like the one shown in Figure 7-3, in other words.

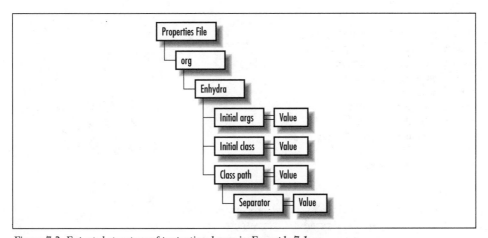

Figure 7-3. Expected structure of properties shown in Example 7-1

While this sounds good, Java provides no means of accessing the name-value pairs in this manner; it does not give the period any special value, but instead treats it as just another character. So while you can do this:

```
String classpathValue = Properties.getProperty("org.enhydra.classpath");
```

You cannot do this:

```
List enhydraProperties = Properties.getProperties("org.enhydra");
```

You would expect (or at least I do!) that the latter would work, and provide you all the subproperties with the structure org.enhydra (org.enhydra.classpath, org.enhydra.initialargs, etc.). Unfortunately, that's not part of the Properties class. For this reason, many developers have had to write their own little wrapper methods around this object, which of course is nonstandard and a bit of a pain. Wouldn't it be nice if this information could be modeled in XML, where operations like the second example are simple? That's exactly what I want to write code to do, and I'll use JDOM to demonstrate that API.

Converting to XML

As in previous chapters, it's easiest to start with a skeleton for the class and build out. For the PropsToXML class, I want to allow a properties file to be supplied for input, and the name of a file for the XML output. The class reads in the properties file, converts it to an XML document using JDOM, and outputs it to the specified filename. Example 7-2 starts the ball rolling.

Example 7-2. The skeleton of the PropsToXML class

```
package javaxml2;

import java.io.FileInputStream;
import java.io.FileOutputStream;
import java.io.IOException;
import java.util.Enumeration;
import java.util.Properties;
import org.jdom.Document;
import org.jdom.Element;
import org.jdom.output.XMLOutputter;

public class PropsToXML {

    /**
     * <p> This will take the supplied properties file, and
     *    convert that file to an XML representation, which is
     *    then output to the supplied XML document filename. </p>
     *
     * @param propertiesFilename file to read in as Java properties.
     * @param xmlFilename file to output XML representation to.
     * @throws <code>IOException</code> - when errors occur.
     */
    public void convert(String propertiesFilename, String xmlFilename)
        throws IOException {

        // Get Java Properties object
        FileInputStream input = new FileInputStream(propertiesFilename);
        Properties props = new Properties();
```

Example 7-2. The skeleton of the PropsToXML class (continued)

```
        props.load(input);

        // Convert to XML
        convertToXML(props, xmlFilename);
    }

    /**
     * <p> This will handle the detail of conversion from a Java
     *     <code>Properties</code> object to an XML document. </p>
     *
     * @param props <code>Properties</code> object to use as input.
     * @param xmlFilename file to output XML to.
     * @throws <code>IOException</code> - when errors occur.
     */
    private void convertToXML(Properties props, String xmlFilename)
        throws IOException {

        // JDOM conversion code goes here
    }

    /**
     * <p> Provide a static entry point for running. </p>
     */
    public static void main(String[] args) {
        if (args.length != 2) {
            System.out.println("Usage: java javaxml2.PropsToXML " +
                "[properties file] [XML file for output]");
            System.exit(0);
        }

        try {
            PropsToXML propsToXML = new PropsToXML();
            propsToXML.convert(args[0], args[1]);
        } catch (Exception e) {
            e.printStackTrace();
        }
    }
}
```

The only new part of this code is the Java `Properties` object, which I've mentioned briefly. The supplied properties filename is used in the `load()` method, and that object is delegated on to a method that will use JDOM, which I'll focus on next.

Creating XML with JDOM

Once the code has the properties in a (more) usable form, it's time to start using JDOM. The first task is to create a JDOM `Document`. For that to occur, you need to create a root element for the document, using JDOM's `Element` class. Since an XML document can't exist without a root element, an instance of the `Element` class is required as input for the `Document` class constructor.

Creating an `Element` requires only the passing of the element's name. There are alternate versions that take in namespace information, and I'll discuss those a little later. For now, it's easiest to use the root element's name, and since this needs to be a top-level, arbitrary name (to contain all the property nestings), I use "properties" in the code. Once this element is created, it's used to create a new JDOM `Document`.

Then, it's on to dealing with the properties in the supplied file. The list of property names is obtained as a Java `Enumeration` through the `Properties` object's `propertyNames()` method. Once that name is available, it can be used to obtain the property value by using the `getProperty()` method. At this point, you've got the root element of the new XML document, the property name to add, and the value for that property. And then, like any other good program, you iterate through all of the other properties until finished. At each step, this information is supplied to a new method, `createXMLRepresentation()`. This performs the logic for handling conversion of a single property into a set of XML elements. Add this code, as shown here, to your source file:

```
private void convertToXML(Properties props, String xmlFilename)
    throws IOException {

    // Create a new JDOM Document with a root element "properties"
    Element root = new Element("properties");
    Document doc = new Document(root);

    // Get the property names
    Enumeration propertyNames = props.propertyNames();
    while (propertyNames.hasMoreElements()) {
        String propertyName = (String)propertyNames.nextElement();
        String propertyValue = props.getProperty(propertyName);
        createXMLRepresentation(root, propertyName, propertyValue);
    }

    // Output document to supplied filename
    XMLOutputter outputter = new XMLOutputter("  ", true);
    FileOutputStream output = new FileOutputStream(xmlFilename);
    outputter.output(doc, output);
}
```

Don't worry about the last few lines that output the JDOM `Document` yet. I'll deal with this in the next section, but first I want to cover the `createXML-Representation()` method, which contains the logic for dealing with a single property, and creating XML from it.

The easiest (and logically, the first) step in moving from a property to XML is to take the name of the property and create an `Element` with that name. You've already seen how to do this; simply pass the name of the element to its constructor. Once the element is created, assign the value of the property as the textual content of the element. This can be done easily enough through the `setText()` method, which of course takes a `String`. Once the element is ready for use, it can be added as a child of the root element through the `addContent()` method. In fact, any legal JDOM construct can be passed to an element's `addContent()` method, as it is overloaded to accept these various types. These include instances of a JDOM `Entity`, `Comment`, `ProcessingInstruction`, and more. But I'll get to those later; for now, add the following method into your source file:

```
/**
 * <p> This will convert a single property and its value to
 *  an XML element and textual value. </p>
 *
 * @param root JDOM root <code>Element</code> to add children to.
 * @param propertyName name to base element creation on.
 * @param propertyValue value to use for property.
 */
private void createXMLRepresentation(Element root,
                                     String propertyName,
                                     String propertyValue) {

    Element element = new Element(propertyName);
    element.setText(propertyValue);
    root.addContent(element);
}
```

At this point, you can actually compile the source file, and then use the resulting `PropsToXML` class. Supply a properties file (you can type in or download the *enhydra.properties* file shown earlier in this chapter), as well as an output filename, as shown here:[*]

```
/javaxml2/build $ java javaxml2.PropsToXML \
                 /javaxml2/ch07/properties/enhydra.properties \
                 enhydraProps.xml
```

This whirs along for a fraction of a second, and then generates an *enhydraProps.xml* file. Open this up; it should look like Example 7-3.[†]

---

[*] If you're not familiar with *NIX, the backslash at the end of each line (\) simply allows for continuation of the command on the next line; Windows users should enter the entire command on one line.

[†] Note that the line wraps in the example are for publishing purposes only; in your document, each property with opening tag, text, and closing tag should be on its own line.

Example 7-3. First version of the enhydraProps.xml document

```
<?xml version="1.0" encoding="UTF-8"?>
<properties>
  <org.enhydra.classpath.separator>":"</org.enhydra.classpath.separator>
  <org.enhydra.initialargs>"./bootstrap.conf"</org.enhydra.initialargs>
  <org.enhydra.initialclass>org.enhydra.multiServer.bootstrap.Bootstrap
</org.enhydra.initialclass>
  <org.enhydra.classpath>"."</org.enhydra.classpath>
  <org.xml.sax.parser>"org.apache.xerces.parsers.SAXParser"
</org.xml.sax.parser>
</properties>
```

In about 50 lines of code, you've gone from Java properties to XML. However, this XML document isn't much better than the properties file; there is still no way to relate the `org.enhydra.initialArgs` property to the `org.enhydra.classpath` property. Our job isn't done yet.

Instead of using the property name as the element name, the code needs to take the property name and split it on the period delimiters. For each of these "sub-names," an element needs to be created and added to the element stack. Then the process can repeat. For the property name `org.xml.sax`, the following XML structure should result:

```
<org>
  <xml>
    <sax>[property Value]</sax>
  </xml>
</org>
```

At each step, using the `Element` constructor and the `addContent()` method does the trick; and once the name is completely deconstructed, the `setText()` method can be used to set the last element's textual value. The best way is to create a new `Element`, called `current`, and use it is a "pointer" (there aren't any pointers in Java—it's just a term); it will always point at the element that content should be added to. At each step, the code also needs to see if the element to be added already exists. For example, the first property, `org.xml.sax`, creates an `org` element. When the next property is added (`org.enhydra.classpath`), the `org` element does not need to be created again.

To facilitate this, the `getChild()` method is used. This method takes the name of the child element to retrieve, and is available to all instances of the `Element` class. If the child specified exists, that element is returned. However, if no child exists, a `null` value is returned, and it is on this `null` value that our code can key. In other words, if the return value is an element, that becomes the `current` element, and no new element needs to be created (it already exists). However, if the return from the getChild() call is null, a new element must be created with the current sub-name, added as content to the current element, and then the current pointer is moved down the tree. Finally, once the iteration is over, the textual value of the property can be added to the leaf element, which turns out to be (nicely) the element that the current pointer references. Add this code to your source file:

```
private void createXMLRepresentation(Element root,
                                     String propertyName,
                                     String propertyValue) {

    /*
    Element element = new Element(propertyName);
    element.setText(propertyValue);
    root.addContent(element);
    */

    int split;
    String name = propertyName;
    Element current = root;
    Element test = null;

    while ((split = name.indexOf(".")) != -1) {
        String subName = name.substring(0, split);
        name = name.substring(split+1);

        // Check for existing element
        if ((test = current.getChild(subName)) == null) {
            Element subElement = new Element(subName);
            current.addContent(subElement);
            current = subElement;
        } else {
            current = test;
        }
    }

    // When out of loop, what's left is the final element's name
    Element last = new Element(name);
    last.setText(propertyValue);
    current.addContent(last);
}
```

With this addition in place, recompile the program and run it again. This time, your output should be a lot nicer, as shown in Example 7-4.

Example 7-4. Updated output from PropsToXML

```
<?xml version="1.0" encoding="UTF-8"?>
<properties>
  <org>
    <enhydra>
      <classpath>
        <separator>":"</separator>
      </classpath>
      <initialargs>"./bootstrap.conf"</initialargs>
      <initialclass>org.enhydra.multiServer.bootstrap.Bootstrap</initialclass>
      <classpath>"."</classpath>
    </enhydra>
    <xml>
      <sax>
        <parser>"org.apache.xerces.parsers.SAXParser"</parser>
      </sax>
    </xml>
  </org>
</properties>
```

And, just as quickly as you've started in on JDOM, you've got the hang of it. However, you might notice that the XML document violates one of the rules of thumb for document design introduced in Chapter 2 (in the section detailing usage of elements versus usage of attributes). You see, each property value has a single textual value. That arguably makes the property values suitable as attributes of the last element on the stack, rather than content. Proving that rules are meant to be broken, I prefer them as content in this case, but that's neither here nor there.

For no other reason than demonstration purposes, let's look at converting the property values to attributes rather than textual content. This turns out to be quite easy, and can be done in one of two ways. The first is to create an instance of the JDOM `Attribute` class. The constructor for that class takes the name of the attribute and its value. Then, the resulting instance can be added to the leaf element with that element's `setAttribute()` method. That approach is shown here:

```
// When out of loop, what's left is the final element's name
Element last = new Element(name);
/* last.setText(propertyValue); */
Attribute attribute = new Attribute("value", propertyValue);
current.setAttribute(attribute);
current.addContent(last);
```

WARNING   If you want to compile the file with these changes, be sure you add
             an import statement for the `Attribute` class:

```
import org.jdom.Attribute;
```

A slightly easier way is to use one of the convenience methods that JDOM offers. Since adding attributes is such a common task, the `Element` class provides an over-loaded version of `setAttribute()` that takes a name and value, and internally creates an `Attribute` object. In this case, that approach is a little clearer:

```
// When out of loop, what's left is the final element's name
Element last = new Element(name);
/* last.setText(propertyValue); */
last.setAttribute("value", propertyValue);
current.addContent(last);
```

This works just as well, but also avoids having to use an extra import statement. You can compile this change in and run the sample program. The new output should match Example 7-5.

Example 7-5. Output of PropsToXML using attributes

```
<?xml version="1.0" encoding="UTF-8"?>
<properties>
  <org>
    <enhydra>
      <classpath>
        <separator value="&quot;:&quot;" />
      </classpath>
      <initialargs value="&quot;./bootstrap.conf&quot;" />
      <initialclass value="org.enhydra.multiServer.bootstrap.Bootstrap" />
      <classpath value="&quot;.&quot;" />
    </enhydra>
    <xml>
      <sax>
        <parser value="&quot;org.apache.xerces.parsers.SAXParser&quot;" />
      </sax>
    </xml>
  </org>
</properties>
```

Each property value is now an attribute of the innermost element. Notice that JDOM converts the quotation marks within the attribute values, which are dis-allowed, to entity references so the document as output is well-formed. However, this makes the output a little less clean, so you may want to switch your code back to using textual data within elements, rather than attributes.

Outputting XML with JDOM

Before we continue, I want to spend a little time talking about the output portion of the code that I skimmed over earlier in the chapter. It's highlighted again here:

```
private void convertToXML(Properties props, String xmlFilename)
    throws IOException {
```

```
    // Create a new JDOM Document with a root element "properties"
    Element root = new Element("properties");
    Document doc = new Document(root);

    // Get the property names
    Enumeration propertyNames = props.propertyNames();
    while (propertyNames.hasMoreElements()) {
        String propertyName = (String)propertyNames.nextElement();
        String propertyValue = props.getProperty(propertyName);
        createXMLRepresentation(root, propertyName, propertyValue);
    }

    // Output document to supplied filename
    XMLOutputter outputter = new XMLOutputter("  ", true);
    FileOutputStream output = new FileOutputStream(xmlFilename);
    outputter.output(doc, output);
}
```

You already know that XMLOutputter is the class to use for handling output to a file, stream, or other static representation. However, I supplied some arguments to the constructor in the code sample; without any arguments, the outputter would perform direct output. There would be no change to the XML used as input. When reading in XML, this most often results in no line breaks and no indentation. The resultant document would have the entire document, except for the XML declaration, on a single line. I'd show you this, but it wouldn't fit on the page, and tends to cause confusion. The outputter has several constructors though:

```
public XMLOutputter();

public XMLOutputter(String indent);

public XMLOutputter(String indent, boolean newlines);

public XMLOutputter(String indent, boolean newlines, String encoding);

public XMLOutputter(XMLOutputter that);
```

Most of these are self-explanatory. The indent parameter allows specification of how many spaces to use for indentation; I used two spaces (" ") in the sample code. The boolean value for newlines determines if line breaks are used (this was on in the sample). If needed, an encoding parameter can be specified, which becomes the value for encoding in the XML declaration:

```
<?xml version="1.0" encoding="UTF-8"?>
```

Additionally, there are mutator methods for all of these properties (setIndent(), setEncoding(), etc.) in the class. There are also versions of the output()

method (the one used in the example code) that take either an OutputStream or a Writer. And there are versions that take the various JDOM constructs as input, so you could output an entire Document, or just an Element, Comment, ProcessingInstruction, or anything else:

```
// Create an outputter with 4 space indentation and new lines
XMLOutputter outputter = new XMLOutputter("    ", true);

// Output different JDOM constructs
outputter.output(myDocument, myOutputStream);
outputter.output(myElement, myWriter);
outputter.output(myComment, myOutputStream);
// etc...
```

In other words, XMLOutputter serves all of your XML output needs. Of course, you can also use DOMOutputter and SAXOutputter, which I'll cover in detail in the next chapter.

XMLProperties

Let's take things to the next logical step, and look at reading XML. Continuing with the example of converting a properties file to XML, you are now probably wondering how to access the information in your XML file. Luckily, there's a solution for that, too! In this section, for the sake of explaining how JDOM reads XML, I want to introduce a new utility class, XMLProperties. This class is essentially an XML-aware version of the Java Properties class; in fact, it extends that class. This class allows access to an XML document through the typical property-access methods like getProperty() and properties(); in other words, it allows Java-style access (using the Properties class) to XML-style storage. In my opinion, this is the best combination you can get.

To accomplish this task, you can start by creating an XMLProperties class that extends the java.util.Properties class. With this approach, making things work becomes simply a matter of overriding the load(), save(), and store() methods. The first of these, load(), reads in an XML document and loads the properties within that document into the superclass object.

WARNING	Don't mistake this class for an all-purpose XML-to-properties converter; it only will read in XML that is in the format detailed earlier in this chapter. In other words, properties are elements with either textual or attribute values but not both; I'll cover both approaches, but you'll have to choose one or the other. Don't try to take all your XML documents, read them in, and expect things to work as planned!

The second method, `save()`, is actually deprecated in Java 2, as it doesn't expose any error information; still, it needs to be overridden for Java 1.1 users. To facilitate this, the implementation in **XMLProperties** simply calls `store()`. And `store()` handles the task of writing the properties information out to an XML document. Example 7-6 is a good start at this, and provides a skeleton within which to work.

Example 7-6. The skeleton of the XMLProperties class

```java
package javaxml2;

import java.io.File;
import java.io.FileReader;
import java.io.FileWriter;
import java.io.InputStream;
import java.io.InputStreamReader;
import java.io.IOException;
import java.io.OutputStream;
import java.io.OutputStreamWriter;
import java.io.Reader;
import java.io.Writer;
import java.util.Enumeration;
import java.util.Iterator;
import java.util.List;
import java.util.Properties;

import org.jdom.Attribute;
import org.jdom.Comment;
import org.jdom.Document;
import org.jdom.Element;
import org.jdom.JDOMException;
import org.jdom.input.SAXBuilder;
import org.jdom.output.XMLOutputter;

public class XMLProperties extends Properties {

    public void load(Reader reader)
        throws IOException {

        // Read XML document into a Properties object
    }

    public void load(InputStream inputStream)
        throws IOException {

        load(new InputStreamReader(inputStream));
    }

    public void load(File xmlDocument)
```

Example 7-6. The skeleton of the XMLProperties class (continued)

```
        throws IOException {

        load(new FileReader(xmlDocument));
    }

    public void save(OutputStream out, String header) {
        try {
            store(out, header);
        } catch (IOException ignored) {
            // Deprecated version doesn't pass errors
        }
    }

    public void store(Writer writer, String header)
        throws IOException {

        // Convert properties to XML and output
    }

    public void store(OutputStream out, String header)
        throws IOException {

        store(new OutputStreamWriter(out), header);
    }

    public void store(File xmlDocument, String header)
        throws IOException {

        store(new FileWriter(xmlDocument), header);
    }
}
```

Take note that I overloaded the `load()` and `store()` methods; while the
`Properties` class only has versions that take an `InputStream` and `OutputStream`
(respectively), I'm a firm believer in providing users options. The extra versions,
which take `File`s and `Reader`s/`Writer`s, make it easier for users to interact, and
add a marginal amount of code to the class. Additionally, these overloaded methods can all delegate to existing methods, which leaves the code ready for loading
and storing implementation.

Storing XML

I'll deal with storing XML first, mainly because the code is already written. The
logic to take a `Properties` object and output it as XML is the purpose of the
`PropsToXML` class, and I'll simply reuse some of that code here to make things
work nicely:

```java
public void store(Writer writer, String header)
    throws IOException {

    // Create a new JDOM Document with a root element "properties"
    Element root = new Element("properties");
    Document doc = new Document(root);

    // Get the property names
    Enumeration propertyNames = propertyNames();
    while (propertyNames.hasMoreElements()) {
        String propertyName = (String)propertyNames.nextElement();
        String propertyValue = getProperty(propertyName);
        createXMLRepresentation(root, propertyName, propertyValue);
    }

    // Output document to supplied filename
    XMLOutputter outputter = new XMLOutputter("  ", true);
    outputter.output(doc, writer);
}

private void createXMLRepresentation(Element root,
                                     String propertyName,
                                     String propertyValue) {

    int split;
    String name = propertyName;
    Element current = root;
    Element test = null;

    while ((split = name.indexOf(".")) != -1) {
        String subName = name.substring(0, split);
        name = name.substring(split+1);

        // Check for existing element
        if ((test = current.getChild(subName)) == null) {
            Element subElement = new Element(subName);
            current.addContent(subElement);
            current = subElement;
        } else {
            current = test;
        }
    }

    // When out of loop, what's left is the final element's name
    Element last = new Element(name);
    last.setText(propertyValue);
    /** Uncomment this for Attribute usage */
    /*
```

```
        last.setAttribute("value", propertyValue);
        */
        current.addContent(last);
    }
```

Not much needs comment. There are a few lines of code highlighted to illustrate some changes, though. The first two changes ensure that the superclass is used to obtain the property names and values, rather than the `Properties` object that was passed into the version of this method in `PropsToXML`. The third change moves from using a string filename to the supplied `Writer` for output. With those few modifications, you're all set to compile the `XMLProperties` source file.

There is one item missing, though. Note that the `store()` method allows specification of a header variable; in a standard Java properties file, this is added as a comment to the head of the file. To keep things parallel, the `XMLProperties` class can be modified to do the same thing. You will need to use the `Comment` class to do this. The following code additions put this change into effect:

```
public void store(Writer writer, String header)
    throws IOException {

    // Create a new JDOM Document with a root element "properties"
    Element root = new Element("properties");
    Document doc = new Document(root);

    // Add in header information
    Comment comment = new Comment(header);
    doc.addContent(comment);

    // Get the property names
    Enumeration propertyNames = propertyNames();
    while (propertyNames.hasMoreElements()) {
        String propertyName = (String)propertyNames.nextElement();
        String propertyValue = getProperty(propertyName);
        createXMLRepresentation(root, propertyName, propertyValue);
    }

    // Output document to supplied filename
    XMLOutputter outputter = new XMLOutputter("  ", true);
    outputter.output(doc, writer);
}
```

The `addContent()` method of the `Document` object is overloaded to take both `Comment` and `ProcessingInstruction` objects, and appends the content to the file. It's used here to add in the `header` parameter as a comment to the XML document being written to.

Loading XML

There's not much left to do here; basically, the class writes out to XML, provides access to XML (through the methods already existing on the `Properties` class), and now simply needs to read in XML. This is a fairly simple task; it boils down to more recursion. I'll show you the code modifications needed, and then walk you through them. Enter the code shown here into your *XMLProperties.java* source file:

```java
public void load(Reader reader)
    throws IOException {

    try {
        // Load XML into JDOM Document
        SAXBuilder builder = new SAXBuilder();
        Document doc = builder.build(reader);

        // Turn into properties objects
        loadFromElements(doc.getRootElement().getChildren(),
            new StringBuffer(""));

    } catch (JDOMException e) {
        throw new IOException(e.getMessage());
    }
}

private void loadFromElements(List elements, StringBuffer baseName) {
    // Iterate through each element
    for (Iterator i = elements.iterator(); i.hasNext(); ) {
        Element current = (Element)i.next();
        String name = current.getName();
        String text = current.getTextTrim();

        // Don't add "." if no baseName
        if (baseName.length() > 0) {
            baseName.append(".");
        }
        baseName.append(name);

        // See if we have an element value
        if ((text == null) || (text.equals(""))) {
            // If no text, recurse on children
            loadFromElements(current.getChildren(),
                            baseName);
        } else {
            // If text, this is a property
            setProperty(baseName.toString(),
                        text);
        }
    }
```

```
                    // On unwind from recursion, remove last name
                    if (baseName.length() == name.length()) {
                        baseName.setLength(0);
                    } else {
                        baseName.setLength(baseName.length() -
                            (name.length() + 1));
                    }
                }
            }
```

The implementation of the load() method (which all overloaded versions delegate to) uses SAXBuilder to read in the supplied XML document. I discussed this earlier in the chapter, and I'll look at it in even more detail in the next; for now, it's enough to realize that it simply reads XML into a JDOM Document object.

The name for a property consists of the names of all the elements leading to the property value, with a period separating each name. Here's a sample property in XML:

```
<properties>
  <org>
    <enhydra>
      <classpath>"."</classpath>
    </enhydra>
  </org>
</properties>
```

The property name can be obtained by taking the element names leading to the value (excluding the properties element, which was used as a root-level container): org, enhydra, and classpath. Throw a period between each, and you get org.enhydra.classpath, which is the property name in question. To accomplish this, I coded up the loadFromElements() method. This takes in a list of elements, iterates through them, and deals with each element individually. If the element has a textual value, that value is added to the superclass object's properties. If it has child elements instead, then the children are obtained, and recursion begins again on the new list of children. At each step of recursion, the name of the element being dealt with is appended to the baseName variable, which keeps track of the property names. Winding through recursion, baseName would be org, then org.enhydra, then org.enhydra.classpath. And, as recursion unwinds, the baseName variable is shortened to remove the last element name. Let's look at the JDOM method calls that make it possible.

First, you'll notice several invocations of the getChildren() method on instances of the Element class. This method returns all child elements of the current element as a Java List. There are versions of this method that also take in the name of an element to search for, and return either all elements with that name

(getChildren(String name)), or just the first child element with that name
(getChild(String name)). There are also namespace-aware versions of the
method, which will be covered in the next chapter. To start the recursion process,
the root element is obtained from the JDOM Document object through the
getRootElement() method, and then its children are used to seed recursion.
Once in the loadFromElements() method, standard Java classes are used to
move through the list of elements (such as java.util.Iterator). To check for
textual content, the getTextTrim() method is used. This method returns the textual content of an element, and returns the element without surrounding
whitespace.* Thus, the content " textual content " (note the surrounding
whitespace) would be returned as "textual content". While this seems somewhat
trivial, consider this more realistic example of XML:

```
<chapter>
  <title>
     Advanced SAX
  </title>
</chapter>
```

The actual textual content of the title element turns out to be several spaces, followed by a line feed, followed by more space, the characters "Advanced SAX",
more space, another line feed, and even more space. In other words, probably not
what you expected. The returned string data from a call to getTextTrim() would
simply be "Advanced SAX", which is what you want in most cases anyway. However, if you do want the complete content (often used for reproducing the input
document exactly as it came in), you can use the getText() method, which
returns the element's content unchanged. If there is no content, the return value
from this method is an empty string (""), which makes for an easy comparison, as
shown in the example code. And that's about it: a few simple method calls and the
code is reading XML with JDOM. Let's see this class in action.

Taking a Test Drive

Once you've got everything in place in the XMLProperties class, compile it. To
test it out, you can enter in or download Example 7-7, which is a class that uses the
XMLProperties class to load an XML document, print some information out
about it, and then write the properties back out as XML.

---

* It also removes more than one space *between* words. The textual content "lots   of   spaces" would be
returned through getTextTrim() as "lots of spaces".

Example 7-7. Testing the XMLProperties class

```java
package javaxml2;

import java.io.FileInputStream;
import java.io.FileOutputStream;
import java.util.Enumeration;

public class TestXMLProperties {

    public static void main(String[] args) {
        if (args.length != 2) {
            System.out.println("Usage: java javaxml2.TestXMLProperties " +
                "[XML input document] [XML output document]");
            System.exit(0);
        }

        try {
            // Create and load properties
            System.out.println("Reading XML properties from " + args[0]);
            XMLProperties props = new XMLProperties();
            props.load(new FileInputStream(args[0]));

            // Print out properties and values
            System.out.println("\n\n---- Property Values ----");
            Enumeration names = props.propertyNames();
            while (names.hasMoreElements()) {
                String name = (String)names.nextElement();
                String value = props.getProperty(name);
                System.out.println("Property Name: " + name +
                                " has value " + value);
            }

            // Store properties
            System.out.println("\n\nWriting XML properies to " + args[1]);
            props.store(new FileOutputStream(args[1]),
                "Testing XMLProperties class");
        } catch (Exception e) {
            e.printStackTrace();
        }
    }
}
```

This doesn't do much; it reads in properties, uses them to print out all the property names and values, and then writes those properties back out—but all in XML. You can run this program on the XML file generated by the PropsToXML class I showed you earlier in the chapter.

WARNING   The version of XMLProperties used here deals with property values
            as textual content of elements (the first version of PropsToXML
            shown), not as attribute values (the second version of PropsToXML).
            You'll need to use that earlier version of PropsToXML, or back out
            your changes, if you are going to use it to generate XML for input to
            the TestXMLProperties class. Otherwise, you won't pick up any
            property values with this code.

Supply the test program with the XML input file and the name of the output file:

```
C:\javaxml2\build>java javaxml2.TestXMLProperties enhydraProps.xml output.xml
Reading XML properties from enhydraProps.xml


---- Property Values ----
Property Name: org.enhydra.classpath.separator has value ":"
Property Name: org.enhydra.initialargs has value "./bootstrap.conf"
Property Name: org.enhydra.initialclass has value
   org.enhydra.multiServer.bootstrap.Bootstrap
Property Name: org.enhydra.classpath has value "."
Property Name: org.xml.sax.parser has value
   "org.apache.xerces.parsers.SAXParser"


Writing XML properties to output.xml
```

And there you have it: XML data formatting, properties behavior.

Backtracking

Before wrapping up on the code, there are a few items I want to address. First, take
a look at the XML file generated by TestXMLProperties, the result of invoking
store() on the properties. It should look similar to Example 7-8 if you used the
XML version of *enhydra.properties* detailed earlier in this chapter.

Example 7-8. Output from TestXMLProperties

```
<?xml version="1.0" encoding="UTF-8"?>
<properties>
  <org>
    <enhydra>
      <classpath>
        <separator>":"</separator>
      </classpath>
      <initialargs>"./bootstrap.conf"</initialargs>
      <initialclass>org.enhydra.multiServer.bootstrap.Bootstrap</initialclass>
      <classpath>"."</classpath>
    </enhydra>
```

Example 7-8. Output from TestXMLProperties (continued)

```
<xml>
  <sax>
    <parser>"org.apache.xerces.parsers.SAXParser"</parser>
  </sax>
</xml>
    </org>
</properties>
<!--Testing XMLProperties class-->
```

Notice anything wrong? The header comment is in the wrong place. Take another look at the code that added in that comment, from the `store()` method:

```
// Create a new JDOM Document with a root element "properties"
Element root = new Element("properties");
Document doc = new Document(root);

// Add in header information
Comment comment = new Comment(header);
doc.addContent(comment);
```

The root element appears before the comment because it is added to the `Document` object first. However, the `Document` object can't be created without supplying a root element—a bit of a chicken-or-egg situation. To work with this, you need to use a new method, `getContent()`. This method returns a `List`, but that `List` contains all the content of the `Document`, including comments, the root element, and processing instructions. Then, you can prepend the comment to this list, as shown here, using methods of the `List` class:

```
// Add in header information
Comment comment = new Comment(header);
doc.getContent().add(0, comment);
```

With this change in place, your output will look as it should:

```
<?xml version="1.0" encoding="UTF-8"?>
<!--Testing XMLProperties class-->
<properties>
  <org>
    <enhydra>
      <classpath>
        <separator>":"</separator>
      </classpath>
      <initialargs>"./bootstrap.conf"</initialargs>
      <initialclass>org.enhydra.multiServer.bootstrap.Bootstrap</initialclass>
      <classpath>"."</classpath>
    </enhydra>
    <xml>
      <sax>
```

```
        <parser>"org.apache.xerces.parsers.SAXParser"</parser>
      </sax>
    </xml>
  </org>
</properties>
```

The getContent() method is also available on the Element class, and returns all content of the element, regardless of type (elements, processing instructions, comments, entities, and Strings for textual content).

Also important are the modifications necessary for XMLProperties to use attributes for property values, instead of element content. You've already seen the code change needed in storage of properties (in fact, the change is commented out in the source code, so you don't need to write anything new). As for loading, the change involves checking for an attribute instead of an element's textual content. This can be done with the getAttributeValue(String name) method, which returns the value of the named attribute, or null if no value exists. The change is shown here:

```
private void loadFromElements(List elements, StringBuffer baseName) {
    // Iterate through each element
    for (Iterator i = elements.iterator(); i.hasNext(); ) {
        Element current = (Element)i.next();
        String name = current.getName();
        // String text = current.getTextTrim();
        String text = current.getAttributeValue("value");

        // Don't add "." if no baseName
        if (baseName.length() > 0) {
            baseName.append(".");
        }
        baseName.append(name);

        // See if we have an attribute value
        if ((text == null) || (text.equals(""))) {
            // If no text, recurse on children
            loadFromElements(current.getChildren(),
                            baseName);
        } else {
            // If text, this is a property
            setProperty(baseName.toString(),
                        text);
        }

        // On unwind from recursion, remove last name
        if (baseName.length() == name.length()) {
            baseName.setLength(0);
        } else {
```

```
                    baseName.setLength(baseName.length() -
                        (name.length() + 1));
            }
        }
    }
```

Compile in the changes, and you're set to deal with attribute values instead of element content. Leave the code in the state you prefer it (as I mentioned earlier, I actually like the values as element content), so if you want textual element content, be sure to back out these changes after seeing how they affect output. Whichever you prefer, hopefully you are starting to know your way around JDOM. And just like SAX and DOM, I highly recommend bookmarking the Javadoc (either locally or online) as a quick reference for those methods you just can't quite remember. In any case, before wrapping up, let's talk a little about a common issue with regard to JDOM: standardization.

Is JDOM a Standard?

More than any other question about JDOM, I am asked whether JDOM is a standard. This is a common question, especially among either those who want to use JDOM (and need justification) or those who don't like JDOM (and need justification). I address some of those issues in this section, so that whatever camp you are in, you know the details about JDOM and its standardization process.

JDOM as a JSR

First and foremost, JDOM is now an official JSR, which is a Java Specification Request. In other words, it is going through the formal standardization process, sponsored by Sun and governed by the JCP (the Java Community Process). You can read all about the JSR and JCP processes at *http://java.sun.com/aboutJava/communityprocess/*. As for JDOM, it is now officially JSR-102 and can be found online at Sun's web site, located at *http://java.sun.com/aboutJava/communityprocess/jsr/jsr_102_jdom.html*.

Once JDOM moves through the JCP, probably in late 2001, several things will happen. First, it will receive a much more elevated status in terms of standards; although the JCP and Sun aren't perfect, they do offer a lot of credence. The JCP has support and members within IBM, BEA, Compaq, HP, Apache, and more. Additionally, it will become very easy to move JDOM into other Java standards. For example, there is interest from Sun in making JDOM part of the next version of JAXP, either 1.2 or 2.0 (I talk more about JAXP in Chapter 9). Finally, future versions of the JDK are slated to have XML as part of their core; in years to come, JDOM may be in every download of Java.

SAX and DOM as Standards

Keep in mind that JDOM isn't getting some sort of elevated status; DOM and SAX are already both a part of JAXP, and so are actually *ahead* of JDOM in that regard. However, it's worth making some comments about the "standardization" of DOM and SAX. First, SAX came out of the public domain, and remains today a de facto standard. Developed primarily on the XML-dev mailing list, no standards body ratified or accepted SAX until it was already in heavy use. While I am by no means criticizing SAX, I am wary of folks who claim that JDOM shouldn't be used because it wasn't developed by a standards body.

On the other hand, DOM was developed by the W3C, and is a formal standard. For that reason, it has a staunch following. DOM is a great solution for many applications. Again, though, the W3C is simply one standards body; the JCP is another, the IETF is yet another, and so on. I'm not arguing the merits of any particular group; I just caution you about accepting *any* standard (JDOM or otherwise) if it doesn't meet your application's needs. Arguments about "standardization" take a backseat to usability. If you like DOM and it serves your needs, then use it. The same goes for SAX and JDOM. What I would prefer that everybody do, though, is stop trying to make decisions for everyone else (and I know I'm defending my API, but I get this sort of thing all the time!). Hopefully, this book takes you deeply enough into all three APIs to help you make an educated decision.

Gotcha!

Not to disappoint, I want to warn you of some common JDOM pitfalls. I hope this will save you a little time in your JDOM programming.

JDOM isn't DOM

First and foremost, you should realize that JDOM isn't DOM. It doesn't wrap DOM, and doesn't provide extensions to DOM. In other words, the two have no technical relation to each other. Realizing this basic truth will save you a lot of time and effort; there are many articles out there today that talk about getting the DOM interfaces to use JDOM, or avoiding JDOM because it hides some of DOM's methods. These statements confuse more people than almost anything else. You don't need to have the DOM interfaces, and DOM calls (like `appendChild()` or `createDocument()`) simply won't work on JDOM. Sorry, wrong API!

Null Return Values

Another interesting facet of JDOM, and one that has raised some controversy, is the return values from methods that retrieve element content. For example, the various getChild() methods on the Element class may return a null value. I mentioned this, and demonstrated it, in the PropsToXML example code. The gotcha occurs when instead of checking if an element exists (as was the case in the example code), you assume that an element already exists. This is most common when some other application or component sends you XML, and your code expects it to conform to a certain format (be it a DTD, XML Schema, or simply an agreed-upon standard). For example, take a look at the following code:

```
Document doc = otherComponent.getDocument();
String price = doc.getRootElement().getChild("item")
                                   .getChild("price")
                                   .getTextTrim();
```

The problem in this code is that if there is no item element under the root, or no price element under that, a null value is returned from the getChild() method invocations. Suddenly, this innocuous-looking code begins to emit NullPointerExceptions, which are quite painful to track down. You can handle this situation in one of two ways. The first is to check for null values at each step of the way:

```
Document doc = otherComponent.getDocument();
Element root = doc.getRootElement();
Element item = root.getChild("item");
if (item != null) {
    Element price = item.getChild("price");
    if (price != null) {
        String price = price.getTextTrim();
    } else {
        // Handle exceptional condition
    }
} else {
    // Handle exceptional condition
}
```

The second option is to wrap the entire code fragment in a try/catch block:

```
Document doc = otherComponent.getDocument();
try {
    String price = doc.getRootElement().getChild("item")
                                       .getChild("price")
                                       .getTextTrim();
} catch (NullPointerException e) {
    // Handle exceptional condition
}
```

While either approach works, I recommend the first; it allows finer-grained error handling, as it is possible to determine exactly which test failed, and therefore exactly what problem occurred. The second code fragment informs you only that somewhere a problem occurred. In any case, careful testing of return values can save you some rather annoying `NullPointerExceptions`.

DOMBuilder

Last but not least, you should be very careful when working with the `DOMBuilder` class. It's not *how* you use the class, but *when* you use it. As I mentioned, this class works for input in a similar fashion to `SAXBuilder`. And like its SAX sister class, it has `build()` methods that take in input forms like a Java `File` or `InputStream`. However, building a JDOM `Document` from a file, URL, or I/O stream is always slower than using `SAXBuilder`; that's because SAX is used to build a DOM tree in `DOMBuilder`, and then that DOM tree is converted to JDOM. Of course, this is much slower than leaving out the intermediary step (creating a DOM tree), and simply going straight from SAX to JDOM.

So, any time you see code like this:

```
DOMBuilder builder = new DOMBuilder();

// Building from a file
Document doc = builder.build(new File("input.xml"));

// Building from a URL
Document doc = builder.build(
    new URL("http://newInstance.com/javaxml2/copyright.xml"));

// Building from an I/O stream
Document doc = builder.build(new FileInputStream("input.xml"));
```

You should run screaming! Seriously, `DOMBuilder` has its place: it's great for taking existing DOM structures and going to JDOM. But for raw, speedy input, it's simply an inferior choice in terms of performance. Save yourself some headaches and commit this fact to memory now!

What's Next?

An advanced JDOM chapter follows. In that chapter, I'll cover some of the finer points of the API, like namespaces, the DOM adapters, how JDOM deals with lists internally, and anything else that might interest those of you who really want to get into the API. It should give you ample knowledge to use JDOM, along with DOM and SAX, in your applications.

In this chapter:
- *Helpful JDOM Internals*
- *JDOM and Factories*
- *Wrappers and Decorators*
- *Gotcha!*
- *What's Next?*

Advanced JDOM

Continuing with JDOM, this chapter introduces some more advanced concepts. In the last chapter, you saw how to read and write XML using JDOM, and also got a good taste of what classes are available in the JDOM distribution. In this chapter, I drill down a little deeper to see what's going on. You'll get to see some of the classes that JDOM uses that aren't exposed in common operations, and you'll start to understand how JDOM is put together. Once you've gotten that basic understanding down, I'll move on to show you how JDOM can utilize factories and your own custom JDOM implementation classes, albeit in a totally different way than DOM. That will take you right into a fairly advanced example using wrappers and decorators, another pattern for adding functionality to the core set of JDOM classes without needing an interface-based API.

Helpful JDOM Internals

The first topic I cover is the architecture of JDOM. In Chapter 7, I showed you a simple UML-type model of the core JDOM classes. However, if you look closely, there are probably some things in the classes that you haven't worked with, or didn't expect. I'm going to cover those particular items in this section, showing how you can get down and dirty with JDOM.

NOTE   JDOM beta 7 was released literally days before this chapter was written. In that release, the Text class was being whiteboarded, but had not been integrated in the JDOM internals. However, this process is happening very quickly, most likely before this book gets into your hands. Even if that is not the case, it will be integrated soon after, and the issues discussed here will then apply. If you have problems with the code snippets in this section, check the version of JDOM you are using, and always try to get the newest possible release.

The Text Class

One class you may have been a bit surprised to see in JDOM is the Text class. If you read the last chapter, you probably caught that one large difference between DOM and JDOM is that JDOM (at least seemingly) directly exposes the textual content of an element, whereas in DOM you get the child Text node and then extract its value. What actually happens, though, is that JDOM models character-based content much like DOM does architecturally; each piece of character content is stored within a JDOM Text instance. However, when you invoke getText() (or getTextTrim() or getTextNormalize()) on a JDOM Element instance, the instance automatically returns the value(s) in its child Text nodes:

```
// Get textual content
String textualContent = element.getText();

// Get textual content, with surrounding whitespace trimmed
String trimmedContent = element.getText().trim();
// or...
String trimmedContent = element.getTextTrim();

// Get textual content, normalized (all interior whitespace compressed to single
//    space. For example, "   this   would be  " would be "this would be"
String normalizedContent = element.getTextNormalize();
```

As a result, it commonly seems that no Text class is actually being used. The same methodology applies when invoking setText() on an element; the text is created as the content of a new Text instance, and that new instance is added as a child of the element. Again, the rationale is that the process of reading and writing the textual content of an XML element is such a common occurrence that it should be as simple and quick as possible.

At the same time, as I pointed out in earlier chapters, a strict tree model makes navigation over content very simple; instanceof and recursion become easy solutions for tree explorations. Therefore, an explicit Text class, present as a child (or children) of Element instances, makes this task much easier. Further, the Text class allows extension, while raw java.lang.String classes are not extensible. For all of these reasons (and several more you can dig into on the jdom-interest mailing lists), the Text class is being added to JDOM. Even though not as readily apparent as in other APIs, it is available for these iteration-type cases. To accommodate this, if you invoke getContent() on an Element instance, you will get all of the content within that element. This could include Comments, ProcessingInstructions, EntityRefs, CDATA sections, and textual content. In this case, the textual content is returned as one or more Text instances rather than directly as Strings, allowing processing like this:

```
public void processElement(Element element) {
    List mixedContent = element.getContent();
```

```
        for (Iterator i = mixedContent.iterator(); i.hasNext(); ) {
            Object o = i.next();
            if (o instanceof Text) {
                processText((Text)o);
            } else if (o instanceof CDATA) {
                processCDATA((CDATA)o);
            } else if (o instanceof Comment) {
                processComment((Comment)o);
            } else if (o instanceof ProcessingInstruction) {
                processProcessingInstruction((ProcessingInstruction)o);
            } else if (o instanceof EntityRef) {
                processEntityRef((EntityRef)o);
            } else if (o instanceof Element) {
                processElement((Element)o);
            }
        }
    }

    public void processComment(Comment comment) {
        // Do something with comments
    }

    public void processProcessingInstruction(ProcessingInstruction pi) {
        // Do something with PIs
    }

    public void processEntityRef(EntityRef entityRef) {
        // Do something with entity references
    }

    public void processText(Text text) {
        // Do something with text
    }

    public void processCDATA(CDATA cdata) {
        // Do something with CDATA
    }
```

This sets up a fairly simple recursive processing of a JDOM tree. You could kick it
off with simply:

```
// Get a JDOM Document through a builder
Document doc = builder.build(input);

// Start recursion
processElement(doc.getRootElement());
```

You would handle Comment and ProcessingInstruction instances at the document level, but you get the idea here. You can choose to use the Text class when it
makes sense, and not worry about it when it doesn't.

The EntityRef Class

Next up on the JDOM internals list is the `EntityRef` class. This is another class that you may not have to use much in common cases, but is helpful to know for special coding needs. This class represents an XML entity reference in JDOM, such as the `OReillyCopyright` entity reference in the *contents.xml* document I have been using in examples:

```
<ora:copyright>&OReillyCopyright;</ora:copyright>
```

This class allows for setting and retrieval of a name, public ID, and system ID, just as is possible when defining the reference in an XML DTD or schema. It can appear anywhere in a JDOM content tree, like the `Elements` and `Text` nodes. However, like `Text` nodes, an `EntityRef` class is often a bit of a pain in the normal case. For example, in the *contents.xml* document, modeled in JDOM, you're usually going to be more interested in the textual value of the reference (the resolved content) rather than the reference itself. In other words, when you invoke `getContent()` on the copyright `Element` in a JDOM tree, you'd like to get "Copyright O'Reilly, 2000" or whatever other textual value is referred to by the entity reference. This is much more useful (again, in the most common cases) than getting a no-content indicator (an empty string), and then having to check for the existence of an `EntityRef`. For this reason, by default, all entity references are expanded when using the JDOM builders (`SAXBuilder` and `DOMBuilder`) to generate JDOM from existing XML. You will rarely see `EntityRefs` in this default case, because you don't want to mess with them. However, if you find you need to leave entity references unexpanded and represented by `EntityRefs`, you can use the `setExpandEntities()` method on the builder classes:

```
// Create new builder
SAXBuilder builder = new SAXBuilder();

// Do not expand entity references (default is to expand these)
builder.setExpandEnitites(false);

// Build the tree with EntityRef objects (if needed, of course)
Document doc = builder.build(inputStream);
```

In this case, you may have `EntityRef` instances in the tree (if you were using the *contents.xml* document, for example). And you can always create `EntityRefs` directly and place them in the JDOM tree:

```
// Create new entity reference
EntityRef ref = new EntityRef("TrueNorthGuitarsTagline");
ref.setSystemID("tngTagline.xml");
```

```
// Insert into the tree
tagLineElement.addContent(ref);
```

When serializing this tree, you get XML like this:

```
<guitar>
  <tagLine>&TrueNorthGuitarsTagline;</tagLine>
</guitar>
```

And when reading the document back in using a builder, the resulting JDOM `Document` would depend on the `expandEntities` flag. If it is set to false, you'd get the original `EntityRef` back again with the correct name and system ID. With this value set to `false` (the default), you'd get the resolved content. A second serialization might result in:

```
<guitar>
  <tagLine>two hands, one heart</tagLine>
</guitar>
```

While this may seem like a lot of fuss over something simple, it's important to realize that whether or not entities are expanded can change the input and output XML you are working with. Always keep track of how the builder flags are set, and what you want your JDOM tree and XML output to look like.

The Namespace Class

I want to briefly cover one more JDOM class, the `Namespace` class. This class acts as both an instance variable and a factory within the JDOM architecture. When you need to create a new namespace, either for an element or for searching, you use the static `getNamespace()` methods on this class:

```
// Create namespace with prefix
Namespace schemaNamespace =
    Namespace.getNamespace("xsd", "http://www.w3.org/XMLSchema/2001");

// Create namespace without prefix
Namespace javaxml2Namespace =
    Namespace.getNamespace("http://www.oreilly.com/javaxml2");
```

As you can see, there is a version for creating namespaces with prefixes and one for creating namespaces without prefixes (default namespaces). Either version can be used, then supplied to the various JDOM methods:

```
// Create element with namespace
Element schema = new Element("schema", schemaNamespace);

// Search for children in the specified namespace
List chapterElements = contentElement.getChildren("chapter", javaxml2Namespace);
```

```
// Declare a new namespace on this element
catalogElement.addNamespaceDeclaration(
    Namespace.getNamespace("tng", "http://www.truenorthguitars.com"));
```

These are all fairly self-explanatory. Also, when XML serialization is performed with the various outputters (SAXOutputter, DOMOutputter, and XMLOutputter), the namespace declarations are automatically handled and added to the resulting XML.

One final note: in JDOM, namespace comparison is based solely on URI. In other words, two Namespace objects are equal if their URIs are equal, regardless of prefix. This is in keeping with the letter and spirit of the XML Namespace specification, which indicates that two elements are in the same namespace if their URIs are identical, regardless of prefix. Look at this XML document fragment:

```
<guitar xmlns="http://www.truenorthguitars.com">
  <ni:owner xmlns:ni="http://www.newInstance.com">
    <ni:name>Brett McLaughlin</ni:name>
    <tng:model xmlns:tng="http://www.truenorthguitars.com>Model 1</tng:model>
    <backWood>Madagascar Rosewood</backWood>
  </ni:owner>
</guitar>
```

Even though they have varying prefixes, the elements guitar, model, and backWood are all in the same namespace. This holds true in the JDOM Namespace model, as well. In fact, the Namespace class's equals() method will return equal based solely on URIs, regardless of prefix.

I've touched on only three of the JDOM classes, but these are the classes that are tricky and most commonly asked about. The rest of the API was covered in the previous chapter, and reinforced in the next sections of this chapter. You should be able to easily deal with textual content, entity references, and namespaces in JDOM now, converting between Strings and Text nodes, resolved content and EntityRefs, and multiple-prefixed namespaces with ease. With that understanding, you're ready to move on to some more complex examples and cases.

JDOM and Factories

Moving right along, recall the discussion from the last chapter on JDOM and factories. I mentioned that you would never see code like this (at least with the current versions) in JDOM applications:

```
// This code does not work!!
JDOMFactory factory = new JDOMFactory();
factory.setDocumentClass("javaxml2.BrettsDocumentClass");
factory.setElementClass("javaxml2.BrettsElementClass");
```

```
Element rootElement = JDOMFactory.createElement("root");
Document document = JDOMFactory.createDocument(rootElement);
```

Well, that remains true. However, I glossed over some pretty important aspects of that discussion, and want to pick it up again here. As I mentioned in Chapter 7, being able to have some form of factories allows greater flexibility in how your XML is modeled in Java. Take a look at the simple subclass of JDOM's `Element` class shown in Example 8-1.

Example 8-1. Subclassing the JDOM Element class

```
package javaxml2;

import org.jdom.Element;
import org.jdom.Namespace;

public class ORAElement extends Element {

    private static final Namespace ORA_NAMESPACE =
        Namespace.getNamespace("ora", "http://www.oreilly.com");

    public ORAElement(String name) {
        super(name, ORA_NAMESPACE);
    }

    public ORAElement(String name, Namespace ns) {
        super(name, ORA_NAMESPACE);
    }

    public ORAElement(String name, String uri) {
        super(name, ORA_NAMESPACE);
    }

    public ORAElement(String name, String prefix, String uri) {
        super(name, ORA_NAMESPACE);
    }
}
```

This is about as simple a subclass as you could come up with; it is somewhat similar to the `NamespaceFilter` class from Chapter 4. It disregards whatever namespace is actually supplied to the element (even if there isn't a namespace supplied!), and sets the element's namespace defined by the URI *http://www. oreilly.com* with the prefix `ora`.* This is a simple case, but it gives you an idea of what is possible, and serves as a good example for this section.

---

* It is slightly different from `NamespaceFilter` in that it changes all elements to a new namespace, rather than just those elements with a particular namespace.

Creating a Factory

Once you've got a custom subclass, the next step is actually using it. As I already mentioned, JDOM considers having to create all objects with factories a bit over-the-top. Simple element creation in JDOM works like this:

```
// Create a new Element
Element element = new Element("guitar");
```

Things remain equally simple with a custom subclass:

```
// Create a new Element, typed as an ORAElement
Element oraElement = new ORAElement("guitar");
```

The element is dropped into the O'Reilly namespace because of the custom subclass. Additionally, this method is more self-documenting than using a factory. It's clear at any point exactly what classes are being used to create objects. Compare that to this code fragment:

```
// Create an element: what type is created?
Element someElement = doc.createElement("guitar");
```

It's not clear if the object created is an `Element` instance, an `ORAElement` instance, or something else entirely. For these reasons, the custom class approach serves JDOM well. For object creation, you can simply instantiate your custom subclass directly. However, the need for factories arises when you are building a document:

```
// Build from an input source
SAXBuilder builder = new SAXBuilder();
Document doc = builder.build(someInputStream);
```

Obviously, here you were not able to specify custom classes through the building process. I suppose you could be really bold and modify the `SAXBuilder` class (and the related `org.jdom.input.SAXHandler` class), but that's a little ridiculous. So, to facilitate this, the `JDOMFactory` interface, in the `org.jdom.input` package, was introduced. This interface defines methods for every type of object creation (see Appendix A for the complete set of methods). For example, there are four methods for element creation, which match up to the four constructors for the `Element` class:

```
public Element element(String name);
public Element element(String name, Namespace ns);
public Element element(String name, String uri);
public Element element(String name, String prefix, String uri);
```

You will find similar methods for `Document`, `Attribute`, `CDATA`, and all the rest. By default, JDOM uses the `org.jdom.input.DefaultJDOMFactory`, which simply returns all of the core JDOM classes within these methods. However, you can easily subclass this implementation and provide your own factory methods. Look at Example 8-2, which defines a custom factory.

Example 8-2. A custom JDOMFactory implementation

```
package javaxml2;

import org.jdom.Element;
import org.jdom.Namespace;
import org.jdom.input.DefaultJDOMFactory;

class CustomJDOMFactory extends DefaultJDOMFactory {

    public Element element(String name) {
        return new ORAElement(name);
    }

    public Element element(String name, Namespace ns) {
        return new ORAElement(name, ns);
    }

    public Element element(String name, String uri) {
        return new ORAElement(name, uri);
    }

    public Element element(String name, String prefix, String uri) {
        return new ORAElement(name, prefix, uri);
    }
}
```

This is a simple implementation; it doesn't need to be very complex. It overrides each of the `element()` methods and returns an instance of the custom subclass, `ORAElement`, instead of the default JDOM `Element` class. At this point, any builder that uses this factory will end up with `ORAElement` instances in the created JDOM `Document` object, rather than the default `Element` instances you would normally see. All that's left is to let the build process know about this custom factory.

Building with Custom Classes

Once you have a valid implementation of `JDOMFactory`, let your builders know to use it by invoking the `setFactory()` method and passing in a factory instance. This method is available on both of the current JDOM builders, `SAXBuilder` and `DOMBuilder`. To see it in action, check out Example 8-3. This simple class takes in an XML document and builds it using the `ORAElement` class and `Custom-JDOMFactory` from Examples 8-1 and 8-2. It then writes the document back out to a supplied output filename, so you can see the effect of the custom classes.

Example 8-3. Building with custom classes using a custom factory

```java
package javaxml2;

import java.io.File;
import java.io.FileWriter;
import java.io.IOException;

import org.jdom.Document;
import org.jdom.JDOMException;
import org.jdom.input.SAXBuilder;
import org.jdom.input.JDOMFactory;
import org.jdom.output.XMLOutputter;

public class ElementChanger {

    public void change(String inputFilename, String outputFilename)
        throws IOException, JDOMException {

        // Create builder and set up factory
        SAXBuilder builder = new SAXBuilder();
        JDOMFactory factory = new CustomJDOMFactory();
        builder.setFactory(factory);

        // Build document
        Document doc = builder.build(inputFilename);

        // Output document
        XMLOutputter outputter = new XMLOutputter();
        outputter.output(doc, new FileWriter(new File(outputFilename)));
    }

    public static void main(String[] args) {
        if (args.length != 2) {
            System.out.println("Usage: javaxml2.ElementChanger " +
                "[XML Input Filename] [XML Output Filename]");
            return;
        }

        try {
            ElementChanger changer = new ElementChanger();
            changer.change(args[0], args[1]);
        } catch (Exception e) {
            e.printStackTrace();
        }
    }
}
```

I ran this on the *contents.xml* file used throughout the first several chapters:

```
bmclaugh@GANDALF
$ java javaxml2.ElementChanger contents.xml newContents.xml
```

This hummed along for a second, and then gave me a new document (*newContents.xml*). A portion of that new document is shown in Example 8-4.

Example 8-4. Output fragment from contents.xml after ElementChanger

```xml
<?xml version="1.0" encoding="UTF-8"?>
<!DOCTYPE book SYSTEM "DTD/JavaXML.dtd">
<!-- Java and XML Contents -->
<ora:book xmlns:ora="http://www.oreilly.com">
  <ora:title ora:series="Java">Java and XML</ora:title>

  <!-- Chapter List -->
  <ora:contents>
    <ora:chapter title="Introduction" number="1">
      <ora:topic name="XML Matters" />
      <ora:topic name="What's Important" />
      <ora:topic name="The Essentials" />
      <ora:topic name="What's Next?" />
    </ora:chapter>
    <ora:chapter title="Nuts and Bolts" number="2">
      <ora:topic name="The Basics" />
      <ora:topic name="Constraints" />
      <ora:topic name="Transformations" />
      <ora:topic name="And More..." />
      <ora:topic name="What's Next?" />
    </ora:chapter>
    <ora:chapter title="SAX" number="3">
      <ora:topic name="Getting Prepared" />
      <ora:topic name="SAX Readers" />
      <ora:topic name="Content Handlers" />
      <ora:topic name="Gotcha!" />
      <ora:topic name="What's Next?" />
    </ora:chapter>
    <ora:chapter title="Advanced SAX" number="4">
      <ora:topic name="Properties and Features" />
      <ora:topic name="More Handlers" />
      <ora:topic name="Filters and Writers" />
      <ora:topic name="Even More Handlers" />
      <ora:topic name="Gotcha!" />
      <ora:topic name="What's Next?" />
    </ora:chapter>
    <!-- Other chapters -->
</ora:book>
```

Each element is now in the O'Reilly namespace, prefixed and referencing the URI specified in the `ORAElement` class.

Obviously, you can take this subclassing to a much higher degree of complexity. Common examples include adding specific attributes or even child elements to every element that comes through. Many developers have existing business interfaces, and define custom JDOM classes that extend the core JDOM classes and also implement these business-specific interfaces. Other developers have built "lightweight" subclasses that discard namespace information and maintain only the bare essentials, keeping documents small (albeit not XML-compliant in some cases). The only limitations are your own ideas in subclassing. Just remember to set up your own factory before building documents, so your new functionality is included.

Wrappers and Decorators

One of the most common requests that comes up about JDOM is related to interfaces. Many, many users have asked for interfaces in JDOM, and that request has been consistently denied. The reasoning is simple: no set of common methods could be arrived at for all JDOM constructs. There has been a reluctance to use the DOM approach, which provides a set of common methods for most constructs. For example, `getChildren()` is on the common DOM `org.w3c.dom.Node` interface; however, it returns `null` when it doesn't apply, such as to a `Text` node. The JDOM approach has been to only provide methods on a basic interface common to all JDOM classes, and no methods fulfilling this requirement have been found. Additionally, for every request to add interfaces, there has been a request to leave the API as is.

However, there are patterns that allow interface-type functionality to be used with JDOM without changing the API drastically (in fact, without changing it at all!). In this section, I want to talk about the most effective of those patterns, which involves using *wrappers* or *decorators*. I'm not going to dive into a lot of design pattern material in this book, but suffice it to say that a wrapper or decorator (I use the two interchangeably in this chapter) is on the *exterior* of existing classes, rather than on the *interior*, as a core JDOM interface would be. In other words, existing behavior is wrapped. In this section, I show you how this pattern allows you to customize JDOM (or any other API) in any way you please.

NOTE   By now, you should be fairly advanced in Java and XML. For that reason, I'm going to move through the example code in this section with a minimal amount of comment. You should be able to figure out what's going on pretty easily, and I'd rather get in more code than more talk.

JDOMNode

To get started, I've defined a JDOMNode interface in Example 8-5. This interface defines very simple behavior that I want accessible for all JDOM nodes, and that I want without having to perform type-casting.

Example 8-5. A node decorator interface

```
package javaxml2;

import java.util.List;
import java.util.Iterator;

// JDOM imports
import org.jdom.Document;

public interface JDOMNode {

    public Object getNode();

    public String getNodeName();

    public JDOMNode getParentNode();

    public String getQName();

    public Iterator iterator();

    public String toString();
}
```

The only method that may look odd is iterator(); it will return a Java Iterator over a node's children, or return an empty list Iterator if there are no children (such as for attributes or text nodes). It's worth noting that I could have just as easily chosen to use the DOM org.w3c.dom.Node interface (if I wanted DOM and JDOM interoperability at a class level), or a different interface specific to my business needs. The sky is the limit on this core interface.

Implementing Classes

The next, more interesting step is to provide implementations of this interface that decorate existing JDOM constructs. These provide wrapping for the concrete classes already in JDOM, and most of the methods on the JDOMNode interface simply are passed through to the underlying (decorated) object. First up is Example 8-6, which decorates a JDOM Element.

Example 8-6. Decorator for JDOM Elements

```
package javaxml2;

import java.util.List;
import java.util.ArrayList;
import java.util.Iterator;

// JDOM imports
import org.jdom.Element;

public class ElementNode implements JDOMNode {

    /** the decorated Element */
    protected Element decorated;

    public ElementNode(Element element) {
        this.decorated = element;
    }

    public Object getNode() {
        return decorated;
    }

    public String getNodeName() {
        if (decorated != null) {
            return decorated.getName();
        }
        return "";
    }

    public JDOMNode getParentNode() {
        if (decorated.getParent() != null) {
            return new ElementNode(decorated.getParent());
        }
        return null;
    }

    public String getQName() {
        if (decorated.getNamespacePrefix().equals("")) {
            return decorated.getName();
        } else {
            return new StringBuffer(decorated.getNamespacePrefix())
                        .append(":")
                        .append(decorated.getName()).toString();
        }
    }

    public Iterator iterator() {
        List list = decorated.getAttributes();
```

Example 8-6. Decorator for JDOM Elements (continued)

```
    ArrayList content = new ArrayList(list);

    // put the element's content in the list in order
    Iterator i = decorated.getMixedContent().iterator();
    while (i.hasNext()) {
        content.add(i.next());
    }
    return content.iterator();
}

public String toString() {
    return decorated.toString();
}
}
```

There's nothing too remarkable here, so let's keep going. In Example 8-7, I've defined a similar class, `AttributeNode`, which decorates a JDOM `Attribute` and implements my core `JDOMNode` class. Notice the several no-op (no-operation) methods for things like getting the children of the attribute; this closely models the DOM approach. Again, keep in mind that these classes could just as easily implement any other interface (think `org.w3c.dom.Attr` in this case) without needing changes within the core JDOM API.

Example 8-7. Decorator for JDOM Attributes

```
package javaxml2;

import java.util.Iterator;
import java.util.Collections;

// JDOM imports
import org.jdom.Attribute;

public class AttributeNode implements JDOMNode {

    /** The decorated attribute */
    protected Attribute decorated;

    public AttributeNode(Attribute attribute) {
        this.decorated = attribute;
    }

    public Object getNode() {
        return decorated;
    }

    public String getNodeName() {
```

Example 8-7. Decorator for JDOM Attributes (continued)

```
        if (decorated != null) {
            return decorated.getName();
        }
        return "";
    }

    public JDOMNode getParentNode() {
        if (decorated.getParent() != null) {
            return new ElementNode(decorated.getParent());
        }
        return null;
    }

    public String getQName() {
        if (decorated.getNamespacePrefix().equals("")) {
            return decorated.getName();
        } else {
            return new StringBuffer(decorated.getNamespacePrefix())
                        .append(":")
                        .append(decorated.getName()).toString();
        }
    }

    public Iterator iterator() {
        return Collections.EMPTY_LIST.iterator();
    }

    public String toString() {
        return decorated.toString();
    }
}
```

Finally, I'll decorate JDOM's textual content (see Example 8-8). At the time of this
writing, the JDOM `Text` class I talked about in the first of this chapter hadn't quite
been integrated into its final form in the JDOM source tree. As a result, I'm actually wrapping a Java `String` in the `TextNode` class. When the `Text` node makes it
in, this needs to be updated to wrap that type, which is a simple operation.

Example 8-8. Decorator for JDOM textual content

```
package javaxml2;

import java.util.Collections;
import java.util.Iterator;

// JDOM imports
import org.jdom.Element;
```

Example 8-8. Decorator for JDOM textual content (continued)

```java
public class TextNode implements JDOMNode {

    /** The decorated String */
    protected String decorated;

    /** The manually set parent of this string content */
    private Element parent = null;

    public TextNode(String string) {
        decorated = string;
    }

    public Object getNode() {
        return decorated;
    }

    public String getNodeName() {
        return "";
    }

    public JDOMNode getParentNode() {
        if (parent == null) {
            throw new RuntimeException(
                "The parent of this String content has not been set!");
        }
        return new ElementNode(parent);
    }

    public String getQName() {
        // text nodes have no name
        return "";
    }

    public Iterator iterator() {
        return Collections.EMPTY_LIST.iterator();
    }

    public TextNode setParent(Element parent) {
        this.parent = parent;
        return this;
    }

    public String toString() {
        return decorated;
    }
}
```

I'm not going to provide decorators for all the other JDOM types because you should be getting the picture by now. Note that I could also have provided a single JDOMNode implementation, ConcreteNode or something like that, that wrapped the various JDOM types all in one class. However, that would require quite a bit of special casing code that isn't suitable here. Instead, there is a one-to-one mapping between JDOM core classes and JDOMNode implementations.

Providing Support for XPath

Now that you've got some interface-based JDOM nodes, I will extend things a little further. This is a common business scenario, in which you need to provide specific functionality on top of an existing API. For a practical example, I tackle XPath. For any JDOMNode implementation, I'd like to be able to get the XPath expression representing that node. To allow for that functionality, I have written another wrapper class, shown in Example 8-9. This class, XPathDisplayNode, wraps an existing node (of any type, because of the interface-based logic), and provides a single public XPath method, getXPath(). This method returns an XPath expression for the wrapped node as a Java string of characters.

Example 8-9. Wrapper for XPath support

```
package javaxml2;

import java.util.Vector;
import java.util.List;
import java.util.Iterator;
import java.util.Stack;

// JDOM imports
import org.jdom.Attribute;
import org.jdom.Element;
import org.jdom.Namespace;

public class XPathDisplayNode {

    /** The JDOMNode this xpath is based on */
    JDOMNode node;

    public XPathDisplayNode(JDOMNode node) {
        this.node = node;
    }

    private String getElementXPath(JDOMNode currentNode) {
        StringBuffer buf = new StringBuffer("/")
            .append(currentNode.getQName());
        Element current = (Element)currentNode.getNode();
        Element parent = current.getParent();
```

Example 8-9. Wrapper for XPath support (continued)

```
        // See if we're at the root element
        if (parent == null ) {
            return buf.toString();
        }

        // Check for other siblings of the same name and namespace
        Namespace ns = current.getNamespace();
        List siblings = parent.getChildren(current.getName(), ns);

        int total = 0;
        Iterator i = siblings.iterator();
        while (i.hasNext()) {
            total++;
            if (current == i.next()) {
                break;
            }
        }

        // No selector needed if this is the only element
        if ((total == 1) && (!i.hasNext())) {
            return buf.toString();
        }

        return buf.append("[")
                  .append(String.valueOf(total))
                  .append("]").toString();
    }

    public String getXPath() {
        // Handle elements
        if (node.getNode() instanceof Element) {
            JDOMNode parent = node.getParentNode();

            // If this is null, we're at the root
            if (parent == null) {
                return "/" + node.getQName();
            }

            // Otherwise, build a path back to the root
            Stack stack = new Stack();
            stack.add(node);
            do {
                stack.add(parent);
                parent = parent.getParentNode();
            } while (parent != null);

            // Build the path
            StringBuffer xpath = new StringBuffer();
```

Example 8-9. Wrapper for XPath support (continued)

```
            while (!stack.isEmpty()) {
                xpath.append(getElementXPath((JDOMNode)stack.pop()));
            }
            return xpath.toString();
        }


        // Handle attributes
        if (node.getNode() instanceof Attribute) {
            Attribute attribute = (Attribute)node.getNode();
            JDOMNode parent = node.getParentNode();
            StringBuffer xpath = new StringBuffer("//")
                .append(parent.getQName())
                .append("[@")
                .append(node.getQName())
                .append("='")
                .append(attribute.getValue())
                .append("']");

            return xpath.toString();
        }


        // Handle text
        if (node.getNode() instanceof String) {
            StringBuffer xpath = new StringBuffer(
                new XPathDisplayNode(node.getParentNode()).getXPath())
                    .append("[child::text()]");
            return xpath.toString();
        }


        // Other node types could follow here
        return "Node type not supported yet.";
    }
}
```

In this class, I provided special casing for each node type; in other words, I didn't implement an `XPathElementNode`, `XPathAttributeNode`, and so on. That's because the similarities in generating this XPath statement are much greater than the advantages of splitting out the code for each type. Of course, this is just the opposite of providing a type-specific node decorator for each JDOM type. You'll want to always try and figure out the difference in your applications, which results in much cleaner code (and often less code, as well).

I'm going to leave the details of working through the process followed in this code up to you. For any node, the XPath expression is calculated and assembled manually, and you should be able to follow the logic pretty easily. That expression is then returned to the calling program, which I cover next.

Endgame

Once you have all your various node types as well as the XPath wrapper, it's time
to do something useful. In this case, I want to provide a document viewer, similar
to the SAXTreeViewer class from Chapter 3, for a JDOM tree. However, I'd also
like to provide the XPath expression for each item in that tree down in the status
bar. Example 8-10 shows how to do this, using the nodes and wrappers discussed
in this section.

Example 8-10. The SimpleXPathViewer class

```
package javaxml2;

import java.awt.*;
import java.io.File;
import javax.swing.*;
import javax.swing.tree.*;
import javax.swing.event.*;
import java.util.Iterator;

// JDOM imports
import org.jdom.*;
import org.jdom.input.SAXBuilder;

public class SimpleXPathViewer extends JFrame {

    /** The event handler inner class */
    EventHandler eventHandler = new EventHandler();

    /** A text field for displaying the XPath for the selectected node */
    private JTextField statusText;

    /** The JTree used to display the nodes of the xml document */
    private JTree jdomTree;

    /** The selection model used to determine which node was clicked */
    private DefaultTreeSelectionModel selectionModel;

    /** The filename containing the xml file to view */
    private String filename;

    /** Temporary hack to get around the lack of a text node */
    private static Element lastElement;

    class EventHandler implements TreeSelectionListener {

        public void valueChanged(TreeSelectionEvent e) {
            TreePath path= selectionModel.getLeadSelectionPath();
```

Example 8-10. The SimpleXPathViewer class (continued)

```java
            // If you are just collapsing the tree, you may not have a new path
            if (path != null) {
                JDOMNode selection=
                    (JDOMNode)((DefaultMutableTreeNode)path.getLastPathComponent())
                        .getUserObject();
                buildXPath(selection);
            }
        };
    };

    public SimpleXPathViewer(String fileName) throws Exception {
        super();
        this.filename = fileName;
        setSize(600, 450);
        initialize();
    }

    private void initialize() throws Exception {
        setTitle("Simple XPath Viewer");

        // Setup the UI
        initConnections();

        // Load the JDOM Document
        Document doc = loadDocument(filename);

        // Create the initial JDOMNode from the Factory method
        JDOMNode root = createNode(doc.getRootElement());

        // Create the root node of the JTree and build it from the JDOM Document
        DefaultMutableTreeNode treeNode =
            new DefaultMutableTreeNode("Document: " + filename);
        buildTree(root, treeNode);

        // Add the node to the tree's model
        ((DefaultTreeModel)jdomTree.getModel()).setRoot(treeNode);
    }

    private void initConnections() {
        setDefaultCloseOperation(javax.swing.WindowConstants.DISPOSE_ON_CLOSE);

        // Setup the JTree and a pane to display it in
        jdomTree = new JTree();
        jdomTree.setName("JDOM Tree");
        jdomTree.addTreeSelectionListener(eventHandler);
        selectionModel = (DefaultTreeSelectionModel)jdomTree.getSelectionModel();
        getContentPane().add(new JScrollPane(jdomTree), BorderLayout.CENTER);
```

Example 8-10. The SimpleXPathViewer class (continued)

```java
    // Setup a text box for use in a status bar
    statusText = new JTextField("Click on an element to view xpath");
    JPanel statusBarPane= new JPanel();
    statusBarPane.setLayout(new BorderLayout());
    statusBarPane.add(statusText, BorderLayout.CENTER );
    getContentPane().add(statusBarPane, BorderLayout.SOUTH);
}

private Document loadDocument(String filename) throws JDOMException {
    SAXBuilder builder = new SAXBuilder();
    builder.setIgnoringElementContentWhitespace(true);
    return builder.build(new File(filename));
}

private JDOMNode createNode(Object node) {
    if (node instanceof Element) {
        lastElement = (Element)node;
        return new ElementNode((Element)node);
    }

    if (node instanceof Attribute) {
        return new AttributeNode((Attribute)node);
    }

    if (node instanceof String) {
        return new TextNode((String)node).setParent(lastElement);
    }

    // All other nodes are not implemented
    return null;
}

private void buildTree(JDOMNode node, DefaultMutableTreeNode treeNode) {
    // If this is a whitespace node or unhandled node, ignore it
    if ((node == null) || (node.toString().trim().equals(""))) {
        return;
    }

    DefaultMutableTreeNode newTreeNode = new DefaultMutableTreeNode(node);

    // Walk over the children of the node
    Iterator i = node.iterator();
    while (i.hasNext()) {
        // Create JDOMNodes on the children and add to the tree
        JDOMNode newNode = createNode(i.next());
        buildTree(newNode, newTreeNode);
    }
```

Example 8-10. The SimpleXPathViewer class (continued)

```
        // After all the children have been added, connect to the tree
        treeNode.add(newTreeNode);
    }

    private void buildXPath(JDOMNode node) {
        statusText.setText(new XPathDisplayNode(node).getXPath());
    }

    public static void main(java.lang.String[] args) {
        try {
            if (args.length != 1) {
                System.out.println("Usage: java javaxml2.SimpleXPathViewer " +
                    "[XML Document filename]");
                return;
            }

            /* Create the frame */
            SimpleXPathViewer viewer= new SimpleXPathViewer(args[0]);

            /* Add a windowListener for the windowClosedEvent */
            viewer.addWindowListener(new java.awt.event.WindowAdapter() {
                    public void windowClosed(java.awt.event.WindowEvent e) {
                        System.exit(0);
                    };
                });
            viewer.setVisible(true);
        } catch (Exception e) {
            e.printStackTrace();
        }
    }
}
```

As usual, I am skipping the Swing details. You can see that once the document is loaded using SAXBuilder, though, the root element of that document is obtained (in the initialize() method). This element is used to create an instance of JDOMNode through the createNode() utility function. The function simply converts between JDOM types and JDOMNode implementations, and took about 15 seconds to code up. Use a similar method in your own programs that use decorators and wrappers.

Once I've got JDOMNode implementations, it's simple to walk the tree, creating visual objects for each node encountered. Additionally, for each node, I've set the status text of the window to the XPath expression for that node. You can compile all of these examples, and run them using this command:

```
C:\javaxml2\build>java javaxml2.SimpleXPathViewer
                    c:\javaxml2\ch08\xml\contents.xml
```

Be sure that JDOM and your XML parser are in your classpath. The result is the Swing UI shown in Figure 8-1. Notice how the status bar reflects the XPath expression for the currently selected node. Play around with this—seeing four or five screenshots in a book isn't nearly as useful as your exploration of the tool.

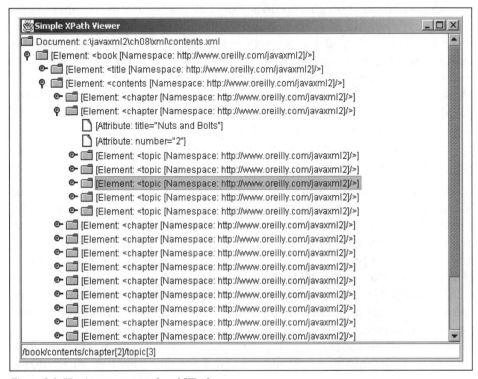

Figure 8-1. Viewing contents.xml and XPaths

And that's it! I know I've gone quickly, but the concepts involved are simple. You can think about how decorators and wrappers might help you with the interface-like functionality you need in your applications. Also check out the JDOM web site at *http://www.jdom.org* for contributions that may include stock wrappers (like this one, or a DOM set of decorators).

Finally, I'd like to thank Philip Nelson, who did the lion's share of the work on the decorator code shown here. Philip has really explored using decorators with JDOM, and was a great help in this section.

Gotcha!

As with the other chapters on APIs, I will address a few more tricky items that relate to the topics in this chapter. These are common problems that can cause you to beat your head against the wall, so try and avoid them.

More on Subclassing

Since I talked about factories and custom classes in this chapter, it's worth point-ing out a few important things about subclassing that can be gotcha items. When you extend a class, and in particular the JDOM classes, you need to ensure that your custom behavior is going to be activated as you want it to. In other words, ensure that there is no path from an application through your subclass and to the superclass that isn't a path you are willing to live with. In almost every case, this involves ensuring that you override each constructor of the superclass. You'll notice that in Example 8-1, the ORAElement class, I overrode all four of the Element class's constructors. This ensured that any application using ORAElement would have to create the object with one of these constructors. While that might seem like a trivial detail, imagine if I had left out the constructor that took in a name and URI for the element. This step effectively reduces the number of ways to construct the object by one. That might seem trivial, but it's not!

Continuing with this hypothetical, you implement a CustomJDOMFactory class, like the one shown in Example 8-2, and override the various element() methods. However, you would probably forget to override element(String name, String uri), since you already forgot to override that constructor in your subclass. Sud-denly, you've got a problem. Every time an element is requested by name and URI (which is quite often in the SAXBuilder process, by the way), you are going to get a plain, vanilla Element instance. However, the other element creation methods all return instances of ORAElement. Just like that, because of one lousy construc-tor, your document is going to have two element implementations, almost cer-tainly not what you wanted. It is crucial to inspect every means of object creation in your subclasses, and generally make sure you override every constructor that is public in the superclass.

Creating Invalid XML

Another tricky case to watch out for when subclassing is inadvertently creating invalid XML. Using JDOM, it's more or less impossible to create XML that is not well-formed, but consider the ORAElement subclass again. This subclass added the ora prefix to every element, which alone could cause it to fail validation. This is probably not a big deal, but you do need to comment out or remove the DOCTYPE declaration to avoid problems when reading the document back in.

Even more importantly, you can get some unexpected results if you aren't careful. Look at this fragment of the XML generated using the ORAElement subclass, which only shows the last little bit of the serialized document:

```
<?xml version="1.0" encoding="UTF-8"?>
<!DOCTYPE book SYSTEM "DTD/JavaXML.dtd">
```

```
<!-- Java and XML Contents -->
<ora:book xmlns:ora="http://www.oreilly.com">
  <ora:title ora:series="Java">Java and XML</ora:title>

  <!-- Other content -->

  <ora:copyright>

<ora:copyright>
  <ora:year value="2001" />
  <ora:content>All Rights Reserved, O'Reilly &amp; Associates</ora:content>
</ora:copyright>
</ora:copyright>
</ora:book>
```

Notice that there are now *two* `ora:copyright` elements! What happened is that an existing element was in place in the O'Reilly namespace (the original `ora:copyright` element). However, the `copyright` element nested within that, with no namespace, was also assigned the `ora` prefix and O'Reilly namespace through the `ORAElement` class. The result is two elements with the same name and namespace, but differing content models. This makes validation very tricky, and is probably not what you intended. These are simple examples, but in more complex documents with more complex subclasses, you'll need to watch carefully what results you are generating, particularly with respect to a DTD, XML Schema, or other form of document constraints.

What's Next?

I'm winding down on the lower-level APIs, and I'll finish up the discussion in the next chapter by covering JAXP, Sun's Java API for XML Processing. JAXP requires use of SAX and DOM, and so logically looks at those APIs. It also serves as a half-way point in the book, and probably a good time to take a short break when you're done with the chapter! I'll cover both JAXP 1.0 and 1.1, now heavily in use, explaining how they work with the APIs you already know and why JAXP can really help out in your application programming. So get ready for another hammer in the old toolbox, and turn the page.

9

In this chapter:
- *API or Abstraction*
- *JAXP 1.0*
- *JAXP 1.1*
- *Gotcha!*
- *What's Next?*

JAXP

When Sun released the Java API for XML Parsing, generally referred to as JAXP, they managed to launch a series of contradictions into the Java world. In one swoop, they released the most important API that wasn't an API to Java developers, and caused great confusion with the simplest API. People switched to a new parser without knowing they had switched to a new parser. There is a lot of confusion surrounding JAXP, not only about how to use it, but even about what it is.

In this chapter, I'll first address some of the confusion about what JAXP is and is not.* Then you'll get a look at JAXP 1.0, which is still used heavily. Once you get the basics, we will move on to JAXP 1.1, the latest version (not quite released as of the writing of this chapter, but almost certainly available by publication time). That will give you a leg up on the new features in the latest version, and in particular the TrAX API included in JAXP 1.1. Buckle up, and be prepared to finally understand the mystery behind JAXP.

API or Abstraction

Before diving into code, it's important to cover some basic concepts. Strictly speaking, JAXP is an API, but it is more accurately called an abstraction layer. It does not provide a new means of parsing XML, add to SAX, DOM, or JDOM, or provide new functionality in handling Java and XML. Instead, it makes it easier to deal with some difficult tasks with DOM and SAX. It also makes it possible to handle vendor-specific tasks encountered when using the DOM and SAX APIs, which in turn allows those APIs to be used in a vendor-neutral way.

---

* If this chapter feels a little bit like déjà vu, you may have read an earlier version of this text at IBM DeveloperWorks. There were originally two articles published at *http://www.ibm.com/developer* that explored JAXP. This chapter is an updated and slightly modified version of those articles.

While I'll go through these features individually, the thing you really need to get a handle on is that JAXP does not provide parsing functionality! Without SAX, DOM, or another XML parsing API, *you cannot parse XML*. I have seen many requests for a comparison of DOM, SAX, or JDOM to JAXP. Making these comparisons is impossible because the first three APIs serve a completely different purpose than JAXP. SAX, DOM, and JDOM all parse XML. JAXP provides a means to get to these APIs and the results of parsing a document. It doesn't offer a new way to parse the document itself. This is a critical distinction to make if you're going to use JAXP correctly. It will also most likely put you miles ahead of many of your fellow XML developers.

If you're still dubious, download the JAXP 1.0 distribution from Sun's web site at *http://java.sun.com/xml* and you'll get an idea of how basic JAXP is. In the included *jar* (*jaxp.jar*), you will find only six classes! How hard could this API be? All of the classes (part of the `javax.xml.parsers` package) sit on top of an existing parser. And two of these classes are for error handling. JAXP is simpler than people think.

Sun's JAXP and Parser

Part of the trouble stems from the fact that Sun's parser is included with the JAXP download. The parser classes are all in the *parser.jar* archive as part of the `com.sun.xml.parser` package and related subpackages. This parser (now code-named Crimson) is *not* part of JAXP. It is part of the JAXP *distribution*, but it is not part of the JAXP *API*. Confusing? A little bit. Think about it this way: JDOM downloads include the Apache Xerces parser. That parser isn't part of JDOM but is used by JDOM, so it's included to ensure that JDOM is usable out of the box. The same principle applies for JAXP, but it isn't as clearly publicized: JAXP comes with Sun's parser so it can be used immediately. However, many people refer to the classes included in Sun's parser as part of the JAXP API itself. For example, a common question on newsgroups is, "How can I use the `XMLDocument` class that comes with JAXP? What is its purpose?" The answer is somewhat complicated.

First, the `com.sun.xml.tree.XMLDocument` class is *not part of JAXP*. It is part of Sun's parser. So the question is misleading from the start. Second, the whole point of JAXP is to provide vendor-independence when dealing with parsers. The same code, using JAXP, could be used with Sun's XML parser, Apache's Xerces XML parser, and Oracle's XML parser. Using a Sun-specific class, then, is a bad idea. It violates the entire point of using JAXP. Are you starting to see how this subject has gotten muddied up? The parser and the API in the JAXP distribution (at least the one from Sun) have been lumped together, and developers mistake classes and features from one as part of the other, and vice versa.

The Old and the New

There is another confusing issue related to JAXP. JAXP 1.0 supports only SAX 1.0 and DOM Level 1. It is generally Sun's policy not to ship any API or product based on a working draft, beta, or other nonfinal version of underlying APIs. When JAXP 1.0 was finalized, Sun settled on SAX 1.0, as SAX 2.0 was still in beta, and DOM Level 1, as Level 2 was still in candidate recommendation. There were a lot of users who layered JAXP on top of existing parsers (like Apache Xerces, for example) that had SAX 2.0 and DOM Level 2 support, and suddenly lost functionality. The result was a lot of questions about how to use features that simply couldn't be used with JAXP. It was also right about this time that SAX 2.0 went from beta to final, and *really* threw things into a mess. However, that hasn't stopped many who didn't need these later versions of DOM and SAX from putting JAXP 1.0 into production, and so I'd be remiss in not covering both the old version (1.0), as well as the new version (1.1), which does support SAX 2.0 and DOM Level 2. The rest of this chapter is split into two parts: the first dealing with JAXP 1.0, and the second with 1.1. Since 1.1 builds on what 1.0 provided in terms of functionality, you should read both sections regardless of the version of the API you're using.

JAXP 1.0

It all begins (and began) with JAXP 1.0. This first version of Sun's API provided, basically, a thin layer over existing APIs that allowed for vendor-neutral parsing of code. For SAX, this isn't a huge deal; now that you are a SAX expert, you are smart enough to use the `XMLReaderFactory` class instead of directly instantiating a vendor's parser class. Of course, as you're also a DOM expert, you know that it's a pain to deal with DOM in a vendor-neutral way, so JAXP helps out quite a bit in this regard. Additionally, JAXP provided some methods for working with validation and namespaces, another vendor-specific task that can now be handled (in most cases) in a much better way.

Starting with SAX

Before getting into how JAXP works with SAX, I will fill you in on some SAX 1.0 details. Remember the `org.xml.sax.helpers.DefaultHandler` class I showed you in Chapter 4 that implemented all the core SAX 2.0 handlers? There was a similar class in SAX 1.0 called `org.xml.sax.HandlerBase`; this class implemented the SAX 1.0 handlers (which were slightly different in that version). As long as you understand this, you'll be all set to deal with JAXP 1.0.

To use JAXP with a SAX-compliant parser, your only task is to extend the `HandlerBase` class and implement the callbacks desired for your application. That's it, no different than doing the same for `DefaultHandler` in SAX 2.0. An instance of your extension class then becomes the core argument for most of the JAXP methods that deal with SAX.

Here's the typical SAX rundown:

- Create a `SAXParser` instance using a specific vendor's parser implementation.

- Register callback implementations (by using a class that extends `HandlerBase`).

- Start parsing and relax as your callback implementations are fired off.

The SAX component of JAXP provides a simple means to do all of this. Without JAXP, a SAX parser instance either must be instantiated directly from a vendor class (such as `org.apache.xerces.parsers.SAXParser`), or it must use a SAX helper class called `ParserFactory` (the SAX 1.0 version of SAX 2.0's `XMLReaderFactory`).

JAXP provides a better alternative. It allows you to use the vendor class as a parser through a Java system property. Of course, when you download a distribution from Sun, you get a JAXP implementation that uses Sun's parser by default. The same JAXP interfaces, but with an implementation built on Apache Xerces, can be downloaded from the Apache XML web site at *http://xml.apache.org*, and they use Apache Xerces by default. Therefore (in either case), changing the parser you are using requires that you change a classpath setting or system property value, but it does *not* require code recompilation. And this is the magic, the abstraction, that JAXP is all about.

WARNING   Where you download the JAXP classes from is important. Even though you can still set system properties to change the parser class, the default parser (when no system properties are present) depends on the implementation—which depends on the location that JAXP comes from. The version from Apache XML uses Xerces by default, while Sun's version uses Crimson by default. If you get these mixed up, you may end up with the wrong parser in your classpath, and get `ClassNotFound` exceptions.

A look at the SAXParserFactory class

The JAXP `SAXParserFactory` class (in the `javax.xml.parsers` class, like all the JAXP classes) is the key to changing parser implementations easily. You must create a new instance of this class (which I will describe how to do in a moment). After the factory is created, it provides a method to obtain a SAX-capable parser. Behind the scenes, the JAXP implementation takes care of the vendor-dependent code, keeping your code unpolluted. This factory provides some other nice features, as well.

In addition to the basic job of creating instances of SAX parsers, the factory allows configuration options to be set. These options affect all parser instances obtained through the factory. The two options available in JAXP 1.0 are setting namespace awareness (setNamespaceAware (boolean awareness)), and turning on validation (setValidating (boolean validating)). Remember that after these options are set, they affect *all* instances obtained from the factory after the method invocation.

Once you have set up the factory, invoking the newSAXParser() method returns a ready-to-use instance of the JAXP SAXParser class. This class wraps an underlying SAX parser (an instance of the SAX class org.xml.sax.Parser). It also protects you from using any vendor-specific additions to the parser class. (Remember our earlier discussion about the xmlDocument class?) This class allows actual parsing behavior to be kicked off. Example 9-1 shows how a SAX factory can be created, configured, and used.

Example 9-1. Using the SAXParserFactory class

```
package javaxml2;

import java.io.File;
import java.io.IOException;
import java.io.OutputStreamWriter;
import java.io.Writer;

// JAXP
import javax.xml.parsers.FactoryConfigurationError;
import javax.xml.parsers.ParserConfigurationException;
import javax.xml.parsers.SAXParserFactory;
import javax.xml.parsers.SAXParser;

// SAX
import org.xml.sax.AttributeList;
import org.xml.sax.HandlerBase;
import org.xml.sax.SAXException;

public class TestSAXParsing {

    public static void main(String[] args) {
        try {
            if (args.length != 1) {
                System.err.println(
                    "Usage: java TestSAXParsing [XML Document filename]");
                System.exit(1);
            }
```

Example 9-1. Using the SAXParserFactory class (continued)

```
                // Get SAX Parser Factory
                SAXParserFactory factory = SAXParserFactory.newInstance();

                // Turn on validation, and turn off namespaces
                factory.setValidating(true);
                factory.setNamespaceAware(false);

                SAXParser parser = factory.newSAXParser();
                parser.parse(new File(args[0]), new MyHandler());

            } catch (ParserConfigurationException e) {
                System.out.println("The underlying parser does not " +
                                   "support the requested features.");
            } catch (FactoryConfigurationError e) {
                System.out.println(
                    "Error occurred obtaining SAX Parser Factory.");
            } catch (Exception e) {
                e.printStackTrace();
            }
        }
    }

class MyHandler extends HandlerBase {
    // SAX callback implementations from DocumentHandler, ErrorHandler,
    //   DTDHandler, and EntityResolver
}
```

Notice in this code that two JAXP-specific problems can occur in using the factory: the inability to obtain or configure a SAX factory, and the inability to configure a SAX parser. The first of these problems, which is represented by a FactoryConfigurationError, usually occurs when the parser specified in a JAXP implementation or system property cannot be loaded. The second problem, ParserConfigurationException, occurs when a requested feature is not available in the parser being used. Both are easy to deal with and shouldn't pose as any difficulty.

A SAXParser is obtained once you get the factory, turn off namespaces, and turn on validation; then parsing begins. Notice that the parse() method of the SAX parser takes an instance of the SAX HandlerBase class that I mentioned earlier (I left the implementation of this class out of the code listing, but you can download the complete source file for *TestSAXParsing.java* at the book's web site). You also pass in the file (as a Java File) to parse, obviously. However, the SAXParser class contains much more than just this single method.

Working with the SAXParser class

Once you have an instance of the SAXParser class, you can do more with it than just passing it a File to parse. Because of the way components in large applications communicate these days, it is not always safe to assume that the creator of an object instance is its user. In other words, one component may create the SAXParser instance, while another component (perhaps coded by another developer) may need to use that same instance. For this reason, methods are provided to determine the settings of a parser instance. The two methods that provide this functionality are isValidating(), which informs the caller if the parser will perform validation, and isNamespaceAware(), which returns an indication if the parser can process namespaces in an XML document. While these methods can give you information about what the parser can do, you do not have the means to change these features. You must do this at the parser factory level.

Additionally, there is a variety of ways to request parsing of a document. Instead of just accepting a File and a SAX HandlerBase instance, the SAXParser's parse() method can also accept a SAX InputSource, a Java InputStream, or a URL in String form, all with a HandlerBase instance as the second argument. Different types of input documents can be treated to different means of parsing.

Finally, the underlying SAX parser (an instance of org.xml.sax.Parser) can be obtained and used directly through the SAXParser's getParser() method. Once this underlying instance is obtained, the usual SAX methods are available. Example 9-2 shows examples of the various uses of the SAXParser class, the core class in JAXP for SAX parsing.

Example 9-2. Using the JAXP SAXParser class

```
// Get a SAX Parser instance
SAXParser saxParser = saxFactory.newSAXParser();

// Find out if validation is supported
boolean isValidating = saxParser.isValidating();

// Find out if namespaces is supported
boolean isNamespaceAware = saxParser.isNamespaceAware();

// ------- Parse, in a variety of ways ---------------- //

// Use a file and a SAX HandlerBase instance
saxParser.parse(new File(args[0]), myHandlerBaseInstance);

// Use a SAX InputSource and a SAX HandlerBase instance
saxParser.parse(mySaxInputSource, myHandlerBaseInstance);

// Use an InputStream and a SAX HandlerBase instance
```

Example 9-2. Using the JAXP SAXParser class (continued)

```
saxParser.parse(myInputStream, myHandlerBaseInstance);

// Use a URI and a SAX HandlerBase instance
saxParser.parse("http://www.newInstance.com/xml/doc.xml",
                myHandlerBaseInstance);

// Get the underlying (wrapped) SAX parser
org.xml.sax.Parser parser = saxParser.getParser();

// Use the underlying parser
parser.setContentHandler(myContentHandlerInstance);
parser.setErrorHandler(myErrorHandlerInstance);
parser.parse(new org.xml.sax.InputSource(args[0]));
```

Up to now, I've talked a lot about SAX, but I haven't unveiled anything remarkable or even that surprising. The fact is, the functionality of JAXP is fairly minor, particularly when SAX is involved. This is fine with me (and should be with you), because minimal functionality means your code is more portable and can be used by other developers, either freely (through open source) or commercially, with any SAX-compliant XML parser. That's it. There's nothing more to using SAX with JAXP. If you already know SAX, you're 98 percent of the way there. You just need to learn two new classes and a couple of Java exceptions, and you're ready to roll. If you've never used SAX, it's easy enough to start now.

Dealing with DOM

The process of using JAXP with DOM is nearly identical to using JAXP with SAX; all you do is change two class names and a method's return type, and you are pretty much there. If you understand how SAX works and understand what DOM is, you won't have any problem. Of course, you've got Chapters 5 and 6 to refer back to, so you're all set. Since JAXP doesn't have to fire SAX callbacks when working with DOM, it is responsible only for returning a DOM Document object from a parsing.

A look at the DOM parser factory

With a basic understanding of DOM and the differences between DOM and SAX, there is little else to say. The code in Example 9-3 will look remarkably similar to the SAX code in Example 9-1. First, an instance of DocumentBuilderFactory is obtained (in the same way that a SAXParserFactory instance was in SAX). Then the factory is configured to handle validation and namespaces (in the same way that it was in SAX). Next, a DocumentBuilder, the DOM analog to SAXParser, is retrieved from the factory. Parsing can then occur, and the resulting DOM Document object is handed off to an instance of the DOMSerializer class (from Chapter 5).

Example 9-3. Using the DocumentBuilderFactory class

```java
package javaxml2;

import java.io.File;
import java.io.IOException;
import java.io.OutputStreamWriter;
import java.io.Writer;

// JAXP
import javax.xml.parsers.FactoryConfigurationError;
import javax.xml.parsers.ParserConfigurationException;
import javax.xml.parsers.DocumentBuilderFactory;
import javax.xml.parsers.DocumentBuilder;

// DOM
import org.w3c.dom.Document;
import org.w3c.dom.DocumentType;
import org.w3c.dom.NamedNodeMap;
import org.w3c.dom.Node;
import org.w3c.dom.NodeList;

public class TestDOMParsing {

    public static void main(String[] args) {
        try {
            if (args.length != 1) {
                System.err.println (
                    "Usage: java TestDOMParsing [filename]");
                System.exit(1);
            }

            // Get Document Builder Factory
            DocumentBuilderFactory factory =
                DocumentBuilderFactory.newInstance();

            // Turn on validation, and turn off namespaces
            factory.setValidating(true);
            factory.setNamespaceAware(false);

            DocumentBuilder builder = factory.newDocumentBuilder();
            Document doc = builder.parse(new File(args[0]));

            // Serialize the DOM tree
            DOMSerializer serializer = new DOMSerializer();
            serializer.serialize(doc, System.out);

        } catch (ParserConfigurationException e) {
            System.out.println("The underlying parser does not " +
                "support the requested features.");
```

Example 9-3. Using the DocumentBuilderFactory class (continued)

```
        } catch (FactoryConfigurationError e) {
            System.out.println("Error occurred obtaining Document " +
                "Builder Factory.");
        } catch (Exception e) {
            e.printStackTrace();
        }
    }
}
```

Two problems can arise from this code: a `FactoryConfigurationError` and a `ParserConfigurationException`. The cause of each is the same as it was in SAX. Either there's a problem present in the implementation classes (`FactoryConfigurationError`), or the parser provided doesn't support the requested features (`ParserConfigurationException`). The only difference between DOM and SAX is that with DOM, you substitute `DocumentBuilderFactory` for `SAXParserFactory`, and `DocumentBuilder` for `SAXParser`.

Working with the DOM parser

Once you have a DOM factory, you can obtain a `DocumentBuilder` instance from it. The methods available to a `DocumentBuilder` instance are very similar to those available to its SAX counterpart. The major difference is that variations of the `parse()` method do not take an instance of the SAX `HandlerBase` class. Instead they return a DOM `Document` instance representing the XML document that was parsed. The only other difference is that two methods are provided for SAX-like functionality: `setErrorHandler()`, which takes a SAX `ErrorHandler` implementation to handle problems that may arise in parsing, and `setEntityResolver()`, which takes a SAX `EntityResolver` implementation to handle entity resolution. Example 9-4 shows examples of these methods in action.

Example 9-4. Using the JAXP DocumentBuilder

```
// Get a DocumentBuilder instance
DocumentBuilder builder = builderFactory.newDocumentBuilder();

// Find out if validation is supported
boolean isValidating = builder.isValidating();

// Find out if namespaces is supported
boolean isNamespaceAware = builder.isNamespaceAware();

// Set a SAX ErrorHandler
builder.setErrorHandler(myErrorHandlerImpl);

// Set a SAX EntityResolver
builder.setEntityResolver(myEntityResolverImpl);
```

Example 9-4. Using the JAXP DocumentBuilder (continued)

```
// ------------ Parse, in a variety of ways ------------------- //

// Use a file
Document doc = builder.parse(new File(args[0]));

// Use a SAX InputSource
Document doc = builder.parse(mySaxInputSource);

// Use an InputStream
Document doc = builder.parse(myInputStream, myHandlerBaseInstance);

// Use a URI
Document doc = builder.parse("http://www.newInstance.com/xml/doc.xml");
```

It really is that straightforward to take what you've learned about SAX and apply it to DOM. So make your bar bets with friends and coworkers on how using JAXP is a piece of cake; you'll win every time.

Changing the Parser

The last topic I need to address in dealing with JAXP is the ability to easily change out the parser used by the factory classes. Changing the parser used by JAXP actually means changing the parser factory, because all `SAXParser` and `DocumentBuilder` instances come from these factories. Since the factories determine which parser is loaded, it's the factories that must change. The implementation of `SAXParserFactory` to be used can be changed by setting the Java system property `javax.xml.parsers.SAXParserFactory`. If this property isn't defined, then the default implementation (whatever parser your vendor specified) is returned. The same principle applies for the `DocumentBuilderFactory` implementation you use. In this case, the `javax.xml.parsers.DocumentBuilder-Factory` system property is queried. And as simple as that, we have gone through it all! This is the whole scope of JAXP 1.0: provide hooks into SAX, provide hooks into DOM, and allow the parser to easily be changed out.

JAXP 1.1

Late in 2000, the expert group for JAXP 1.1 formed, and work got underway to move JAXP 1.0 to a better, more effective solution for parsing and handling XML documents. As I write this chapter, JAXP 1.1 has just become downloadable in a final form from Sun's web site at *http://java.sun.com/xml*. Many of the changes to the API center around parsing, which makes sense, given that the "P" in JAXP stands for "parsing." But the most significant changes in JAXP 1.1 center around XML transformations, which I cover in the last part of this chapter. In terms of additions to 1.0 functionality, the changes are fairly minor. The biggest addition is support for SAX 2.0, which went final in May of 2000, and DOM Level 2, which was finalized in November of 2000. Remember that JAXP 1.0 supported only SAX 1.0 and DOM Level 1. This lack of updated standards has been one of the biggest criticisms of JAXP 1.0, and is probably why the 1.1 version has appeared so quickly.

In addition to updating JAXP to the newest versions of SAX and DOM, several small changes have been made in the API feature list. Almost all of these changes are the result of feedback from the various companies and individuals on the JAXP expert group. These changes also all deal with configuring the parsers returned from JAXP's two factories, `SAXParserFactory` and `Document-BuilderFactory`. I cover these now, as well as the update in standards support for SAX and DOM, and then we look at the new TrAX API that is part of JAXP 1.1.

Updating the Standards

The most anticipated change from JAXP 1.0 to 1.1 is the updated support for the SAX and DOM standards. Of critical note is that SAX 2.0 handles namespaces, while SAX 1.0 did not.* This namespace support enables the use of numerous other XML vocabularies, such as XML Schema, XLink, and XPointer. While it was possible to use these vocabularies in SAX 1.0, the burden was on the developer to split an element's local (or qualified) name from its namespace, and keep track of namespaces throughout the document. SAX 2.0 provides this information to the developer, dramatically simplifying these programming tasks. The same goes for DOM Level 2: namespace support, as well as a wealth of other methods on the DOM classes, is available.

The good news is that these changes are generally transparent to the developer using JAXP. In other words, standards updates happen somewhat "automatically," without user intervention. Simply specifying a SAX 2.0–compliant parser to the `SAXParserFactory` and a DOM Level 2–compliant parser to the `DocumentBuilderFactory` class takes care of the update in functionality.

The road to SAX 2.0

There are a few significant changes related to these standards updates, particularly with regard to SAX. In SAX 1.0, the parser interface implemented by vendors and XML parser projects was `org.xml.sax.Parser`. The JAXP class `SAXParser`,

---

* Careful readers will note that JAXP 1.0 offered namespace processing through the `setNamespaceAware()` methods on `SAXParserFactory` and `DocumentBuilderFactory`. The JAXP code had to do this task "by hand" instead of relying on the SAX or DOM APIs. With SAX 2.0 and DOM Level 2, this process is standardized, and therefore much more reliable, as well as cleaner, than the JAXP 1.0 implementation. It's a good thing.

then, provided a method to get this underlying implementation class through the getParser() method. The signature for that method looks like this:

```
public interface SAXParser {

    public org.xml.sax.Parser getParser();

    // Other methods
}
```

However, in the change from SAX 1.0 to 2.0, the Parser interface was deprecated and replaced with a new interface, org.xml.sax.XMLReader (the one that you are familiar with from earlier chapters). This made the getParser() method useless for obtaining an instance of the SAX 2.0 XMLReader class. To support this new interface, a new method has been added to the JAXP SAXParser class. Not surprisingly, this method is named getXMLReader() and looks like:

```
public interface SAXParser {

    public org.xml.sax.XMLReader getXMLReader();

    public org.xml.sax.Parser getParser();

    // Other methods
}
```

In the same way, JAXP 1.0 used the parse() method by supplying an instance of the HandlerBase class (or a subclass, to be more accurate). Of course in SAX 2.0, the HandlerBase class has been replaced by DefaultHandler. To accommodate this change, all of the parse() methods on the SAXParser class have been complemented with versions of the same method that take an instance of the DefaultHandler class to support SAX 2.0. To help you see this difference, take a look at Example 9-5, which shows a good chunk of the SAXParser interface.

Example 9-5. The parse( ) methods of the SAXParser interface

```
public interface SAXParser {

    // The SAX 1.0 parse methods
    public void parse(File file, HandlerBase handlerBase);
    public void parse(InputSource inputSource, HandlerBase handlerBase);
    public void parse(InputStream inputStream, HandlerBase handlerBase);
    public void parse(InputStream inputStream, HandlerBase handlerBase,
                      String systemID);
    public void parse(String uri, HandlerBase handlerBase);

    // The SAX 2.0 parse methods
    public void parse(File file, DefaultHandler defaultHandler);
```

Example 9-5. The parse( ) methods of the SAXParser interface (continued)

```
public void parse(InputSource inputSource,
                  DefaultHandler defaultHandler);
public void parse(InputStream inputStream,
                  DefaultHandler defaultHandler);
public void parse(InputStream inputStream,
                  DefaultHandler defaultHandler,
                  String systemID);
public void parse(String uri, DefaultHandler defaultHandler);

// Other methods

}
```

All these methods for parsing may seem a bit confusing, but it's only tricky if you're working with *both* versions of SAX. If you are using SAX 1.0, you'll be working with the `Parser` interface and `HandlerBase` class, and it will be obvious which methods to use. Similarly, when using SAX 2.0, it will be obvious that the methods that accept `DefaultHandler` instances and return `XMLReader` instances should be used. So take all this as a reference and don't worry too much about it! There are some other changes to the SAX portion of the API, as well.

Changes in SAX classes

To complete the discussion of the changes to existing JAXP functionality, I need to go over a few new methods that are available to JAXP SAX users. First, the `SAXParserFactory` class has a new method, `setFeature()`. As you recall from JAXP 1.0, the `SAXParserFactory` class allows configuration of `SAXParser` instances returned from the factory. In addition to the methods already available in 1.0 (`setValidating()` and `setNamespaceAware()`), this new method allows SAX 2.0 features to be requested for new parser instances. For example, a user may request the *http://apache.org/xml/features/validation/schema* feature, which allows XML Schema validation to be turned on or off. This can now be performed directly on a `SAXParserFactory`, as shown here:

```
SAXParserFactory myFactory = SAXParserFactory.newInstance();

// Turn on XML Schema validation
myFactory.setFeature(
    "http://apache.org/xml/features/validation/schema", true);

// Now get an instance of the parser with schema validation enabled
SAXParser parser = myFactory.newSAXParser();
```

A `getFeature()` method is provided to complement the `setFeature()` method and allow querying of particular features. This method returns a simple `boolean` value.

In addition to providing a means to set SAX features (with true or false values), JAXP 1.1 supports the setting of SAX properties (with object values). For example, using an instance of a SAX parser, you could set the property *http://xml.org/ sax/properties/lexical-handler*, assigning that property an implementation of a SAX LexicalHandler interface. Because properties like this lexical one are parser-specific instead of factory-specific (as features were), a setProperty() method is provided on the JAXP SAXParser class rather than on the SAXParserFactory class. And as with features, a getProperty() complement is provided to return the value associated with a specific property, also on the SAXParser class.

Updates to the DOM

A number of new methods are available for the DOM portion of JAXP, as well. These methods have been added to existing JAXP classes to support both DOM Level 2 options, as well as common configuration situations that have arisen in the last year. I won't cover all of these options and the corresponding methods here since many are used only in very unusual situations and won't be needed in most of your applications. I encourage you to check these out in the latest JAXP specification. With the coverage of standards updates, SAX changes, and additional DOM methods, you're ready to read about the most substantial change in JAXP 1.1: the TrAX API.

The TrAX API

So far, I've covered the changes to XML parsing in JAXP. Now I can turn to XML transformations in JAXP 1.1. Perhaps the most exciting development in the newest version of Sun's API is that JAXP 1.1 allows vendor-neutral XML document transformations. While this vendor-neutrality may cloud the definition of JAXP as simply a parsing API, it is a much-needed facility since XSL processors currently employ different methods and means for enabling user and developer interaction. In fact, XSL processors have even greater variance across providers than their XML parser counterparts.

Originally, the JAXP expert group sought to provide a simple Transform class with a few methods to allow specification of a stylesheet and subsequent document transformations. This first effort turned out to be rather shaky, but I'm happy to report that we (the JAXP expert group) are going much further in our continued efforts. Scott Boag and Michael Kay, two of the XSL processor gurus (working on Apache Xalan and SAXON, respectively), have worked with many others to develop TrAX, which supports a much wider array of options and features, and provides complete support for almost all XML transformations—all under the JAXP umbrella. The result is the addition of the `javax.xml.transform` package, and a few subpackages, to the JAXP API.

Like the parsing portion of JAXP, performing XML transformations requires three basic steps:

- Obtain a `Transformer` factory
- Retrieve a `Transformer`
- Perform operations (transformations)

Working with the factory

For the transformation portion of JAXP, the factory you will work with is represented by the class `javax.xml.transform.TransformerFactory`. This class is analogous to the `SAXParserFactory` and `DocumentBuilderFactory` classes that I already covered in both the JAXP 1.0 and 1.1 sections. Of course, simply obtaining a factory instance to work with is a piece of cake:

```
TransformerFactory factory = TransformerFactory.newInstance();
```

Nothing special here, just basic factory design principles at work, in conjunction with a singleton pattern.

Once the factory is available, various options can be set upon the factory. Those options will affect all instances of `Transformer` (which is covered in a minute) created by that factory. You can also obtain instances of `javax.xml.transform.Templates` through the `TransformerFactory`. Templates are an advanced JAXP/TrAX concept, and covered at the end of the chapter.

The first of the options you can work with are *attributes*. These are not XML attributes, but are similar to the properties used in SAX. Attributes allow options to be passed to the underlying XSL processor, which may be Apache Xalan, SAXON, or Oracle's XSL processor (or, theoretically, any TrAX-compliant processor). They are largely vendor-dependent, though. Like the parsing side of JAXP, a `setAttribute()` method is provided as well as a counterpart, `getAttribute()`. Also like `setProperty()`, the mutator method (`setAttribute()`) takes an attribute name and `Object` value. And like `getProperty()`, the accessor method (`getAttribute()`) takes an attribute name and returns the associated `Object` value.

Setting an `ErrorListener` is the second option available. Defined in the `javax.xml.transform.ErrorListener` interface, an `ErrorListener` allows problems in transformation to be caught and handled programmatically. If this sounds like `org.xml.sax.ErrorHandler`, it is very similar. Example 9-6 shows this interface.

Example 9-6. The ErrorListener interface

```
package javax.xml.transform;

public interface ErrorListener {
    public void warning(TransformerException exception)
        throws TransformerException;
    public void error(TransformerException exception)
        throws TransformerException;
    public void fatalError(TransformerException exception)
        throws TransformerException;
}
```

Creating an implementation of this interface, filling the three callback methods, and using the `setErrorListener()` method on the `TransformerFactory` instance you are working with sets you up to deal with any errors that occur during transformation.

Finally, a method is provided to set and retrieve the URI resolver for the instances generated by the factory. The interface defined in `javax.xml.transform.URIResolver` also behaves similarly to a SAX counterpart, `org.xml.sax.EntityResolver`. The interface has a single method, shown in Example 9-7.

Example 9-7. The URIResolver interface

```
package javax.xml.transform;

public interface URIResolver {
    public Source resolve(String href, String base)
        throws TransformerException;
}
```

This interface, when implemented, allows URIs found in XSL constructs like `xsl:import` and `xsl:include` to be handled. Returning a `Source` (which I'll cover in a moment), you can instruct your transformer to search for the specified document in various locations when a particular URI is encountered. For example, when an include of the URI *http://www.oreilly.com/oreilly.xsl* is encountered, you might instead return the local document *alternateOreilly.xsl* and prevent the need for network access. Implementations of the `URIResolver` interface can be set using the `TransformerFactory`'s `setURIResolver()` method, and retrieved using the `getURIResolver()` method.

Finally, once you set the options of your choice, you can obtain an instance, or instances, of a `Transformer` through the `newTransformer()` method of the factory, as shown here:

```
// Get the factory
TransformerFactory factory = TransformerFactory.newInstance();
```

```
// Configure the factory
factory.setErrorResolver(myErrorResolver);
factory.setURIResolver(myURIResolver);

// Get a Transformer to work with, with the options specified
Transformer transformer =
    factory.newTransformer(new StreamSource("foundation.xsl"));
```

As you can see, this method takes the stylesheet as input to use in all transformations for that `Transformer` instance. In other words, if you wanted to transform a document using stylesheet A and stylesheet B, you would need two `Transformer` instances, one for each stylesheet. If you wanted to transform multiple documents with the same stylesheet (call it stylesheet C), however, you would need only a single `Transformer` instance, associated with stylesheet C. Don't worry about the `StreamSource` class; that's coming next.

Transforming XML

Once you have an instance of a `Transformer`, you can go about actually performing XML transformations. This consists of two basic steps:

* Set the XSL stylesheet to use

* Perform the transformation, specifying the XML document and result target

As I have demonstrated, the first step is really the easiest. A stylesheet can be supplied when obtaining a `Transformer` instance from the factory. The location of this stylesheet must be specified by providing a `javax.xml.transform.Source` instance (actually an instance of an implementation of the `Source` interface) for its location. The `Source` interface, which you've seen in a few code samples, is the means of locating an input, be it a stylesheet, document, or other information set. TrAX provides the `Source` interface and three concrete implementations:

* `javax.xml.transform.stream.StreamSource`

* `javax.xml.transform.dom.DOMSource`

* `javax.xml.transform.sax.SAXSource`

The first of these, `StreamSource`, reads input from some type of I/O device. Constructors are provided for accepting an `InputStream`, a `Reader`, or a `String` system ID as input. Once created, the `StreamSource` can be passed to the `Transformer` for use. This will probably be the `Source` implementation you use most commonly in programs. It's great for reading a document from a network, input stream, user input, or other static representation of XSL stylesheets.

The next `Source` implementation, `DOMSource`, provides for reading from an existing DOM tree. It provides a constructor for taking in a DOM `org.w3c.dom.Node`, and will read from that `Node` when used. This is ideal for supplying an existing

DOM tree to a transformation, perhaps if parsing has already occurred and an XML document is already in memory as a DOM structure, or if you've built a DOM tree programmatically.

SAXSource provides for reading input from SAX producers. This Source implementation takes either a SAX org.xml.sax.InputSource, or an org.xml.sax. XMLReader as input, and uses the events from these sources. This is ideal for situations in which a SAX content handler is already in use, and callbacks are set up and need to be triggered prior to transformations.

Once you've obtained an instance of a Transformer (by providing the stylesheet to use through an appropriate Source), you're ready to perform a transformation. The transform() method is used as shown here:

```
// Get the factory
TransformerFactory factory = TransformerFactory.newInstance();

// Configure the factory
factory.setErrorResolver(myErrorResolver);
factory.setURIResolver(myURIResolver);

// Get a Transformer to work with, with the options specified
Transformer transformer =
    factory.newTransformer(new StreamSource("foundation.xsl"));

// Perform transformation on myDocument, and print out result
transfomer.transform(new StreamSource("asimov.xml"),
                     new StreamResult("results.xml"));
```

The transform() method takes two arguments: a Source implementation, and a javax.xml.transform.Result implementation. You should already be seeing the symmetry in how this works and have an idea about the functionality within the Result interface. The Source provides the XML document to be transformed, and the Result provides an output target for the transformation. Like Source, there are three concrete implementations of the Result interface provided with TrAX and JAXP:

* javax.xml.transform.stream.StreamResult

* javax.xml.transform.dom.DOMResult

* javax.xml.transform.sax.SAXResult

The StreamResult class takes as a construction mechanism either an OutputStream (like System.out for easy debugging!), a Java File, a String system ID, or a Writer. DOMResult takes a DOM Node to output the transformation to (presumably as a DOM org.w3c.dom.Document), and SAXResult takes a SAX ContentHandler instance to fire callbacks to, resulting from the transformed XML. All are analogous to their Source counterparts.

While the previous example shows transforming from a stream to a stream, any combination of sources and results is possible. Here are a few examples:

```
// Perform transformation on jordan.xml, and print out result
transformer.transform(new StreamSource("jordan.xml"),
                    new StreamResult(System.out));

// Transform from SAX and output results to a DOM Node
transformer.transform(new SAXSource(
                    new InputSource(
                        "http://www.oreilly.com/catalog.xml")),
                    new DOMResult(DocumentBuilder.newDocument()));

// Transform from DOM and output to a File
transformer.transform(new DOMSource(domTree),
                    new StreamResult(
                        new FileOutputStream("results.xml")));

// Use a custom source and result (JDOM)
transformer.transform(new org.jdom.trax.JDOMSource(myJdomDocument),
                    new org.jdom.trax.JDOMResult(
                        new org.jdom.Document()));
```

TrAX provides tremendous flexibility in moving from various input types to various output types, and in using XSL stylesheets in a variety of formats, such as files, in-memory DOM trees, SAX readers, and so on.

Odds and ends

Before closing shop on JAXP, there are a few bits and pieces of TrAX I haven't yet talked about. I won't treat these completely, as they are less commonly used, but I will touch on them briefly. First, TrAX introduces an interface called SourceLocator, also in the javax.xml.transform package. This class functions for transformations exactly as the Locator class did for SAX parsing: it supplies information about where action is occurring. Most commonly used for error reporting, the interface looks like this:

```
package javax.xml.transform;

public interface SourceLocator {
    public int getColumnNumber();
    public int getLineNumber();
    public String getPublicId();
    public String getSystemId();
}
```

I won't comment much on this interface, as it's pretty self-explanatory. However, you should know that in the javax.xml.transform.dom package, there is a sub-interface called DOMLocator. This interface adds the getOriginatingNode()

method, which returns the DOM node being processed. This makes error handling quite easy when working with a DOMSource, and is useful in applications that work with DOM trees.

TrAX also provides a concrete class, javax.xml.transform.OutputKeys, which defines several constants for use in output properties for transformations. These constants can then be used for setting properties on a Transformer or a Templates object. That leads me to the last subject dealing with TrAX.

The Templates interface in TrAX is used when a set of output properties is desired across multiple transformations, or when a set of transformation instructions can be used repeatedly. By supplying a Source to a TransformerFactory's newTemplates() method, you get an instance of the Templates object:

```
// Get a factory
TransformerFactory factory = TransformerFactory.newInstance();

// Get a Templates object
Templates template = factory.newTemplates(new StreamSource("html.xsl"));
```

At this point, the template object would be a compiled representation of the transformation detailed in *html.xsl* (in this example, a stylesheet that converts XML to HTML). By using a Templates object, transformations can be performed from this template across threads, and you also get some optimizations, because instructions are precompiled. Once you have gone that far, you need to generate a Transformer, but from the Templates object, rather than the factory:

```
// Get a transformer
Transformer transformer = template.newTransformer();

// Transform
transformer.transform(new DOMSource(orderForm),
                      new StreamResult(res.getOutputStream()));
```

Here, there is no need to supply a Source to the newTransformer() method, as the transformer is simply a set of (already) compiled instructions. From there, it's business as usual. In this example, a DOM tree that represents an order form is supplied to the transformation, processed using the *html.xsl* stylesheet, and then sent to a servlet's output stream for display. Pretty slick, huh? As a general rule, if you are going to use a stylesheet more than twice, use a Templates object; it will pay off in performance. Additionally, anytime you are dealing with threads, Templates are the only way to go.

Gotcha!

The API chapters wouldn't be complete without letting you know about some problems that I frequently run into or that I'm asked about. Hopefully they'll help save you some time, and maybe make your code more bug-proof. Read on, and see where JAXP catches folks these days.

Default Parsers and JAXP Implementations

It's worth saying again: the implementation of JAXP determines the default parser. If you switch the JAXP implementation, you often end up switching the parser that is used, if you haven't set any system properties for JAXP. Your classpath may have to change, or you will get all sorts of `ClassNotFoundExceptions`.

To avoid this problem completely, you could simply set the relevant JAXP system property to the parser factory you want to use, and regardless of what implementation you choose, you'll get expected behavior. Or better yet, put a *jaxp.properties* file in the *lib* directory of your Java installation.* This file can be as simple as this:

```
javax.xml.parsers.SAXParserFactoryorg.apache.xerces.XercesFactory
```

By changing the factory implementation, you change the parser wrapper that is returned from calls to `newSAXParser()`. And lest you try the example file given, the `org.apache.xerces.XercesFactory` class doesn't exist; it's just for example purposes. It happened to fit within the confines of the code block!

Features on Factories, Properties on Parsers

One common mistake is to mix up factories and properties in the JAXP world. The best way to remember the correct application is to memorize the phrase "features on factories, properties on parsers." You would be amazed at the number of mails I get insisting that the sender has a "corrupt" version of JAXP, because the following code won't compile:

```
SAXParserFactory factory = SAXParserFactory.newInstance();
factory.setProperty(
    "http://apache.org/xml/properties/dom/document-class-name",
    "org.apache.xerces.dom.DocumentImpl");
```

Of course, this is a property, and therefore must be set on a `SAXParser` instance, not a `SAXParserFactory` instance. The reverse, of course, holds true for setting features on parsers:

```
SAXParser parser = factory.newSAXParser();
parser.setFeature("http://xml.org/sax/features/namespaces", true);
```

---

* This option assumes that you have set the `JAVA_HOME` environment variable to the installation directory of your JDK. It assumes that because it's a good, if not mandatory, practice and will help you out in the long term. JAXP looks, in actuality, for `%JAVA_HOME%/lib/jaxp.properties`.

In either case, it is user error, not a strange download problem where all but a few methods came across OK (I generally refer these people to some good books on I/O). This is also a good case of the Javadocs not being used when they should. I'm a firm believer in the value of Javadoc.

What's Next?

Because JAXP is an abstraction layer on top of the APIs already discussed in the earlier chapters, there's no need to go into "Advanced JAXP." Additionally, the JAXP concepts are simple enough to not warrant an additional chapter. With this tour through the various "low-level" Java and XML APIs, you should have all the hammers and wrenches needed for your XML programming.

However, there's certainly more to XML than low-level APIs these days. In addition to vertical applications of XML, there are a number of high-level APIs coming out that build on top of the concepts (and APIs) in the first half of this book to provide more convenience to the developer. These more specific concepts and programming tools are the backbone of the second half of this book. I'll begin the discussion in Chapter 10 by talking about presentation frameworks, something that provides a lot of eye candy on top of XML. Read on, and we'll all be graphic designers for a chapter or so.

10

Web Publishing Frameworks

This chapter begins our examination of specific Java and XML topics. I have covered the basics of using XML from Java, looking at the SAX, DOM, JDOM, and JAXP APIs to manipulate XML, and the fundamentals of using and creating XML itself. Now that you have a grasp on using XML from your code, I want to spend time on specific applications. The next six chapters cover the most significant applications of XML, and, in particular, how those applications are implemented in the Java space. While there are literally thousands of important applications of XML, the topics in these chapters are those continually in the spotlight, with the potential to significantly change the way traditional development processes occur.

The More Things Change, the More They Stay the Same

Readers of the first edition will find that much of the Cocoon discussion in this chapter is the same. Although I promised Cocoon 2 would be out by now and expected to be writing a chapter on it, things haven't progressed as quickly as expected. Stefano Mazzochi, the driving force behind Cocoon, finally got around to finishing school (good choice, Stefano!), and development on Cocoon 2 slowed as a result. Cocoon 1.x is still the current development path, so stick with it for now. I've updated the section on Cocoon 2 to reflect what is coming. Keep an eye out for more Cocoon-related books from O'Reilly in the months to come.

The first hot topic I look at is the XML application that has generated the most excitement in the XML and Java communities: the web publishing framework. Although I have continually emphasized that generating presentation from content is perhaps overhyped compared to the value of the portable data that XML provides, using XML for presentation styling is still very important. This importance increases when looking at web-based applications.

Virtually every major application I can find is either completely web-based or at least has a web frontend. At the same time, users are demanding more functionality, and marketing departments are demanding more flexibility in look and feel. The result has been the rise of the web artist; this new role is different from the webmaster in that little to no Perl, ASP, JavaScript, or other scripting language coding is part of the job description. The web artist's entire day is comprised of HTML and WML creation, modification, and development.* The rapid changes in business and market strategy can require a complete application or site overhaul as often as once a week, often forcing the web artist to spend days changing hundreds of HTML pages. While Cascading Style Sheets (CSS) have helped, the difficulty of maintaining consistency across these pages requires a huge amount of time. Even if this less-than-ideal situation were acceptable, no computer developer wants to spend his or her life making markup language changes to web pages.

With the advent of server-side Java, the problem has only grown. Servlet developers find themselves spending long hours modifying their `out.println()` statements to output HTML, and often glance hatefully at the marketing department when changes to a site's look require modifications to their code. The entire Java Server Pages (JSP) specification arguably stemmed from this situation; however, JSP is not a solution, as it only shifts the frustration to the content author, who constantly has to avoid making incidental changes to embedded Java code. In addition, JSP does not provide the clean separation between content and presentation it promises. A means to generate pure data content was called for, as well as a means to have that content uniformly styled either at predetermined times (*static content generation*) or dynamically at runtime (*dynamic content generation*).

Of course, you may be nodding your head at this familiar problem if you have ever done any web development, and hopefully your mind is wandering into the XSL and XSLT technology space. The problem is that an engine must exist to handle content generation, particularly in the dynamic sense. Having hundreds of XML documents on a site does no good if there is no mechanism to apply transformations on request. Add the need for servlets and other server-side components to output XML that should be consistently styled, and you have defined a small set of requirements for the web publishing framework. In this chapter, I take a look at this framework, how it allows you to avoid long hours of HTML coding, and how it helps you convert all of those "web artists" into XML and XSL gurus, allowing applications to change look and feel as often as desired.

---

* "HTML and WML" includes the tangential technologies used with the markup language. These complementary technologies, like Flash and Shockwave, are not trivial, so I'm by no means belittling these content authors.

A web publishing framework attempts to address these complicated issues. Just as a web server is responsible for responding to a URL request for a file, a web publishing framework is responsible for responding to a similar request; however, instead of responding with a file, it often will respond with a *published* version of a file. In this case, a published file refers to a file that may have been transformed with XSLT, massaged at an application level, or converted into another format such as a PDF. The requestor does not see the raw data that may underlie the published result, but also does not have to explicitly request that publication occur. Often, a URI base (such as *http://yourHost.com/publish*) signifies that a publishing engine that sits on top of the web server should handle requests. As you may suspect, the concept is much simpler than the actual implementation of a framework like this, and finding the correct framework for your needs is not a trivial task.

Selecting a Framework

You might expect to find a list of hundreds of possible solutions. As you've seen, the Java language offers an easy interface into XML through several APIs. Additionally, Java servlets offer a simple means of handling web requests and responses. However, the list of frameworks is small, and the list of good, stable ones is even smaller. One of the best resources for seeing what products are currently available is XML Software's list at *http://xmlsoftware.com/publishing/*. This list changes so frequently that it is not worth repeating here. Still, some important criteria for determining what framework is right for you are worth mentioning.

Stability

Don't be surprised if you (still!) have a hard time finding a product whose version tag is greater than 2.x. In fact, you may have to search diligently to even find a second-generation framework. While a higher version number is not a guarantee of stability, it often reflects the amount of time, effort, and review that a framework has undergone. The XML publishing system is such a new beast that the market has been flooded with 1.0 and 1.1 products that simply are not stable enough for practical use.

You can often ascertain the stability of a product by investigating other products from the same vendor. Often a vendor releases an entire suite of tools; if their other tools do not offer SAX 2.0 and DOM Level 2 support, or are all also 1.0 and 1.1 products, you might be wise to pass on the framework until it has matured and conformed to newer XML standards. Try to steer away from platform-specific technologies. If the framework is tied to a platform (such as Windows, or even a specific flavor of Unix), you aren't dealing with a pure Java solution. Remember that a publishing framework must serve clients on any platform; why use a product that can't run on any platform?

Integration with Other XML Tools and APIs

Once you know your framework is stable enough for your needs, make sure it supports a variety of XML parsers and processors. If your framework is tied to a specific parser or processor, you will be limited to one specific implementation of a technology. This is a bad thing. Although frameworks often integrate well with a particular parser vendor, determine if parsers can be interchanged. If you have a favorite processor (or one left to you from previous projects), make sure it can still be used.

Support for SAX and DOM is a must, and many frameworks now support JDOM and JAXP as well. Even if you have a favorite API, the more options you have, the better! Also, try to find a framework whose developers are monitoring the specifications of XML Schema, XLink, XPointer, and other XML vocabularies. This will indicate if you can expect to see revisions of the framework that add support for these XML specifications, an important indication of the framework's longevity. Don't be afraid to ask questions about how quickly new specifications are expected to be integrated into the product, and insist on a firm answer.

Production Presence

The last and perhaps most important question to answer when looking for a web publishing framework is whether it is used in production applications. If you aren't supplied with at least a few reference applications or sites that are using the framework, don't be surprised if there aren't any. Vendors (and developers, in the open source realm) should be happy and proud to let you know where to check out their frameworks in action. Hesitance in this area is a sign that you may be more of a pioneer with a product than you wish to be. For example, Apache Cocoon provides just such a list online, at *http://xml.apache.org/cocoon/livesites.html*.

Making the Decision

Once you have evaluated these criteria, you will probably have a clear choice. Very few frameworks can positively answer all the questions raised here, not to mention your application-specific concerns. In fact, as of July 2001, less than ten publishing frameworks exist that support the latest versions of SAX (Version 2.0), DOM (Level 2), and JAXP (Version 1.1) are in production use at even one application site, and have at least three significant revisions of code under their belt. These are not listed here because, honestly, in six months they may not exist, or may be radically changed. The world of web publishing frameworks is in such flux that trying to recommend four or five options and assuming they will be in existence months from now has a greater chance of misleading you than helping you.

However, one publishing framework has been consistently successful within the Java and XML community. When considering the open source community in particular, this framework is often the choice of Java developers. The Apache Cocoon project, founded by Stefano Mazzocchi, has been a solid framework since its inception. Developed while most of us were still trying to figure out what XML was, Cocoon is now entering its second generation as an XML publishing framework based completely in Java. It also is part of the Apache XML project, and has default support for Apache Xerces and Apache Xalan. It allows any conformant XML parser to be used, and is based on the immensely popular Java servlet architecture. In addition, there are several production sites using Apache Cocoon (in its 1.x form) that push the boundaries of traditional web application development yet still perform extremely well. For this reason, and again in keeping with the spirit of open source software, I use Apache Cocoon as the framework of choice in this chapter.

In previous chapters, the choice of XML parser and processor was fairly open; in other words, examples would work on different vendor implementations with only small modifications to code. However, the web publishing framework is not standardized, and each framework implements wildly different features and conventions. For this reason, the examples in this chapter using Apache Cocoon are not portable; however, the popularity of the concepts and design patterns used within Cocoon do merit an entire chapter. If you do not choose Cocoon, at least look over the examples. The concepts in web publishing are usable across any vendor implementation, even if the specifics of the code are not.

Installation

In other chapters, installation instructions generally involved pointing you at a web site where you could obtain a distribution of the software and letting you add the included *jar* file to your classpath. Installing a framework such as Cocoon is not quite as simple, and the procedures are documented here. Additionally, Cocoon has instructions online for various other servlet engines; check these out at *http://xml.apache.org/cocoon/install.html*.

Source Code or Binaries

The first thing you need to do is decide if you want the source code or binaries for Cocoon. This decision actually can be boiled down even further: do you want the very latest features, or the most reliable build? If you are a hardcore developer who wants to dig into Cocoon, you should get a copy of CVS and pull the latest Cocoon source code from the *xml.apache.org* CVS repository. Rather than detail this process, as it probably involves the minority of you, I'll simply refer you to the *CVS Pocket Reference* by Gregor Purdy (O'Reilly). This will get you set up, in concert with the instructions online at *http://xml.apache.org/cvs.html*.

For those interested in trying Cocoon out or actually running it in production, download the latest Cocoon binary from *http://xml.apache.org/cocoon/dist*. As I write, the latest version, 1.8.2, is available for Windows (*Cocoon-1.8.2.zip*) and Linux/Unix (*Cocoon-1.8.2.tar.gz*). Once you download the archive, expand it to a temporary directory that you can work with. The most important thing to note here is the *lib/* directory that's created. This directory includes all of the libraries needed to run Cocoon using your servlet engine.

NOTE   If you don't have a *lib/* directory, or if it doesn't contain several *jar* files within it, you may have an older version of Cocoon. It's only in the newer releases (1.8 and up) that the download contains these libraries (which make life significantly easier, by the way!).

Configuring the Servlet Engine

Once you have built Cocoon, configure your servlet engine to use Cocoon and tell it which requests Cocoon should handle. I'll look at setting up Cocoon to work with the Jakarta Tomcat servlet engine here; as this is the reference implementation for the Java Servlet API (Version 2.2), you should be able to mimic these steps for your own servlet engine if you are not using the Tomcat implementation.

The first step is to copy all of the libraries needed for Cocoon at runtime into Tomcat's library directory. This is located at *TOMCAT_HOME/lib*, where *TOMCAT_HOME* is the directory of your Tomcat installation. On my Windows machine, this is *c:\java\jakarta-tomcat*, and on Linux it's */usr/local/jakarta-tomcat*. However, this does not mean simply copy everything in Cocoon's *lib/* directory over (unless you want to); the required *jar* files needed at runtime are:

- *bsfengines.jar* (Bean Scripting Framework)
- *bsf.jar* (Bean Scripting Framework)
- *fop_0_15_0.jar* (FOP)
- *sax-bugfix.jar* (SAX fixes to error handling)
- *turbine-pool.jar* (Turbine)
- *w3c.jar* (W3C)
- *xalan_1_2_D02.jar* (Xalan)
- *xerces_1_2.jar* (Xerces)

Additionally, copy Cocoon's *bin/cocoon.jar* file into this same directory (*TOMCAT_HOME/lib*). At that point, you'll have all the libraries needed to run Cocoon.

The latest versions of Tomcat (I'm using 3.2.1) automatically load all libraries in the Tomcat *lib/* directory, which means you don't have to mess with the classpath. If you are using a servlet engine that doesn't support this automatic loading, add each *jar* to the servlet engine's classpath.

Once the required libraries are in place, let the servlet engine know which context to run Cocoon under. This essentially tells the servlet engine where to look for files requested through the Cocoon engine. This is handled by modifying the *server.xml* file, located in Tomcat's *conf/* directory. Add the following directive in at the end of the file, within the `ContextManager` element:

```
<Server>
  <!-- Other Server elements -->

  <ContextManager>
    <!-- Other Context directives -->

    <Context path="/cocoon"
             docBase="webapps/cocoon"
             debug="0"
             reloadable="true" >
    </Context>
  </ContextManager>
</Server>
```

In other words, requests based on the URI */cocoon* (such as */cocoon/index.xml*) should be mapped to the context within the specified directory (*webapps/cocoon*). Of course, you'll need to create the directories for the context you've just defined. So add a *cocoon* and *cocoon/WEB-INF* directory to Tomcat's *webapps* directory. You should have a directory structure similar to Figure 10-1.

With this setup, you'll need to copy a few files from the Cocoon distribution into the context. Copy Cocoon's *conf/cocoon.properties* and *src/WEB-INF/web.xml* files into the *TOMCAT_HOME/webapps/cocoon/WEB-INF/* directory. Once this is in place, you only need to modify the *web.xml* file that you just copied. Change the reference in it to point to the *cocoon.properties* file you just copied over:

```
<web-app>
 <servlet>
  <servlet-name>org.apache.cocoon.Cocoon</servlet-name>
  <servlet-class>org.apache.cocoon.Cocoon</servlet-class>
  <init-param>
   <param-name>properties</param-name>
   <param-value>WEB-INF/cocoon.properties</param-value>
  </init-param>
 </servlet>

 <servlet-mapping>
  <servlet-name>org.apache.cocoon.Cocoon</servlet-name>
  <url-pattern>*.xml</url-pattern>
 </servlet-mapping>
</web-app>
```

At this point, you have one last, rather annoying, step to perform. Tomcat automatically loads all the *jar* files in its *lib/* directory, and it does it alphabetically, according to the name of the *jar* file. The problem is that Cocoon requires a DOM

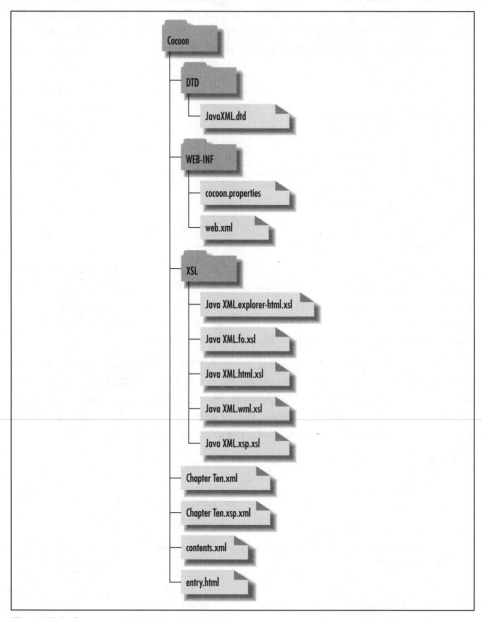

Figure 10-1. Cocoon context directory structure

Level 2 implementation (such as the one in Xerces, included with Cocoon in *xerces_1_2.jar*); however, Tomcat uses a DOM Level 1 implementation, included in *parser.jar*. Of course, because of the alphabetical listing, *parser.jar* gets loaded before *xerces_1_2.jar*, and Cocoon bombs out. To solve this, rename your *parser.jar* archive something that will get loaded after Xerces; I used *z_parser.jar*. This step ensures that the classes are still available to Tomcat, but that the DOM Level 2 classes are loaded first and used by Cocoon.

Once you complete these steps, test Cocoon by loading up the Cocoon information URI, which reports details about Cocoon's installation. Access *http://[hostname: port]/cocoon/Cocoon.xml*. In a default installation, this would be *http://localhost:8080/ cocoon/Cocoon.xml*. Your browser should give you results similar to those in Figure 10-2.

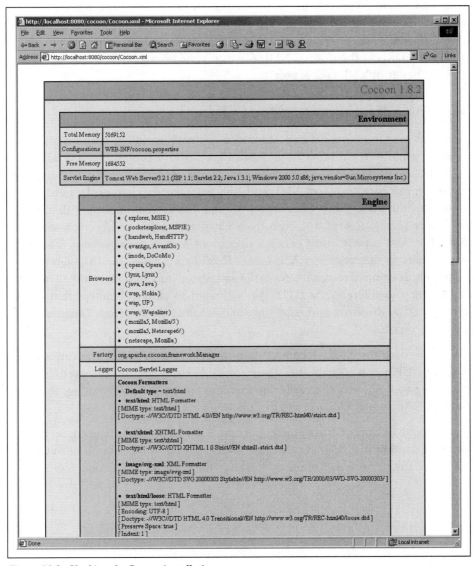

Figure 10-2. Checking the Cocoon installation

Once this is set up, you're ready to put some real content into place. With the setup you already have, all requests that end in *.xml* and are within the defined Cocoon context will be handled by the Cocoon servlet.

Using a Publishing Framework

Using a good publishing framework like Cocoon doesn't require any special instruction; it is not a complex application that users must learn to adapt to. In fact, all Cocoon's uses are based on simple URLs entered into a standard web browser. Generating dynamic HTML from XML, viewing XML transformed into PDF files, and even generating VRML applications from XML is simply a matter of typing the URL to the desired XML file into your browser and watching Cocoon and the power of XML take action.

Viewing XML Converted to HTML

Now that your framework is in place and is correctly handling requests ending in *.xml,* we begin to see it publish our XML files. Cocoon comes with several sample XML files and associated XSL stylesheets in the project's *samples/* subdirectory. However, you have your own XML and XSL from earlier chapters by now, so let's transform the XML table of contents for this book (*contents.xml*) with the XSL stylesheet (*JavaXML.html.xsl*), both from Chapter 2. Locate where you saved the XML file, and copy it into Cocoon's document root, *webapps/cocoon/*. The document refers to the stylesheet *XSL/JavaXML.html.xsl.* Create the *XSL/* directory in your web document root, and copy the stylesheet into that directory. The XML document also references a DTD; you will need to either comment that out, or create a *DTD/* directory and copy the *JavaXML.dtd* file, also from Chapter 2, into that directory.

Once you have the XML document and its stylesheet in place, you can access it with the URL *http://<hostname>:<port>/cocoon/contents.xml* in your web browser. Assuming you followed the earlier instructions to get Cocoon running, the transformed XML should look like Figure 10-3.

This should be almost trivial; once Cocoon is set up and configured, serving up dynamic content is a piece of cake! The mapping from XML extensions to Cocoon works for any requests within the context in which you set up Cocoon.

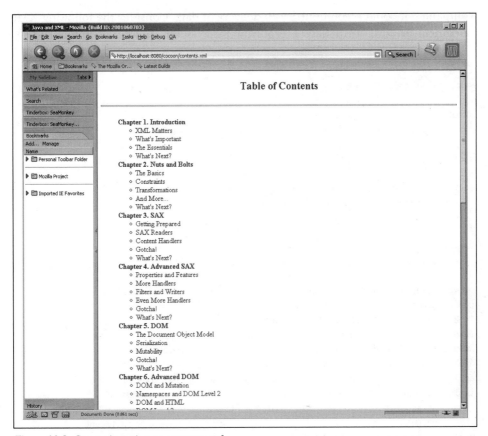

Figure 10-3. Cocoon in action on contents.xml

Viewing PDFs from XML

In the discussions concerning using XML for presentation, I've focused on XML converted to HTML. However, that's just scratching the surface of formats that XML can be converted to. Not only is a variety of markup languages supported as final document formats, but in addition, Java provides libraries for converting XML to some non-markup-based formats. The most popular and stable library in this category is the Apache XML group's Formatting Objects Processor, FOP. This gives Cocoon or any other publishing framework the ability to turn XML documents into Portable Document Format (PDF) documents, which are generally viewed with Adobe Acrobat (*http://www.adobe.com*).

The importance of converting a document from XML into a PDF cannot be overstated; particularly for document-driven web sites, such as print media or publishing companies, it could revolutionize web delivery of data. Consider the following XML document, an XML-formatted excerpt from this chapter, shown in Example 10-1.

Example 10-1. XML version of Java and XML

```
<?xml version="1.0"?>

<?cocoon-process type="xslt"?>
<?xml-stylesheet href="XSL/JavaXML.fo.xsl" type="text/xsl"?>

<book>
 <cover>
  <title>Java and XML</title>
   <author>Brett McLaughlin</author>
 </cover>

 <contents>
  <chapter title="Web Publishing Frameworks" number="10">

   <paragraph> This chapter begins looking at specific Java and XML
topics. So far, I have covered the basics of using XML from Java,
looking at the SAX, DOM, JDOM, and JAXP APIs to manipulate XML and the
fundamentals of using and creating XML itself. Now that you have a grasp
on using XML from your code, I want to spend time on specific
applications. The next six chapters represent the most significant
applications of XML, and, in particular, how those applications are
implemented in the Java space. While there are literally thousands of
important applications of XML, the topics in these chapters are those
that continually seem to be in the spotlight, and that have a significant
potential to change the way traditional development processes occur.
   </paragraph>

   <sidebar title="The More Things Change, the More They Stay the Same">
Readers of the first edition of this book will find that
much of this chapter on Cocoon is the same as the first edition. Although
I promised you that Cocoon 2 would be out by now, and although I expected
to be writing a chapter on Cocoon 2, things haven't progressed as quickly
as expected. Stefano Mazzochi, the driving force behind Cocoon, finally
got around to finishing school (good choice, Stefano!), and so
development on Cocoon 2 has significantly slowed. The result is that
Cocoon 1.x is still the current development path, and you should stick
with it for now. I've updated the section on Cocoon 2 to reflect what is
coming, and you should keep an eye out for more Cocoon-related books from
O'Reilly in the months to come.</sidebar>

   <paragraph> I'll begin this look at hot topics with the one XML
application that seems to have generated the largest amount of excitement
in the XML and Java communities: the web publishing framework. Although
I have continually emphasized that generating presentation from content
```

Example 10-1. XML version of Java and XML (continued)

```
is perhaps over-hyped when compared to the value of the portable data
that XML provides, using XML for presentation styling is still very
important. This importance increases when looking at web-based
applications.</paragraph>
  </chapter>


  </contents>
</book>
```

You saw how an XSL stylesheet allows you to transform this document into HTML. But converting an entire chapter of a book into HTML could result in a gigantic HTML document, and certainly an unreadable format; potential readers wanting online delivery of a book generally prefer a PDF document. On the other hand, generating PDF statically from the chapter means that changes to the chapter must be matched with subsequent PDF file generation. Keeping a single XML document format means the chapter can be easily updated (with any XML editor), formatted into SGML for printing hard copy, transferred to other companies and applications, and included in other books or compendiums. Now add the ability for web users to type in a URL and access the book in PDF format to this robust set of features, and you have a complete publishing system.

Although I don't cover formatting objects and the FOP for Java libraries in detail, you can review the entire formatting objects definition within the XSL specification at the W3C at *http://www.w3.org/TR/xsl/*. Example 10-2 is an XSL stylesheet that uses formatting objects to specify a transformation from XML to a PDF document, appropriate for the XML version of this chapter.

Example 10-2. XSL stylesheet for PDF transformation

```
<xsl:stylesheet version="1.0"
  xmlns:xsl="http://www.w3.org/1999/XSL/Transform"
  xmlns:fo="http://www.w3.org/1999/XSL/Format">

  <xsl:template match="book">
    <xsl:processing-instruction name="cocoon-format">
      type="text/xslfo"
    </xsl:processing-instruction>
    <fo:root xmlns:fo="http://www.w3.org/1999/XSL/Format">
      <fo:layout-master-set>
      <fo:simple-page-master
        master-name="right"
        margin-top="75pt"
        margin-bottom="25pt"
        margin-left="100pt"
        margin-right="50pt">
        <fo:region-body margin-bottom="50pt"/>
```

Example 10-2. XSL stylesheet for PDF transformation (continued)

```
            <fo:region-after extent="25pt"/>
      </fo:simple-page-master>
      <fo:simple-page-master
        master-name="left"
        margin-top="75pt"
        margin-bottom="25pt"
        margin-left="50pt"
        margin-right="100pt">
        <fo:region-body margin-bottom="50pt"/>
        <fo:region-after extent="25pt"/>
      </fo:simple-page-master>
      <fo:page-sequence-master master-name="psmOddEven">
        <fo:repeatable-page-master-alternatives>
          <fo:conditional-page-master-reference
              master-name="right"
              page-position="first"/>
          <fo:conditional-page-master-reference
              master-name="right"
              odd-or-even="even"/>
          <fo:conditional-page-master-reference
              master-name="left"
              odd-or-even="odd"/>
          <!-- recommended fallback procedure -->
          <fo:conditional-page-master-reference
              master-name="right"/>
        </fo:repeatable-page-master-alternatives>
      </fo:page-sequence-master>
      </fo:layout-master-set>

      <fo:page-sequence master-name="psmOddEven">

        <fo:static-content flow-name="xsl-region-after">
          <fo:block text-align-last="center" font-size="10pt">
            <fo:page-number/>
          </fo:block>
        </fo:static-content>

        <fo:flow flow-name="xsl-region-body">
          <xsl:apply-templates/>
        </fo:flow>
      </fo:page-sequence>

    </fo:root>
</xsl:template>

<xsl:template match="cover">
  <fo:block font-size="10pt"
            space-before.optimum="10pt">
```

Example 10-2. XSL stylesheet for PDF transformation (continued)

```
      <xsl:value-of select="title"/>
      (<xsl:value-of select="author"/>)
    </fo:block>
  </xsl:template>

<xsl:template match="contents">
  <xsl:apply-templates/>
</xsl:template>

<xsl:template match="chapter">
  <fo:block font-size="24pt"
            text-align-last="center"
            space-before.optimum="24pt">
    <xsl:value-of select="@number" />.
    <xsl:value-of select="@title" />
    <xsl:apply-templates/>
  </fo:block>
</xsl:template>

<xsl:template match="paragraph">
  <fo:block font-size="12pt"
            space-before.optimum="12pt"
            text-align="justify">
    <xsl:apply-templates/>
  </fo:block>
</xsl:template>

<xsl:template match="sidebar">
  <fo:block font-size="14pt"
            font-style="italic"
            color="blue"
            space-before.optimum="16pt"
            text-align="center">
    <xsl:value-of select="@title" />
  </fo:block>
  <fo:block font-size="12pt"
            color="blue"
            space-before.optimum="16pt"
            text-align="justify">
    <xsl:apply-templates/>
  </fo:block>
  </xsl:template>
</xsl:stylesheet>
```

If you create both of these files, saving the chapter as *chapterTen.xml,* and the XSL stylesheet as *JavaXML.fo.xsl* within a subdirectory called *XSL/,* you can see the result of the transformation in a web browser. Make sure you have the Adobe

Acrobat Reader and plug-in for your web browser, and then access the XML document just created. Figure 10-4 shows the results.

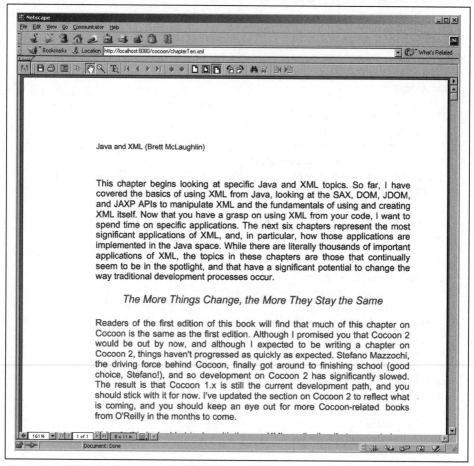

Figure 10-4. PDF transformation result from chapterTen.xml

Browser-Dependent Styling

In addition to specifically requesting certain types of transformations, such as a conversion to a PDF, Cocoon allows for dynamic processing to occur based on the request. A common example of this is applying different formatting based on the media of the client. In a traditional web environment, this allows an XML document to be transformed differently based on the browser being used. A client using Internet Explorer could be served a different presentation than a client using Netscape; with the recent wars between versions of HTML, DHTML, and Java-Script brewing between Netscape and Microsoft, this is a powerful feature to have available. Cocoon provides built-in support for many common browser types.

Locate the *cocoon.properties* file you referenced earlier, open it, and scroll to the bottom of the file. You will see the following section (this may be slightly different for newer versions):

```
##########################################
# User Agents (Browsers)                 #
##########################################

# NOTE: numbers indicate the search order. This is VERY VERY IMPORTANT
# since some words may be found in more than one browser description.
# (MSIE is presented as "Mozilla/4.0 (Compatible; MSIE 4.01; ...")
#
# for example, the "explorer=MSIE" tag indicates that the XSL stylesheet
# associated to the media type "explorer" should be mapped to those
# browsers that have the string "MSIE" in their "user-Agent" HTTP header.

browser.0 = explorer=MSIE
browser.1 = pocketexplorer=MSPIE
browser.2 = handweb=HandHTTP
browser.3 = avantgo=AvantGo
browser.4 = imode=DoCoMo
browser.5 = opera=Opera
browser.6 = lynx=Lynx
browser.7 = java=Java
browser.8 = wap=Nokia
browser.9 = wap=UP
browser.10 = wap=Wapalizer
browser.11 = mozilla5=Mozilla/5
browser.12 = mozilla5=Netscape6/
browser.13 = netscape=Mozilla
```

The keywords after the first equals sign are the items to take note of: `explorer`, `lynx`, `java`, and `mozilla5`, for example, all differentiate between different user-agents, the codes the browsers send with requests for URLs. As an example of applying stylesheets based on this property, you can create a sample XSL stylesheet to apply when the client accesses the XML table of contents (*contents.xml*) document with Internet Explorer. Copy the original XML-to-HTML stylesheet, *JavaXML.html.xsl*, to *JavaXML.explorer-html.xsl*. Then make the modifications shown in Example 10-3.

Example 10-3. Modified XSL stylesheet for Internet Explorer

```
<?xml version="1.0"?>

<xsl:stylesheet xmlns:javaxml2="http://www.oreilly.com/javaxml2"
                xmlns:xsl="http://www.w3.org/1999/XSL/Transform"
                xmlns:ora="http://www.oreilly.com"
                version="1.0"
>
```

Example 10-3. Modified XSL stylesheet for Internet Explorer (continued)

```
<xsl:template match="javaxml2:book">
<xsl:processing-instruction name="cocoon-format">
  type="text/html"
</xsl:processing-instruction>
  <html>
    <head>
      <title>
        <xsl:value-of select="javaxml2:title" /> (Explorer Version)
      </title>
    </head>
    <body>
      <xsl:apply-templates select="*[not(self::javaxml2:title)]" />
    </body>
  </html>
</xsl:template>


<xsl:template match="javaxml2:contents">
  <center>
   <h2>Table of Contents (Explorer Version)</h2>
   <small>
     Try <a href="http://www.mozilla.org">Mozilla</a> today!
   </small>
  </center>
  <!-- Other XSL directives -->
</xsl:template>


<!-- Other XSL template matches -->

</xsl:stylesheet>
```

While this is a trivial example, dynamic HTML could be inserted for Internet Explorer 5.5, and standard HTML could be used for Netscape Navigator or Mozilla, which have less DHTML support. With this in place, you need to let your XML document know that if the media type (or user-agent) matches up with the explorer type defined in the properties file, a different XSL stylesheet should be used. The additional processing instruction shown in Example 10-4 handles this, and can be added to the *contents.xml* file.

Example 10-4. Modified contents.xml with media type discernment

```
<?xml version="1.0"?>
<!DOCTYPE Book SYSTEM "DTD/JavaXML.dtd">
<?xml-stylesheet href="XSL/JavaXML.html.xsl" type="text/xsl"?>
<?xml-stylesheet href="XSL/JavaXML.explorer-html.xsl" type="text/xsl"
                media="explorer"?>

<?cocoon-process type="xslt"?>
```

Example 10-4. Modified contents.xml with media type discernment (continued)

```
<!-- Java and XML Contents -->
<book xmlns="http://www.oreilly.com/javaxml2"
      xmlns:ora="http://www.oreilly.com"
>
  <!-- XML content -->
</book>
```

Accessing the XML in your Netscape browser yields the same results as before; however, if you access the page in Internet Explorer, you will see that the document has been transformed with the alternate stylesheet, and looks like Figure 10-5.

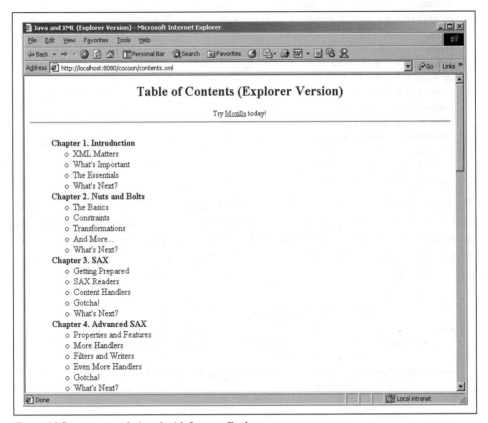

Figure 10-5. contents.xml viewed with Internet Explorer

WAP and XML

One of the real powers in this dynamic application of stylesheets lies in the use of wireless devices. Remember our properties file?

```
#########################################
# User Agents (Browsers)                #
#########################################

# NOTE: numbers indicate the search order. This is VERY VERY IMPORTANT
# since some words may be found in more than one browser description.
# (MSIE is presented as "Mozilla/4.0 (Compatible; MSIE 4.01; ...")
#
# for example, the "explorer=MSIE" tag indicates that the XSL stylesheet
# associated to the media type "explorer" should be mapped to those
# browsers that have the string "MSIE" in their "user-Agent" HTTP header.

browser.0 = explorer=MSIE
browser.1 = pocketexplorer=MSPIE
browser.2 = handweb=HandHTTP
browser.3 = avantgo=AvantGo
browser.4 = imode=DoCoMo
browser.5 = opera=Opera
browser.6 = lynx=Lynx
browser.7 = java=Java
browser.8 = wap=Nokia
browser.9 = wap=UP
browser.10 = wap=Wapalizer
browser.11 = mozilla5=Mozilla/5
browser.12 = mozilla5=Netscape6/
browser.13 = netscape=Mozilla
```

The highlighted entries detect that a wireless agent, such as an Internet-capable phone, is being used to access content. Just as Cocoon detected whether the incoming web browser was Internet Explorer or Netscape, responding with the correct stylesheet, a WAP device can be handled by yet another stylesheet. Add another stylesheet reference in to your *contents.xml* document:

```
<?xml version="1.0"?>
<!DOCTYPE Book SYSTEM "DTD/JavaXML.dtd">
<?xml-stylesheet href="XSL/JavaXML.html.xsl" type="text/xsl"?>
<?xml-stylesheet href="XSL/JavaXML.explorer-html.xsl" type="text/xsl"
                 media="explorer"?>
<?xml-stylesheet href="XSL/JavaXML.wml.xsl" type="text/xsl"
                 media="wap"?>

<?cocoon-process type="xslt"?>

<!-- Java and XML Contents -->
<book xmlns="http://www.oreilly.com/javaxml2"
      xmlns:ora="http://www.oreilly.com"
>
  <!-- XML table of contents -->
</book>
```

Now you need to create this newly referenced stylesheet for WAP devices. The Wireless Markup Language (WML) is typically used when building a stylesheet for a WAP device. WML is a variant on HTML, but has a slightly different method of representing different pages. When a wireless device requests a URL, the returned response must be within a `wml` element. In that root element, several *cards* can be defined, each through the WML `card` element. The device downloads multiple cards at one time (often referred to as a *deck*) so that it does not have to go back to the server for the additional screens. Example 10-5 shows a simple WML page using these constructs.

Example 10-5. Simple WML page

```
<wml>
 <card id="index" title="Home Page">
  <p align="left">
   <i>Main Menu</i><br />
   <a href="#title">Title Page</a><br />
   <a href="#myPage">My Page</a><br />
  <p>
 </card>

 <card id="title" title="My Title Page">
  Welcome to my Title Page!<br />
  So happy to see you.
 </card>

 <card id="myPage" title="Hello World">
  <p align="center">
   Hello World!
  </p>
 </card>
</wml>
```

This simple example serves requests with a menu, and two screens accessed from links within that menu. The complete WML 1.1 specification is available online, along with all other related WAP specifications, at *http://www.wapforum.org/what/technical_1_1.htm*. You can also pick up a copy of *Learning WML and WMLScript* by Martin Frost (O'Reilly). Additionally, the UP.SDK can be downloaded from *http://www.phone.com/products/upsdk.html*; this is a software emulation of a wireless device that allows testing of your WML pages. With this software, you can develop an XSL stylesheet to output WML for WAP devices, and test the results by pointing your UP.SDK browser to *http://<hostname>:<port>/contents.xml*.

Because phone displays are much smaller than computer screens, you want to show only a subset of the information in our XML table of contents. Example 10-6 is an XSL stylesheet that outputs three cards in WML. The first card is a menu with links to the other two cards. The second card generates a table of contents listing from our *contents.xml* document. The third card is a simple copyright screen. This stylesheet can be saved as *JavaXML.wml.xsl* in the *XSL/* subdirectory of your Cocoon context.

Example 10-6. WML stylesheet

```
<?xml version="1.0"?>

<xsl:stylesheet version="1.0"
                xmlns:xsl="http://www.w3.org/1999/XSL/Transform"
                xmlns:javaxml2="http://www.oreilly.com/javaxml2"
                xmlns:ora="http://www.oreilly.com"
                exclude-result-prefixes="javaxml2 ora"
>

 <xsl:template match="javaxml2:book">
  <xsl:processing-instruction name="cocoon-format">
    type="text/wml"
  </xsl:processing-instruction>

  <wml>
   <card id="index" title="{javaxml2:title}">
    <p align="center">
     <i><xsl:value-of select="javaxml2:title"/></i><br />
     <a href="#contents">Contents</a><br/>
     <a href="#copyright">Copyright</a><br/>
    </p>
   </card>

   <xsl:apply-templates select="javaxml2:contents" />

   <card id="copyright" title="Copyright">
    <p align="center">
     Copyright 2000, O&apos;Reilly &amp; Associates
    </p>
   </card>
  </wml>
 </xsl:template>

<xsl:template match="javaxml2:contents">
 <card id="contents" title="Contents">
  <p align="center">
   <i>Contents</i><br />
   <xsl:for-each select="javaxml2:chapter">
    <xsl:value-of select="@number" />.
    <xsl:value-of select="@title" /><br />
   </xsl:for-each>
```

Example 10-6. WML stylesheet (continued)

```
    </p>
  </card>
 </xsl:template>

</xsl:stylesheet>
```

Other than the WML tags, most of this example should look familiar. There is also a processing instruction for Cocoon, with the target specified as `cocoon-format`. The data sent, `type="text/wml"`, instructs Cocoon to output this stylesheet with a content header specifying that the output is `text/wml` (instead of the normal `text/html` or `text/plain`). There is one other important addition, an attribute added to the root element of the stylesheet:

```
<?xml version="1.0"?>

<xsl:stylesheet version="1.0"
             xmlns:xsl="http://www.w3.org/1999/XSL/Transform"
             xmlns:javaxml2="http://www.oreilly.com/javaxml2"
             xmlns:ora="http://www.oreilly.com"
             exclude-result-prefixes="javaxml2 ora"
  >
```

By default, any XML namespace declarations other than the XSL namespace are added to the root element of the transformation output. In this example, the root element of the transformed output, `wml`, would have the namespace declarations associated with the `javaxml2` and `ora` prefixes added to it:

```
<wml xmlns:javaxml2="http://www.oreilly.com/javaxml2"
     xmlns:ora="http://www.oreilly.com"
  >
    <!-- WML content -->
</wml>
```

This addition causes a WAP browser to report an error, as `xmlns:javaxml2` and `xmlns:ora` are not allowed attributes for the `wml` element. WAP browsers are not as forgiving as HTML browsers, and the rest of the WML content would not be shown. However, you must declare the namespace so the XSL stylesheet can handle template matching for the input document, which does use the `javaxml`-associated namespace. To handle this problem, XSL allows the attribute `exclude-result-prefixes` to be added to the `xsl:stylesheet` element. The namespace prefix specified to this attribute will not be added to the transformed output, which is exactly what you want. Your output would now look like this:

```
<wml>
    <!-- WML content -->
</wml>
```

This is understood perfectly by a WAP browser. If you've downloaded the UP.SDK browser, you can point it to your XML table of contents, and see the results. Figure 10-6 shows the main menu that results from the transformation using the WML stylesheet when a WAP device requests the *contents.xml* file through Cocoon.

Figure 10-6. Main menu for Java and XML

WARNING   In the UP.SDK browser versions that I tested, the browser would not resolve the entity reference OReillyCopyright. I had to comment this line out in my XML to make the examples work. You will probably have to do the same, until the simulator fixes this bug.

Figure 10-7 shows the generated table of contents, accessed by clicking the "Link" button when the "Contents" link is indicated in the display.

Figure 10-7. WML table of contents

Visit *http://www.openwave.com** and *http://www.wapforum.org* for more information on WML and WAP; both sites have extensive online resources for wireless device development.

By now, you should have a pretty good idea of the variety of output that can be created with Cocoon. With a minimal amount of effort and an extra stylesheet, the same XML document can be served in multiple formats to multiple types of clients; this is one of the reasons the web publishing framework is such a powerful tool. Without XML and a framework like this, separate sites would have to be created for each type of client. Now that you have seen how flexible the generation of output is when using Cocoon, I will move on to how Cocoon provides technology that allows for dynamic creation and customization of the input to these transformations.

---

* Careful readers will notice the lack of references to phone.com; that's because phone.com has now become a part of OpenWave, at *http://www.openwave.com*.

XSP

XSP stands for Extensible Server Pages, and is perhaps the most important development coming out of the Cocoon project. JavaServer Pages (JSP) allows tags and inline Java code to be inserted into an otherwise normal HTML page; when the JSP page is requested, the code is executed and the results are inserted right into the output HTML.* This has taken the Java and ASP worlds by storm, ostensibly simplifying server-side Java programming and allowing a separation of output and logic. However, there are still some significant problems. First, JSP does not really provide a separation of content and presentation. This is the same problem I have been talking about: changes to a banner, font color, or text size require the JSP (with the inline Java and JavaBean references) to be modified. JSP also mingles content (pure data) with presentation in the same way static HTML does. Second, there is no ability to transform the JSP into any other format, or use it across applications, because the JSP specification is designed primarily for delivery of output.

XSP remedies these problems. XSP is simply XML at its heart. Take a look at the sample XSP page in Example 10-7.

Example 10-7. A simple XSP page

```
<?xml version="1.0"?>
<?cocoon-process type="xsp"?>
<?cocoon-process type="xslt"?>
<?xml-stylesheet href="myStylesheet.xsl" type="text/xsl"?>
```

```
<xsp:page language="java"
          xmlns:xsp="http://www.apache.org/1999/XSP/Core"
>

 <xsp:logic>
  private static int numHits = 0;

  private synchronized int getNumHits() {
   return ++numHits;
  }
 </xsp:logic>

 <page>
  <title>Hit Counter</title>

  <p>I've been requested <xsp:expr>getNumHits()</xsp:expr> times.</p>
 </page>
</xsp:page>
```

---

* This is a drastic oversimplification; the JSP is actually precompiled into a servlet, and a PrintWriter handles output. For more information on JSP, refer to *JavaServer Pages* by Hans Bergsten (O'Reilly).

All XML conventions are followed. For now, think of the `xsp:logic` element content as "off-limits" to the XML parser; I'll discuss that later. Other than that, the entire document is simply XML with some new elements. In fact, it references an XSL stylesheet that has nothing remarkable about it, as you can see in Example 10-8.

Example 10-8. XSL stylesheet for the XSP page

```
<?xml version="1.0"?>

<xsl:stylesheet version="1.0"
                xmlns:xsl="http://www.w3.org/1999/XSL/Transform"
>

  <xsl:template match="page">
    <xsl:processing-instruction name="cocoon-format">
      type="text/html"
    </xsl:processing-instruction>
    <html>
      <head>
        <title><xsl:value-of select="title"/></title>
      </head>
      <body>
        <xsl:apply-templates select="*[not(self::title)]" />
      </body>
    </html>
  </xsl:template>

  <xsl:template match="p">
    <p align="center">
      <xsl:apply-templates />
    </p>
  </xsl:template>

</xsl:stylesheet>
```

Thus, XSP easily handles the first major problem of JSP: it separates content from presentation. This separation allows developers to handle content generation (the XSP page can be generated from a servlet or other Java code as well as being static), while XML and XSL authors can handle presentation and styling through modification of the XSL stylesheet applied to the XSP page. Just as easily, XSP solves the other significant deficiency of JSP: because XSP processing occurs before any stylesheets are applied, the resultant XML document can be transformed into any other format. XSP maintains all the advantages of XML, as the XSP page can be transferred between applications as well as being used just for presentation.

Creating an XSP Page

Now that you have had a taste of XSP, you can build your own XSP page. For this example, I'll continue looking at the XML documents already created. Let's revisit the XML document constructed earlier. This document represents a portion of this chapter and was transformed into a PDF document. Instead of simply using this document for display, assume that the author wants to let his editor view the document as it is being written. However, in addition to the text of the book, the editor should be able to see comments from the author that the public should not see: for example, questions about style and formatting. First, add the following comment to the *chapterTen.xml* file you built earlier:

```
<?xml version="1.0"?>

<?cocoon-process type="xslt"?>
<?xml-stylesheet href="XSL/JavaXML.fo.xsl" type="text/xsl"?>

<book>
 <cover>
  <title>Java and XML</title>
  <author>Brett McLaughlin</author>
 </cover>

 <contents>
  <chapter title="Web Publishing Frameworks" number="10">

   <paragraph> This chapter begins looking at specific Java and XML
topics. So far, I have covered the basics of using XML from Java,
looking at the SAX, DOM, JDOM, and JAXP APIs to manipulate XML and the
fundamentals of using and creating XML itself. Now that you have a grasp
on using XML from your code, I want to spend time on specific
applications. The next six chapters represent the most significant
applications of XML, and, in particular, how those applications are
implemented in the Java space. While there are literally thousands of
important applications of XML, the topics in these chapters are those
that continually seem to be in the spotlight, and that have a significant
potential to change the way traditional development processes occur.
   </paragraph>

   <authorComment>Mike - Do you think the following sidebar is a little
much? I could easily leave it out if it's still clear without it.
   </authorComment>

   <sidebar title="The More Things Change, the More They Stay the Same">
Readers of the first edition of this book will find that
much of this chapter on Cocoon is the same as the first edition. Although
I promised you that Cocoon 2 would be out by now, and although I expected
to be writing a chapter on Cocoon 2, things haven't progressed as quickly
```

as expected. Stefano Mazzochi, the driving force behind Cocoon, finally
got around to finishing school (good choice, Stefano!), and so
development on Cocoon 2 has significantly slowed. The result is that
Cocoon 1.x is still the current development path, and you should stick
with it for now. I've updated the section on Cocoon 2 to reflect what is
coming, and you should keep an eye out for more Cocoon-related books from
O'Reilly in the months to come.</sidebar>

       <paragraph> I'll begin this look at hot topics with the one XML
application that seems to have generated the largest amount of excitement
in the XML and Java communities: the web publishing framework. Although
I have continually emphasized that generating presentation from content
is perhaps over-hyped when compared to the value of the portable data
that XML provides, using XML for presentation styling is still very
important. This importance increases when looking at web-based
applications.</paragraph>
  </chapter>

 </contents>
</book>

With this comment in your XML document, add a corresponding entry into your
XSL stylesheet, *JavaXML.fo.xsl*:

```
<xsl:template match="sidebar">
  <fo:block font-size="14pt"
            font-style="italic"
            color="blue"
            space-before.optimum="16pt"
            text-align="center">
    <xsl:value-of select="@title" />
  </fo:block>
  <fo:block font-size="12pt"
            color="blue"
            space-before.optimum="16pt"
            text-align="justify">
    <xsl:apply-templates/>
  </fo:block>
</xsl:template>

<xsl:template match="authorComment">
  <fo:block font-size="10pt"
            font-style="italic"
            color="red"
            space-before.optimum="12pt"
            text-align="justify">
    <xsl:apply-templates/>
  </fo:block>
</xsl:template>
```

The comments appear slightly smaller than the rest of the text, italicized, and in red. Now it's possible to turn your XML document into an XSP page (as in Example 10-9) by adding processing instructions for Cocoon and surrounding the elements within a new root element, xsp:page.

Example 10-9. Turning chapterTen.xml into an XSP page

```
<?xml version="1.0"?>

<?cocoon-process type="xsp"?>
<?cocoon-process type="xslt"?>
<?xml-stylesheet href="XSL/JavaXML.fo.xsl" type="text/xsl"?>

<xsp:page language="java"
          xmlns:xsp="http://www.apache.org/1999/XSP/Core"
>
<book>
 <cover>
  <title>Java and XML</title>
  <author>Brett McLaughlin</author>
 </cover>

 <contents>
  <chapter title="Web Publishing Frameworks" number="10">
  <!-- Text of chapter -->
  </chapter>
 </contents>
</book>
</xsp:page>
```

Before adding XSP logic to determine whether to show the comment, build a simple HTML page letting the viewer indicate if he is the book's editor. In a real application, this could be a page that handles authentication and determines a user's role; for this example, it lets the user select author, editor, or just a curious reader, and enter a password for verification. An HTML page that does this is shown in Example 10-10. Save this file as *entry.html* in your context's document root.

Example 10-10. Entry page for chapterTen.xml XSP page

```
<html>
 <head>
  <title>Welcome to the Java and XML Book in Progress</title>
 </head>

 <body>
  <h1 align="center"><i>Java and XML</i> Book in Progress</h1>
  <center>
   <form action="/cocoon/chapterTen.xml" method="POST">
    Select your role:
```

Example 10-10. Entry page for chapterTen.xml XSP page (continued)

```
    <select name="userRole">
     <option value="author">I'm the Author</option>
     <option value="editor">I'm the Editor</option>
     <option value="reader">I'm a Reader</option>
    </select>
    <br />
    Enter your password:
    <input type="password" name="password" size="8" />
    <br /><br />
    <input type="submit" value="Take me to the Book!" />
   </form>
  </center>
 </body>
</html>
```

Also notice that this HTML submits the form data directly to your XSP page. In this example, the XSP acts like a servlet. It reads the request parameters, determines what user role was selected, authenticates that role using the password supplied, and finally determines whether the author comments should be shown. To begin, define a boolean variable; this variable holds the result of comparing the request parameters to see if the user is an author or editor and supplied a correct password. The value of the variable is checked, and if it is true, the authorComment element is displayed; surround the authorComment element with the XSP directives shown here:

```
<xsp:logic>
 boolean authorOrEditor = false;

 // Perform logic to see if user is an author or editor

 if (authorOrEditor) {
   <xsp:content>
     <authorComment>Mike - Do you think the following sidebar is
     a little much? I could easily leave it out if it's still
     clear without it.</authorComment>
   </xsp:content>
 }
</xsp:logic>
```

This shouldn't look strange; other than the XSP-specific tags, you're just defining a variable and checking its value. If the variable evaluates to true, the authorComment element is added to the XSP page's output; otherwise, the element is not included in the output. One interesting thing to note is that the actual XML document output is surrounded within the xsp:logic block with an xsp: content element (which in turn is within the outer xsp:page element), ensuring that the XSP processor does not try to interpret any elements or text within the block as XSP structures. The same code in JSP might look like this:

```
<%
 if (authorOrEditor) {
%>
        <authorComment>Mike - Do you think the following sidebar is
        a little much? I could easily leave it out if it's still
        clear without it.</authorComment>
<%
 }
%>
```

This is not very structured, as the JSP block ends before the `authorComment` element begins; then a new block is appended after the element, which closes the brackets opened in the first JSP block. It is very easy to mismatch coding structures or forget to add matching JSP blocks. The XSP paradigm forces every open element to be closed (standard XML well-formedness) and one block of code is matched with one element.

With these logical structures in place, the XSP page just needs to interpret the request parameters. You can use the built-in XSP variable `request`, which mimics the `javax.servlet.http.HttpServletRequest` object. The following code additions read the values of the `userRole` and `password` request parameters (if they exist). The value of `userRole` is then compared with the roles that can see the comments ("author" and "editor"). If a match occurs, the password is checked as well. If the password matches the key for the supplied role, the `boolean` variable is set to true, and the `authorComment` element is part of the XML output:

```
<xsp:logic>
 boolean authorOrEditor = false;

  // Perform logic to see if user is an author or editor
<![CDATA[
String[] roleValues = request.getParameterValues("userRole");
String[] passwordValues = request.getParameterValues("password");
if ((roleValues != null) && (passwordValues != null)) {
  String userRole = roleValues[0];
  String password = passwordValues[0];
  if (userRole.equals("author") && password.equals("brett")) {
    authorOrEditor = true;
  } else
    if (userRole.equals("editor") && password.equals("mike")) {
    authorOrEditor = true;
  }
}
]]>
```

```
        if (authorOrEditor) {
  ...
```

Notice that I enclose a good bit of this logic within a CDATA tag. Remember that XSP is still evaluated as XML, and must follow the rules of an XML document; however, the double quotes and ampersands used in the Java fragments are not allowed in XML documents. Instead of escaping these characters and getting a very strange XSP fragment, you can use the CDATA tag and write standard Java code. Without it, you would have to code as follows:

```
<xsp:logic>
 boolean authorOrEditor = false;

 String[] roleValues =
   request.getParameterValues(&quot;userRole&quot;);
 String[] passwordValues =
   request.getParameterValues(&quot;password&quot;);
 if ((roleValues != null) &amp;&amp;
     (passwordValues != null)) {
   String userRole = roleValues[0];
   String password = passwordValues[0];
   if (userRole.equals("author") &amp;&amp;
       password.equals("brett")) {
     authorOrEditor = true;
   } else
   if (userRole.equals("editor") &amp;&amp;
       password.equals("mike")) {
     authorOrEditor = true;
   }
 }
 ...
</xsp:logic>
```

Now test the entry page and the resultant PDF generated from the XML. You should get output similar to Figure 10-8 if you direct your web browser to *http:// <hostname>:<port>/cocoon/entry.html.*

Select the role of author and use the password "brett", or select the editor role with the password "mike". Either case gives you the PDF output shown in Figure 10-9.

The one thing that has not yet been done is to isolate the page's logic from its content. Just as JSP allows inclusion of JavaBeans to abstract the content and presentation from the logic of an application component, XSP allows tag libraries to be created. These tag libraries allow XML tags to trigger the matching code within a tag library.

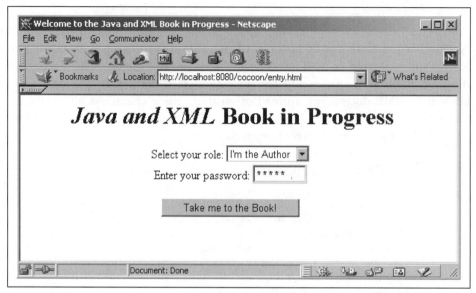

Figure 10-8. Entry page for chapterTen.xml XSP page

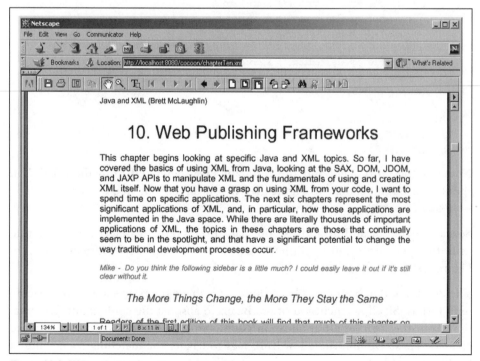

Figure 10-9. XSP output with author or editor role

Using XSP Tag Libraries

In addition to showing comments based on the user's identity, the XSP page should indicate that the chapter is in a draft state. The current date can be shown to indicate the date of the draft (then the date is frozen when the chapter is considered complete). Instead of adding inline Java tags to load the current date, simply create a custom tag library for this purpose. It's also worth looking at the process of creating an XSP element that takes in the chapter number and title and formats the complete title. This function will handle the insertion of the draft date, as well. To do this, you first need to create a tag library that is available to the XSP page. Much of the tag library is based on an XSL stylesheet. You can start with the skeleton shown in Example 10-11, which passes anything it receives through as output. Save this skeleton as *JavaXML.xsp.xsl* in the *XSL/* subdirectory. Be sure to include the `javaxml2` namespace declaration, as it will be used to match elements within that namespace used in the XSP pages.

Example 10-11. Skeleton of XSP tag library

```
<?xml version="1.0"?>

<xsl:stylesheet version="1.0"
  xmlns:xsl="http://www.w3.org/1999/XSL/Transform"
  xmlns:xsp="http://www.apache.org/1999/XSP/Core"
  xmlns:javaxml2="http://www.oreilly.com/javaxml2"
>
  <xsl:template match="xsp:page">
    <xsp:page>
      <xsl:copy>
        <xsl:apply-templates select="@*"/>
      </xsl:copy>

      <xsl:apply-templates/>
    </xsp:page>
  </xsl:template>

  <xsl:template match="@*|*|text()|processing-instruction()">
    <xsl:copy>
      <xsl:apply-templates
          select="@*|*|text()|processing-instruction()"/>
    </xsl:copy>
  </xsl:template>

</xsl:stylesheet>
```

By matching the `xsp:page` tag, it's possible to ensure that all elements are matched and handled within this stylesheet; this is referred to as a *logicsheet* in XSP parlance. Now add Java methods for the templates within this logicsheet to call:

```
<xsl:template match="xsp:page">
  <xsp:page>
    <xsl:copy>
      <xsl:apply-templates select="@*"/>
    </xsl:copy>

    <xsp:structure>
      <xsp:include>java.util.Date</xsp:include>
      <xsp:include>java.text.SimpleDateFormat</xsp:include>
    </xsp:structure>

    <xsp:logic>
      private static String getDraftDate() {
        return (new SimpleDateFormat("MM/dd/yyyy"))
          .format(new Date());
      }

      private static String getTitle(int chapterNum,
                                     String chapterTitle) {
        return chapterNum + ". " + chapterTitle;
      }
    </xsp:logic>

    <xsl:apply-templates/>
  </xsp:page>
</xsl:template>
```

Several new XSP elements are introduced here. First, `xsp:structure` is used to surround several `xsp:include` statements. These work just like their Java counterpart, `import`, making the specified Java classes available for use by their unqualified names (rather than the complete packaged names). Once these are available, the logicsheet defines and implements two methods: one that creates a chapter title from the chapter number and textual title, and one that returns the current date as a formatted `String`. These methods are available to any elements within this logicsheet.

Now define the element that specifies when an XSP result should replace an XML element. The `javaxml2`-associated namespace is already declared in the root element, so it can be used as the namespace for the new tag library elements. Add the following template into your logicsheet:

```
<!-- Create formatted title -->
<xsl:template match="javaxml2:draftTitle">
```

```
<xsp:expr>getTitle(<xsl:value-of select="@chapterNum" />,
                    "<xsl:value-of select="@chapterTitle" />")
</xsp:expr> (<xsp:expr>getDraftDate()</xsp:expr>)
</xsl:template>

<xsl:template match="@*|*|text()|processing-instruction()">
  <xsl:copy>
    <xsl:apply-templates
        select="@*|*|text()|processing-instruction()"/>
  </xsl:copy>
</xsl:template>
```

When a document with this tag library uses the element javaxml2:draftTitle
(or just draftTitle if the default namespace is mapped to *http://www.oreilly.com/
javaxml2*), the result of the method getTitle() is prepended to the value of the
getDraftDate() method. The javaxml2:draftTitle element also expects two
attributes to be declared: the chapter number and the textual title of the chapter.
Signify to the XSP processor that you are calling a defined method by enclosing
the method call within a set of <xsp:expr> tags. To indicate that the second argument (the chapter title) is a String, it should be enclosed within quotes. Since
the chapter number should be treated as an int, it is left without quotation marks.

Once you have completed the XSP logicsheet (available online at the book's web
site as well), you need to make it accessible to Cocoon. This can be done one of
two ways. The first is to specify the location of the file as a URI, which allows the
servlet engine (and therefore Cocoon) to locate the logicsheet. For example, to
add the XSP logicsheet to Cocoon's set of resources through its URI, you could
add the following lines to the *cocoon.properties* file on a Unix-based system:

```
# Set the libraries associated with the given namespace.
# Use the syntax:
#   processor.xsp.logicsheet.<namespace-tag>.<language> = URL to file
# where "URL to file" is usually starting with file:// if you locate
# your custom library in your file system.
processor.xsp.logicsheet.context.java  = resource://org/apache/cocoon/processor/
  xsp/library/java/context.xsl
processor.xsp.logicsheet.cookie.java   = resource://org/apache/cocoon/processor/
  xsp/library/java/cookie.xsl
processor.xsp.logicsheet.global.java   = resource://org/apache/cocoon/processor/
  xsp/library/java/global.xsl
processor.xsp.logicsheet.request.java  = resource://org/apache/cocoon/processor/
  xsp/library/java/request.xsl
processor.xsp.logicsheet.response.java = resource://org/apache/cocoon/processor/
  xsp/library/java/response.xsl
processor.xsp.logicsheet.session.java  = resource://org/apache/cocoon/processor/
  xsp/library/java/session.xsl
processor.xsp.logicsheet.util.java     =
  resource://org/apache/cocoon/processor/xsp/library/java/util.xsl
```

```
processor.xsp.logicsheet.sql.java      =
    resource://org/apache/cocoon/processor/xsp/library/sql/sql.xsl
processor.xsp.logicsheet.esql.java     =
    resource://org/apache/cocoon/processor/xsp/library/sql/esql.xsl
processor.xsp.logicsheet.fp.java       =
    resource://org/apache/cocoon/processor/xsp/library/fp/fp.xsl


processor.xsp.library.JavaXML.java =
    file:///usr/local/jakarta-tomcat/webapps/cocoon/XSL/JavaXML.xsp.xsl
```

For Windows systems, this would be:

```
# Set the libraries associated with the given namespace.
# Use the syntax:
#   processor.xsp.logicsheet.<namespace-tag>.<language> = URL to file
# where "URL to file" is usually starting with file:// if you locate
# your custom library in your file system.
processor.xsp.logicsheet.context.java  = resource://org/apache/cocoon/processor/
xsp/library/java/context.xsl
processor.xsp.logicsheet.cookie.java   = resource://org/apache/cocoon/processor/
xsp/library/java/cookie.xsl
processor.xsp.logicsheet.global.java   = resource://org/apache/cocoon/processor/
xsp/library/java/global.xsl
processor.xsp.logicsheet.request.java  = resource://org/apache/cocoon/processor/
xsp/library/java/request.xsl
processor.xsp.logicsheet.response.java = resource://org/apache/cocoon/processor/
xsp/library/java/response.xsl
processor.xsp.logicsheet.session.java  = resource://org/apache/cocoon/processor/
xsp/library/java/session.xsl
processor.xsp.logicsheet.util.java     =
    resource://org/apache/cocoon/processor/xsp/library/java/util.xsl
processor.xsp.logicsheet.sql.java      =
    resource://org/apache/cocoon/processor/xsp/library/sql/sql.xsl
processor.xsp.logicsheet.esql.java     =
    resource://org/apache/cocoon/processor/xsp/library/sql/esql.xsl
processor.xsp.logicsheet.fp.java       =
    resource://org/apache/cocoon/processor/xsp/library/fp/fp.xsl


processor.xsp.library.javaxml2.java =
    file:///C:/java/jakarta-tomcat/webapps/cocoon/XSL/JavaXML.xsp.xsl
```

While this is handy for testing, it is not a very good solution for uncoupling your logicsheets from the servlet engine, and also adds quite a bit of maintenance overhead when adding new logicsheets: a new line would have to be added to the *cocoon.properties* file for new logicsheets to be available. Allowing specification of a resource in the servlet engine's classpath is an alternative method for loading logicsheets. This lets you add custom logicsheets to a *jar* file, and that *jar* file to the servlet engine classpath (which in Tomcat simply means adding that archive to the *lib/* directory!). In addition, new logicsheets can be put within the *jar* file, providing a central location for storing your custom XSP logicsheets. From the *XSL/* subdirectory in your web server's document root, perform the following command to create a *jar* file that contains your logicsheet:

```
jar cvf logicsheets.jar JavaXML.xsp.xsl
```

Move the created *logicsheets.jar* archive into your *TOMCAT_HOME/lib/* directory with the other Cocoon libraries. That will ensure that Tomcat loads the library on startup. With your logicsheet available, you can now let Cocoon know where to look for `javaxml2`-associated namespace references within XSP pages. Edit the *cocoon.properties* file; locate the section that lists the various Cocoon XSP resources, and add the new logicsheet reference:

```
# Set the libraries associated with the given namespace.
# Use the syntax:
#   processor.xsp.logicsheet.<namespace-tag>.<language> = URL to file
# where "URL to file" is usually starting with file:// if you locate
# your custom library in your file system.
processor.xsp.logicsheet.context.java  = resource://org/apache/cocoon/processor/
xsp/library/java/context.xsl
processor.xsp.logicsheet.cookie.java   = resource://org/apache/cocoon/processor/
xsp/library/java/cookie.xsl
processor.xsp.logicsheet.global.java   = resource://org/apache/cocoon/processor/
xsp/library/java/global.xsl
processor.xsp.logicsheet.request.java  = resource://org/apache/cocoon/processor/
xsp/library/java/request.xsl
processor.xsp.logicsheet.response.java = resource://org/apache/cocoon/processor/
xsp/library/java/response.xsl
processor.xsp.logicsheet.session.java  = resource://org/apache/cocoon/processor/
xsp/library/java/session.xsl
processor.xsp.logicsheet.util.java     =
   resource://org/apache/cocoon/processor/xsp/library/java/util.xsl
processor.xsp.logicsheet.sql.java      =
   resource://org/apache/cocoon/processor/xsp/library/sql/sql.xsl
processor.xsp.logicsheet.esql.java     =
   resource://org/apache/cocoon/processor/xsp/library/sql/esql.xsl
processor.xsp.logicsheet.fp.java       =
   resource://org/apache/cocoon/processor/xsp/library/fp/fp.xsl

processor.xsp.logicsheet.javaxml2.java = resource://JavaXML.xsp.xsl
```

Because the logicsheet is not nested within any subdirectories in the *logicsheets.jar* file, you can simply use the name of the logicsheet as its resource path. Finally, restart your servlet engine (this also ensures that Tomcat auto-loads the new library). This will reload the *cocoon.properties* file, and the logicsheet will be available for use. As the Cocoon engine is used to handle requests, any XSP page that declares that it uses the `javaxml2` namespace will have access to the logicsheet specified as the `javaxml2` library. So the XSP page needs to add a namespace declaration for the `javaxml2` namespace:

```
<?xml version="1.0"?>

<?cocoon-process type="xsp"?>
<?cocoon-process type="xslt"?>
<?xml-stylesheet href="XSL/JavaXML.fo.xsl" type="text/xsl"?>

<xsp:page language="java"
          xmlns:xsp="http://www.apache.org/1999/XSP/Core"
          xmlns:javaxml2="http://www.oreilly.com/javaxml2"
>
<book>
  <!-- Book content -->
</book>
</xsp:page>
```

With the tag library now available for use, you can finally add in the `javaxml2:` `draftTitle` element to your XML document, *chapterTen.xml*:

```
<contents>
  <chapter title="Web Publishing Frameworks" number="10">
    <javaxml2:draftTitle chapterNum="10"
                         chapterTitle="Web Publishing Framework" />
    ...
```

Replace the hardcoded chapter title with the element defined in the XSP tag library with the following change to your *JavaXML.fo.xsl* stylesheet:

```
<xsl:template match="chapter">
  <fo:block font-size="24pt"
            text-align-last="center"
            space-before.optimum="24pt">
<!--
    <xsl:value-of select="@number" />.
    <xsl:value-of select="@title" />
-->
    <xsl:apply-templates/>
  </fo:block>
</xsl:template>
```

This should generate the title with the chapter number, chapter title, and the date of the draft. Accessing this new version of the XSP page results in the output shown in Figure 10-10.

I have only scratched the surface of XSP. Even this simple example allows the title to be converted to a different form by modifying only the XSP logicsheet—not the content or presentation of the page—when the chapter is complete. In the same way, XSP allows the creation of very strict contracts separating presentation from

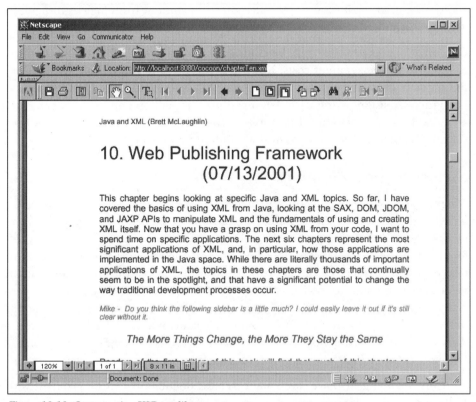

Figure 10-10. Output using XSP tag library

content from application logic. Adding server-side Java components such as Enterprise JavaBeans can bring business logic into the equation. Rather than using a less flexible solution like JSP that is coupled to HTML and a presentation format, using XSP allows a looser coupling of components and thus is a better solution for application development. XSP also promises to be key in the upcoming Cocoon 2.0, which I look at now.

Cocoon 2.0 and Beyond

Cocoon 2.0, the next generation of Cocoon, promises to be a giant leap forward for the web publishing framework. Cocoon 1.x, which is primarily based on XML being transformed via XSL, still has some serious limitations. First, it does not significantly reduce the management costs of large sites. While one XML document can be transformed into different client views, a significant number of documents will still exist. Generally, either long URIs (such as */content/publishing/books/javaxml/contents.xml*), a large number of virtual path mappings (*/javaxml* mapped to */content/publishing/books/javaxml*), or a combination of the two result. In addition, a strict separation of presentation from content from logic is difficult to accomplish, and even more difficult to manage.

Cocoon 2 focuses on enforcing the contracts between these different layers, therefore reducing management costs. XSP is a centerpiece in this design. In addition, the sitemap allows the distinction between XSP, XML, and static HTML pages to be hidden from the prying user. Advanced precompilation and memory considerations will also be introduced to make Cocoon 2 even more of an advance over Cocoon 1.x than Cocoon 1.x was over a standard web server.

Servlet Engine Mappings

A significant change in Cocoon 2 is that it no longer requires a simple mapping for XML documents. While this works well in the 1.x model, it still leaves management of non-XML documents to the webmaster, possibly someone completely different from the person responsible for the XML documents. Cocoon 2 seeks to take over management of the entire web site. For this reason, the main Cocoon servlet (`org.apache.cocoon.servlet.CocoonServlet` in the 2.0 model) is generally mapped to a URI, such as *Cocoon*. This could also be mapped to the root of the web server itself (simply "/") to completely control a site. The URL requested then follows the servlet mapping: *http://myHost.com/Cocoon/myPage.xml* or *http://myHost.com/Cocoon/myDynamicPage.xsp*, for example.

With this mapping in place, even static HTML documents can be grouped with XML documents, allowing the management of all files on the server to be handled by a central person or group. If HTML, WML, and XML documents must be mixed in a directory, no confusion needs to occur, and uniform URIs can be used. Cocoon 2 will happily serve HTML as well as any other document type; with a mapping from the root of a server to Cocoon, the web publishing framework actually becomes invisible to the client.

The Sitemap

Another important introduction to Cocoon 2 is the *sitemap*. In Cocoon, a sitemap provides a central location for administration of a web site. Cocoon uses this sitemap to decide how to process the request URIs it receives. For example, when Cocoon receives a request like *http://myCocoonSite.com/Cocoon/javaxml/chapterOne.html*, the Cocoon servlet dissects the request and determines that the actual URI requested is */javaxml/chapterOne.html*. However, suppose that the file *chapterOne.html* should map not to a static HTML file, but to the transformation of an XML document (as in the earlier examples). The sitemap can handle this, quite easily! Take a look at the sitemap shown in Example 10-12.

Example 10-12. Sample Cocoon 2 sitemap

```
<sitemap>
 <process match="/javaxml/*.html">
  <generator type="file" src="/docs/javaxml/*.xml"
  <filter type="xslt">
   <parameter name="stylesheet" value="/styles/JavaXML.html.xsl"/>
  </filter>
  <serializer type="html"/>
 </process>

 <process match="/javaxml/*.pdf">
  <generator type="file" src="/docs/javaxml/*.xml"
  <filter type="xslt">
   <parameter name="stylesheet" value="/styles/JavaXML.pdf.xsl"/>
  </filter>
  <serializer type="fop"/>
 </process>
</sitemap>
```

In this example, Cocoon matches the URI */javaxml/chapterOne.html* to the sitemap directive /javaxml/*.html. It determines that this is an actual file, and the source for the file should be determined by using the mapping /docs/javaxml/ *. xml, which translates to */docs/javaxml/chapterOne.xml* (the filename we want transformed). The XSLT filter is then applied; the stylesheet to use, *JavaXML.html. xsl*, is also specified in the sitemap. The resulting transformation is then displayed to the user. In addition, the XML file could be an XSP file processed before being converted to XML and then styled.

This same process can render a PDF from the request *http://myCocoonSite.com/ Cocoon/javaxml/chapterOne.pdf*, all with a few extra lines in the sitemap (shown in the previous example). The processing instructions in the individual XML documents can be completely removed, a significant change from Cocoon 1.x. First, uniform application of stylesheets and processing can occur based on a directory location. Simply creating XML and placing it in the */docs/javaxml/* directory in the example means the document can be accessed as HTML or PDF. It is also trivial to change the stylesheet used for all documents, something very difficult and tedious to do in Cocoon 1.x. Instead of making a change to each XML document, only the single line in the sitemap needs to be changed.

The Cocoon sitemap is still being developed, and there will probably be quite a few additional enhancements and changes to its format and structure by the time Cocoon 2.0 goes final. To get involved, join the mailing lists at *cocoon-users@xml. apache.org* and *cocoon-dev@xml.apache.org*. The Apache XML project at *http://xml. apache.org* has details about how to participate in these lists and the Cocoon project.

Producers and Processors

One final improvement that Cocoon 2 will include is precompiled and event-based *producers* and *processors*. In Cocoon, a producer handles the transformation of a request URI into an XML document stream. A processor then takes an input stream (currently the XML document in a DOM tree) into output readable by the client. I haven't covered producers and processors in the Cocoon 1.x model because they are going to drastically change in the Cocoon 2.0 model; any producers and processors currently being used will most likely be useless and have to be rewritten in Cocoon 2.0.

Cocoon 2 moves from using DOM for these structures to using the more event-based SAX, wrapped within a DOM structure. As a producer in 1.x had to generate an XML document in memory, the corresponding DOM structure could get extremely large. This eventually drained system resources, particularly when performing complex tasks such as large transformations or handling formatting objects· (PDF generation). For these reasons, DOM will be a simple wrapper around SAX-based events in Cocoon 2, allowing producers and processors to be very slim and efficient.

In addition, producers and processors will be precompiled versions of other formats. For example, XSL stylesheets can be precompiled into processors, and XSP pages can be precompiled into producers. This further increases performance while removing load from the client. These and other changes continue to use a component model, allowing Cocoon to be a very flexible, very pluggable framework. Keep up on the latest changes by monitoring the Cocoon web site.

What's Next?

The next chapter looks at a technology that allows XML to be used as a data format in an important request and response model: XML Remote Procedure Calls. XML-RPC allows clients in a distributed system to request that tasks be executed on a server (or servers) on another portion of the network. Until recently, RPC has declined in popularity, mostly due to the surge of RMI-based technologies in the Java space (most notably, EJB). However, with XML as a data format, XML-RPC is a new solution for many problems that could not be solved cleanly or efficiently without RPC. I'll show you XML-RPC next, and in particular, the Java implementation of the technology.

11

XML-RPC

XML-RPC is actually a specific flavor of RPC, which stands for *remote procedure calls.* If you are new to programming, or have worked with the Java language only a short time, remote procedure calls may be new for you; if you've been around the block in the development world, you may be a bit rusty, as RPC has fallen out of vogue in recent years. In this chapter I look at why those three little letters in front of RPC are revolutionizing what was becoming a computing dinosaur, and how to use XML-RPC from the world of Java. I also spend some time at the end of this chapter looking at real-world applications of XML-RPC, trying to shed some light not only on how to use this technology, but when to use it.

If you are part of the tidal wave of object-oriented development that has come along in the past three to five years, even hearing the word "procedure" may send shivers down your back. Procedural languages such as PL/SQL and ANSI C are not popular for a long list of very good reasons. You have probably been scolded for calling a Java method a function or procedure before, and almost certainly know better than to write "spaghetti code," code that has method after method chained together in a long line. RPC has fallen by the wayside much as these languages and techniques have. There are new, object-oriented ways of achieving the same results, often with better design and performance. Surprisingly, though, the rise of XML has brought with it the rise and prominence of APIs specifically built for XML-RPC, and a gradual trend toward using XML-RPC in specific situations despite the connotations it carries.

Before trying to use these APIs, it is worth spending some time looking at what RPC is and how it compares to similar Java technologies, most notably *remote method invocation* (RMI). If you do choose to use XML-RPC in your applications (and you almost surely will want to at some point), be assured that you will probably have to justify your choice to other developers, particularly those who may have just read books on EJB or RMI. Certainly there are places for all these technologies. Understanding the proper application of each is critical to your success not only as a developer, but as a team member and mentor. Keeping in mind these reasons for understanding the concepts behind these remote methodologies, let's take a look at the two most popular ways to operate upon objects across a network: RPC and RMI.

RPC Versus RMI

If you haven't been under a rock for the last several years, you should be aware that EJB and RMI have taken the Java world by storm. The entire EJB (Enterprise JavaBeans) specification is founded upon RMI principles, and you will be hard-pressed to write a three-tier application without using RMI, even if indirectly. In other words, if you don't know how to use RMI yet, you may want to pick up *Java Enterprise in a Nutshell* by David Flanagan, Jim Farley, William Crawford, and Kris Magnusson, or *Java Distributed Computing* by Jim Farley (both published by O'Reilly) and spend some time looking into this useful technology.

What Is RMI?

In short, RMI is *remote method invocation*. RMI allows a program to invoke methods on an object when the object is not located on the same machine as the program. This is at the heart of distributed computing in the Java world, and is the backbone of EJB as well as many enterprise application implementations. Without getting into too much detail, RMI uses client stubs to describe the methods a remote object has available for invocation. The client acts upon these stubs (which are Java interfaces), and RMI handles the "magic" of translating requests to a stub into a network call. This call invokes the method on the machine with the actual object, and then streams the result back across the network. Finally, the stub returns this result to the client that made the original method call, and the client moves on. The main idea is that the client doesn't typically worry about the RMI and network details; it uses the stub as if it were the actual object with implemented methods. RMI (using JRMP™, Java's remote protocol) makes all this network communication happen behind the scenes, allowing the client to deal with a generic exception (`java.rmi.RemoteException`) and spend more time handling business rules and application logic. RMI can also use different protocols such as Internet Inter-ORB Protocol (IIOP), allowing communication between Java and CORBA objects, often in different languages such as C or C++.

RMI carries a cost, though. First, using RMI is resource-intensive. JRMP provides very poor performance, and writing a remote protocol to replace it is not a simple task. As clients issue RMI calls, sockets must be opened and maintained, and the number of sockets can affect system performance, particularly when the system is accessible via a network (which then requires more sockets to be opened for HTTP access). RMI also requires a server or provider to bind objects to. Until an object is bound to a name on one of these providers, the object is not accessible to other programs. This requires using an RMI registry, a Lightweight Directory Access Protocol (LDAP) directory server, or a variety of other Java Naming and Directory Interface (JNDI) services. Finally, RMI can involve a lot of coding, even with all the helpful RMI server classes you get with the JDK; a remote interface describing the methods available to be invoked must be coded (as well as quite a few other interfaces if you are using EJB). This also means that adding an additional method to the server class results in a change to the interface and recompilation of the client stubs, something that is often not desirable and sometimes not possible.

What Is RPC?

RPC is *remote procedure calls*. Where RMI lets you interoperate directly with a Java object, RPC is built in more of a dispatch fashion. Instead of dealing with objects, RPC lets you use standalone methods across a network. Although this limits interactivity, it does make for a slightly simpler interface to the client. You can think of RPC as a way to use "services" on remote machines, while RMI allows you to use "servers" on remote machines. The subtle difference is that RMI typically is driven entirely by the client, with events occurring when methods are invoked remotely. RPC is often built more as a class or set of classes that works to perform tasks with or without client intervention; however, at times these classes service requests from clients, and execute "mini" tasks for the clients. I will show you some examples shortly to clarify these definitions.

RPC, while not as interactive an environment as RMI, does offer some significant advantages. RPC allows disparate systems to work together. While RMI allows the use of IIOP for connecting Java to CORBA servers and clients, RPC allows literally any type of application intercommunication, because the transport protocol can be HTTP. Since virtually every language in use today has some means of communicating via HTTP, RPC is very attractive for programs that must connect to legacy systems. RPC is also typically more lightweight than RMI (particularly when using XML as the encoding, which I'll cover next); while RMI often has to load entire Java classes over the network (such as code for applets and custom helper classes for EJB), RPC only has to pass across the request parameters and the resulting response, generally encoded as textual data. RPC also fits very nicely into the API model, allowing systems that are not part of your specific application to still access information from your application. This means that changes to your server do not have to result in changes to other clients' application code; with pure textual data transfer and requests, additional methods can be added without client recompilation, and minor changes are sufficient to use these new methods.

The problem with RPC has traditionally been the encoding of data in transfer; imagine trying to represent a Java `Hashtable` or `Vector` in a very lightweight way through textual formats. When you consider that these structures can, in turn, hold other Java object types, the data representation quickly becomes tricky to write; it also has to remain a format that is usable by all the disparate programming languages, or the advantages of RPC are lessened. Until recently, an inverse relationship had been developing between the quality and usability of the encoding and its simplicity; in other words, the easier it became to represent complex objects, the more difficult it became to use the encoding in multiple programming languages without proprietary extensions and code. Elaborate textual representations of data were not standardized and required completely new implementations in every language to be usable. You can see where this discussion is leading.

XML-RPC

The greatest obstacle to using RPC has traditionally been its encoding. But then XML came along with a solution. XML provided not only a very simple, textual representation of data, but a standard for the structure of that data. Concerns about proprietary solutions became moot when the W3C released the XML 1.0 specification, reassuring RPC coders that XML was not going anywhere. In addition, SAX provided a lightweight, standard way to access XML, making it much easier to implement RPC libraries. This left only transmission over HTTP (something people have been doing for many years) and the specific encoding and decoding APIs for XML-RPC implementers to write. After a few beta implementations of XML-RPC libraries, it became clear that XML was also a very fast and lightweight encoding, resulting in better performance for XML-RPC libraries than expected. XML-RPC is now a viable and stable solution for remote procedure calls.

For you, the Java developer, XML-RPC provides a way to handle simple creation of "hooks" into your application and its services, for your own use as well as for other application clients in different divisions or even different companies. It also uncouples these APIs from Java if clients are unable to use the Java language directly. Finally, XML-RPC removes RMI from the technologies that have to be learned to use distributed services (at least initially). I'll spend this chapter looking at how to implement an XML-RPC server and client; I'll show an example of how a server can operate independently of clients, yet still provide XML-RPC accessible interfaces to interoperate with and query its data. Although I'm not going to look at RMI in depth in this chapter, I continually compare the XML-RPC solution to RMI, pointing out why XML-RPC is a better solution for some specific types of tasks.

Saying Hello

You are probably interested in seeing if XML-RPC might be the right solution for some of your development problems. To elaborate on XML-RPC, we'll now look at building some actual working Java code using XML-RPC. In the great tradition of programming, I'll start with a simple "Hello World" type program. I'll show you how to define an XML-RPC server, and have that server register a handler. This handler takes in a Java `String` parameter and the user's name, and returns "Hello" and the user's name; for example, the method might return "Hello Shirley" when invoked. Then you'll need to make this handler available for XML-RPC clients. Finally, I'll demonstrate building a simple client to connect to the server and request the method invocation.

In a practical case, the XML-RPC server and handler would be on one machine, probably a heavy-duty server, and the client on another machine, invoking the procedure calls remotely. However, if you don't have multiple machines available, you can still use the examples locally. Although this will be much faster than an actual client and server, you can still see how the pieces fit together and get a taste of XML-RPC.

XML-RPC Libraries

A lot of work has already gone into RPC, and more recently XML-RPC. Like using SAX, DOM, and JDOM for XML handling, there is no reason to reinvent the wheel when there are good, even exceptional, Java packages in existence for your desired purpose. The center for information about XML-RPC and links to libraries for Java as well as many other languages can be found at *http://www.xmlrpc.com*. Sponsored by Userland (*http://www.userland.com*), this site has a public specification on XML-RPC, information on what datatypes are supported, and some tutorials on XML-RPC use. Most importantly, it directs you to the XML-RPC package for Java. Following the link on the main page, you are directed to Hannes Wallnofer's site at *http://classic.helma.at/hannes/xmlrpc/*.

On Hannes's site is a description of the classes in his XML-RPC package and instructions. Download the archive file and expand the files into your development area or IDE. You should then be able to compile these classes; there is one Java servlet example that requires the servlet classes (*servlet.jar* for Servlet API 2.2). You can obtain these classes with the Tomcat servlet engine by pointing your web browser to *http://jakarta.apache.org*. If you do not wish to play with the servlet example, the servlet classes are not required for the programs in this chapter.

The core distribution (which does not include the applet or regular expression examples in the downloaded archive) is made up of thirteen classes, all in the `helma.xmlrpc` package. These are in a ready-to-use format in the *lib/xmlrpc.jar* file of the distribution. The classes within that distribution are detailed briefly in Table 11-1.

Table 11-1. The XML-RPC classes

Class	Purpose
XmlRpc	Core class allowing method calls on handlers by an XML-RPC server.
XmlRpcClient	Class for client to use for RPC communication over HTTP, including proxy and cookie support.
XmlRpcClientLite	Class for client to use when a less-featured HTTP client is needed (no cookies, proxy support).
XmlRpcServer	Class for servers to use to receive RPC calls.
XmlRpcServlet	Provides the functionality of XmlRpcServer in a servlet format.
XmlRpcProxyServlet	Acts as an XML-RPC servlet proxy.
XmlRpcHandler	Base interface for controlling XML-RPC interactions by handlers.
AuthenticatedXmlRpcHandler	Same as XmlRpcHandler, but allows for authentication.
Base64	Encodes and decodes between bytes and base 64 encoding characters.
Benchmark	Times roundtrip XML-RPC interactions for a specific SAX driver.
WebServer	A lightweight HTTP server for use by XML-RPC servers.

The SAX classes (from earlier examples) and a SAX driver are not included in the distribution, but they are required for operation. In other words, you need a complete XML parser implementation that supports SAX. I continue to use Apache Xerces in these examples, although the libraries support any SAX 1.0–compatible driver.

Once you have all the source files compiled, ensure that the XML-RPC classes, SAX classes, and your XML parser classes are all in your environment's classpath. This should have you ready to write your own custom code and start the process of "saying hello." Keep the XML-RPC source files handy, as looking at what is going on under the hood can aid in your understanding of the examples.

Writing the Handler

The first thing you need to do is write the class and method you want invoked remotely. This is usually called a *handler*. Beware, though, as the XML-RPC server mechanism that dispatches requests is also often called a handler; again, naming ambiguity rears its ugly head. A clearer distinction can be drawn as follows: an *XML-RPC handler* is a method or set of methods that takes an XML-RPC request, decodes its contents, and dispatches the request to a class and method. A *response handler*, or simply *handler*, is any method that can be invoked by an XML-RPC handler. With the XML-RPC libraries for Java, you do not need to write an XML-RPC handler because one is included as part of the `helma.xmlrpc.XmlRpcServer` class. You only need to write a class with one or more methods to register with the server.

It might surprise you to learn that creating a response handler requires no subclassing or other special treatment in your code. Any method can be invoked via XML-RPC as long as its parameter and return types are supported (able to be encoded) by XML-RPC. Table 11-2 lists all currently supported Java types that can be used in XML-RPC method signatures.

Table 11-2. Supported Java types in XML-RPC

XML-RPC datatype	Java type
int	int
boolean	boolean
string	String
double	double
dateTime.iso8601	Date
struct	Hashtable
array	Vector
base64	byte[]
nil	null

Although this list includes only a small number of types, they handle most of the XML-RPC requests made over a network. The method in this example only needs to take in a `String` (the name to say "hello" to), and return a `String`, and so fits these requirements. This is enough information to write a simple handler class, shown in Example 11-1.

Example 11-1. Handler class with remote method

```
package javaxml2;

public class HelloHandler {

    public String sayHello(String name) {
        return "Hello " + name;
    }
}
```

This is as simple as it seems. The method signature takes in and returns legal XML-RPC parameters, so you can safely register it with your (soon to be created) XML-RPC server and know it will be callable via XML-RPC.

Writing the Server

With your handler ready, you need to write a program to start up an XML-RPC server, listen for requests, and dispatch these requests to the handler. For this example, I use the `helma.xmlrpc.WebServer` class as the request handler. Although you could use a Java servlet, using this lightweight web server implementation allows you to avoid running a servlet engine on the XML-RPC server. I'll spend more time at the end of this chapter discussing servlets in the context of an XML-RPC server. For the server, the example allows the specification of a port to start the server on, and then has the server listen for XML-RPC requests until shut down. Finally, you need to register the class you just created with the server, and specify any other application-specific parameters to the server.

Create the skeleton for this class (shown in Example 11-2) now; you'll need to import the `WebServer` class and also ensure that a port number is given to the program on the command line when the server is started.

Example 11-2. Skeleton for XML-RPC server

```
package javaxml2;

import helma.xmlrpc.WebServer;

public class HelloServer {

    public static void main(String[] args) {
        if (args.length < 1) {
            System.out.println(
                "Usage: java javaxml2.HelloServer [port]");
            System.exit(-1);
        }

        // Start the server on specified port
    }
}
```

Before starting the server, specify the SAX driver for use in parsing and encoding XML. The default SAX driver for these libraries is James Clark's XP parser, available online at *http://www.jclark.com*. In this code, I instead request the Apache Xerces parser by specifying the SAX `Parser` implementation class[*] to the XML-RPC engine. This is done through the `setDriver()` method, a static method

---

[*] Currently this XML-RPC library does not support SAX 2.0 or implement the `XMLReader` interface. As the Apache Xerces `SAXParser` class implements both the SAX 1.0 `Parser` interface and SAX 2.0 `XMLReader` interface, no code needs to be changed in the examples if SAX 2.0 updates are made to the libraries. However, if you are using a different vendor's parser, you may need to specify a SAX 2.0 class if the XML-RPC libraries are modified to use SAX 2.0.

belonging to the `XmlRpc` class. This class underpins the `WebServer` class, but must be imported and used directly to make this change in SAX drivers. A `ClassNotFoundException` can be thrown by this method, so must be caught in case the driver class cannot be located in your classpath at runtime. Add the necessary import statement and methods to your `HelloServer` class now:

```java
package javaxml2;

import helma.xmlrpc.WebServer;
import helma.xmlrpc.XmlRpc;

public class HelloServer {

    public static void main(String[] args) {
        if (args.length < 1) {
            System.out.println(
                "Usage: java javaxml2.HelloServer [port]");
            System.exit(-1);
        }

        try {
            // Use the Apache Xerces SAX Driver
            XmlRpc.setDriver("org.apache.xerces.parsers.SAXParser");

            // Start the server

        } catch (ClassNotFoundException e) {
            System.out.println("Could not locate SAX Driver");
        }
    }
}
```

At this point, you are ready to add the main portion of the code, which creates the HTTP listener that services XML-RPC requests, and then registers some handler classes that are available for remote procedure calls. Creating the listener is very simple; the `WebServer` helper class I have been discussing can be instantiated by supplying it the port to listen to, and just that easily, the server is servicing XML-RPC requests. Although no classes are available to be called yet, you do have a working XML-RPC server. Let's add in the line to create and start the server, as well as a status line for display purposes. You'll also need to add another import statement and exception handler, this one for `java.io.IOException`. Because the server must start up on a port, it can throw an `IOException` if the port is inaccessible or if other problems occur in server startup. The modified code fragment looks like this:

```java
package javaxml2;

import java.io.IOException;
```

```
import helma.xmlrpc.WebServer;
import helma.xmlrpc.XmlRpc;

public class HelloServer {

    public static void main(String[] args) {
        if (args.length < 1) {
            System.out.println(
                "Usage: java javaxml2.HelloServer [port]");
            System.exit(-1);
        }

        try {
            // Use the Apache Xerces SAX Driver
            XmlRpc.setDriver("org.apache.xerces.parsers.SAXParser");

            // Start the server
            System.out.println("Starting XML-RPC Server...");
            WebServer server = new WebServer(Integer.parseInt(args[0]));

        } catch (ClassNotFoundException e) {
            System.out.println("Could not locate SAX Driver");
        } catch (IOException e) {
            System.out.println("Could not start server: " +
                e.getMessage());
        }
    }
}
```

Compile this class and give it a try; it is completely functional, and should print out the status line and then pause, waiting for requests. You now need to add the handler class to the server so that it can receive requests.

One of the most significant differences between RMI and RPC is the way methods are made available. In RMI, a remote interface has the method signature for each remote method. If a method is implemented on the server class, but no matching signature is added to the remote interface, the new method cannot be invoked by an RMI client. This makes for a large amount of code modification and recompilation in the development of RMI classes. This process is quite a bit different, and is generally considered easier and more flexible, in RPC. When a request comes in to an RPC server, the request contains a set of parameters and a textual value, usually in the form "classname.methodname." This signifies to the RPC server that the requested method is in the class "classname" and is named "methodname." The RPC server tries to find a matching class and method that take parameter types that match the types within the RPC request as input. Once a match is made, the method is called, and the result is encoded and sent back to the client.

Thus, the method requested is never explicitly defined in the XML-RPC server, but rather in the request from the client. Only a class instance is registered with the XML-RPC server. You can add methods to that class, restart the XML-RPC server with no code changes (allowing it to register an updated class instance), and then immediately request the new methods within your client code. As long as you can determine and send the correct parameters to the server, the new methods are instantly accessible. This is one of the advantages of XML-RPC over RMI, in that it can more closely represent an API; there are no client stubs, skeletons, or interfaces that must be updated. If a method is added, the method signature can be published to the client community and used immediately.

Now that you've read about how easily an RPC handler can be used, I demonstrate how to register one in the `HelloHandler` example. The `WebServer` class allows the addition of a handler through the `addHandler()` method. This method takes a name as input to register the handler class to, and an instance of the handler class itself. This is typically accessed by instantiating a new class with its constructor (using the `new` keyword), although in the next section I'll look at using other methods, in the event that an instance should be shared instead of created by each client. In the current example, instantiating a new class is an acceptable solution. Register the `HelloHandler` class to the name "hello". You can include status lines to show what is occurring in the server as it adds the handler:

```
try {
    // Use the Apache Xerces SAX Driver
    XmlRpc.setDriver("org.apache.xerces.parsers.SAXParser");

    // Start the server
    System.out.println("Starting XML-RPC Server...");
    WebServer server = new WebServer(Integer.parseInt(args[0]));

    // Register the handler class
    server.addHandler("hello", new HelloHandler());
    System.out.println(
        "Registered HelloHandler class to \"hello\"");

    System.out.println("Now accepting requests...");

} catch (ClassNotFoundException e) {
    System.out.println("Could not locate SAX Driver");
} catch (IOException e) {
    System.out.println("Could not start server: " +
        e.getMessage());
}
```

Now recompile this source file and start up the server. Your output should look similar to Example 11-3.*

Example 11-3. Starting the server

```
$ java javaxml2.HelloServer 8585
Starting XML-RPC Server...
Registered HelloHandler class to "hello"
Now accepting requests...
```

It's that simple! You can now write a client for the server, and test communications across a network using XML-RPC. This is another advantage of XML-RPC; the barrier for entry into coding servers and clients is low, compared to the complexity of using RMI. Read on, and see creating a client is just as straightforward.

Writing the Client

With the server running and accepting requests, you done the hardest part of coding the XML-RPC application (believe it or not, that was the hard part!). Now you need to construct a simple client to call the sayHello() method remotely. This is made simple by using the helma.xmlrpc.XmlRpcClient. This class takes care of many of the details on the client side that its analogs, XmlRpcServer and WebServer, do on the server. To write your client, you need this class as well as the XmlRpc class; this client must handle encoding of the request, so again set the SAX driver class to use with the setDriver() method. Begin your client code with these required import statements, checking for an argument to pass as the parameter to the sayHello() method on the server, and some exception handling. Create the Java source file shown in Example 11-4 and save it as *HelloClient.java*.

Example 11-4. A client for the XML-RPC server

```
package javaxml2;

import helma.xmlrpc.XmlRpc;
import helma.xmlrpc.XmlRpcClient;

public class HelloClient {

    public static void main(String args[]) {
        if (args.length < 1) {
            System.out.println(
                "Usage: java HelloClient [your name]");
            System.exit(-1);
        }
```

---

* If you are on a Unix machine, you must be logged in as the root user to start a service up on a port lower than 1024. To avoid these problems, consider using a higher numbered port, as shown in Example 11-3.

Example 11-4. A client for the XML-RPC server (continued)

```
    try {
        // Use the Apache Xerces SAX Driver
        XmlRpc.setDriver("org.apache.xerces.parsers.SAXParser");

        // Specify the Server

        // Create request

        // Make a request and print the result

    } catch (ClassNotFoundException e) {
        System.out.println("Could not locate SAX Driver");
    }
    }
}
```

As with the rest of the code in this chapter, this is simple and straightforward. To create an XML-RPC client, you need to instantiate the `XmlRpcClient` class, which requires the hostname of the XML-RPC server to connect to. This should be a complete URL, including the *http://* protocol prefix. In creating the client, a `java.net.MalformedURLException` can be thrown when this URL is in an unacceptable format. You can add this class to the list of imported classes, instantiate the client, and add the required exception handler:

```
package javaxml2;

import java.net.MalformedURLException;

import helma.xmlrpc.XmlRpc;
import helma.xmlrpc.XmlRpcClient;

public class HelloClient {

    public static void main(String args[]) {
        if (args.length < 1) {
            System.out.println(
                "Usage: java HelloClient [your name]");
            System.exit(-1);
        }

        try {
            // Use the Apache Xerces SAX Driver
            XmlRpc.setDriver("org.apache.xerces.parsers.SAXParser");

            // Specify the server
```

```
            XmlRpcClient client =
                new XmlRpcClient("http://localhost:8585/");

            // Create request

            // Make a request and print the result

        } catch (ClassNotFoundException e) {
            System.out.println("Could not locate SAX Driver");
        } catch (MalformedURLException e) {
            System.out.println(
                "Incorrect URL for XML-RPC server format: " +
                e.getMessage());
        }
    }
}
```

Although no actual RPC calls are being made, you now have a fully functional client application. You can compile and run this application, although you won't see any activity, as no connection is made until a request is initiated.

WARNING   Make sure you use the port number in your source code that you plan to specify to the server when you start it up. Obviously, this is a poor way to implement connectivity between the client and server; changing the port the server listens to requires changing the source code of our client! In your own applications, make this a user-defined variable; I've kept it simple for example purposes.

The ease with which this client and our server come together is impressive. Still, this program is not of much use until it actually makes a request and receives a response. To encode the request, invoke the `execute()` method on your `XmlRpcClient` instance. This method takes in two parameters: the name of the class identifier and method to invoke, which is a single `String` parameter, and a `Vector` containing the method parameters to pass in to the specified method. The class identifier is the name you registered to the `HelloHandler` class on the XML-RPC server; this identifier can be the actual name of the class, but it is often something more readable and meaningful to the client, and in this case it was "hello". The name of the method to invoke is appended to this, separated from the class identifier with a period, in the form *[class identifier].[method name]*. The parameters must be in the form of a Java `Vector`, and should include any parameter objects that are needed by the specified method. In the simple `sayHello()` method, this is a `String` with the name of the user, which should have been specified on the command line.

Once the XML-RPC client encodes this request, it sends the request to the XML-RPC server. The server locates the class that matches the request's class identifier, and looks for a matching method name. If a matching method name is found, the parameter types for the method are compared with the parameters in the request. If a match occurs, the method is executed. If multiple methods are found with the same name, the parameters determine which method is invoked; this process allows normal Java overloading to occur in the handler classes. The result of the method invocation is encoded by the XML-RPC server, and sent back to the client as a Java Object (which in turn could be a Vector of Objects!). This result can be cast to the appropriate Java type, and used in the client normally. If a matching class identifier/method/parameter signature is not found, an XmlRpcException is thrown back to the client. This ensures the client is not trying to invoke a method or handler that does not exist, or sending incorrect parameters.

All this happens with a few additional lines of Java code. You must import the Xml-RpcException class, as well as java.io.IOException; the latter is thrown when communication between the client and server causes error conditions. You can then add the Vector class and instantiate it, adding to it a single String parameter. This allows your code to invoke the execute() method with the name of the handler, the method to call, and its parameters; the result of this call is cast to a String, which is printed out to the screen. In this example, the local machine is running the XML-RPC server on port 8585:

```
package javaxml2;

import java.io.IOException;
import java.net.MalformedURLException;
import java.util.Vector;

import helma.xmlrpc.XmlRpc;
import helma.xmlrpc.XmlRpcClient;
import helma.xmlrpc.XmlRpcException;

public class HelloClient {

    public static void main(String args[]) {
        if (args.length < 1) {
            System.out.println(
                "Usage: java HelloClient [your name]");
            System.exit(-1);
        }

        try {
            // Use the Apache Xerces SAX Driver
            XmlRpc.setDriver("org.apache.xerces.parsers.SAXParser");

            // Specify the server
            XmlRpcClient client =
```

```
                    new XmlRpcClient("http://localhost:8585/");

            // Create request
            Vector params = new Vector();
            params.addElement(args[0]);

            // Make a request and print the result
            String result =
                (String)client.execute("hello.sayHello", params);

          System.out.println("Response from server: " + result);

        } catch (ClassNotFoundException e) {
            System.out.println("Could not locate SAX Driver");
        } catch (MalformedURLException e) {
            System.out.println(
                "Incorrect URL for XML-RPC server format: " +
                e.getMessage());
        } catch (XmlRpcException e) {
            System.out.println("XML-RPC Exception: " + e.getMessage());
        } catch (IOException e) {
            System.out.println("IO Exception: " + e.getMessage());
        }
    }
}
```

That's all that is required to make this work. Now compile your source code and
open a command shell for running the example.

Talk to Me

Make sure that you have the XML-RPC classes and your example classes in your environment's classpath. Also, confirm that Apache Xerces or your chosen SAX driver is
in your classpath and accessible, as the examples must load these classes for parsing.
Once that is set up, start the HelloServer class by giving it a port number. On Windows, use the *start* command to start the server in a separate process:

```
c:\javaxml2\build>start java javaxml2.HelloServer 8585
Starting XML-RPC Server...
Registered HelloHandler class to "hello"
Now accepting requests...
```

On Unix, use the background processing command (&) to make sure you can run
your client as well (or open another terminal window and duplicate your environment settings):

```
$ java javaxml2.HelloServer &
Starting XML-RPC Server...
Registered HelloHandler class to "hello"
Now accepting requests...
```

You can then run your client by specifying your name to the program as a command-line argument. You should quickly see a response (similar to that shown in Example 11-5) as the HelloServer receives your client's request, handles it, and returns the result of the sayHello() method, which is then printed by the client.

Example 11-5. Running the HelloClient class

```
$ java javaxml2.HelloClient Leigh
Response from server: Hello Leigh
```

You have just seen XML-RPC in action. Certainly this is not a particularly useful example, but it should have given you an idea of the basics and shown you the simplicity of coding an XML-RPC server and client in Java. With these fundamentals, I want to move on to a more realistic example. In the next section, I'll show you how to build a more useful server, and take a look at what XML-RPC handlers often look like. I'll then demonstrate creating a client (similar to our HelloClient) to test the new code.

Putting the Load on the Server

As instructional as the "hello" example has been in demonstrating how to use XML-RPC with Java, it isn't very realistic. In addition to being a trivial example, the server is not very flexible and the handler itself doesn't give any indication of how a practical XML-RPC handler might operate. Here I'll try to give an example of using XML-RPC in a production environment by increasing the usefulness of the handler and the usability of the server. While it's not code you might add to your current project, this example begins to demonstrate how XML-RPC might be of use, and how to build applications that can use XML-RPC but are not limited by it.

A Shared Handler

The HelloHandler class was simple, but useless in a practical application. Most XML-RPC uses relate to letting events occur on a server that is more suited for complex tasks, while allowing a thin client to request procedures to be executed and then use the returned results. In addition, it is possible that part or even all of the computations needed to respond to a request can be done in advance; in other words, the handler class may be running tasks and ensuring that results are already available when a method call comes in. As a Java coder, threads and shared instance data should leap to your mind. Here I'll take a look at a very simple Scheduler class to illustrate these principles.

The scheduler should allow clients to add and remove events. Clients can then query the scheduler for a list of all events in the queue. To make this more practical (and to have a task for the server to perform later), querying the current events returns them sorted by the time they occurred. An event for this example is simply a `String` event name and a time for the event (in a `java.util.Date` format). Though this is not a complete scheduler implementation, it can demonstrate how to let the server do behind-the-scenes work for clients.

First, code the `addEvent()` and `removeEvent()` methods. Because these are both client-triggered events, there is nothing particularly remarkable about them; what is worth thinking about is how to store these events in the `Scheduler` class. Although the XML-RPC server will instantiate this class, and that instance will be used for all XML-RPC calls coming into that server, it is possible and even probable that other classes or even XML-RPC servers may interact with the scheduler. If the scheduler stores a list of events as a member variable, multiple instances will not be able to share data. To solve this problem in this example, it's best to make the class's storage static, causing it to be shared across all `Scheduler` class instances. To store both an event name and an event time, a `Hashtable` would seem appropriate, allowing the use of key-value pairs. In addition to this `Hashtable`, the class stores the names of the events in a `Vector`. Although this uses some extra storage space (and memory in the Java Virtual Machine), the class can sort the `Vector` and not have to deal with sorting the `Hashtable`; the advantage is that it's simple to swap the event names in the `Vector` (a single swap) and not have to swap the event times in the `Hashtable` (*two* swaps for each exchange). With that information, you're ready to code the skeleton of this class, and add these first two methods to allow addition and removal of events. For now, add the storage as well, but I'll leave the implementation of the retrieval and sorting of events for later. Example 11-6 is a code listing for this new handler.

Example 11-6. The Scheduler class

```
package javaxml2;

import java.util.Date;
import java.util.Hashtable;
import java.util.Vector;

public class Scheduler {

    /** List of event names (for sorting) */
    private static Vector events = new Vector();

    /** Event details (name, time) */
    private static Hashtable eventDetails = new Hashtable();

    public Scheduler() {
    }
```

Example 11-6. The Scheduler class (continued)

```
    public boolean addEvent(String eventName, Date eventTime) {
        // Add this event to the list of events
        if (!events.contains(eventName)) {
            events.addElement(eventName);
            eventDetails.put(eventName, eventTime);
        }

        return true;
    }

    public synchronized boolean removeEvent(String eventName) {
        events.remove(eventName);
        eventDetails.remove(eventName);

        return true;
    }
}
```

The addEvent() method adds the name of the event to both storage objects, and the time to the Hashtable. The removeEvent() method does the opposite. Both methods return a boolean value. Although in the example this value is always true, in a more complex implementation, this value could be used to indicate problems in the addition or removal of events.

With the ability to add and remove events, you now need to add a method that returns a list of events. This method returns all events added to the event store, regardless of the client or application that added them; in other words, these could be events added by a different XML-RPC client, a different XML-RPC server, another application, or a standalone implementation of this same scheduler. Since the method has to return a single Object result, it can return a Vector of formatted String values that contain the name of each event and its time. In a more useful implementation this might return the Vector of events or some other form of the events in a typed format (with the date as a Date object, etc.). This method acts more as a view of the data, though, and does not allow the client to further manipulate it. To return this list of events, the method uses the event store and the java.text.SimpleDateFormat class, which allows textual formatting of Date objects. Iterating through all events, a String is created with the event name and the time it is set for; each String is inserted into the Vector result list, and this list is returned to the client. Now add the required import statement and the code to return the events in the store to the scheduler code:

```
package javaxml2;

import java.text.SimpleDateFormat;
```

```
import java.util.Date;
import java.util.Hashtable;
import java.util.Vector;

public class Scheduler {

    // Existing method implementations

    public Vector getListOfEvents() {
        Vector list = new Vector();

        // Create a Date Formatter
        SimpleDateFormat fmt =
            new SimpleDateFormat("hh:mm a MM/dd/yyyy");

        // Add each event to the list
        for (int i=0; i<events.size(); i++) {
            String eventName = (String)events.elementAt(i);
            list.addElement("Event \"" + eventName +
                            "\" scheduled for " +
                            fmt.format(
                                (Date)eventDetails.get(eventName)));
        }

        return list;
    }
}
```

At this point, you could use this class as an XML-RPC handler without any problems. However, the point of this exercise is to look at how work can be done by the server while the client is performing other tasks. The getListOfEvents() method assumes the event list (the Vector variable events) is correctly ordered when this method is called, and that sorting has already occurred. I haven't shown you any code to sort the events yet, but more importantly, there isn't any code to trigger this sorting. Furthermore, as the event store increases, sorting is time-consuming, and the client should not wait for it to complete. First it makes sense to add a method that the class can use to sort the events. For simplicity, a bubble sort is used. (Discussion of sorting algorithms is beyond the scope of this book, so this code is presented without any explanation of its workings.) At the end of the method, though, the Vector variable events is sorted in order of the time the events within it occur. For information on this and other sorting algorithms, refer to *Algorithms in Java* by Robert Sedgewick and Tim Lindholm (Addison Wesley). The algorithm and method to handle sorting of the events are presented here, and should be added to your code:

```
package javaxml2;

import java.text.SimpleDateFormat;
```

```java
import java.util.Date;
import java.util.Enumeration;
import java.util.Hashtable;
import java.util.Vector;

public class Scheduler {

    /** List of event names (for sorting) */
    private static Vector events = new Vector();

    /** Event details (name, time) */
    private static Hashtable eventDetails = new Hashtable();

    /** Flag to indicate if events are sorted */
    private static boolean eventsSorted;

    // Existing method implementations

    private synchronized void sortEvents() {
        if (eventsSorted) {
            return;
        }

        // Create array of events as they are (unsorted)
        String[] eventNames = new String[events.size()];
        events.copyInto(eventNames);

        // Bubble sort these
        String tmpName;
        Date date1, date2;
        for (int i=0; i<eventNames.length - 1; i++) {
            for (int j=0; j<eventNames.length - i - 1; j++) {
                // Compare the dates for these events
                date1 = (Date)eventDetails.get(eventNames[j]);
                date2 = (Date)eventDetails.get(eventNames[j+1]);
                if (date1.compareTo(date2) > 0) {

                    // Swap if needed
                    tmpName = eventNames[j];
                    eventNames[j] = eventNames[j+1];
                    eventNames[j+1] = tmpName;

                }
            }
        }

        // Put into new Vector (ordered)
```

```
        Vector sortedEvents = new Vector();
        for (int i=0; i<eventNames.length; i++) {
            sortedEvents.addElement(eventNames[i]);
        }

        // Update the global events
        events = sortedEvents;
        eventsSorted = true;


    }
}
```

In addition to the core algorithm, the code imports the `java.util.Enumeration`
class and adds a `boolean` member variable, `eventsSorted`. This flag allows short-
circuiting of the execution of the sorting when the events are already ordered.
Although you have not yet added code to update this flag, it's easy to do so. The
sorting method already indicates that events are sorted at its completion. The
class's constructor should initially set this value to true, indicating that all events
are in order. It is only when events are added that the list may become unordered,
so in the `addEvents()` method you'll need to set this flag to false if an event is
added. This lets the `Scheduler` class know that something should occur to trigger
the sort. When the `getListOfEvents()` method is invoked, the events will be
ordered and ready for retrieval. You should add code to the constructor and the
method for adding events that will update this flag:

```
package javaxml2;

import java.text.SimpleDateFormat;
import java.util.Date;
import java.util.Enumeration;
import java.util.Hashtable;
import java.util.Vector;

public class Scheduler {

    public Scheduler() {
        eventsSorted = true;
    }

    public boolean addEvent(String eventName, Date eventTime) {
        // Add this event to the list of events
        if (!events.contains(eventName)) {
            events.addElement(eventName);
            eventDetails.put(eventName, eventTime);
            eventsSorted = false;
        }
```

```
        return true;
    }


    // Other method implementations
}
```

You do not need to make any changes to the `removeEvent()` method, as removing an entry does not affect the order of the events. The ideal mechanism to handle server-side processing while freeing the client for further action is a thread that sorts events. With this thread started in the JVM, client processing can continue without waiting for the thread to complete. This is particularly important in a multithreaded environment where synchronization and threads waiting for object locks are in use. In this example, I've avoided threading issues, but you can add the relevant code to handle these issues fairly easily. You'll want to create an inner class that extends `Thread`, and does nothing but invoke the `sortEvents()` method. You can then add to the `addEvents()` method the code that creates and starts this thread when events are added. Then any additional events trigger a resorting of the events, but allow the client to continue with its actions (which might include adding additional events, in turn starting more threads to sort the data). When the client does request the list of events, the events should be sorted when returned, all without the client ever waiting on this action to occur or spending processing power to make it happen. The addition of the inner class to sort, as well as the code to run that class as a thread in our `addEvents()` method, rounds out the `Scheduler` class and is shown here:

```
package javaxml2;

import java.text.SimpleDateFormat;
import java.util.Date;
import java.util.Enumeration;
import java.util.Hashtable;
import java.util.Vector;

public class Scheduler {

    // Existing variables and methods

    public boolean addEvent(String eventName, Date eventTime) {
        // Add this event to the list of events
        if (!events.contains(eventName)) {
            events.addElement(eventName);
            eventDetails.put(eventName, eventTime);
            eventsSorted = false;

            // Start thread on server sorting
            SortEventsThread sorter = new SortEventsThread();
```

```
        sorter.start();
    }

    return true;
}

class SortEventsThread extends Thread {

    public void run() {
        sortEvents();
    }
}
}
```

Now when you compile the modified source code, you'll have a threaded sched-uler that performs the process-intensive task of sorting on the server, allowing any clients to work uninterrupted while the sorting occurs. This is still a simple exam-ple of using a handler class properly, but it does introduce the concepts of resource distribution and letting a server handle the workload when possible. To complement this more advanced handler class, I'll next demonstrate building a more robust XML-RPC server.

A Configurable Server

The XML-RPC server class still needs some work. The current version requires you to specifically add handler classes to the server in the code. This means the addi-tion of a new handler class requires coding and recompilation. Not only is this undesirable from a change-control perspective, but it is annoying and time-con-suming. Obtaining the newest code from a source control system, adding the change, and testing to add one or two handlers is not practical, and won't win you friends among management. What is preferred is to have a robust server that can read this sort of information from a configuration file and load the needed classes at runtime. We will build a lightweight server to do this now.

To begin, you'll want to create a new server class. You can either start from scratch, or copy and paste from the HelloServer class given earlier in this chapter. Start by setting up our framework, adding the required import statements, and instantiating the server, similar to the earlier example; however, you should not add any code that registers handlers, as there will be a helper method to load the needed information from a file. The one change from the earlier version is that this class requires an additional command-line parameter that should be the name of a file. The server will read this file in using methods I'll cover later, and add handlers to the server. You can create the LightweightXmlRPcServer class, which continues to use the thin WebServer helper class, with the code shown in Example 11-7.

Example 11-7. A reusable XML-RPC server

```
package javaxml2;

import java.io.IOException;

import helma.xmlrpc.XmlRpc;
import helma.xmlrpc.WebServer;

public class LightweightXmlRpcServer {

    /** The XML-RPC server utility class */
    private WebServer server;

    /** Port number to listen on */
    private int port;

    /** Configuration file to use */
    private String configFile;

    public LightweightXmlRpcServer(int port, String configFile) {
        this.port = port;
        this.configFile = configFile;
    }

    public void start() throws IOException {
        try {
            // Use Apache Xerces SAX Parser
            XmlRpc.setDriver("org.apache.xerces.parsers.SAXParser");

            System.out.println("Starting up XML-RPC Server...");
            server = new WebServer(port);

            // Register handlers

        } catch (ClassNotFoundException e) {
            throw new IOException("Error loading SAX parser: " +
                e.getMessage());
        }
    }

    public static void main(String[] args) {

        if (args.length < 2) {
            System.out.println(
                "Usage: " +
                "java com.oreilly.xml.LightweightXmlRpcServer " +
                "[port] [configFile]");
```

Example 11-7. A reusable XML-RPC server (continued)

```
            System.exit(-1);
        }

        LightweightXmlRpcServer server =
            new LightweightXmlRpcServer(Integer.parseInt(args[0]),
                                        args[1]);

        try {
            // Start the server
            server.start();
        } catch (IOException e) {
            System.out.println(e.getMessage());
        }
    }
}
```

Nothing remarkable here. The code ensures that the required parameters are passed in and then starts the server on the requested port. It's now time to add in methods to load the handlers from a file, and then add those handlers one by one to the server.

Because each handler needs a name and an associated class, you can create a configuration file that has these two pieces of information. With Java, it is easy to load and instantiate a class with its complete package and name. This means you can completely represent a new handler with a pair of textual values. Within this file, you can add both the original HelloHandler class as well as the new Scheduler class. Since you are writing the file parser as well, it's safe to arbitrarily decide to use commas as delimiters and the pound sign (#) as a comment marker. In fact, you can use whatever format you wish as long as you write code that uses your conventions in parsing the file.

NOTE   You may be surprised that I'm not using an XML file format here. There are several reasons for this. First, I'm going to talk about SOAP in the next chapter, which uses XML throughout. Using a non-XML format here provides a good contrast between the two methodologies. Second, you're certainly prepared at this point to write your own XML parsing code, so this task is a good exercise. And third, I'm a realist; you'll be amazed at how many times "XML frameworks" and "XML applications" use non-XML formats. So get used to it now, as you're sure to encounter it time and time again.

Create the configuration file shown in Example 11-8, which will add the HelloHandler class under the class identifier "hello" and the Scheduler class under the class identifier "scheduler", and save it as *xmlrpc.conf*.

Example 11-8. XML-RPC configuration file

```
# Hello Handler: sayHello()
hello,javaxml2.HelloHandler

# Scheduler: addEvent(), removeEvent(), getEvents()
scheduler,javaxml2.Scheduler
```

For documentation purposes, I've specified the methods available to each handler in comments. This allows future maintainers of this configuration file to know what methods are available for each handler.

Java's I/O classes make it easy to load this file and read its contents. It's simple to create a helper method that reads the specified file and stores the pairs of values in a Java Hashtable. The object can then be passed on to another helper that loads and registers each handler. This example method does not do extensive error checking as a production-ready server might, and it simply ignores any line without a pair of comma-separated values. It is easy to add error handling if you want to use this code in your applications. Once it finds a line with a pair of values, the line is broken up and the class identifier and class name are stored as an entry within the Hashtable. Add the import statements for the required utility classes and then the new getHandlers() method to the LightweightServer class now:

```
package javaxml2;

import java.io.BufferedReader;
import java.io.FileReader;
import java.io.IOException;
import java.util.Hashtable;

import helma.xmlrpc.XmlRpc;
import helma.xmlrpc.WebServer;

public class LightweightXmlRpcServer {

    // Existing method implementations

    private Hashtable getHandlers() throws IOException {

        Hashtable handlers = new Hashtable();

        BufferedReader reader =
            new BufferedReader(new FileReader(configFile));
        String line = null;

        while ((line = reader.readLine()) != null) {
            // Syntax is "handlerName, handlerClass"
```

```
        int comma;

        // Skip comments
        if (line.startsWith("#")) {
            continue;
        }

        // Skip empty or useless lines
        if ((comma = line.indexOf(",")) < 2) {
            continue;
        }

        // Add the handler name and the handler class
        handlers.put(line.substring(0, comma),
                     line.substring(comma+1));
    }

    return handlers;
}
}
```

Instead of adding code to save the result of this method, you can use that result as input to a method that iterates through the `Hashtable` and adds each handler to the server. The code needed to accomplish this task is not complicated; the only notable thing is that the `addHandler()` method of `WebServer` requires an instantiated class as a parameter. The code is required to take the name of the class to register from the `Hashtable`, load that class into the JVM with `Class.forName()`, and then instantiate that class with `newInstance()`. This is the methodology used in class loaders and other dynamic applications in Java, but may be unfamiliar to you if you are new to Java or have not had to dynamically instantiate classes from a textual name before. Once the class is loaded in this way, it and the class identifier are passed to the `addHandler()` method, and the iteration continues. Once the contents of the `Hashtable` are loaded, the server is set up and ready to go. I've used the `Enumeration` class to cycle through the keys in the `Hashtable`, so you'll need to add this import statement to your source file:

```
package javaxml2;

import java.io.BufferedReader;
import java.io.FileReader;
import java.io.IOException;
import java.util.Enumeration;
import java.util.Hashtable;

import helma.xmlrpc.XmlRpc;
import helma.xmlrpc.WebServer;
```

```java
public class LightweightXmlRpcServer {

    // Existing method implementations

    private void registerHandlers(Hashtable handlers) {
        Enumeration handlerNames = handlers.keys();

        // Loop through the requested handlers
        while (handlerNames.hasMoreElements()) {
            String handlerName = (String)handlerNames.nextElement();
            String handlerClass = (String)handlers.get(handlerName);

            // Add this handler to the server
            try {
                server.addHandler(handlerName,
                    Class.forName(handlerClass).newInstance());

                System.out.println("Registered handler " + handlerName +
                                    " to class " + handlerClass);
            } catch (Exception e) {
                System.out.println("Could not register handler " +
                                    handlerName + " with class " +
                                    handlerClass);
            }
        }
    }
}
```

This is simply a complement to the getHandlers() method; in fact, it takes the result of that method as input. It uses the String values within the Hashtable and registers each. Now the server is running and will have any handlers in the configuration file loaded and available for remote calls. You could just as easily have consolidated these methods into one larger method. However, the purposes of the two methods are significantly different; while one, getHandlers(), deals with parsing a file, the other, registerHandlers(), deals with registering handlers once information about the handlers is available. With this methodology, you can change the way you parse the configuration file (or even have it read from a database or other medium) without having to worry about the way the handlers are registered.

Once you have added these two helper methods, add their invocation to the start() method of your server class:

```java
public void start() throws IOException {
    try {
        // Use Apache Xerces SAX Parser
        XmlRpc.setDriver("org.apache.xerces.parsers.SAXParser");
```

```
                    System.out.println("Starting up XML-RPC Server...");
                    server = new WebServer(port);

                    // Register handlers
                    registerHandlers(getHandlers());

            } catch (ClassNotFoundException e) {
                throw new IOException("Error loading SAX parser: " +
                    e.getMessage());
            }
        }
```

Compile this code, ensure you have created the configuration file, and your server
is ready for use.

A Useful Client

The new client has no new concepts or techniques in it; just as the `HelloClient`
class was simple, so is the `SchedulerClient` class. It needs to start up an XML-
RPC client, invoke handler methods, and print out the result of those handlers.
The complete code for the client is here. Comments indicate what is occurring,
and since this is all ground already covered, you can simply enter the code in
Example 11-9 into your editor and compile it.

Example 11-9. The SchedulerClient class

```
package javaxml2;

import java.io.IOException;
import java.net.MalformedURLException;
import java.util.Calendar;
import java.util.Date;
import java.util.Enumeration;
import java.util.Hashtable;
import java.util.Vector;

import helma.xmlrpc.XmlRpc;
import helma.xmlrpc.XmlRpcClient;
import helma.xmlrpc.XmlRpcException;

public class SchedulerClient {

    public static void addEvents(XmlRpcClient client)
        throws XmlRpcException, IOException {

        System.out.println("\nAdding events...\n");

        // Parameters for events
```

Example 11-9. The SchedulerClient class (continued)

```
        Vector params = new Vector();

        // Add an event for next month
        params.addElement("Proofread final draft");

        Calendar cal = Calendar.getInstance();
        cal.add(Calendar.MONTH, 1);
        params.addElement(cal.getTime());

        // Add the event
        if (((Boolean)client.execute("scheduler.addEvent", params))
                        .booleanValue()) {
            System.out.println("Event added.");
        } else {
            System.out.println("Could not add event.");
        }

        // Add an event for tomorrow
        params.clear();
        params.addElement("Submit final draft");

        cal = Calendar.getInstance();
        cal.add(Calendar.DAY_OF_MONTH, 1);
        params.addElement(cal.getTime());

        // Add the event
        if (((Boolean)client.execute("scheduler.addEvent", params))
                        .booleanValue()) {
            System.out.println("Event added.");
        } else {
            System.out.println("Could not add event.");
        }

    }

    public static void listEvents(XmlRpcClient client)
        throws XmlRpcException, IOException {

        System.out.println("\nListing events...\n");

        // Get the events in the scheduler
        Vector params = new Vector();
        Vector events =
            (Vector)client.execute("scheduler.getListOfEvents", params);
        for (int i=0; i<events.size(); i++) {
```

Example 11-9. The SchedulerClient class (continued)

```
              System.out.println((String)events.elementAt(i));
          }
      }

      public static void main(String args[]) {

          try {
              // Use the Apache Xerces SAX Parser Implementation
              XmlRpc.setDriver("org.apache.xerces.parsers.SAXParser");

              // Connect to server
              XmlRpcClient client =
              new XmlRpcClient("http://localhost:8585/");

              // Add some events
              addEvents(client);

              // List events
              listEvents(client);

          } catch (Exception e) {
              System.out.println(e.getMessage());
          }
      }
}
```

As you are entering this code, notice that the events are added in reverse order of the event time. The server rearranges these events with the sortEvents() method to facilitate correctly ordered results when the getListOfEvents() method is called. The server takes care of this sorting next.

Talk to Me (Again)

Once you have entered the code for the handler, server, and client, compile all of the source files. You also need to create the configuration file that lists handlers to register with the XML-RPC server discussed previously in this chapter, in the section "A Configurable Server." First, start up the XML-RPC server as a separate process:

```
c:\javaxml2\build>start java javaxml2.LightweightXmlRpcServer 8585
                    c:\javaxml2\ch11\conf\xmlrpc.conf
```

On Unix, use:

```
$ java javaxml2.LightweightServer 8585 conf/xmlrpc.conf &
```

You should see the server indicate that the handlers in the supplied configuration file are registered to the names you provided:

```
Starting up XML-RPC Server...
Registered handler scheduler to class javaxml2.Scheduler
Registered handler hello to class javaxml2.HelloHandler
```

NOTE   If you never stopped the previous XML-RPC server, `HelloServer`, you will get an error trying to start another server on the same port. Be sure to stop the `HelloServer` before trying to start the `LightweightXmlRpcServer`.

Finally, execute your client and see the results:

```
$ java javaxml2.SchedulerClient

Adding events...

Event added.
Event added.

Listing events...

Event "Submit final draft" scheduled for 10:55 AM 05/09/2001
Event "Proofread final draft" scheduled for 10:55 AM 06/08/2001
```

You should not notice a significant pause as your client adds and lists events, yet the server still sorts the events in a separate thread within the server JVM (and bubble sorting is not a quick algorithm, by the way). You have written your first useful XML-RPC application!

The Real World

I'll conclude this chapter with a short look at some important details of using XML-RPC in the real world. This continues the focus on allowing you to use XML not because it is the newest and neatest technology, but because it is the best for solving certain situations. All of the knowledge within this book, the XML specifications, and other XML books will not make your application operate as well as it could if you do not know when and how to use XML and XML-RPC correctly! This section highlights some of the common issues that arise in using XML-RPC.

Where's the XML in XML-RPC?

After working through this chapter, you may have been surprised that you didn't have to write any SAX, DOM, or JDOM code. In fact, you used very little XML directly at all. This is because the XML-RPC libraries were responsible for the encoding and decoding of the requests that your clients sent to and from the servers. While this may seem a little bit of a letdown, as you didn't write any code that directly manipulates XML, you are definitely using XML technology. The simple request to the sayHello() method was actually translated to an HTTP call that looks like Example 11-10.

Example 11-10. XML for XML-RPC request

```
POST /RPC2 HTTP/1.1
User-Agent: Tomcat Web Server/3.1 Beta (Sun Solaris 2.6)
Host: newInstance.com
Content-Type: text/xml
Content-length: 234

<?xml version="1.0"?>
<methodCall>
  <methodName>hello.sayHello</methodName>
  <params>
    <param>
      <value><string>Brett</string></value>
    </param>
  </params>
</methodCall>
```

The XML-RPC libraries on the server receive this and decode it, matching it with a handler method (if one is available that matches). The requested Java method is then invoked, and the server encodes the result back into XML, as shown in Example 11-11.

Example 11-11. XML underlying an XML-RPC response

```
HTTP/1.1 200 OK
Connection: close
Content-Type: text/xml
Content-Length: 149
Date: Mon, 11 Apr 2000 03:32:19 CST
Server: Tomcat Web Server/3.1 Beta-Sun Solaris 2.6

<?xml version="1.0"?>
<methodResponse>
  <params>
    <param>
      <value><string>Hello Brett</string></value>
    </param>
  </params>
</methodResponse>
```

This communication all happens without you having to worry about the details.

Shared Instances

In the examples, I looked at using static data objects to share data across multiple instances of the same class. However, there are times when an instance itself is shared. This may not be because of an XML-RPC need, but because of a need to use the class differently on the server. For example, the singleton design pattern in Java mandates that only one instance of a class ever be created, and that instance is shared across all applications. This is usually accomplished by using a static method called getInstance() instead of constructing the object:

```
Scheduler scheduler;

// Get the single instance, which is managed in the Scheduler class
scheduler = Scheduler.getInstance();

// Add an event for right now
scheduler.addEvent("Picnic", new Date());
```

To ensure that no classes directly instantiate the Scheduler class, the constructor is usually made private or protected. While this forces clients to use this code to get an instance, it can also cause confusion when using the class as an XML-RPC handler. Remember that registering a handler has always been accomplished with the instantiation of the handler class. However, the WebServer class requires only a valid instance as a parameter, not necessarily a new instance. For example, the following code is a perfectly acceptable way to add a handler:

```
WebServer server = new WebServer(8585);

// Create a handler class
HelloHandler hello = new HelloHandler();
server.addHandler("hello", hello);
```

The server class does not distinguish between these methodologies, as long as the handler class is instantiated when it gets passed into the addHandler() method. So you can make a small change to this code if you want to add an instance of the singleton Scheduler class described previously:

```
WebServer server = new WebServer(8585);

// Pass in the singleton instance
server.addHandler("scheduler", Scheduler.getInstance());
```

This passes in the shared instance just as if the class were being instantiated through a constructor with the new keyword, and preserves any information shared across the singleton class. Many classes used in services such as XML-RPC are built as singletons to avoid the use of static data variables, as a shared instance allows the data to be stored in member variables; the single instance then operates upon those member variables for all client requests.

To Servlet or Not To Servlet

The use of a servlet as an XML-RPC server has become a popular option recently. For more details on servlets, see Jason Hunter's *Java Servlet Programming* (O'Reilly). In fact, the XML-RPC Java classes that you downloaded include a servlet with the distribution. It is both legal and common to use a servlet in this way, having the servlet do nothing but field XML-RPC requests. However, it is not always the best idea.

If you have a machine that must serve other HTTP requests for Java tasks, then a servlet engine is a good choice for handling the details of these requests. In this case, running a servlet as an XML-RPC server is a good idea. However, one of the advantages of XML-RPC is it allows handler classes with complex, process-intensive tasks to be separated from other application code. The Scheduler class could be placed on a server with classes that performed complex indexing, algorithmic modeling, and perhaps graphical transformations. All of these functions are very expensive for application clients to perform. However, adding a servlet engine and accepting application requests for other tasks as well as the XML-RPC handling greatly reduces the processing power available to these handler classes. In this case, the only requests that should be coming to the server are for these handler classes.

In the case where only XML-RPC requests are accepted (as indicated previously), it is rarely a good idea to use a servlet for the XML-RPC server. The provided Web-Server class is small, light, and designed specifically for handling XML-RPC requests over HTTP. A servlet engine is designed to accept any HTTP request, and is not tuned as well for XML-RPC requests in particular. Over time, you will begin to see performance degradation in the servlet engine as compared to the WebServer class. Unless you have a compelling reason to use a servlet for other non-XML-RPC tasks, stick with the lightweight XML-RPC server designed for the purpose you need.

What's Next?

Now that you have a handle on RPC and XML-RPC, it's time to take the next logical step. That step is SOAP, the Simple Object Access Protocol. SOAP builds upon XML-RPC to add support for custom object types, better error reporting, and more features. It's also quite the rage these days. In the next chapter, I'll give you the lowdown so you'll be prepared.

12

SOAP

SOAP is the Simple Object Access Protocol. If you haven't heard of it by now, you've probably been living under a rock somewhere. It's become the newest craze in web programming, and is integral to the web services fanaticism that has taken hold of the latest generation of web development. If you've heard of .NET from Microsoft or the peer-to-peer "revolution," then you've heard about technologies that rely on SOAP (even if you don't know it). There's not one but *two* SOAP implementations going on over at Apache, and Microsoft has hundreds of pages on their MSDN web site devoted to it (*http://msdn.microsoft.com*).

In this chapter, I explain what SOAP is, and why it is such an important part of where the web development paradigm is moving. That will help you get the fundamentals down, and prepare you for actually working with a SOAP toolkit. From there, I briefly run over the SOAP projects currently available, and then delve into the Apache implementation. This chapter is not meant to be the complete picture on SOAP; the next chapter fills in lots of gaps. Take this as the first part of a miniseries; many of your questions at the end of this chapter will be answered in the next.

Starting Out

The first thing to do is get an understanding of what SOAP is. You can read through the complete W3C note submission, which is fairly lengthy, at *http://www. w3.org/TR/SOAP*. When you take away all of the hype, SOAP is just a protocol. It's a simple protocol (to use, not necessarily to write), based on the idea that at some point in a distributed architecture, you'll need to exchange information. Additionally, in a system that is probably overtaxed and process-heavy, this protocol is lightweight, requiring a minimal amount of overhead. Finally, it allows all this to occur over HTTP, which allows you to get around tricky issues like firewalls and keep away from having all sorts of sockets listening on oddly numbered ports. Once you get that down, everything else is just details.

Of course, I'm sure you're here for the details, so I won't leave them out. There are three basic components to the SOAP specification: the SOAP envelope, a set of encoding rules, and a means of interaction between request and response. Begin to think about a SOAP message as an actual letter; you know, those antiquated things in envelopes with postage and an address scrawled across the front? That analogy helps SOAP concepts like "envelope" make a lot more sense. Figure 12-1 seeks to illustrate the SOAP process in terms of this analog.

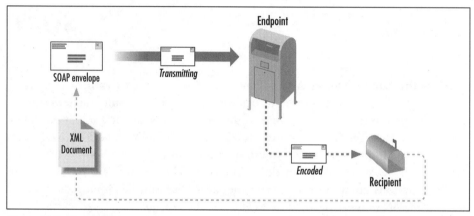

Figure 12-1. The SOAP message process

With this picture in your head, let's look at the three components of the SOAP specification. I cover each briefly and provide examples that illustrate these concepts more completely. Additionally, it's these three key components that make SOAP so important and valuable. Error handling, support for a variety of encodings, serialization of custom parameters, and the fact that SOAP runs over HTTP make it more attractive in many cases than the other choices for a distributed protocol.* Additionally, SOAP provides a high degree of interoperability with other applications, which I delve into more completely in the next chapter. For now, I want to focus on the basic pieces of SOAP.

The Envelope

The SOAP envelope is analogous to the envelope of an actual letter. It supplies information about the message that is being encoded in a SOAP payload, including data relating to the recipient and sender, as well as details about the message

---

* There's a lot of talk about running SOAP over other protocols, like SMTP (or even Jabber). This isn't part of the SOAP standard, but it may be added in the future. Don't be surprised if you see it discussed.

itself. For example, the header of the SOAP envelope can specify exactly how a message must be processed. Before an application goes forward with processing a message, the application can determine information about a message, including whether it will even be able to process the message. Distinct from the situation with standard XML-RPC calls (remember that? XML-RPC messages, encoding, and the rest are all wrapped into a single XML fragment), with SOAP actual interpretation occurs in order to determine something about the message. A typical SOAP message can also include the encoding style, which assists the recipient in interpreting the message. Example 12-1 shows the SOAP envelope, complete with the specified encoding.

Example 12-1. The SOAP envelope

```
<soap:Envelope
   xmlns:soap="http://schemas.xmlsoap.org/soap/envelope/"
   soap:encodingStyle="http://myHost.com/encodings/secureEncoding"
>
  <soap:Body>
    <article xmlns="http://www.ibm.com/developer">
      <name>Soapbox</name>
      <url>
        http://www-106.ibm.com/developerworks/library/x-soapbx1.html
      </url>
    </article>
  </soap:Body>
</soap:Envelope>
```

You can see that an encoding is specified within the envelope, allowing an application to determine (using the value of the encodingStyle attribute) whether it can read the incoming message situated within the Body element. Be sure to get the SOAP envelope namespace correct, or SOAP servers that receive your message will trigger version mismatch errors, and you won't be able to interoperate with them.

Encoding

The second major element that SOAP brings to the table is a simple means of encoding user-defined datatypes. In RPC (and XML-RPC), encoding can only occur for a predefined set of datatypes: those that are supported by whatever XML-RPC toolkit you download. Encoding other types requires modifying the actual RPC server and clients themselves. With SOAP, however, XML schemas can be used to easily specify new datatypes (using the complexType structure discussed way back in Chapter 2), and those new types can be easily represented in XML as part of a SOAP payload. Because of this integration with XML Schema,

you can encode any datatype in a SOAP message that you can logically describe in
an XML schema.

Invocation

The best way to understand how SOAP invocation works is to compare it with
something you already know, such as XML-RPC. If you recall, an XML-RPC call
would look something like the code fragment shown in Example 12-2.

Example 12-2. Invocation in XML-RPC

```
// Specify the XML parser to use
XmlRpc.setDriver("org.apache.xerces.parsers.SAXParser");

// Specify the server to connect to
XmlRpcClient client =
    new XmlRpcClient("http://rpc.middleearth.com");

// Create the parameters
Vector params = new Vector();
params.addElement(flightNumber);
params.addElement(numSeats);
params.addElement(creditCardType);
params.addElement(creditCardNum);

// Request reservation
Boolean boughtTickets =
    (Boolean)client.execute("ticketCounter.buyTickets", params);

// Deal with the response
```

I've coded up a simple ticket counter–style application. Now, look at
Example 12-3, which shows the same call in SOAP.

Example 12-3. Invocation in SOAP

```
// Create the parameters
Vector params = new Vector();
params.addElement(
    new Parameter("flightNumber", Integer.class, flightNumber, null));
params.addElement(
    new Parameter("numSeats", Integer.class, numSeats, null));
params.addElement(
    new Parameter("creditCardType", String.class, creditCardType, null));
params.addElement(
    new Parameter("creditCardNumber", Long.class, creditCardNum, null));
```

Example 12-3. Invocation in SOAP (continued)

```
// Create the Call object
Call call = new Call();
call.setTargetObjectURI("urn:xmltoday-airline-tickets");
call.setMethodName("buyTickets");
call.setEncodingStyleURI(Constants.NS_URI_SOAP_ENC);
call.setParams(params);

// Invoke
Response res = call.invoke(new URL("http://rpc.middleearth.com"), "");

// Deal with the response
```

As you can see, the actual invocation itself, represented by the `Call` object, is resident in memory. It allows you to set the target of the call, the method to invoke, the encoding style, the parameters, and more not shown here. It is more flexible than the XML-RPC methodology, allowing you to explicitly set the various parameters that are determined implicitly in XML-RPC. You'll see quite a bit more about this invocation process in the rest of the chapter, including how SOAP provides fault responses, an error hierarchy, and of course the returned results from the call.

With that brief introduction, you probably know enough to want to get on with the fun stuff. Let me show you the SOAP implementation I'm going to use, explain why I made that choice, and get to some code.

Setting Up

Now that you have some basic concepts down, it's time to get going on the fun part, the code. You need a project or product for use, which turns out to be simpler to find than you might think. If you want a Java-based project providing SOAP capability, you don't have to look that far. There are two groups of products out there: commercial and free. As in most of the rest of the book, I'm steering away from covering commercial products. This isn't because they are bad (on the contrary, some are wonderful); it's because I want every reader of this book to be able to use every example. That calls for accessibility, something commercial products don't provide; you have to pay to use them, or download them and at some point the trial period runs out.

That brings us to open source projects. In that realm, I see only one available: Apache SOAP. Located online at *http://xml.apache.org/soap*, this project seeks to provide a SOAP toolkit in Java. Currently in a Version 2.2 release, you can download it from the Apache web site. That's the version and project I use for the examples throughout this chapter.

Other Options

Before moving on to the installation and setup of Apache SOAP, I will answer a few questions that might be rattling around in your head. It's probably clear why I'm not using a commercial product. However, you may be thinking of a couple of other open source or related options that you might want to use, and wondering why I am not covering those.

What about IBM SOAP4J?

First on the list of options is IBM's SOAP implementation, IBM SOAP4J. IBM's work is actually the basis of the current Apache SOAP project, much as IBM XML4J fed into what is now the Apache Xerces XML parser project. Expect the IBM implementation to resurface, wrapping the Apache SOAP project's implementation. This is similar to what is happening with IBM's XML4J; it currently just provides IBM packaging over Xerces. This makes some additional levels of vendor-backing available to the open source version, although the two (Apache and IBM) projects are using the same codebase.

Isn't Microsoft a player?

Yes. Without a doubt, Microsoft and its SOAP implementation, as well as the whole .NET initiative (covered more in the next chapter), are very important. In fact, I wanted to spend some time covering Microsoft's SOAP implementation in detail, but it only supports COM objects and the like, without Java support. For this reason, coverage of it doesn't belong in a book on Java and XML. However, Microsoft (despite the connotations we developers tend to have about the company) is doing important work in web services, and you'd be making a mistake in writing it off, at least in this particular regard. If you need to communicate with COM or Visual Basic components, I highly recommend checking out the Microsoft SOAP toolkit, found online at *http://msdn.microsoft.com/library/default.asp?url=/nhp/Default. asp?contentid=28000523* along with a lot of other SOAP resources.

What's Axis?

Those of you who monitor activity in Apache may have heard of Apache Axis. Axis is the next-generation SOAP toolkit, also being developed under the Apache XML umbrella. With SOAP (the specification, not a specific implementation) undergoing fairly fast and radical change these days, tracking it is difficult. Trying to build a version of SOAP that meets current requirements and moves with new development is also awfully tough. As a result, the current Apache SOAP offering is somewhat limited in its construction. Rather than try to rearchitect an existing toolkit, the Apache folks started fresh with a new codebase and project; thus, Axis was born. Additionally, the naming of SOAP was apparently going to change, from SOAP to XP and then to XMLP. As a result, the name of this new SOAP project was uncoupled from the specification name; thus, you have "Axis." Of course, now it looks like the W3C is going back to calling the specification SOAP (Version 1.2, or Version 2.0), so things are even more confusing!

Think of IBM SOAP4J as architecture 1 of the SOAP toolkit. Following that is Apache SOAP (covered in this chapter), which is architecture 2. Finally, Axis provides a next-generation architecture, architecture 3. This project is driven by SAX, while Apache SOAP is based upon DOM. Additionally, Axis provides a more user-friendly approach in header interaction, something missing in Apache SOAP. With all of these improvements, you're probably wondering why I'm not covering Axis. It's simply too early. Axis is presently trying to get together a 0.51 release. It's not a beta, or even an alpha, really; it's very early on. While I'd love to cover all the new Axis features, there's no way your boss is going to let you put in a pre-alpha release of open source software in your mission-critical systems, now is there? As a result, I've chosen to focus on something you *can* use, *today*: Apache SOAP. I'm sure when Axis does finalize, I'll update this chapter in a subsequent revision of the book. Until then, let's focus on a solution you can use.

Installation

There are two forms of installation with regard to SOAP. The first is running a SOAP client, using the SOAP API to communicate with a server that can receive SOAP messages. The second is running a SOAP server, which can receive messages from a SOAP client. I cover installation of both cases in this section.

The client

To use SOAP on a client, you first need to download Apache SOAP, available online at *http://xml.apache.org/dist/soap*. I've downloaded Version 2.2, in the binary format (in the *version-2.2* subdirectory). You should then extract the contents of the archive into a directory on your machine; my installation is in the *javaxml2* directory (*c:\javaxml2* on my Windows machine, */javaxml2* on my Mac OS X machine). The result is */javaxml2/soap-2_2*. You'll also need to download the Java-Mail package, available from Sun at *http://java.sun.com/products/javamail/*. This is for the SMTP transfer protocol support included in Apache SOAP. Then, download the JavaBeans Activation Framework (JAF), also from Sun, available online at *http://java.sun.com/products/beans/glasgow/jaf.html*. I'm assuming that you still have Xerces or another XML parser available for use.

Expand both the JavaMail and JAF packages, and then add the included *jar* files to your classpath, as well as the *soap.jar* library. Each of these *jar* files is either in the root directory or in the *lib/* directory of the relevant installation. At the end, your classpath should look something like this:

```
$ echo $CLASSPATH
/javaxml2/soap-2_2/lib/soap.jar:/javaxml2/lib/xerces.jar:
/javaxml2/javamail-1.2/mail.jar:/javaxml2/jaf-1.0.1/activation.jar
```

On Windows, it should look like:

```
c:\>echo %CLASSPATH%
c:\javaxml2\soap-2_2\lib\soap.jar;c:\javaxml2\lib\xerces.jar;
c:\javaxml2\javamail-1.2\mail.jar;c:\javaxml2\jaf-1.0.1\activation.jar
```

Finally, add the *javaxml2/soap-2_2/* directory to your classpath if you want to run the SOAP examples. I cover setup for specific examples in this chapter as I get to them.

The server

To build a SOAP-capable set of server components, you first need a servlet engine. As in earlier chapters, I'll use Apache Tomcat (available from *http://jakarta.apache. org*) throughout this chapter for examples. You'll then need to add everything needed on the client to the server's classpath. The easiest way to do that is to drop *soap.jar*, *activation.jar*, and *mail.jar*, as well as your parser, in your servlet engine's library directory. On Tomcat, this is simply the *lib/* directory, which contains libraries that should be autoloaded. If you want to support scripting (which is not covered in this chapter, but is in the Apache SOAP examples), you'll need to put *bsf.jar* (available online at *http://oss.software.ibm.com/developerworks/projects/bsf*) and *js.jar* (available from *http://www.mozilla.org/rhino/*) in the same directory.

Now restart your servlet engine, and you're ready to write SOAP server components.

The router servlet and admin client

In addition to basic operation, Apache SOAP includes a router servlet as well as an admin client; even if you don't want to use these, I recommend you install them so you can test your SOAP installation. This process is servlet-engine–specific, so I just cover the Tomcat installation here. However, installation instructions for several other servlet engines are available online at *http://xml.apache.org/soap/docs/index.html*.

Installation under Tomcat is simple; just take the *soap.war* file in the *soap-2_2/ webapps* directory, and drop it in your *$TOMCAT_HOME/webapps* directory. That's it! To test the installation, point your web browser to *http://localhost:8080/soap/ servlet/rpcrouter*. You should get a response like that shown in Figure 12-2.

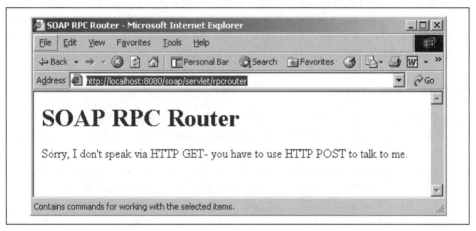

Figure 12-2. The RPC router servlet

Although this looks like an error, it does indicate that things are working correctly. You should get the same response pointing your browser to the admin client, at *http://localhost:8080/soap/servlet/messagerouter*.

As a final test of both the server and client, ensure you have followed all the setup instructions so far. Then execute the following Java class as shown, supplying your servlet URL for the RPC router servlet:

```
C:\>java org.apache.soap.server.ServiceManagerClient
        http://localhost:8080/soap/servlet/rpcrouter list
Deployed Services:
```

You should get the empty list of services, as shown here. If you get any other message, consult the long list of possible errors at *http://xml.apache.org/soap/docs/ trouble/index.html*. A fairly complete list of problems that you can run into is there. If you do get the empty list of services, then you're set up and ready to continue with the examples in the rest of this chapter.

Getting Dirty

There are three basic steps in writing any SOAP-based system, and I'll look at each in turn:

- Decide on SOAP-RPC or SOAP messaging
- Write or obtain access to a SOAP service
- Write or obtain access to a SOAP client

The first step is to decide if you want to use SOAP for RPC-style calls, in which a remote procedure is invoked on a server, or for messaging, in which a client simply sends pieces of information to a server. I'll detail these processes in the next section. Once you've made that design decision, you need to access, or code up, a service. Of course, since we're all Java pros here, this chapter shows you how to code up your own. Finally, you need to write the client for this service, and watch things take off.

RPC or Messaging?

Your first task is actually not code-related but design-related. You need to determine if you want an RPC service or a messaging one. The first, RPC, is something you should be pretty familiar with after the last chapter. A client invokes a remote procedure on a server somewhere, and then gets some sort of response. In this scenario, SOAP is simply acting as a more extensible XML-RPC system, allowing better error handling and passing of complex types across the network. This is a concept you should already understand, and because it turns out that RPC systems are simple to write in SOAP, I'll start off there. This chapter describes how to write an RPC service, and then an RPC client, and put the system in action.

The second style of SOAP processing is message-based. Instead of invoking remote procedures, it provides for transfer of information. As you can imagine, this is pretty powerful, and doesn't depend on a client knowing about a particular method on some server. It also models distributed systems more closely, allowing packets of data (packet in the figurative sense, not in the network sense) to be passed around, keeping various systems aware of what other systems are doing. It is also more complicated than the simpler RPC-style programming, so I'll cover it in the next chapter with other business-to-business details after you're well grounded in SOAP-RPC programming.

Like most design issues, the actual process of making this decision is left up to you. Look at your application and determine exactly what you want SOAP to do for you. If you have a server and a set of clients that just need to perform tasks remotely, then RPC is probably well suited for your needs. However, in larger systems that are exchanging data rather than performing specific business functions on request, SOAP's messaging capabilities may be a better match.

An RPC Service

With the formalities out of the way, it's time to get going, fast and furious. As you'll recall from the last chapter, in RPC you need a class that is going to have its methods invoked remotely.

Code artifacts

I'll start by showing you some *code artifacts* to have available on the server. These artifacts are classes with methods that are exposed to RPC clients.* Rather than use the simple class from last chapter, I offer a slightly more complex example to show you what SOAP can do. In that vein, Example 12-4 is a class that stores a CD inventory, such as an application for an online music store might use. I'm introducing a basic version here, and will add to it later in the chapter.

Example 12-4. The CDCatalog class

```
package javaxml2;

import java.util.Hashtable;

public class CDCatalog {

    /** The CDs, by title */
    private Hashtable catalog;

    public CDCatalog() {
        catalog = new Hashtable();

        // Seed the catalog
        catalog.put("Nickel Creek", "Nickel Creek");
        catalog.put("Let it Fall", "Sean Watkins");
        catalog.put("Aerial Boundaries", "Michael Hedges");
        catalog.put("Taproot", "Michael Hedges");
    }

    public void addCD(String title, String artist) {
        if ((title == null) || (artist == null)) {
            throw new IllegalArgumentException("Title and artist cannot be null.");
        }
```

---

* You can use scripts through the Bean Scripting Framework, but for the sake of space I won't cover that here. Check out the upcoming O'Reilly SOAP book, as well as the online documentation at *http://xml. apache.org/soap*, for more details on script support in SOAP.

Example 12-4. The CDCatalog class (continued)

```
        catalog.put(title, artist);
    }

    public String getArtist(String title) {
        if (title == null) {
            throw new IllegalArgumentException("Title cannot be null.");
        }

        // Return the requested CD
        return (String)catalog.get(title);
    }

    public Hashtable list() {
        return catalog;
    }
}
```

This allows for adding a new CD, searching for an artist by a CD title, and getting all current CDs. Take note that the list() method returns a Hashtable, and there is nothing special I have to do to make that work; Apache SOAP provides automatic mapping of the Hashtable Java type, much as XML-RPC did.

Compile this class, and make sure you've got everything typed in (or downloaded, if you choose) correctly. Notice that the CDCatalog class has no knowledge about SOAP. This means you can take your existing Java classes and expose them through SOAP-RPC, which reduces the work required on your end to move to a SOAP-based architecture if needed.

Deployment descriptors

With the Java coding done, you now need to define a deployment descriptor. This specifies several key things to a SOAP server:

- The URN of the SOAP service for clients to access

- The method or methods available to clients

- The serialization and deserialization handlers for any custom classes

The first is similar to a URL, and required for a client to connect to any SOAP server. The second is exactly what you expect: a list of methods letting the client know what are allowable artifacts for a SOAP client. It also lets the SOAP server, which I'll cover in a moment, know what requests to accept. The third is a means of telling the SOAP server how to handle any custom parameters; I'll come back to this in the next section when I add some more complex behavior to the catalog.

I'll show you the deployment descriptor and detail each item within it. Example 12-5 is the deployment descriptor for the CDCatalog service we're creating.

Example 12-5. The CDCatalog deployment descriptor

```
<isd:service xmlns:isd="http://xml.apache.org/xml-soap/deployment"
             id="urn:cd-catalog"
>
  <isd:provider type="java"
                scope="Application"
                methods="addCD getArtist list"
  >
    <isd:java class="javaxml2.CDCatalog" static="false" />
  </isd:provider>

  <isd:faultListener>org.apache.soap.server.DOMFaultListener</isd:faultListener>
</isd:service>
```

First, I referenced the Apache SOAP deployment namespace, and then supplied a URN for my service through the id attribute. This should be something unique across services, and descriptive of the service. I showed about as much originality in naming the service as Dave Matthews did with his band, but it gets the job done. Then, I specified through the java element the class to expose, including its package name (through the class attribute), and indicated that the methods being exposed were not static ones (through the static attribute).

Next, I specified a fault listener implementation to use. Apache's SOAP implementation provides two; I used the first, DOMFaultListener. This listener returns any exception and fault information through an additional DOM element in the response to the client. I'll get back to this when I look at writing clients, so don't worry too much about it right now. The other fault listener implementation is org.apache.soap.server.ExceptionFaultListener. This listener exposes any faults through an additional parameter returned to the client. Since quite a few SOAP-based applications are already going to be working in Java and XML APIs like DOM, it's common to use the DOMFaultListener in most cases.

Deploying the service

At this point, you've got a working deployment descriptor and a set of code artifacts to expose, and you can deploy your service. Apache SOAP comes with a utility to do this task, provided you have done the setup work. First, you need a deployment descriptor for your service, which I just talked about. Second, you need to make the classes for your service available to the SOAP server. The best way to do this is to *jar* up the service class from the last section:

```
jar cvf javaxml2.jar javaxml2/CDCatalog.class
```

Take this *jar* file and drop it into your *lib/* directory (or wherever libraries are auto-loaded for your servlet engine), and restart your servlet engine.

WARNING   When you do this, you have created a snapshot of your class file. Changing the code in the *CDCatalog.java* file and recompiling it will not cause the servlet engine to pick up the changes. You'll need to re-*jar* the archive and copy it over to your *lib/* directory each time code changes are made to ensure your service is updated. You'll also want to restart your servlet engine to make sure the changes are picked up by the engine as well.

With your service class (or classes) accessible by your SOAP server, you can now deploy the service, using Apache SOAP's `org.apache.soap.server.Service-Manager` utility class:

```
C:\javaxml2\Ch12>java org.apache.soap.server.ServiceManagerClient
    http://localhost:8080/soap/servlet/rpcrouter deploy xml\CDCatalogDD.xml
```

The first argument is the SOAP server and RPC router servlet, the second is the action to take, and the third is the relevant deployment descriptor. Once this has executed, verify your service was added:

```
(gandalf)/javaxml2/Ch12$ java org.apache.soap.server.ServiceManagerClient
    http://localhost:8080/soap/servlet/rpcrouter list
Deployed Services:
      urn:cd-catalog
      urn:AddressFetcher
      urn:xml-soap-demo-calculator
```

At a minimum, this should show any and all services you have available on the server. Finally, you can easily undeploy the service, as long as you know its name:

```
C:\javaxml2\Ch12>java org.apache.soap.server.ServiceManagerClient
    http://localhost:8080/soap/servlet/rpcrouter undeploy urn:cd-catalog
```

Every time you update your service code, you must undeploy and then redeploy to ensure the SOAP server is running the newest copy.

An RPC Client

Next up is the client. I'm going to keep things simple, and just write a couple of command-line programs that invoke SOAP-RPC. It would be impossible to try and guess your business case, so I just focus on the SOAP details and let you work out integration with your existing software. Once you have the business portion of your code working, there are some basic steps you'll take in every SOAP-RPC call:

- Create the SOAP-RPC call
- Set up any type mappings for custom parameters

- Set the URI of the SOAP service to use

- Specify the method to invoke

- Specify the encoding to use

- Add any parameters to the call

- Connect to the SOAP service

- Receive and interpret a response

That may seem like a lot, but most of the operations are one- or two-line method invocations. In other words, talking to a SOAP service is generally a piece of cake. Example 12-6 shows the code for the **CDAdder** class, which allows you to add a new CD to the catalog. Take a look at the code, and then I'll walk you through the juicy bits.

Example 12-6. The CDAdder class

```
package javaxml2;

import java.net.URL;
import java.util.Vector;
import org.apache.soap.Constants;
import org.apache.soap.Fault;
import org.apache.soap.SOAPException;
import org.apache.soap.rpc.Call;
import org.apache.soap.rpc.Parameter;
import org.apache.soap.rpc.Response;

public class CDAdder {

    public void add(URL url, String title, String artist)
        throws SOAPException {

        System.out.println("Adding CD titled '" + title + "' by '" +
            artist + "'");

        // Build the Call object
        Call call = new Call();
        call.setTargetObjectURI("urn:cd-catalog");
        call.setMethodName("addCD");
        call.setEncodingStyleURI(Constants.NS_URI_SOAP_ENC);

        // Set up parameters
        Vector params = new Vector();
        params.addElement(new Parameter("title", String.class, title, null));
        params.addElement(new Parameter("artist", String.class, artist, null));
        call.setParams(params);
```

Example 12-6. The CDAdder class (continued)

```
        // Invoke the call
        Response response;
        response = call.invoke(url, "");

        if (!response.generatedFault()) {
            System.out.println("Successful CD Addition.");
        } else {
            Fault fault = response.getFault();
            System.out.println("Error encountered: " + fault.getFaultString());
        }
    }

    public static void main(String[] args) {
        if (args.length != 3) {
            System.out.println("Usage: java javaxml2.CDAdder [SOAP server URL] " +
                "\"[CD Title]\" \"[Artist Name]\"");
            return;
        }

        try {
            // URL for SOAP server to connect to
            URL url = new URL(args[0]);

            // Get values for new CD
            String title = args[1];
            String artist = args[2];

            // Add the CD
            CDAdder adder = new CDAdder();
            adder.add(url, title, artist);
        } catch (Exception e) {
            e.printStackTrace();
        }
    }
}
```

This program captures the URL of the SOAP server to connect to, as well as information needed to create and add a new CD to the catalog. Then, in the add() method, the code creates the SOAP Call object, on which all the interesting interaction occurs. The target URI of the SOAP service and the method to invoke are set on the call, and both match up to values from the service's deployment descriptor from Example 12-5. Next, the encoding is set, which should always be the constant Constants.NS_URI_SOAP_ENC unless you have very unique encoding needs.

The program creates a new Vector populated with SOAP Parameter objects. Each of these represents a parameter to the specified method, and since the addCD() method takes two String values, this is pretty simple. Supply the name of the parameter (for use in the XML and debugging), the class for the parameter, and the value. The fourth argument is an optional encoding, if a single parameter needs a special encoding. For no special treatment, the value `null` suffices. The resulting `Vector` is then added to the `Call` object.

Once your call is set up, use the `invoke()` method on that object. The return value from this method is an `org.apache.soap.Response` instance, which is queried for any problems that resulted. This is fairly self-explanatory, so I'll leave it to you to walk through the code. Once you've compiled your client and followed the instructions earlier in this chapter for setting up your classpath, run the example as follows:

```
C:\javaxml2\build>java javaxml2.CDAdder
    http://localhost:8080/soap/servlet/rpcrouter
    "Riding the Midnight Train" "Doc Watson"

Adding CD titled 'Riding the Midnight Train' by 'Doc Watson'
Successful CD Addition
```

Example 12-7 is another simple class, `CDLister`, which lists all current CDs in the catalog. I won't go into detail on it, as it's very similar to Example 12-6, and is mainly a reinforcement of what I've already talked about.

Example 12-7. The CDLister class

```java
package javaxml2;

import java.net.URL;
import java.util.Enumeration;
import java.util.Hashtable;
import java.util.Vector;
import org.apache.soap.Constants;
import org.apache.soap.Fault;
import org.apache.soap.SOAPException;
import org.apache.soap.rpc.Call;
import org.apache.soap.rpc.Parameter;
import org.apache.soap.rpc.Response;

public class CDLister {

    public void list(URL url) throws SOAPException {
        System.out.println("Listing current CD catalog.");

        // Build the Call object
        Call call = new Call();
        call.setTargetObjectURI("urn:cd-catalog");
        call.setMethodName("list");
        call.setEncodingStyleURI(Constants.NS_URI_SOAP_ENC);
```

Example 12-7. The CDLister class (continued)

```
        // No parameters needed

        // Invoke the call
        Response response;
        response = call.invoke(url, "");

        if (!response.generatedFault()) {
            Parameter returnValue = response.getReturnValue();
            Hashtable catalog = (Hashtable)returnValue.getValue();
            Enumeration e = catalog.keys();
            while (e.hasMoreElements()) {
                String title = (String)e.nextElement();
                String artist = (String)catalog.get(title);
                System.out.println("  '" + title + "' by " + artist);
            }
        } else {
            Fault fault = response.getFault();
            System.out.println("Error encountered: " + fault.getFaultString());
        }
    }

    public static void main(String[] args) {
        if (args.length != 1) {
            System.out.println("Usage: java javaxml2.CDAdder [SOAP server URL]");
            return;
        }

        try {
            // URL for SOAP server to connect to
            URL url = new URL(args[0]);

            // List the current CDs
            CDLister lister = new CDLister();
            lister.list(url);
        } catch (Exception e) {
            e.printStackTrace();
        }
    }
}
```

The only difference in this method from the CDAdder class is that the Response object has a return value (the Hashtable from the list() method). This is returned as a Parameter object, which allows a client to check its encoding and then extract the actual method return value. Once that's done, the client can use the returned value like any other Java object, and in the example simply runs through the CD catalog and prints out each one. You can now run this additional client to see it in action:

```
C:\javaxml2\build>java javaxml2.CDLister
     http://localhost:8080/soap/servlet/rpcrouter
Listing current CD catalog.
  'Riding the Midnight Train' by Doc Watson
  'Taproot' by Michael Hedges
  'Nickel Creek' by Nickel Creek
  'Let it Fall' by Sean Watkins
  'Aerial Boundaries' by Michael Hedges
```

That's really all there is to basic RPC functionality in SOAP. I'd like to push on a bit, though, and talk about a few more complex topics.

Going Further

Although you can now do everything in SOAP you knew how to do in XML-RPC, there is a lot more to SOAP. As I said in the beginning of the chapter, two important things that SOAP brings to the table are the ability to use custom parameters with a minimal amount of effort, and more advanced fault handling. In this section, I cover both of these topics.

Custom Parameter Types

The most limiting thing with the CD catalog, at least at this point, is that it stores only the title and artist for a given CD. It is much more realistic to have an object (or set of objects) that represents a CD with the title, artist, label, track listings, perhaps a genre, and all sorts of other information. I'm not going to build this entire structure, but will move from a title and artist to a CD object with a title, artist, and label. This object needs to be passed from the client to the server and back, and demonstrates how SOAP can handle these custom types. Example 12-8 shows this new class.

Example 12-8. The CD class

```
package javaxml2;

public class CD {

    /** The title of the CD */
    private String title;

    /** The artist performing on the CD */
    private String artist;
```

Example 12-8. The CD class (continued)

```java
    /** The label of the CD */
    private String label;

    public CD() {
        // Default constructor
    }

    public CD(String title, String artist, String label) {
        this.title = title;
        this.artist = artist;
        this.label = label;
    }

    public String getTitle() {
        return title;
    }

    public void setTitle(String title) {
        this.title = title;
    }

    public String getArtist() {
        return artist;
    }

    public void setArtist(String artist) {
        this.artist = artist;
    }

    public String getLabel() {
        return label;
    }

    public void setLabel(String label) {
        this.label = label;
    }

    public String toString() {
        return "'" + title + "' by " + artist + ", on " +
            label;
    }
}
```

This requires a whole slew of changes to the CDCatalog class as well. Example 12-9 shows a modified version of this class with the changes that use the new CD support class highlighted.

Example 12-9. An updated CDCatalog class

```java
package javaxml2;

import java.util.Hashtable;

public class CDCatalog {

    /** The CDs, by title */
    private Hashtable catalog;

    public CDCatalog() {
        catalog = new Hashtable();

        // Seed the catalog
        addCD(new CD("Nickel Creek", "Nickel Creek", "Sugar Hill"));
        addCD(new CD("Let it Fall", "Sean Watkins", "Sugar Hill"));
        addCD(new CD("Aerial Boundaries", "Michael Hedges", "Windham Hill"));
        addCD(new CD("Taproot", "Michael Hedges", "Windham Hill"));
    }

    public void addCD(CD cd) {
        if (cd == null) {
            throw new IllegalArgumentException("The CD object cannot be null.");
        }
        catalog.put(cd.getTitle(), cd);
    }

    public CD getCD(String title) {
        if (title == null) {
            throw new IllegalArgumentException("Title cannot be null.");
        }

        // Return the requested CD
        return (CD)catalog.get(title);
    }

    public Hashtable list() {
        return catalog;
    }
}
```

In addition to the obvious changes, I've also updated the old getArtist(String title) method to getCD(String title), and made the return value a CD object. This means the SOAP server will need to serialize and deserialize this new class, and the client will be updated. First, I look at an updated deployment descriptor that details the serialization issues related to this custom type. Add the following lines to the deployment descriptor for the CD catalog, as well as changing the available method names to match the updated CDCatalog class:

```
<isd:service xmlns:isd="http://xml.apache.org/xml-soap/deployment"
             id="urn:cd-catalog"
>
  <isd:provider type="java"
                scope="Application"
                methods="addCD getCD list"
  >
    <isd:java class="javaxml2.CDCatalog" static="false" />
  </isd:provider>

  <isd:faultListener>org.apache.soap.server.DOMFaultListener</isd:faultListener>

  <isd:mappings>
    <isd:map encodingStyle="http://schemas.xmlsoap.org/soap/encoding/"
            xmlns:x="urn:cd-catalog-demo" qname="x:cd"
            javaType="javaxml2.CD"
            java2XMLClassName="org.apache.soap.encoding.soapenc.BeanSerializer"
            xml2JavaClassName="org.apache.soap.encoding.soapenc.BeanSerializer"/>
  </isd:mappings>
</isd:service>
```

The new element, mappings, specifies how a SOAP server should handle custom parameters such as the CD class. First, define a map element for each custom parameter type. For the encodingStyle attribute, at least as of Apache SOAP 2.2, you should always supply the value *http://schemas.xmlsoap.org/soap/encoding/*, the only encoding currently supported. You need to supply a namespace for the custom type and then the name of the class, with this namespace prefix, for the type. In my case, I used a "dummy" namespace and the simple prefix "x" for this purpose. Then, using the javaType attribute, supply the actual Java class name: javaxml2.CD in this case. Finally, the magic occurs in the java2XMLClassName and xml2JavaClassName attributes. These specify a class to convert from Java to XML and from XML to Java, respectively. I've used the incredibly handy BeanSerializer class, also provided with Apache SOAP. If your custom parameter is in a JavaBean format, this serializer and deserializer will save you from having to write your own. You need to have a class with a default constructor (remember that I defined an empty, no-args constructor within the CD class), and expose all the data in that class through setXXX and getXXX style methods. Since the CD class fits the bill here, the BeanSerializer works perfectly.

| NOTE | It's no accident that the CD class follows the JavaBean conventions. Most data classes fit easily into this format, and I knew I wanted to avoid writing my own custom serializer and deserializer. These are a pain to write (not overly difficult, but easy to mess up), and I recommend you go to great lengths to try and use the Bean conventions in your own custom parameters. In many cases, the Bean conventions only require that a default constructor (with no arguments) is present in your class. |

Now recreate your service *jar* file. Then, redeploy your service:

```
(gandalf)/javaxml2/Ch12$ java org.apache.soap.server.ServiceManagerClient
     http://localhost:8080/soap/servlet/rpcrouter xml/CDCatalogDD.xml
```

| WARNING | If you have kept your servlet engine running and the service deployed all this time, you'll need to restart the servlet engine to activate the new classes for the SOAP service, and redeploy the service. |

At this point, all that's left is modifying the client to use the new class and methods. Example 12-10 is an updated version of the client class CDAdder. The changes from the previous version of the class are highlighted.

Example 12-10. The updated CDAdder class

```
package javaxml2;

import java.net.URL;
import java.util.Vector;
import org.apache.soap.Constants;
import org.apache.soap.Fault;
import org.apache.soap.SOAPException;
import org.apache.soap.encoding.SOAPMappingRegistry;
import org.apache.soap.encoding.soapenc.BeanSerializer;
import org.apache.soap.rpc.Call;
import org.apache.soap.rpc.Parameter;
import org.apache.soap.rpc.Response;
import org.apache.soap.util.xml.QName;

public class CDAdder {

    public void add(URL url, String title, String artist, String label)
        throws SOAPException {

        System.out.println("Adding CD titled '" + title + "' by '" +
            artist + "', on the label " + label);
```

Example 12-10. The updated CDAdder class (continued)

```
        CD cd = new CD(title, artist, label);

        // Map this type so SOAP can use it
        SOAPMappingRegistry registry = new SOAPMappingRegistry();
        BeanSerializer serializer = new BeanSerializer();
        registry.mapTypes(Constants.NS_URI_SOAP_ENC,
            new QName("urn:cd-catalog-demo", "cd"),
            CD.class, serializer, serializer);

        // Build the Call object
        Call call = new Call();
        call.setSOAPMappingRegistry(registry);
        call.setTargetObjectURI("urn:cd-catalog");
        call.setMethodName("addCD");
        call.setEncodingStyleURI(Constants.NS_URI_SOAP_ENC);

        // Set up parameters
        Vector params = new Vector();
        params.addElement(new Parameter("cd", CD.class, cd, null));
        call.setParams(params);

        // Invoke the call
        Response response;
        response = call.invoke(url, "");

        if (!response.generatedFault()) {
            System.out.println("Successful CD Addition.");
        } else {
            Fault fault = response.getFault();
            System.out.println("Error encountered: " + fault.getFaultString());
        }
    }

    public static void main(String[] args) {
        if (args.length != 4) {
            System.out.println("Usage: java javaxml2.CDAdder [SOAP server URL] " +
                "\"[CD Title]\" \"[Artist Name]\" \"[CD Label]\"");
            return;
        }

        try {
            // URL for SOAP server to connect to
            URL url = new URL(args[0]);

            // Get values for new CD
            String title = args[1];
```

Example 12-10. The updated CDAdder class (continued)

```
            String artist = args[2];
            String label = args[3];

            // Add the CD
            CDAdder adder = new CDAdder();
            adder.add(url, title, artist, label);
        } catch (Exception e) {
            e.printStackTrace();
        }
    }
}
```

The only really interesting change is in dealing with the mapping of the CD class:

```
            // Map this type so SOAP can use it
            SOAPMappingRegistry registry = new SOAPMappingRegistry();
            BeanSerializer serializer = new BeanSerializer();
            registry.mapTypes(Constants.NS_URI_SOAP_ENC,
                new QName("urn:cd-catalog-demo", "cd"),
                CD.class, serializer, serializer);
```

This is how a custom parameter can be encoded and sent across the wire. I already discussed how the `BeanSerializer` class could be used to handle parameters in the JavaBean format, such as the CD class. To specify that to the server, I used the deployment descriptor; however, now I need to let the client know to use this serializer and deserializer. This is what the `SOAPMappingRegistry` class allows. The `mapTypes()` method takes in an encoding string (again, using the constant NS_URI_SOAP_ENC is the best idea here), and information about the parameter type a special serialization should be used for. First, a `QName` is supplied. This is why the odd namespacing was used back in the deployment descriptor; you need to specify the same URN here, as well as the local name of the element (in this case "CD"), then the Java `Class` object of the class to be serialized (`CD.class`), and finally the class instance for serialization and deserialization. In the case of the `BeanSerializer`, the same instance works for both. Once all this is set up in the registry, let the `Call` object know about it through the `setSOAPMapping-Registry()` method.

You can run this class just as before, adding the CD label, and things should work smoothly:

```
C:\javaxml2\build>java javaxml2.CDAdder
    http://localhost:8080/soap/servlet/rpcrouter
    "Tony Rice" "Manzanita" "Sugar Hill"
Adding CD titled 'Tony Rice' by 'Manzanita', on the label Sugar Hill
Successful CD Addition.
```

I'll leave it up to you to modify the `CDLister` class in the same fashion, and the downloadable samples have this updated class as well.

NOTE	You might think that since the `CDLister` class doesn't deal directly with a `CD` object (the return value of the `list()` method was a `Hashtable`), you don't need to make any changes. However, the returned `Hashtable` contains instances of CD objects. If SOAP doesn't know how to deserialize these, your client is going to give you an error. Therefore, you must specify a `SOAPMappingRegistry` instance on the `Call` object to make things work.

Better Error Handling

Now that you're tossing around custom objects, making RPC calls, and generally showing up everyone else in the office, let me talk about a less exciting topic: error handling. In any network transaction, many things can go wrong. The service isn't running, an error occurs on the server, objects can't be found, classes are missing, and a whole lot of other problems can arise. Until now, I just used the `fault.getString()` method to report errors. But this method isn't always very helpful. To see it in action, comment out the following line in the `CDCatalog` constructor:

```
public CDCatalog() {
    //catalog = new Hashtable();

    // Seed the catalog
    addCD(new CD("Nickel Creek", "Nickel Creek", "Sugar Hill"));
    addCD(new CD("Let it Fall", "Sean Watkins", "Sugar Hill"));
    addCD(new CD("Aerial Boundaries", "Michael Hedges", "Windham Hill"));
    addCD(new CD("Taproot", "Michael Hedges", "Windham Hill"));
}
```

Recompile, restart your server engine, and redeploy. The result is that a `NullPointerException` occurs when the class constructor tries to add a CD to an uninitialized `Hashtable`. Running the client will let you know an error has occurred, but not in a very meaningful way:

```
(gandalf)/javaxml2/build$ java javaxml2.CDLister
    http://localhost:8080/soap/servlet/rpcrouter
Listing current CD catalog.
Error encountered: Unable to resolve target object: null
```

This isn't exactly the type of information you need to track down the problem. However, the framework is in place to do a better job of error handling; remember the `DOMFaultListener` you specified as the value of the `faultListener` element? This is where it comes into play. The returned `Fault` object in the case of a problem (as in this one) contains a DOM `org.w3c.dom.Element` with detailed error information. First, add an import statement for `java.util.Iterator` to your client source code:

```
import java.net.URL;
import java.util.Enumeration;
import java.util.Hashtable;
import java.util.Iterator;
import java.util.Vector;
import org.apache.soap.Constants;
import org.apache.soap.Fault;
import org.apache.soap.SOAPException;
import org.apache.soap.encoding.SOAPMappingRegistry;
import org.apache.soap.encoding.soapenc.BeanSerializer;
import org.apache.soap.rpc.Call;
import org.apache.soap.rpc.Parameter;
import org.apache.soap.rpc.Response;
import org.apache.soap.util.xml.QName;
```

Next, make the following change to how errors are handled in the `list()` method:

```
        if (!response.generatedFault()) {
            Parameter returnValue = response.getReturnValue();
            Hashtable catalog = (Hashtable)returnValue.getValue();
            Enumeration e = catalog.keys();
            while (e.hasMoreElements()) {
                String title = (String)e.nextElement();
                CD cd = (CD)catalog.get(title);
                System.out.println("  '" + cd.getTitle() + "' by " +
cd.getArtist( ) +
                    " on the label " + cd.getLabel());
            }
        } else {
            Fault fault = response.getFault();
            System.out.println("Error encountered: " + fault.getFaultString());

            Vector entries = fault.getDetailEntries();
            for (Iterator i = entries.iterator(); i.hasNext(); ) {
                org.w3c.dom.Element entry = (org.w3c.dom.Element)i.next();
                System.out.println(entry.getFirstChild().getNodeValue());
            }
        }
```

By using the `getDetailEntries()` method, you get access to the raw data supplied by the SOAP service and server about the problem. The code iterates through these (there is generally only a single element, but it pays to be careful) and grabs the DOM `Element` contained within each entry. Essentially, here's the XML you are working through:

```
<SOAP-ENV:Fault>
  <faultcode>SOAP-ENV:Server.BadTargetObjectURI</faultcode>
```

```
    <faultstring>Unable to resolve target object: null</faultstring>
    <stacktrace>Here's what we want!</stackTrace>
  </SOAP-ENV:Fault>
```

In other words, the Fault object gives you access to the portion of the SOAP envelope that deals with errors. Additionally, Apache SOAP provides a Java stack trace
if errors occur, and that provides the detailed information needed to trouble-
shoot problems. By grabbing the stackTrace element and printing the Text
node's value from that Element, your client will now print out the stack trace from
the server. Compile these changes and rerun the client. You should get the following output:

```
C:\javaxml2\build>java javaxml2.CDLister http://localhost:8080/soap/servlet/rpcr
outer
Listing current CD catalog.
Error encountered: Unable to resolve target object: null
java.lang.NullPointerException
        at javaxml2.CDCatalog.addCD(CDCatalog.java:24)
        at javaxml2.CDCatalog.<init>(CDCatalog.java:14)
        at java.lang.Class.newInstance0(Native Method)
        at java.lang.Class.newInstance(Class.java:237)
```

This goes on for a bit, but you can see the juicy bits of information indicating that
a NullPointerException occurred, and even get the line numbers on the server
classes where the problems happened. The result of this fairly minor change is a
much more robust means of handling errors. That should prepare you for tracking down bugs on your server classes. Oh, and be sure to change your CDCatalog
class back to a version that won't cause these errors before moving on!

What's Next?

The next chapter is a direct continuation of these topics. More than ever, XML is
becoming the cornerstone of business-to-business activity, and SOAP is key to that.
In the next chapter, I'll introduce two important technologies to you, UDDI and
WSDL. If you have no idea what those are, you're in the right place. You'll learn
how they all fit together to form the backbone of web services architectures. Get
ready to finally find out what the web services, peer-to-peer craze is all about.

13

Web Services

In the last chapter, I focused on SOAP as a standalone technology; your application was a SOAP client talking to a SOAP server, based on nothing but Java and a servlet engine. While this is a perfectly good solution for applications in which you write all the clients and all the services, it is fairly limited for interoperating with other applications. If you've heard anything about SOAP, it's the interoperability aspect that has gotten it such good press lately. The last chapter was incomplete; it did not teach you how to do true servicing of other applications using SOAP as a transport mechanism. This chapter fills in the rest of the picture, and solves the remaining problems in interoperability.

To get you started, I apply some simple definitions to the overused term "web services." Although it's hard to quantify this term right now, since everyone is using it for their own particular flavor of software and architecture, some general principles apply. In almost every definition of web services, you'll find that there is a need for an exchange of information with other applications. This exchange needs a set of standards, and the two that are the most important (at least right now) are UDDI and WSDL. I cover both and show you how they fit in with SOAP. Finally, I'll try and pull all these various acronyms and technologies together into one concrete example to finish off the chapter.

Web Services

Web services seems to have become the next big thing in computing these days, so I've made room for this chapter in the second edition of this book. However, trying to define the term is somewhat tricky; from one person's perspective, it may be correct, but from everyone else's it's probably completely off-base. I'm left with trying to boil down the hype and differences in implementation to a simple set of concepts that remain true across the board.

Web services is about interoperability. More and more, applications must communicate with each other. But the problems in communication grow, instead of shrink, with every new day of technology innovation. As more languages, increasingly complex data structures, and varied business needs develop, the difference between one system and another (even if they are performing the same business task!) also grows. For systems to interoperate, there must be a common language. This isn't a language in the sense that Java is a language; programs not written in Java must have just as much access as those that are in Java. Instead, it's a language that anyone with a dictionary can access; even if the words aren't the same, applications have access to the words, which can be translated into something that *can* be understood.

XML solves the problem of data transfer, and is one piece of that language. It is accepted and usable in almost every programming language around: C, Perl, Python, LISP, Java, Pascal, C#, Visual Basic. . . the list goes on and on. However, web service frameworks seek to go quite a bit further. The key to interoperability is not just data, but *what* data. What information can I get from your system? What can you find out from mine? In other words, there must be a means of broadcasting what services an application makes available. And this is where we have, until recently, had a gaping hole.

However, recent additions to the web services realm have begun to fill this hole. First, UDDI provides a means of discovering other services and registering your services for others to discover. Second, WSDL offers a way to provide the needed information about a discovered service to allow a client to interact with it. I've purposely left out the explanation of what UDDI and WSDL stand for and mean for now, because I want to focus on the big picture.

Figure 13-1 shows how the process flows. To begin, a service provider codes up a service (like you did in the last chapter). This service could be as simple as adding CDs to a catalog, or as complex as storing the VIN (vehicle identification numbers) for all automobiles registered in Massachusetts that are used by the government. As long as the service is web-accessible, it's a candidate for a service registry. This is all part of the UDDI portion of the picture. UDDI also allows a user to search all registered services for a specific service name, like "cd-catalog" or "govt-bin-numbers." The registry returns all the matching services.

Hopefully, the client has found the desired service. But interaction takes more than just a name; it requires the URL to connect to and the parameters required, as well as the return value. This is accomplished through XML in a WSDL format, which I cover as well. And then, your client interacts with the located service, knowing (because of WSDL) you are using the service correctly. Life is grand, and all because of web services. Of course, I've skimmed over all the hard parts, but I'll delve into some of that complexity now that you have the big picture.

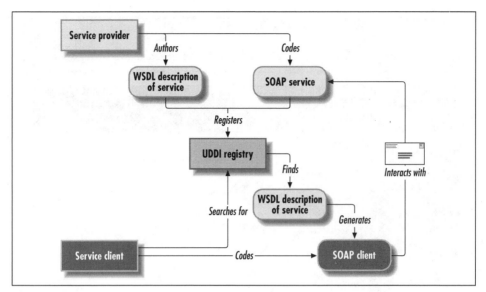

Figure 13-1. The web services process

UDDI

With no further suspense, I want to define what UDDI is. It stands for *Universal Discovery, Description, and Integration,* and is most often associated with the word "registry." The primary place to learn about UDDI is its web site, *http://www.uddi. org* (shown in Figure 13-2), also the home of the UDDI registry that is so important in registering and locating services. This site describes the UDDI project, which seeks to create and define a complete framework for the exchange of data I've been talking about in this chapter. The initiative is supported by both IBM and Microsoft, so it looks like it's around for the long haul.

The core of this is the network of services about which UDDI stores information. The ability to register a new service and search for an existing one is part and parcel of this registry, and is available online at the UDDI web site. All that is required is a simple

registration process. Neither IBM nor Microsoft require a company or even an individual to pay high fees to make their services publicly available. Because of this, there are many, many more services being registered every day than a "for-profit" system would engender.

That's all that there really is to UDDI. There is little complexity in the use of UDDI; the hard stuff is all in implementation, which you and I aren't really interested as a service provider or consumer. There are several UDDI implementations available that can be downloaded and run locally, and I prefer jUDDI over the others. You

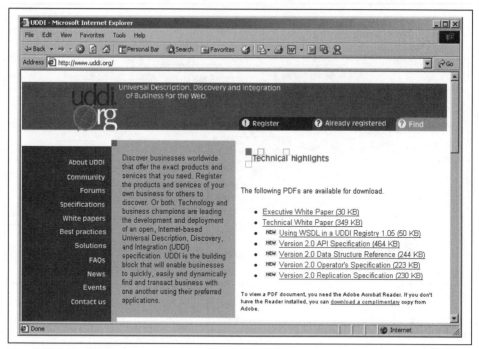

Figure 13-2. The UDDI web site

can check out this Java-based open source project at *http://www.juddi.org*. Additionally, IBM's web services toolkit (covered in the section "WSDL" later in this chapter) includes a trial version of a private UDDI registry. I'm not going to cover jUDDI or the IBM UDDI registry here, because they don't aid in understanding how to use UDDI, but rather how to implement it. If you have an interest in seeing what drives a UDDI registry, I'd recommend you check out jUDDI. If you are just interested in writing web services and making them available to others, though, I wouldn't worry too much about it. Finally, I leave out the specifics of registering and searching for services until the final section, in which I walk you through a fairly complex real-world example using SOAP, UDDI, and WSDL.

WSDL

WSDL is the *Web Services Description Language*. The entire specification is online at *http://www.w3.org/TR/wsdl*, and describes everything you need to know about a service in order to interact with it. Like UDDI, it's a fairly simple piece of technology on its own (really, it's not even technology; it's just markup), but becomes extremely important in the overall web services picture. The WSDL file describes several critical pieces of information a service client would need:

- The name of the service, including its URN

- The location the service can be accessed at (usually an HTTP URL address)

- The methods available for invocation

- The input and output parameter types for each method

Each of these pieces of data on their own are fairly useless, but together, they represent the complete client picture of the service. Additionally, a WSDL document incorporates elements of XML Schema, XML-RPC–style parameters, and quite a bit of everything else you've read about so far. Example 13-1 is a portion of a WSDL schema for the CD catalog from the last chapter; it only describes the getCD() method of the service. It's not complete, but it should give you an idea of what a WSDL document looks like.

Example 13-1. Portion of a WSDL document

```
<?xml version="1.0"?>

<definitions name="CDCatalog"
             targetNamespace="http://www.oreilly.com/javaxml2/cd-catalog.wsdl"
             xmlns:cd="http://www.oreilly.com/javaxml2/cd-catalog.wsdl"
             xmlns:soap="http://schemas.xmlsoap.org/wsdl/soap/"
             xmlns:cdXSD="http://www.oreilly.com/javaxml2/cd-catalog.xsd"
             xmlns="http://schemas.xmlsoap.org/wsdl/"
>
  <types>
    <schema targetNamespace="http://www.oreilly.com/javaxml2/cd-catalog.xsd"
            xmlns="http://www.w3.org/2000/10/XMLSchema">
      <element name="Title">
        <complexType>
          <all><element name="title" type="string" /></all>
        </complexType>
      </element>
      <element name="CD">
        <complexType>
          <all>
            <element name="title" type="string" />
            <element name="artist" type="string" />
            <element name="label" type="string" />
          </all>
        </complexType>
      </element>
    </schema>
  </types>
```

Example 13-1. Portion of a WSDL document (continued)

```
<message name="getCDInput">
  <part name="body" element="cdXSD:Title" />
</message>

<message name="getCDOutput">
  <part name="body" element="cdXSD:CD" />
</message>

<portType name="CDCatalogPortType">
  <operation name="getCD">
    <input message="cd:getCDInput" />
    <output message="cd:getCDOutput" />
  </operation>
</portType>

<binding name="CDCatalogBinding" type="cd:CDCatalogPortType">
  <soap:binding style="rpc"
                transport="http://schemas.xmlsoap.org/soap/http" />
  <operation name="getCD">
    <soap:operation soapAction="urn:cd-catalog" />
    <input>
      <soap:body use="encoded"
          encodingStyle="http://schemas.xmlsoap.org/soap/encoding/"
          namespace="urn:cd-catalog" />
    </input>
    <output>
      <soap:body use="encoded"
          encodingStyle="http://schemas.xmlsoap.org/soap/encoding/"
          namespace="urn:cd-catalog" />
    </output>
  </operation>
</binding>

<service name="CDCatalog">
  <documentation>CD Catalog Service from Java and XML</documentation>
  <port name="CDCatalogPort" binding="cd:CDCatalogBinding">
    <soap:address location="http://newInstance.com/soap/servlet/rpcrouter" />
  </port>
</service>
</defintions>
```

As you can see, this is a fairly verbose format for describing a service; however, it's also easy to understand. First, any types that must be passed across the wire are described using the types element, and an XML Schema-style syntax.

WARNING   Currently, WSDL specifications are using the 2000 version of the
             XML Schema specification, and not the finalized April 2001 XML
             Schema specification. You'll need to use the slightly older schema
             constructs until the WSDL specification is brought completely up to
             date.

Next, the `message` element is used to define interaction from the client to the
server, and the server to the client. These are combined in the `portType` element
to define available operations (you would find additional available methods in this
section as well). The `binding` element details how the operations can be accessed
and the URN where they are accessible, and the `service` element brings all of this
together. Thinking about this process as a hierarchy will help keep everything
straight in your head.

SOAP's All You Got?

Don't get the idea that a SOAP service is the only type of web service around.
It's certainly possible to build a program (or programs) that interact with clients through some other means, and represent that interaction through a
WSDL file. For example, an XML-RPC service fits the bill pretty nicely; even
though it doesn't have an envelope and custom parameter support, it still can
easily interact with clients and represent its input and output parameters in
WSDL. However, almost all the services I've seen (and I've seen a lot!) are
SOAP, so it is certainly the overriding trend. Still, keep in the back of your
mind the ability to use any program as a service, not just SOAP ones.

Currently, the Apache SOAP implementation does not directly use WSDL documents. In other words, you can't consume a WSDL document and automatically
get a client class, for example. While some of the other platforms, such as
Microsoft, are further along, Apache's Axis project is working on this functionality. For now, you'll need to interpret the WSDL document on your own, and then
manually code up a client. That's more fun anyway.

Putting It All Together

With that fairly basic understanding of WSDL added to the UDDI discussion,
you're ready for a complete web services example. In this section, I detail the process of writing a SOAP service (a messaging one, this time), registering it with a
UDDI registry, finding it using UDDI, getting the WSDL descriptor, and then
interacting with the service via a client.

For the example, I add a little more complexity. Here's the scenario. CDs-R-Us is a new company that wants to provide CDs to distributors around the world. Since they are (noticeable) late to market, they seek to gain business by providing a high-tech interface, using web services to make interaction easy. They are going to provide the ability to send XML messages requesting CDs through SOAP. Their applications will fulfill these orders by looking up the CD on their catalog server (running, of course, a heavy-duty version of the CDCatalog service from last chapter), and then returning an invoice. There are actually two SOAP transactions going on: one from the client to CDs-R-Us, which is messaging-based, and one internal to CDs-R-Us, which is RPC-based. Figure 13-3 shows the complete process flow. They also want to register their messaging service with a UDDI registry so potential clients can find them.

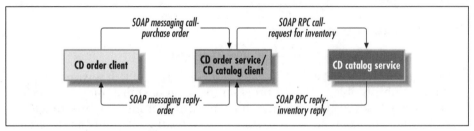

Figure 13-3. Process flow for the example application

A Messaging Service

Since we'll be using `CDCatalog` from last chapter for the RPC client, I can skip right to the new code, the messaging service. This should receive an XML purchase order and make a request to the catalog service on another machine on CDs-R-Us's local network; in other words, the messaging service is also a SOAP-RPC client. This is perfectly legal in the web services world and quite common. One business receives information from another, and in turn starts an interaction with *another* business. If this still seems odd, ask your home builder how many subcontractors he employs, and then ask each of them how many subcontractors *they* employ; it would probably blow your mind!

First, let's define the purchase order (PO) format that CDs-R-Us requires. The XML Schema for the PO document is shown in Example 13-2.

Example 13-2. po.xsd XML Schema

```
<?xml version="1.0" encoding="UTF-8"?>

<xs:schema xmlns:xs="http://www.w3.org/2001/XMLSchema"
           xmlns="http://www.cds-r-us.com"
           targetNamespace="http://www.cds-r-us.com">
```

Example 13-2. po.xsd XML Schema (continued)

```
<xs:element name="purchaseOrder">
  <xs:complexType>
    <xs:sequence>
      <xs:element ref="recipient" />
      <xs:element ref="order" />
    </xs:sequence>
    <xs:attribute name="orderDate" type="xs:string" />
  </xs:complexType>
</xs:element>

<xs:element name="recipient">
  <xs:complexType>
    <xs:sequence>
      <xs:element ref="name" />
      <xs:element ref="street" />
      <xs:element ref="city" />
      <xs:element ref="state" />
      <xs:element ref="postalCode" />
    </xs:sequence>
    <xs:attribute name="country" type="xs:string" />
  </xs:complexType>
</xs:element>

<xs:element name="name" type="xs:string"/>
<xs:element name="street" type="xs:string" />
<xs:element name="city" type="xs:string" />
<xs:element name="state" type="xs:string" />
<xs:element name="postalCode" type="xs:short" />

<xs:element name="order">
  <xs:complexType>
    <xs:sequence>
      <xs:element ref="cd" maxOccurs="unbounded" />
    </xs:sequence>
  </xs:complexType>
</xs:element>

<xs:element name="cd">
  <xs:complexType>
    <xs:attribute name="artist" type="xs:string" />
    <xs:attribute name="title" type="xs:string" />
  </xs:complexType>
</xs:element>
</xs:schema>
```

With that schema in place, a typical PO would look something like Example 13-3.

Example 13-3. Example PO for CDs

```
<purcahseOrder orderDate="07.23.2001"
    xmlns="http://www.cds-r-us.com"
    xmlns:xsi="http://www.w3.org/2001/XMLSchema-instance"
    xsi:schemaLocation="http://www.cds-r-us.com po.xsd"
>
  <recipient country="USA">
    <name>Dennis Scannell</name>
    <street>175 Perry Lea Side Road</street>
    <city>Waterbury</city>
    <state>VT</state>
    <postalCode>05676</postalCode>
  </recipient>
  <order>
    <cd artist="Brooks Williams" title="Little Lion" />
    <cd artist="David Wilcox" title="What You Whispered" />
  </order>
</purchaseOrder>
```

The service should accept an XML document like Example 13-3, figure out what information is relevant, and then pass that information on to the CD catalog service through RPC. Once it gets a response, it formulates some sort of invoice or acknowledgment for the messaging client, and sends that message back. I keep things simple for the purpose of this example, but you can easily see where to add additional processing as we walk through the code.

Writing a service that accepts XML messages is a bit different from writing one that accepts RPC requests; with messaging, you need to interact more directly with the request and response objects, and your class needs to know about SOAP. Remember that in the RPC-style processing, the class receiving requests didn't know a thing about RPC or SOAP, and was therefore encapsulated fairly well. With a messaging-style service, all methods that can be interacted with must follow this convention:

```
public void methodName(SOAPEnvelope env, SOAPContext req, SOAPContext res)
    throws java.io.IOException, javax.mail.MessagingException;
```

This should feel somewhat similar to how servlets work; you get a request and response object to interact with, as well as the actual SOAP envelope for the message sent across the wire. You can see the expected IOException that may be thrown when network and related errors occur; additionally, a MessagingException (from the JavaMail package) can result from problems with the SOAP message envelope. Additionally, the method name must be the same as the name of the root element of the message content!* This is easy to forget; in

---

* This is a requirement of Apache's SOAP implementation, not of the actual SOAP specification. However, it's fairly standard and a good programming practice, so I'd get used to following it now.

our case, it means that the method receiving XML must be called
purchaseOrder, since that is the root element in Example 13-3. With this knowledge, it's possible to set up the skeleton for a message service. This skeleton is
shown in Example 13-4; in addition to putting in the framework for receiving a
SOAP message, it also has the logic to make the appropriate call to the CDCatalog
service on another machine. I've left a comment as a placeholder for the messaging code we'll look at in a moment.

Example 13-4. Skeleton for CDs-R-Us messaging service

```java
package javaxml2;

import java.io.IOException;
import java.net.MalformedURLException;
import java.net.URL;
import java.util.Hashtable;
import java.util.LinkedList;
import java.util.List;
import java.util.Vector;
import javax.mail.MessagingException;

// SOAP imports
import org.apache.soap.Constants;
import org.apache.soap.Envelope;
import org.apache.soap.Fault;
import org.apache.soap.SOAPException;
import org.apache.soap.encoding.SOAPMappingRegistry;
import org.apache.soap.encoding.soapenc.BeanSerializer;
import org.apache.soap.rpc.Call;
import org.apache.soap.rpc.Parameter;
import org.apache.soap.rpc.Response;
import org.apache.soap.rpc.SOAPContext;
import org.apache.soap.util.xml.QName;

public class OrderProcessor {

    /** Mapping for CD class */
    private SOAPMappingRegistry registry;

    /** The serializer for the CD class */
    private BeanSerializer serializer;

    /** The RPC Call object */
    private Call call;

    /** Parameters for call */
    private Vector params;
```

Example 13-4. Skeleton for CDs-R-Us messaging service (continued)

```java
    /** Response from RPC call */
    private Response rpcResponse;

    /** The URL to connect to */
    private URL rpcServerURL;

    public void initialize() {
        // Set up internal URL for SOAP-RPC
        try {
            rpcServerURL =
                new URL("http://localhost:8080/soap/servlet/rpcrouter");
        } catch (MalformedURLException neverHappens) {
            // ignored
        }

        // Set up a SOAP mapping to translate CD objects
        registry = new SOAPMappingRegistry();
        serializer = new BeanSerializer();
        registry.mapTypes(Constants.NS_URI_SOAP_ENC,
            new QName("urn:cd-catalog-demo", "cd"),
            CD.class, serializer, serializer);

        // Build a Call to the internal SOAP service
        call = new Call();
        call.setSOAPMappingRegistry(registry);
        call.setTargetObjectURI("urn:cd-catalog");
        call.setMethodName("getCD");
        call.setEncodingStyleURI(Constants.NS_URI_SOAP_ENC);

        // Set up input
        params = new Vector();
    }

    public void purchaseOrder(Envelope env, SOAPContext req, SOAPContext res)
            throws IOException, MessagingException {

        // Set up SOAP environment
        initialize();

        // Set up list of CDs successfully ordered
        List orderedCDs = new LinkedList();

        // Set up hashtable of failed orders
        Hashtable failedCDs = new Hashtable();

        // Parse incoming message and get list of CDS ordered
```

Example 13-4. Skeleton for CDs-R-Us messaging service (continued)

```
    // Loop through each ordered CD from the PO request
        String artist = "";
        String title = "";

        // Set up input
        params.clear();
        params.addElement(new Parameter("title", String.class, title, null));
        call.setParams(params);

        try {
            // Invoke the call
            rpcResponse = call.invoke(rpcServerURL, "");

            if (!rpcResponse.generatedFault()) {
                Parameter returnValue = rpcResponse.getReturnValue();
                CD cd = (CD)returnValue.getValue();

                // See if the CD is available
                if (cd == null) {
                    failedCDs.put(title, "Requested CD is not available.");
                    continue;
                }

                // Verify it's by the right artist
                if (cd.getArtist().equalsIgnoreCase(artist)) {
                    // Add this CD to the successful orders
                    orderedCDs.add(cd);
                } else {
                    // Add this to the failed orders
                    failedCDs.put(title, "Incorrect artist for specified CD.");
                }
            } else {
                Fault fault = rpcResponse.getFault();
                failedCDs.put(title, fault.getFaultString());
            }
        } catch (SOAPException e) {
            failedCDs.put(title, "SOAP Exception: " + e.getMessage());
        }

    // At the end of the loop, return something useful to the client
    }
}
```

NOTE   In this example and in the rest of the chapter, I use the hostname
            http://localhost:8080 to represent a SOAP service running on your
            local machine. Most of you will be testing the example locally, and
            this will help you avoid putting in fictional hostnames and getting
            frustrated when things don't work.

            In a real environment you would expect the client to connect to a
            CDs-R-Us machine, like *http://www.cds-r-us.com*, and the messaging
            service to connect to an internal machine running the CD catalog,
            such as *http://catalog.cds-r-us.com*, perhaps behind an external fire-
            wall. Still, I'd rather your code work right away than try and put false
            hostnames in the example code. That's why everything uses the local
            machine as the hostname.

I briefly run through what is going on here, and then get to the interesting aspect:
the messaging interaction. First, the `initialize()` method is used to set up an
RPC call for each client. This `Call` object is used and reused, so no resources are
wasted on a single client. At the same time, each client gets their own `Call` object,
ensuring that synchronization and threading issues don't surface. Next, some storage is set up: a `List` for successful orders, and a `Hashtable` for failed ones. The
`Hashtable` has the title of the ordered CD as the key, and error information as
the value. Then, the SOAP message from the client would be read (here's where
I've left a placeholder, for now). For each CD ordered, a looping process begins.
The CD title and artist are extracted from the message, and an RPC call is invoked
to obtain the requested CD object. Depending on the result from the request to
the CD catalog, the CD is added to the list of successful or failed orders. At the
end of the loop, a message would be constructed and sent back to the client.

It's worth noting that the `CDCatalog` is a simple version, and not complete in this
context. A real CD catalog service would probably check for a CD in its inventory,
ensure copies are available, remove one CD from the inventory, report its SKU,
etc. In this case, all the CD catalog service does is check for the requested CD in its
list of available CDs. Still, you get the idea.

Now that this skeleton is in place, you are ready to interact with the user's message. Let's take care of some additional classes that will be used. Add the import
statements shown here:

```
import java.io.IOException;
import java.io.StringWriter;
import java.net.MalformedURLException;
import java.net.URL;
import java.util.Enumeration;
import java.util.Hashtable;
import java.util.Iterator;
import java.util.LinkedList;
import java.util.List;
```

```
import java.util.Vector;
import javax.mail.MessagingException;

// DOM
import org.w3c.dom.Document;
import org.w3c.dom.Element;
import org.w3c.dom.NodeList;
import org.w3c.dom.Text;

// SOAP imports
import org.apache.soap.Constants;
import org.apache.soap.Envelope;
import org.apache.soap.Fault;
import org.apache.soap.SOAPException;
import org.apache.soap.encoding.SOAPMappingRegistry;
import org.apache.soap.encoding.soapenc.BeanSerializer;
import org.apache.soap.rpc.Call;
import org.apache.soap.rpc.Parameter;
import org.apache.soap.rpc.Response;
import org.apache.soap.rpc.SOAPContext;
import org.apache.soap.util.xml.QName;
```

The code needs to use DOM to work with the XML in the message sent by the client; that message is what I want to look at first. You remember the XML shown in Example 13-3, which is the content of the message that the service expects to receive. However, the message will be wrapped in some SOAP specifics, and ends up looking like Example 13-5 before it's sent. The extra information is used by SOAP to allow interpretation of the message.

Example 13-5. The SOAP-ready document from Example 13-3

```
<s:Envelope xmlns:s="http://schemas.xmlsoap.org/soap/envelope/">
 <s:Body>
  <purchaseOrder orderDate="07.23.2001"
      xmlns="urn:cd-order-service"
  >
    <recipient country="USA">
      <name>Dennis Scannell</name>
      <street>175 Perry Lea Side Road</street>
      <city>Waterbury</city>
      <state>VT</state>
      <postalCode>05676</postalCode>
    </recipient>
    <order>
      <cd artist="Brooks Williams" title="Little Lion" />
      <cd artist="David Wilcox" title="What You Whispered" />
    </order>
  </purchaseOrder>
 </s:Body>
</s:Envelope>
```

The actual message is in the body of the SOAP envelope. The corollaries to these structures in Apache SOAP are `org.apache.soap.Envelope` and `org.apache.soap.Body`. To get the entries in the body, use `envelope.getBody().getBodyEntries()`, which returns a `Vector`. The first (and only) item in this `Vector` in this example turns out to be a DOM `Element`, which is the Java equivalent for the XML `purchaseOrder` element. That, of course, is exactly what we want. Once that element is obtained, you can use normal DOM methods to walk the DOM tree and get each ordered CD. Add the following code to your `purchaseOrder()` method, which extracts and iterates through each CD requested by the client:

```java
public void purchaseOrder(Envelope env, SOAPContext req, SOAPContext res)
    throws IOException, MessagingException {

    // Set up SOAP environment
    initialize();

    // Set up list of CDs successfully ordered
    List orderedCDs = new LinkedList();

    // Set up hashtable of failed orders
    Hashtable failedCDs = new Hashtable();

    // Get the purchaseOrder element - always the first body entry
    Vector bodyEntries = env.getBody().getBodyEntries();
    Element purchaseOrder = (Element)bodyEntries.iterator().next();

    // In a real application, do something with the buyer information

    // Get the CDs ordered
    Element order =
        (Element)purchaseOrder.getElementsByTagName("order").item(0);
    NodeList cds = order.getElementsByTagName("cd");

    // Loop through each ordered CD from the PO request
    for (int i=0, len=cds.getLength(); i<len; i++) {
        Element cdElement = (Element)cds.item(i);
        String artist = cdElement.getAttribute("artist");
        String title = cdElement.getAttribute("title");

        // Set up input for SOAP-RPC call, shown in Example 13-4
        params.clear();
        params.addElement(new Parameter("title", String.class, title, null));
        call.setParams(params);

        try {
            // Existing RPC code from code, shown in Example 13-4
        } catch (SOAPException e) {
```

```
        failedCDs.put(title, "SOAP Exception: " + e.getMessage());
      }
    }

    // At the end of the loop, return something useful to the client
  }
```

Once this code completes, the list of ordered CDs that were successful is in the orderedCDs List, and the failed orders are in the failedCDs Hashtable. Since the client already knows how to "speak" XML (it sent an XML message), it makes sense to send an XML response. Rather than constructing a response from scratch, formatting it for SOAP, and manually responding, it's possible to use the Envelope object the code just read from. Add in the code shown here, which generates a response:

```
public void purchaseOrder(Envelope env, SOAPContext req, SOAPContext res)
    throws IOException, MessagingException {

  // Existing code for Messaging parsing, shown above

  // Loop through each ordered CD from the PO request
  for (int i=0, len=cds.getLength(); i<len; i++) {
    Element cdElement = (Element)cds.item(i);
    String artist = cdElement.getAttribute("artist");
    String title = cdElement.getAttribute("title");

    // Set up input
    params.clear();
    params.addElement(new Parameter("title", String.class, title, null));
    call.setParams(params);

    try {
      // Existing RPC code from code, shown in Example 13-4
    } catch (SOAPException e) {
      failedCDs.put(title, "SOAP Exception: " + e.getMessage());
    }
  }

  // At the end of the loop, return something useful to the client
  Document doc = new org.apache.xerces.dom.DocumentImpl();
  Element response = doc.createElement("response");
  Element orderedCDsElement = doc.createElement("orderedCDs");
  Element failedCDsElement = doc.createElement("failedCDs");
  response.appendChild(orderedCDsElement);
  response.appendChild(failedCDsElement);

  // Add the ordered CDs
  for (Iterator i = orderedCDs.iterator(); i.hasNext(); ) {
    CD orderedCD = (CD)i.next();
    Element cdElement = doc.createElement("orderedCD");
```

```
        cdElement.setAttribute("title", orderedCD.getTitle());
        cdElement.setAttribute("artist", orderedCD.getArtist());
        cdElement.setAttribute("label", orderedCD.getLabel());
        orderedCDsElement.appendChild(cdElement);
    }

    // Add the failed CDs
    Enumeration keys = failedCDs.keys();
    while (keys.hasMoreElements()) {
        String title = (String)keys.nextElement();
        String error = (String)failedCDs.get(title);
        Element failedElement = doc.createElement("failedCD");
        failedElement.setAttribute("title", title);
        failedElement.appendChild(doc.createTextNode(error));
        failedCDsElement.appendChild(failedElement);
    }

    // Set this as the content of the envelope
    bodyEntries.clear();
    bodyEntries.add(response);
    StringWriter writer = new StringWriter();
    env.marshall(writer, null);

    // Send the envelope back to the client
    res.setRootPart(writer.toString(), "text/xml");
}
```

This builds up a new XML tree with the successful and failed orders within it. It then sets the tree as the content of the envelope's Body, replacing the original request from the client. Next, the envelope has to be converted to a textual format, which can be sent as the response using the SOAPContext res object. SOAP provides a means of doing this, through the marshall() method. Supplying the method a StringWriter means that the value "dropped into" that writer can be extracted as a String for use later. The second argument is an instance of org.apache.soap. util.xml.XMLJavaMappingRegistry. An example is the SOAPMappingRegistry class, a subclass of XMLJavaMappingRegistry used earlier and in the last chapter; since no special types need to be mapped, a null argument suffices.

Finally, the result of all this work and serialization is set as the content of the response, through the setRootPart() element. The second value of this method is the HTML-style content type. Since the code sends back XML, the correct value is "text/xml". Once the client gets that response, it can figure out the content is in an XML format and decode it. Other than setting this content on the SOAPContext response object, you don't need to do anything else in order to communicate back to the client. Once this method completes, the SOAP server will automatically return that object to the client, along with any information you've put within it. This is also a lot like working with the HttpServletResponse object in servlets, if you are familiar with that methodology.

At this point, you can compile the `OrderProcessor` class, and deploy it to your SOAP server:

```
java org.apache.soap.server.ServiceManagerClient
    http://localhost:8080/soap/servlet/rpcrouter deploy xml/OrderProcessorDD.xml
```

Once this is done, you're ready to register the service with a UDDI registry.

Registering with UDDI

To begin the process of registering your service, make sure it is publicly accessible. You can't register a service that is only available on your local machine (*http:// localhost:8080* and the like). If you are in the testing or experimentation phase, read through this section and file it away for later use. If you are ready to actually register a service on a network somewhere, be sure you know the hostname of the machine where it can be accessed. Then hop online and visit *http://www.uddi.org.*

Once you're at the UDDI website, click the "Register" link at the top right of the screen (see Figure 13-2 if you are lost at this point). Then select the node to register your service within. Right now, registering in one makes it accessible in all, so this is a fairly meaningless decision. I chose IBM in my case, and click the "Go" button. At this point, you'll need an account to access the IBM registry. If you don't have one, it's free to sign up and get one; click the "Register" button over on the left, and follow the instructions there. Once you're registered, login through the "Login" link on the left (see Figure 13-4). You also must provide an activation key, supplied via email after registration on your first login.

Once you make it through the registration and account activation process, you're ready to publish your service. First select whether you want to add a new business; this is generally a good idea. I've added a new business, shown in Figure 13-5.

You can then add services and attach them to your business, which adds an additional layer of organization to your searches. You can optionally add business contacts, locations, and more. Once that's done, you are ready to add your service to the registry.

Select "Add a new service" and enter in the name of your service; in this example, it would be `cd-order-service`. You'll be given options to enter the description, access point, and service location for the service. I entered "This service allows ordering CDs via a purchase order" as my description. For my access point, I selected "http" and then "newInstance.com/soap/servlet/rpcrouter" for the access point. Do the same for your service, using your own hostname and URL. You can then specify a service locator, which is a formal set of standards for categorizing your service; I'm not going to get into this here, but you can read up on it at the

Figure 13-4. Logging into the IBM UDDI registry

web site. Once you're finished entering information, you should have something that looks similar to Figure 13-6.

At this point things begin to get a little less efficent. Unfortunately, there is no capability to upload a WSDL document describing your service: that would allow a description, in technical terms, to be made available with your service for those who may want to be clients of the service. The only information allowed is the service name and access point (or points, if it's available at multiple locations). However, this does make it possible for anyone with a UDDI registration and login to search for a service and a related business. So you've registered your service, and it's available for anyone else to search for.

Searching a UDDI Registry

The opposite side of this coin is looking for a service; I'm moving from the service provider realm into that of the client, the service consumer. If you want to use SOAP, WSDL, and the rest, visit the UDDI web site's registry online and login, then search for services (like the one you just registered). This is simple: just click

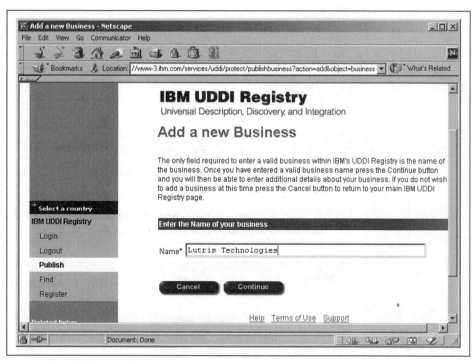

Figure 13-5. Adding a new business to the UDDI registry

the "Find" link, select the node to search within (again, I chose "IBM"), and enter the name of the service to look for. You'll need to login if you haven't already.

This is another area where web services is still evolving; searches are pretty basic, and can only be done based on a service name. If I name my service "Reading Library Service" and you enter "book" as the search text, you'll never find my service. You would need to enter "reading" or "library" to get my service. Still, it is a good start. Once you've registered your service, you can enter "cd" as your search text. Specify that you want to find services, as opposed to businesses or service types. Then, click the "Find" button on the search screen. You should get results similar to those shown in Figure 13-7 (which includes the CD service I added, and may include other readers' services once this book is out).

You can click on the service name and find the access point I entered earlier, as well as any other information I supplied (such as whether I selected a service type or category). Again, you might expect to be able to download WSDL from this service description, but that's not currently an option. At this point, you contact the business which has a service you are interested in, determine available methods to use from them, and set up any cost-based arragements required to use their services.

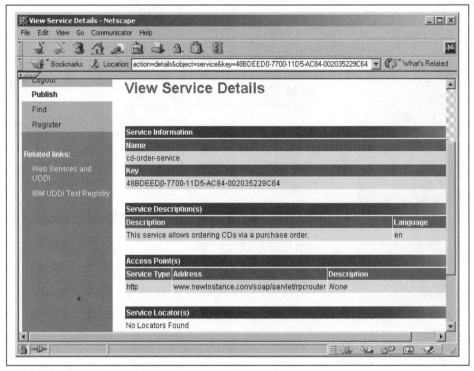

Figure 13-6. Results from adding a service

The UDDI registries still have some work left; however, the infrastructure is in place for a powerful means of registering and searching for web services. Additionally, as WSDL becomes available to upload (for service providers) and download (for service consumers), personal interaction will not be required to use a service. Despite the lack of human contact and immersion in LCD screens, this means more services are used, which in turn causes more services to be developed.

WSDL

Now I spend some time talking about how useful WSDL documents are. I'll tell you how to take one and run a simple tool, like the IBM WSTK mentioned earlier in the chapter, and generate a Java client. I'd like to describe how WSDL is a lifesaver, right now, today! However, that's not yet the case; instead, I'll let you know what is going on with Java and WSDL, so you'll be prepared when all the pieces fall into place.

Expect to see an array of tools beginning to appear that allow you to take a Java service, like the `OrderProcessor` or `CDCatalog` classes, and generate WSDL for those services. In fact, some of these tools are already available. IBM's WSTK is one I've already mentioned, and there are other packages from The Mind Electric (Glue, at *http://www.themindelectric.com*), Silverstream (*http://www.silverstream.com*),

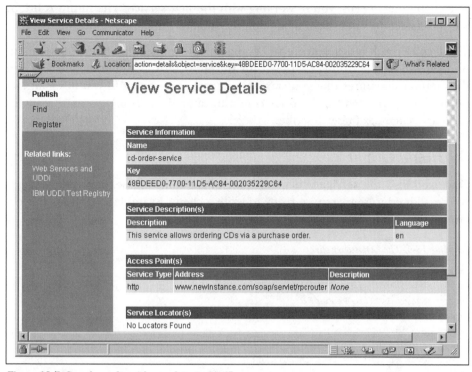

Figure 13-7. Search results with search text of "cd"

and SOAPWiz (*http://www.bju.edu/cps/faculty/sschaub/soapwiz/*). I tried these with varying levels of success. In simple cases like CDCatalog, the tools could usually generate WSDL (although IBM's toolkit choked on the method retuning a Hashtable). This is because the methods expect as input, and return as output, fairly primitive Java types like String and CD, which is made up of primitives.

The problems began when I tried to use these tools on the OrderProcessor class. Since this class is message-based, instead of RPC-based, it has some complex types as input: Envelope and SOAPContext. Because these are complex types, which in turn are made up of complex types, WSDL generators tend to get confused very fast, and generally end up choking and spewing out stack traces. The tools still have some work to do in order to handle message-based SOAP services or extremely complex RPC-based services.

The end result is twofold: first, it should get you excited about the future. As tools emerge that can handle these more complex types, it will be easy to generate WSDL from even complex SOAP services. Then, those same tools can even generate clients that speak to these services. Imagine searching the UDDI registry for a service, downloading its WSDL descriptor, and using a tool to generate a client that speaks to the service. With only a small amount of code modification specific to your business needs, you're working with the new service. The future is bright for web services (as well as for a book on the subject, I imagine!).

The second result is that you are still going to have to pick up a phone and talk to someone about their service, at least for the short term. Once someone tells you the method signatures that you can interact with, or sends it to you in email (we programmer-types tend to be poor communicators in person), you are ready to code up a client, as I now describe.

Writing a Client

Once you find the service you want, a set of methods to use, and the messages you're allowed to send, you're ready to write a client. Example 13-6 shows this client, ready to compile and use.

Example 13-6. The CDOrderer client

```
package javaxml2;

import java.io.BufferedReader;
import java.io.FileReader;
import java.io.IOException;
import java.net.URL;
import javax.xml.parsers.DocumentBuilder;

// SAX and DOM imports
import org.w3c.dom.Document;
import org.xml.sax.InputSource;
import org.xml.sax.SAXException;

// SOAP imports
import org.apache.soap.Constants;
import org.apache.soap.Envelope;
import org.apache.soap.SOAPException;
import org.apache.soap.messaging.Message;
import org.apache.soap.transport.SOAPTransport;
import org.apache.soap.util.xml.XMLParserUtils;

public class CDOrderer {

    public void order(URL serviceURL, String msgFilename)
        throws IOException, SAXException, SOAPException {

        // Parse the XML message
        FileReader reader = new FileReader(msgFilename);
        DocumentBuilder builder = XMLParserUtils.getXMLDocBuilder();
        Document doc = builder.parse(new InputSource(reader));
```

Example 13-6. The CDOrderer client (continued)

```
        if (doc == null) {
            throw new SOAPException(Constants.FAULT_CODE_CLIENT,
                "Error parsing XML message.");
        }

        // Create the message envelope
        Envelope msgEnvelope = Envelope.unmarshall(doc.getDocumentElement());

        // Send the message
        Message msg = new Message();
        msg.send(serviceURL, "urn:cd-order-service", msgEnvelope);

        // Handle the response
        SOAPTransport transport = msg.getSOAPTransport();
        BufferedReader resReader = transport.receive();

        String line;
        while ((line = resReader.readLine()) != null) {
            System.out.println(line);
        }
    }

    public static void main(String[] args) {
        if (args.length != 1) {
            System.out.println("Usage: java javaxml2.CDOrderer " +
                "[XML Message Filename]");
            return;
        }

        try {
            URL serviceURL =
                new URL("http://localhost:8080/soap/servlet/messagerouter");

            CDOrderer orderer = new CDOrderer();
            orderer.order(serviceURL, args[0]);
        } catch (Exception e) {
            e.printStackTrace();
        }
    }
}
```

This is a very simple, trivial client. It reads in an XML message supplied on the command line, and converts that to a SOAP `Envelope`. The `org.apache.soap.messaging.Message` object is used to encapsulate the envelope and send it to the service URN and hostname specified. The response is obtained through the `SOAPTransport` from the `Message`, and I simply echoed the resulting message to the screen. In your own applications, you could write this to another XML file, extract it and use DOM or JDOM to manipulate it, and then continue processing.

Instead of directly instantiating an instance of `org.apache.xerces.dom.`
`DocumentImpl`, I used the JAXP `DocumentBuilder` class and SOAP's `XMLUtils`
class to avoid a vendor-specific piece of code. This is a better practice than that shown in the `OrderProcessor` class, where the Xerces class is directly referenced. I show both just to give you a good idea of the difference; I recommend changing the code in `OrderProcessor` to mimic the client shown here.

Once you've ensured all the required SOAP client classes are in your classpath, and compiled the `CDOrderer` class, you are ready to try things out. Ensure that the services at `urn:cd-order-service` and `urn:cd-catalog` are deployed and available. Additionally, you may want to add one or both of the CDs in the *po.xml* document, from Example 13-2 and Example 13-3. I tried it once with a single CD added to the catalog, to see both a successful and failed order, and then with both added to see it succeed on both:

```
C:\javaxml2\build>java javaxml2.CDAdder
    http://localhost:8080/soap/servlet/rpcrouter
    "Little Lion" "Brooks Williams" "Signature Sounds"
Adding CD titled 'Little Lion' by 'Brooks Williams', on the label
    Signature Sounds
Successful CD Addition.
```

Make sure you have the SOAP-suitable XML shown in Example 13-5 saved; I used the filename *poMsg.xml* in my *xml* directory. Finally, you're ready to run the client:

```
bmclaugh@GANDALF
$ java javaxml2.CDOrderer c:\javaxml2\ch13\xml\poMsg.xml
<?xml version='1.0' encoding='UTF-8'?>
<s:Envelope xmlns:s="http://schemas.xmlsoap.org/soap/envelope/">
<s:Body>
<response>
 <orderedCDs>
  <orderedCD artist="Brooks Williams" label="Signature Sounds"
            title="Little Lion"/>
 </orderedCDs>
 <failedCDs>
  <failedCD title="What You Whispered">Requested CD is not available.</failedCD>
 </failedCDs>
</response>
</s:Body>
</s:Envelope>
```

The program spits out the XML response from the server; I formatted my response to make it more readable. You should get a similar output (in this example, I've added the Brooks Williams CD but not the David Wilcox CD to the catalog, as shown previously) in your tests.

At this point, you should be feeling pretty comfortable with writing both SOAP servers and client. Additionally, you probably realize that UDDI and WSDL are not that complex. Used with SOAP, they provide a nice framework for web services and interbusiness communication. I also recommend you take a look at some of the more advanced properties of Apache SOAP, or the SOAP implementation you are using. For example, Apache SOAP supports using SMTP (the Simple Mail Transport Protocol) as a transport for RPC and messaging. I don't cover this, because it's a more advanced SOAP topic, and because the specification does not yet cover SMTP as a transport. In other words, it's implementation-dependent, and I avoid those cases as much as possible. In any case, getting to know the ins and outs of your SOAP implementation only increases the effectiveness of your web services.

Where Do I Go From Here?

If you're like me, you probably are ready for about three or four more chapters of this stuff. A chapter on working with UDDI registries programmatically, another chapter on working with WSDL, some more examples. . . it would be fun. Of course, then this would be a book on web services, not Java and XML. However, there are several resources online you should check out to get to the next level. First, try *http://www.webservices.org*, which has a lot of additional introductory material. Then check out IBM's site on the subject, at *http://www.ibm.com/developerworks/webservices*; if you are working with Microsoft clients (C#, Visual Basic, and COM objects), you'll want to visit *http://www.microsoft.com/soap*. In other words, use this chapter as a solid jumping off point, visit the web services sites mentioned here, and look for upcoming books from O'Reilly on SOAP.

What's Next?

With a working understanding of web services, you're ready to conquer the world, right? Well, not quite. As with anything else in Java, there are as many ways to do business-to-business and service-based communication as there are people doing it. I'd rather not imply that the latest craze (SOAP, UDDI, and WSDL) is the end-all, be-all solution, so in the next chapter I'll introduce a completely different way to tackle intercommunication problems, using various languages, servlets, and RSS (Rich Site Summary). That should round out your knowledge base considerably.

14

Content Syndication

In the last two chapters, I tried to give you a "web services" view of the world. In other words, you saw how to write applications that communicated with each other through the various web services technologies like WSDL, UDDI, and SOAP. However, as you also saw, some things in this worldview are still a bit shaky, like WSDL generation and support (providing you're using open standards like Apache SOAP). Today, you may want to consider other options for business-to-business communication. In this chapter, I present an alternative solution for communicating across businesses to round out your skillset.

In this chapter, I look at using different XML specifications to provide this sort of communication across application and company lines, using some companies invented for the purpose. To begin with, I'll examine the Foobar Public Library, a library that allows its suppliers to enter online new books being shipped to the library. These books are then added to the library's data store for later use. Unfortunately, the library is having a hard time finding good Java developers, so it has implemented a Perl-based CGI solution. New books are entered online and then stored by a Perl script. Already, you can see that alternatives to web services would be handy, as finding a good Perl SOAP implementation is not easy (at least not yet!).

I'll also look at another company, *mytechbooks.com*. *mytechbooks.com* sells technical and computing books (such as this one) online through various partnerships with large bookstores. It has recently signed an agreement with the Foobar Public Library to obtain books from the library. *mytechbooks.com* will pay for the shipping and inventory costs of the books, while the library agrees to order extra books at its discounted costs; these extra books are then sold by *mytechbooks.com*. *mytechbooks. com* needs to be able to access the new books entered into the Foobar Public Library by suppliers to know when new offerings are available, and then advertise those new offerings. However, *mytechbooks.com* has no idea how to interface with

THE FOOBAR PUBLIC LIBRARY

the Foobar Public Library's Perl-based system. Additionally, there are no protected network connections between the two organizations, so normal HTTP must be used for communication. And just to get us out of the web services world, *mytechbooks.com* wants to wait until web services is more fleshed out, and has WSDL support integrated in more firmly, so wants a more stable solution (or at least one that has been in use a little longer).

Finally, I'll look at customers of *mytechbooks.com*. The bookstore targets people who are active online, so wants to advertise on sites like Netscape Netcenter; it also wants to allow people to easily obtain information from its site when new offerings are available. However, as in the situation with the Foobar Public Library, the people at *mytechbooks.com* have no idea how to achieve this goal. Seeing as they've read O'Reilly books and articles on *http://www.oreillynet.com*, they've heard RSS's spec lead, Rael Dornfest, talk about how cool RSS is, and want to try it. Of course, Rael is right, so that's what I talk about in this chapter.

We tackle this common scenario by starting with the Foobar Public Library and examining its Perl system. Moving out to *mytechbooks.com* and then the customers of the bookstore, I show you how to enable this business-to-business (to-customer) application by using XML as a communication tool between each layer.

The Foobar Public Library

To start the creation of a business-to-business system, I describe the system currently in place at the Foobar Public Library. Before diving into the code, though, it's necessary to examine the library's requirements so that you do not create a system it cannot support.

Evaluating the Requirements

All too often, good solutions to a problem are not appropriate solutions for the company with the problem. The Foobar Library is a perfect example of this: certainly a Java servlet that could communicate with servlets built by *mytechbooks.com* could quickly solve the two organizations' problems. However, this ignores the library's requirements. Before creating a solution, the library detailed its requirements:

- The solution must be Perl-based; no Java engineers are on staff.
- The solution must not involve new software or library installations.
- The solution must not impact the existing order-entry system (no interface changes).

While these are not extremely stringent requirements, they force a solution other than Java servlets. You must avoid using Java as a solution. Of course, as this is a book on XML, you should be thinking that storing the data about new books in an

XML format could allow the library to then supply that XML to clients through an
HTTP request, thus enabling those clients to use the data in any way they wish. In
fact, this is a much better solution than servlet-to-servlet communication, as the
XML can be used by any company or client in its applications, rather than tying
the library (and its books) to a specific company. This then defines the goal for
updating the Foobar Public Library's system: save the entered information as XML
data, and then provide HTTP access to that XML data for clients and customers.

Entering the Books

We need to examine the existing HTML interface for suppliers entering new books
into the system. Example 14-1 shows the static HTML used to generate this form.

Example 14-1. Static HTML for Foobar Public Library interface

```
<html>

<head>
  <title>Foobar Public Library: Add Books</title>
  <style>
<!--
body        { font-family: Arial }
h1          { color: #000080 }
-->
  </style>
</head>

<body link="#FFFF00" vlink="#FFFF00" alink="#FFFF00">
 <table border="0" width="100%" cellpadding="0" cellspacing="0">
  <tr>
   <td width="15%" bgcolor="#000080" valign="top" align="center">
    <b><i>
     <font color="#FFFFFF" size="4">Options</font>
    </i></b>
   <p><b>
     <font color="#FFFFFF">
      <a href="/javaxml/foobar">Main Menu</a>
     </font>
   </p></b>
   <p><b>
     <font color="#FFFFFF">
      <a href="/javaxml/foobar/catalog.html">Catalog</a>
     </font>
    </b></p>
    <p><b>
     <i><font color="#FFFF00">Add Books</font></i>
    </b></p>
    <p><b>
```

Example 14-1. Static HTML for Foobar Public Library interface (continued)

```
    <font color="#FFFFFF">
     <a href="/javaxml/foobar/logout.html">Log Out</a>
    </font>
   </p></td>
   <td width="*" valign="top" align="center">
    <h1 align="center">The Foobar Public Library</h1>
    <h3 align="center"><i>- Add Books -</i></h3>

<!-- This will need to point at your CGI directory and script, which
     we look at next -->
    <form method="POST" action="/cgi/addBook.pl">

     <table border="0" cellpadding="5" width="100%">
      <tr>
       <td width="100%" valign="top" align="center" colspan="2">
        Title 
        <input type="text" name="title" size="20">
        <hr width="85%" />
       </td>
      </tr>
      <tr>
       <td width="50%" valign="top" align="right">Author 
        <input type="text" name="author" size="20">
       </td>
       <td width="50%" valign="top" align="left">Subject 
        <select size="1" name="subject">
         <option>Fiction</option>
         <option>Biography</option>
         <option>Science</option>
         <option>Industry</option>
         <option>Computers</option>
        </select></td>
      </tr>
      <tr>
       <td width="50%" valign="top" align="right">Publisher 
        <input type="text" name="publisher" size="20">
       </td>
       <td width="50%" valign="top" align="left">ISBN 
        <input type="text" name="isbn" size="20">
       </td>
      </tr>
      <tr>
       <td width="50%" valign="top" align="right">Price 
        <input type="text" name="price" size="20">
       </td>
       <td width="50%" valign="top" align="left">Pages 
        <input type="text" name="numPages" size="20">
       </td>
```

Example 14-1. Static HTML for Foobar Public Library interface (continued)

```
        </tr>
        <tr>
         <td width="100%" valign="top" align="center" colspan="2">
          Description 
           <textarea rows="2" name="description" cols="20"></textarea>
         </td>
        </tr>
       </table>
       <p>
         <input type="submit" value="Add this Book" name="addBook">
         <input type="reset" value="Reset Form" name="reset">
         <input type="button" value="Cancel" name="cancel">
       </p>
     </form>
    </td>
   </tr>
  </table>
 </body>
</html>
```

This file, saved as *addBooks.html*, provides the portion of the library application allowing suppliers to add new books they are sending to the library.

NOTE   In Example 14-1 and throughout the rest of the chapter, complete
          code and HTML listings are given so that you can create the exam-
          ple applications and walk through the process of enabling XML
          communication across the applications. Additionally, the code exam-
          ples in this chapter assume you are using the filenames supplied in
          the text; you will need to change the code and examples if you use
          your own filenames. Code that may need to be changed to refer-
          ence different filenames or scripts is emphasized in the listings to
          help you walk through the examples.

The HTML in Example 14-1, when accessed through a web server, results in the output shown in Figure 14-1. Although we do not look at the other menu options, the supplier can also view the library's catalog, go to the application's main menu, and log out of the application by using the menu on the left of the screen.

This form allows the supplier to enter the details about each book it is sending to the library. The supplier enters the book's essentials (title, author, publisher, pages, and a description), as well as a subject to categorize the book, and sales details, which include the price and ISBN number.

Once this information has been entered, it is submitted to a Perl CGI script:

```
<form method="POST" action="/cgi/addBook.pl">
```

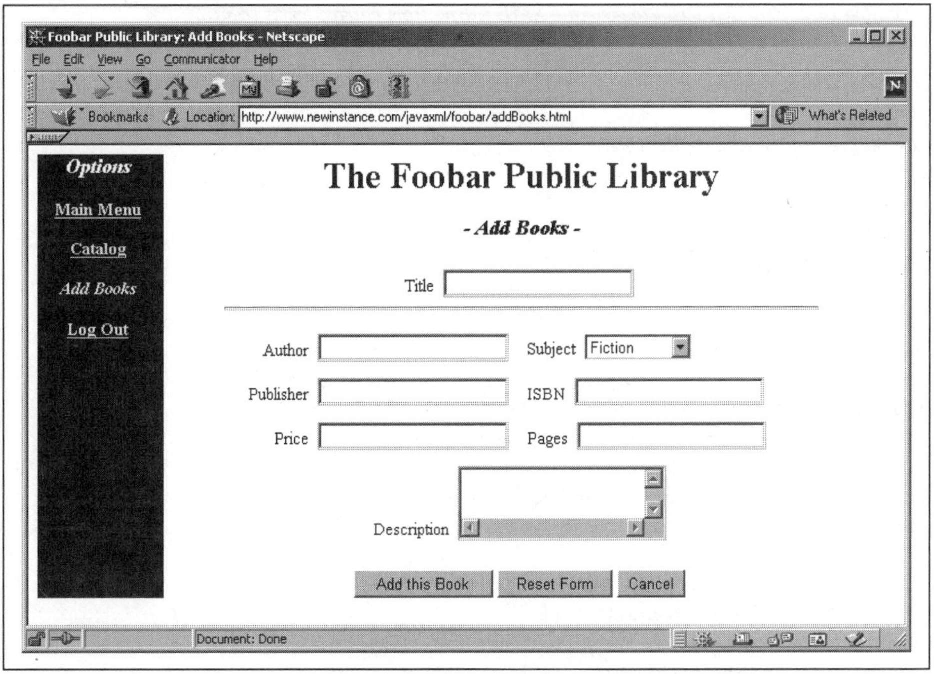

Figure 14-1. HTML user interface for Foobar Public Library

This script, then, must produce XML output. The easiest solution would be to download a Perl library that handled XML parsing, such as Xerces-Perl; however, remember that one requirement of the library was that no libraries or software could be added. While this may seem silly and frustrating, keep in mind that many companies have very strict lock-downs on their production systems. In this case, the Foobar Public Library is just beginning to introduce applications on the Internet, and it does not have resources to support additional software.

Luckily, the code only has to output XML; this is done fairly easily by generating a file with information on the entered books by brute force. Things would be much trickier if parsing incoming XML were required. Because the library needs to keep any existing books, each new entry is appended to an existing file, instead of creating a new file upon a new request. Writing the Perl is almost trivial, and the complete Perl program to read the request parameters and append the information to an existing file is shown in Example 14-2.

Example 14-2. Perl CGI script to generate XML entries from entered books

```
#!/usr/local/bin/perl

# This should be the directory you wish to write files to
$baseDir = "/home/bmclaugh/javaxml/foobar/books/";
```

Example 14-2. Perl CGI script to generate XML entries from entered books (continued)

```perl
# This should be the filename to use
$filename = "books.txt";


$bookFile = $baseDir . $filename;


# Get the user's input
use CGI;
$query = new CGI;


$title = $query->param('title');
$author = $query->param('author');
$subject = $query->param('subject');
$publisher = $query->param('publisher');
$isbn = $query->param('isbn');
$price = $query->param('price');
$numPages = $query->param('numPages');
$description = $query->param('description');


# Save the book to a file in XML
if (open(FILE, ">>" . $bookFile)) {
  print FILE "<book subject=\"" . $subject . "\">\n";
  print FILE " <title><![CDATA[" . $title . "]]></title>\n";
  print FILE " <author><![CDATA[" . $author . "]]></author>\n";
  print FILE " <publisher><![CDATA[" . $publisher . "]]></publisher>\n";
  print FILE " <numPages>" . $numPages . "</numPages>\n";
  print FILE " <saleDetails>\n";
  print FILE "   <isbn>" . $isbn . "</isbn>\n";
  print FILE "   <price>" . $price . "</price>\n";
  print FILE " </saleDetails>\n";
  print FILE " <description>";
  print FILE "<![CDATA[" . $description . "]]>";
  print FILE "</description>\n";
  print FILE "</book>\n\n";


  # Give the user a confirmation
  print <<"EOF";
Content-type: text/html


  <html>
   <head>
    <title>Foobar Public Library: Confirmation</title>
   </head>
   <body>
    <h1 align="center">Book Added</h1>
    <p align="center">
     Thank you.  The book you submitted has been added to the Library.
    </p>
   </body>
```

Example 14-2. Perl CGI script to generate XML entries from entered books (continued)

```
  </html>
EOF

} else {
  print <<"EOF";
Content-type: text/html

  <html>
   <head>
    <title>Foobar Public Library: Error</title>
   </head>
   <body>
    <h1 align="center">Error in Adding Book</h1>
    <p align="center">
     We're sorry.  The book you submitted has <i>not</i> been added to
     the Library.
    </p>
   </body>
  </html>
EOF
}
close (FILE);
```

This program, saved as *addBook.pl*, is invoked by a form submitted when the supplier enters a new book. The script defines the file to write to, and then assigns the request parameter values to local variables:

```
$title = $query->param('title');
$author = $query->param('author');
$subject = $query->param('subject');
$publisher = $query->param('publisher');
$isbn = $query->param('isbn');
$price = $query->param('price');
$numPages = $query->param('numPages');
$description = $query->param('description');
```

Once these values are easily accessible, the script opens the file defined earlier in append mode (signified by >> preceding the filename) and writes raw XML-formatted information about the entered book to the end of the file:

```
print FILE "<book subject=\"" . $subject . "\">\n";
print FILE " <title><![CDATA[" . $title . "]]></title>\n";
print FILE " <author><![CDATA[" . $author . "]]></author>\n";
print FILE " <publisher><![CDATA[" . $publisher . "]]></publisher>\n";
print FILE " <numPages>" . $numPages . "</numPages>\n";
print FILE " <saleDetails>\n";
print FILE "  <isbn>" . $isbn . "</isbn>\n";
print FILE "  <price>" . $price . "</price>\n";
print FILE " </saleDetails>\n";
```

```
print FILE " <description>";
print FILE "<![CDATA[" . $description . "]]>";
print FILE "</description>\n";
print FILE "</book>\n\n";
```

The subject is used as an attribute on the enclosing element, book, and the rest of the information is entered in as elements. Because a book's title, author, description, and publisher may include quotation marks, apostrophes, ampersands, and other characters that would have to be escaped, the code encloses that data within a CDATA section so as not to have to worry about escaping the data.

Additionally, you should notice that no XML declaration or root element is created, as multiple books will exist in a single file. Because it is a bit difficult to check if the file exists, write the declaration and root element if the file is new, and then write out the ending element (which has to be overwritten at each new entry), the file is left as an XML document fragment. For example, here is what the file might look like after two books have been entered:

```
<book subject="Computers">
 <title><![CDATA[Java Servlet Programming]]></title>
 <author><![CDATA[Jason Hunter]]></author>
 <publisher><![CDATA[O'Reilly & Associates]]></publisher>
 <numPages>753</numPages>
 <saleDetails>
  <isbn>0596000405</isbn>
  <price>44.95</price>
 </saleDetails>
 <description><![CDATA[This book is a superb introduction to Java
   servlets and their various communications mechanisms.]]></description>
 </book>

<book subject="Fiction">
 <title><![CDATA[Second Foundation]]></title>
 <author><![CDATA[Isaac Asimov]]></author>
 <publisher><![CDATA[Bantam Books]]></publisher>
 <numPages>279</numPages>
 <saleDetails>
  <isbn>0553293362</isbn>
  <price>5.59</price>
 </saleDetails>
 <description><![CDATA[fter the First Foundation was taken over by the
   Mule, only the Second Foundation stood between order and the utter
   destruction the Mule would bring.]]></description>
 </book>
```

Although not a complete XML document, this fragment is well-formed and could be inserted into an XML document with the header and root element already set. In fact, when I look at providing a listing of books in the next section, that is precisely how I'll handle output of the fragment.

The rest of the script outputs HTML indicating whether the book was successfully added or if errors occurred. Once a book has been added to the XML storage, the supplier receives the simple confirmation message shown in Figure 14-2.

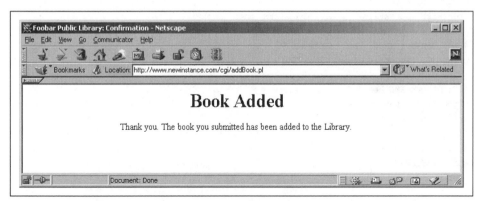

Figure 14-2. Confirmation message when a book is added

Now that there is an XML document fragment with information about new books, you'll need to take that file and provide it to requestors.

Providing a Listing of Available Books

We again can use Perl as a mechanism to provide clients and customers with an XML listing of new books. I'm making the assumption that some other portion of the library's application periodically reads the XML data and updates the library's catalog; at this point, that application component is responsible for removing the entries within the file (or the file itself) so that the books within it are no longer regarded as new entries. With this assumption, all a second Perl script has to do is read the XML fragment and add the data within it to an XML document that is output to the screen. As I already mentioned, the script also needs to add an XML declaration and a root element to surround the content within the new books file. This new script, shown in Example 14-3, reads the file created by the *addBook.pl* script and outputs the content within an XML document when it is requested over HTTP.

Example 14-3. Perl CGI script to output XML document with new book listings

```
#!/usr/local/bin/perl

# This should be the directory you wish to write files to
$baseDir = "/home/bmclaugh/javaxml/foobar/books/";

# This should be the filename to use
$filename = "books.txt";
```

Example 14-3. Perl CGI script to output XML document with new book listings (continued)

```perl
$bookFile = $baseDir . $filename;

# First open the file
open(FILE, $bookFile) || die "Could not open $bookFile.\n";

# Let browser know what is coming
print "Content-type: text/plain\n\n";

# Print out XML header and root element
print "<?xml version=\"1.0\"?>\n";
print "<books>\n";

# Print out books
while (<FILE>) {
  print "$_";
}

# Close root element
print "</books>\n";

close(FILE);
```

This script, saved as *supplyBooks.pl*, accepts a request, reads the file created by *addBook.pl*, and outputs XML upon an HTTP request. The result of requesting this script in a web browser (with several books added) is shown in Figure 14-3.

As you can see, this easily turned the library's simple Perl-based application into a component capable of supplying useful information to its clients, including the *mytechbooks.com* technical bookstore. Additionally, we were able to accomplish this without installing new software, changing the architecture of the library's system or application, or even writing a line of Java!

mytechbooks.com

With the Foobar Public Library allowing access to an XML listing of its new books, *mytechbooks.com* is moving closer to its goal of providing up-to-date content to its customers. In addition, *mytechbooks.com* already has an established standard for using Java for application development. This makes the process of accessing and using the XML from the library even easier, as Java has the excellent support for XML we have been looking at throughout this book. You'll need to allow *mytechbooks.com* to provide an online listing of new books first, and then look at how to get this information out to its customers automatically.

Figure 14-3. XML output from supplyBooks.pl

Filtering XML Data

If you remember, the Foobar Public Library allowed books on several different subjects to be entered into its system; *mytechbooks.com* wants only the books about computer-related subjects. Fortunately, the library captured this information in the subject attribute of the book element for each book in its XML data. The first task is to filter out any book whose subject is not "Computers". Once the technical books have been obtained, they should be formatted into an HTML page that can be shown to customers visiting *mytechbooks.com*.

For this company and application, there is no static HTML, since the page showing new listings must be generated each time it is accessed. I'm going to use a servlet here for handling these responses. Although Apache Cocoon would be an excellent choice for converting the XML data from the library into an HTML response, *mytechbooks.com* is under tremendous time pressure to make these book listings available, and does not want to introduce such a large change into its system immediately; instead, it would prefer to use XML parsers and processors and then add Cocoon in as a second-phase addition. This means that you'll have to handle conversion from XML to HTML as well as the filtering of the data and the addition of other presentation-specific items, such as a company logo and menu bar.

However, taking all the information at your disposal about XML and XSL, you remember that even without Cocoon you can use XSL to transform an XML document into HTML. Applying a transformation would also allow you to filter out the books that do not have the subject criteria that *mytechbooks.com* desires. With this in mind, it's simple to create an XSL stylesheet that can be applied to the XML response from the Foobar Public Library. Example 14-4 shows the beginning of this stylesheet, which handles generation of the HTML specific to the *mytechbooks.com* web site.

Example 14-4. XSL stylesheet for Foobar Public Library book listings

```
<?xml version="1.0"?>

<xsl:stylesheet xmlns:xsl="http://www.w3.org/1999/XSL/Transform"
                version="1.0"
>

  <xsl:template match="books">
   <html>
    <head>
     <title>mytechbooks.com - Your Computer Bookstore</title>
    </head>
    <body background="/javaxml/techbooks/images/background.gif"
          link="#FFFFFF" vlink="#FFFFFF" alink="#FFFFFF">
     <h1 align="center">
      <font face="Arial" color="#00659C">
       &lt;mytechbooks.com&gt;
      </font>
     </h1>
     <p align="center">
      <i><b>
       Your source on the Web for computing and technical books.
      </b></i>
     </p>
     <p align="center">
      <b><font size="4" color="#00659C">
       <u>New Listings</u>
      </font></b>
     </p>
```

Example 14-4. XSL stylesheet for Foobar Public Library book listings (continued)

```
<table border="0" cellpadding="5" cellspacing="5">
 <tr>
  <td valign="top" align="center" nowrap="nowrap" width="115">
   <p align="center">
    <font color="#FFFFFF"><b>
     <a href="/javaxml/techbooks/">Home</a>
    </b></font>
   </p>
   <p align="center">
    <font color="#FFFFFF"><b>
     <a href="/javaxml/techbooks/current.html">Current Listings</a>
    </b></font>
   </p>
   <p align="center">
    <b><font color="#FFFFFF">
     <i>New Listings</i>
    </font></b>
   </p>
   <p align="center">
    <font color="#FFFFFF"><b>
     <a href="/javaxml/techbooks/contact.html">Contact Us</a>
    </b></font>
   </p>
  </td>
  <td valign="top" align="left">
   <table border="0" cellpadding="5" cellspacing="5">
    <tr>
     <td width="450" align="left" valign="top">
      <p>
       <b>
        Welcome to <font face="courier">mytechbooks.com</font>,
        your source on the Web for computing and technical books.
        Our newest offerings are listed on the left.  To purchase
        any of these fine books, simply click on the
        &quot;Buy this Book!&quot; link, and you will be taken to
        the shopping cart for our store.  Enjoy!
       </b>
      </p>
      <p>
       <b>
        You should also check out our current listings, information
        about the store, and you can call us with your questions.
        Use the links on the menu to the left to access this
        information.  Thanks for shopping!
       </b>
      </p>
```

Example 14-4. XSL stylesheet for Foobar Public Library book listings (continued)

```
        </td>
        <td align="left">

      <!-- Handle creation of content for each new *computer* book -->

        </td>
       </tr>
      </table>
     </td>
    </tr>
   </table>
  </body>
 </html>
</xsl:template>

</xsl:stylesheet>
```

While this doesn't yet filter the incoming XML data or transform that data, it does take care of the HTML interface for the user. Often it is much easier to take care of these presentation details first, and then add the transformation-specific logic afterwards.

NOTE   When developing XSL stylesheets, particularly for web applications, you should test the results with your XSLT Processor using its command-line capabilities. This can help you ensure that the stylesheet is transforming your document as you expect at each step of its development; trying to debug a large stylesheet's problems once it is complete is much more difficult. For this example, you could access the *supplyBooks.pl* script in a web browser, save the results to an XML file, and test that and the stylesheet as you follow the examples.

Similar to the Foobar Public Library's application, this provides a menu on the left with hyperlinks to other portions of the application, contains some text about the company and its offerings, and then leaves a right column open for the addition of new book listings.

Before filtering the content, you need to add a template for outputting HTML content from a single book element's entry. As you recall, an entry looks like this:

```
<book subject="Computers">
 <title><![CDATA[Running Linux]]></title>
 <author><![CDATA[Matt Welsh]]></author>
 <publisher><![CDATA[O'Reilly & Associates]]></publisher>
 <numPages>729</numPages>
 <saleDetails>
  <isbn> 156592469X</isbn>
```

```
  <price>39.95</price>
 </saleDetails>
 <description><![CDATA[In the tradition of all O'Reilly books, Running
  Linux features clear, step-by-step instructions that always seem to
  provide just the right amount of information.]]></description>
</book>
```

You can then convert this to HTML with the following XSL template:

```
<?xml version="1.0"?>

<xsl:stylesheet xmlns:xsl="http://www.w3.org/1999/XSL/Transform"
                version="1.0"
>

 <xsl:template match="books">
   <!-- Presentation of User Interface -->
 </xsl:template>

 <xsl:template match="book">
  <table border="0" cellspacing="1" bgcolor="#000000">
   <tr>
    <td>
     <table border="0" cellpadding="3" cellspacing="0">
      <tr>
       <td width="100%" bgcolor="#00659C" nowrap="nowrap" align="center">
        <b><font color="#FFFFFF">
         <xsl:value-of select="title" />
        </font></b>
       </td>
      </tr>
      <tr>
       <td width="100%" align="center" nowrap="nowrap" bgcolor="#FFFFFF">
        <font color="#000000"><b>
         Author: <xsl:value-of select="author" /><br />
         Publisher: <xsl:value-of select="publisher" /><br />
         Pages: <xsl:value-of select="numPages" /><br />
         Price: <xsl:value-of select="saleDetails/price" /><br />
         <br />
        </b></font>
        <xsl:element name="a">
         <xsl:attribute name="href">/servlets/BuyBookServlet?isbn=
          <xsl:value-of select="saleDetails/isbn" />
         </xsl:attribute>
         <font color="#00659C">Buy the Book!</font>
        </xsl:element>
       </td>
      </tr>
     </table>
    </td>
```

```
    </tr>
   </table>
   <br />
  </xsl:template>

 </xsl:stylesheet>
```

This template matches the `book` element, and then creates a table with a heading in one row, and contents in the second row. The entire table is within another table with a black background, which results in the appearance of the table being surrounded by a beveled black border. The title is inserted into the header of the table, and the information about the book (author, publisher, pages, and price) is added to the content of the table. Finally, a link to a Java servlet, `BuyBook-Servlet`, is provided to allow easy access to purchasing the book. The value of the book's `isbn` element is supplied as an argument to this servlet, which enables it to load the book being purchased.

WARNING   In your XSL stylesheet, you should ensure that the line indicating the use of `BuyBookServlet` and the line with the `xsl:value-of` element selecting the book's ISBN number is actually one single line. If not, spaces and a carriage return could be inserted into the resultant URL, causing incorrect information to be passed to the servlet. The example stylesheet has this information broken into two lines because of the space constraints of the printed page.

The last addition you need to make to your stylesheet is to ensure that the new template is applied, and that only books with the subject "Computers" are passed to the new template. You can reference the value of the `subject` attribute with the @ symbol in your stylesheet, and filter the requests with the `select` attribute on the `xsl:apply-templates` element:

```
   </td>
   <td align="left">

    <!-- Handle creation of content for each new *computer* book -->
    <xsl:apply-templates select="book[@subject='Computers']" />

   </td>
  </tr>
 </table>
```

This references the value of the attribute and compares it to a literal, enclosed within single quotes because the entire XPath expression is enclosed within double quotes. Because you are accessing an attribute of a nested element, you'll need to reference the element by name, and surround the expression on the element's attribute with brackets. This will ensure that only books with a subject of "Computers" have templates applied, and are therefore included in the HTML output. Once the stylesheet is complete, it can be saved as *computerBooks.xsl* and referenced programmatically by a Java servlet, which I'll show you how to write next.

XSLT from a Servlet

With your stylesheet ready for use, you need to add Java code to apply it to the XML data from the Foobar Public Library. This data is accessed easily by using Java's `java.net.URL` class to make an HTTP request to the library's system. Once you have this set up, all that is left is to actually apply the XSL transformation programmatically. Example 14-5 shows the Java servlet code that loads the XML data from the library, and indicates where the transformation code would be inserted

Example 14-5. Java Servlet for transforming book listings into HTML

```java
package com.techbooks;

import java.io.FileInputStream;
import java.io.InputStream;
import java.io.IOException;
import java.io.PrintWriter;
import java.net.URL;
import javax.servlet.*;
import javax.servlet.http.*;

public class ListBooksServlet extends HttpServlet {

    /** Host to connect to for books list */
    private static final String hostname = "newInstance.com";
    /** Port number to connect to for books list */
    private static final int portNumber = 80;
    /** File to request (URI path) for books list */
    private static final String file = "/cgi/supplyBooks.pl";

    /** Stylesheet to apply to XML */
    private static final String stylesheet =
        "/home/bmclaugh/javaxml/techbooks/XSL/computerBooks.xsl";

    public void service(HttpServletRequest req, HttpServletResponse res)
        throws ServletException, IOException {

        res.setContentType("text/html");

        // Connect and get XML listing of books
        URL getBooksURL = new URL("http", hostname, portNumber, file);
```

Example 14-5. Java Servlet for transforming book listings into HTML (continued)

```
        InputStream in = getBooksURL.openStream();

        // Transform XML for InputStream into HTML output
    }
}
```

This simple servlet requests the Foobar Public Library's application through an HTTP request, and gets the XML response in an `InputStream`.* This stream should then be used as a parameter to the XSLT processor, as well as the XSL stylesheet defined as a constant in the servlet.

There is currently no Java API that specifies how XSLT transformations can occur programmatically; however, each processor vendor should have classes that allow a transformation to be invoked from your Java code. I continue to look at using the Apache Xalan processor here; you should consult your processor's vendor for the method or methods to invoke in your own programs.

For Apache Xalan, the `XSLTProcessor` class is provided in the `org.apache.xalan.xslt` package for just this purpose. It takes as parameters an `XSLTInput-Source` wrapping the XML file to process, an `XSLTInputSource` wrapping the XSL stylesheet to apply, and an `XSLTResultTarget` to use for output of the transformation. All three of these helper classes are in the `org.apache.xalan.xslt` package as well. They can conveniently be created by passing in an `InputStream` (to `XSLTInputSource`) or an `OutputStream` (to `XSLTResultTarget`). You have the XML document as an `InputStream`, you can wrap the XSL stylesheet within a `FileInputStream`, and the servlet API provides easy access to the `Servlet-OutputStream` object through the `getOutputStream()` method on the `HttpServletResponse` object. The last detail to address is obtaining an instance of `XSLTProcessor`. Because there are several underlying mechanisms that can be used for processing, this class is not instantiated directly, but rather obtained through the `XSLTProcessorFactory` class, also in the `org.apache.xalan.xslt` package. You should be familiar with factory classes by now, so all that is left is to import the classes you'll need and add the processing method calls to the servlet:

```
package com.techbooks;

import java.io.FileInputStream;
import java.io.InputStream;
import java.io.IOException;
import java.io.PrintWriter;
import java.net.URL;
```

---

* For more information on the URL class and Java I/O, see *Java I/O* by Elliotte Rusty Harold (O'Reilly).

```
import javax.servlet.*;
import javax.servlet.http.*;

// Import Xalan XSLT Processor components
import org.apache.xalan.xslt.XSLTInputSource;
import org.apache.xalan.xslt.XSLTProcessor;
import org.apache.xalan.xslt.XSLTProcessorFactory;
import org.apache.xalan.xslt.XSLTResultTarget;

public class ListBooksServlet extends HttpServlet {

    /** Host to connect to for books list */
    private static final String hostname = "newInstance.com";
    /** Port number to connect to for books list */
    private static final int portNumber = 80;
    /** File to request (URI path) for books list */
    private static final String file = "/cgi/supplyBooks.pl";

    /** Stylesheet to apply to XML */
    private static final String stylesheet =
        "/home/bmclaugh/javaxml/techbooks/XSL/computerBooks.xsl";

    public void service(HttpServletRequest req, HttpServletResponse res)
        throws ServletException, IOException {

        res.setContentType("text/html");

        // Connect and get XML listing of books
        URL getBooksURL = new URL("http", hostname, portNumber, file);
        InputStream in = getBooksURL.openStream();

        // Transform XML for InputStream into HTML output
        try {
            XSLTProcessor processor = XSLTProcessorFactory.getProcessor();

            // Transform XML with XSL stylesheet
            processor.process(new XSLTInputSource(in),
                          new XSLTInputSource(
                              new FileInputStream(stylesheet)),
                          new XSLTResultTarget(
                              res.getOutputStream())));

        } catch (Exception e) {
            PrintWriter out = res.getWriter();
            out.println("Error: " + e.getMessage());
            out.close();
        }
    }
}
```

NOTE   I could have also used JAXP 1.1's TrAX API for performing this translation. However, JAXP 1.1 is still pretty new as of this writing, and I see few people adopting it (yet). Additionally, most servlet engines, especially Tomcat, still ship with JAXP 1.0, and many are relying on that default behavior rather than supplying a newer version of JAXP.

When this new servlet is requested, it in turn requests the XML data from the Foobar Public Library. This data (a listing of the newly available books) is then transformed and output to the screen as HTML. The response from the servlet should look similar to Figure 14-4.

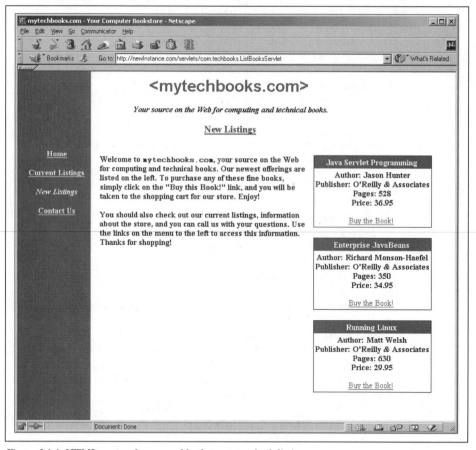

Figure 14-4. HTML output from mytechbooks.com new book listing

Along with the menu links on the left (not implemented in this example), the newest book listings are printed in a very nice format, all with up-to-date information (thanks to the changes at the Foobar Public Library!) as well as links to buy the book with a few mouseclicks. Now *mytechbooks.com* customers can easily browse the new book listings online; all that is left is to push this information out to these customers, so they don't even have to type in a URL. I'll look at solving this difficult problem next.

Push Versus Pull

So far, I have looked at building applications assuming that the application clients would always pull data and content. In other words, a user had to type a URL into a browser (in the case of the *mytechbooks.com* new book listings), or an application like the *mytechbooks.com* servlet had to make an HTTP request for XML data (in the case of the Foobar Public Library). While this is not a problem, it is not always the best way for a company like *mytechbooks.com* to sell books. Clients pulling data have to remember to visit sites they would buy items from, and often don't revisit those sites for days, weeks, or even months. While those clients may often purchase a large number of goods and services when they do remember, on average, those purchases do not result in as much revenue as if small purchases were made more frequently.

Realizing this trend, *mytechbooks.com* wants to be able to push data to its clients. Pushing data involves letting the client know (without any client action) that new items are available or that specials are being run. This in turn allows the client to make more frequent purchases without having to remember to visit a web page. However, pushing data to clients is difficult in a web medium, as the Internet does not behave as a thick client: it is harder to send pop-up messages or generate alerts for users. What *mytechbooks.com* has discovered, though, is the popularity of personalized "start pages" like Netscape's My Netscape and Yahoo's My Yahoo pages. In talking with Netscape, *mytechbooks.com* has been hearing about a technology called Rich Site Summary (RSS), and thinks that may be the answer to its need to push data out to clients.

Rich Site Summary

Rich Site Summary (RSS) is a particular flavor of XML. It has its own DTD, and defines what is called a *channel.* A channel is a way to represent data about a specific subject, and provides for a title and description of the channel, an image or logo, and then several *items* within the channel. Each item, then, is something of particular interest about the channel, or a product or service available. Because the allowed elements of an item are fairly generic (`title`, `description`, `hyperlink`), almost anything can be represented as an item of a channel. An RSS channel is not intended to provide a complete site's content, but rather a short blurb about a company or service, suitable for display in a portal-style framework, or as a sidebar on a web site. In fact, the different "widgets" at Netscape's Netcenter are all RSS channels, and Netscape allows the creation of new RSS channels that can be registered with Netcenter. Netscape also has a built-in system for displaying RSS channels in an HTML format, which of course fits into its Netcenter start pages.

At this point, you may be a little concerned that RSS is to Netscape as Microsoft's XML parser is to Microsoft: difficult to integrate with other tools or vendors. Although originally developed by Netscape specifically for Netcenter, the XML structure of RSS has made it usable by any application that can read a DTD. In fact, many portal-style web sites and applications are beginning to use RSS, such as the Apache Jetspeed project (*http://jakarta.apache.org/jetspeed*), an open source Enterprise Information Portal system. Jetspeed takes the same RSS format that Netscape uses, and renders it in a completely different manner. Because of the concise grammar of RSS, this is easily done.

As many users have start pages, or homepages, or similar places on the Web that they frequent, *mytechbooks.com* would like to create an RSS channel that provides new book listings, and then allows interested clients to jump straight to buying an item that catches their eye. This is an effective means to push data, as products like Netcenter will automatically update RSS channel content as often as the user desires.

Creating an XML RSS Document

The first thing you need to do to use RSS is create an RSS file. This is almost too simple to be believed: other than referencing the correct DTD and following that DTD, there is nothing at all complicated about creating an RSS document. Example 14-6 shows a sample RSS file that *mytechbooks.com* has modeled.

Example 14-6. Sample RSS document for mytechbooks.com

```
<?xml version="1.0" encoding="UTF-8"?>

<rdf:RDF xmlns:rdf="http://www.w3.org/1999/02/22-rdf-syntax-ns#"
         xmlns="http://purl.org/rss/1.0/"
>
 <channel>
  <title>mytechbooks.com New Listings</title>
  <link>http://www.newInstance.com/javaxml2/techbooks</link>
  <description>
   Your online source for technical material, computers,
   and computing books!
  </description>

  <image rdf:resource="http://newInstance.com/javaxml2/logo.gif" />

  <items>
   <rdf:Seq>
    <rdf:li resource="http://www.newInstance.com/javaxml2/techbooks" />
   </rdf:Seq>
  </items>
 </channel>

 <image rdf:about="http://newInstance.com/javaxml2/logo.gif">
```

Example 14-6. Sample RSS document for mytechbooks.com (continued)

```
  <title>mytechbooks.com</title>
  <url>http://newInstance.com/javaxml2/logo.gif</url>
  <link>http://newInstance.com/javaxml2/techbooks</link>
 </image>

 <item rdf:about="http://www.newInstance.com/javaxml2/techbooks">
  <title>Java Servlet Programming</title>
  <link>
   http://newInstance.com/javaxml2/techbooks/buy.xsp?isbn=156592391X
  </link>
  <description>
   This book is a superb introduction to Java servlets
   and their various communications mechanisms.
  </description>
 </item>
</rdf:RDF>
```

The root element must be RDF, in the RDF namespace, as shown in the example. Within the root element, one single `channel` element must appear. This has elements that describe the channel (`title`, `link`, and `description`), an optional image that can be associated with the channel (as well as information about that image), and then as many as 15 `item` elements,* each detailing one item related to the channel. Each item has a `title`, `link`, and `description` element, all of which are self-explanatory. An optional text box and button to submit the information in the book can be added as well, although these are not included in the example. For complete details of allowed elements and attributes, visit the RSS 1.0 specification online at *http://groups.yahoo.com/group/rss-dev/files/specification.html.*

NOTE   As in previous examples, actual RSS channel documents should avoid having whitespace within the `link` and `url` elements, but rather have all information on a single line. Again, the formatting in the example does not reflect this due to printing and sizing constraints.

There is one somewhat tricky thing to watch out for, though. You'll notice that the `item` element (or elements) is actually not nested within the `channel` element at all. To create a link between items in the document and the channel, you'll want to use some RDF (the Resource Description Framework, which RSS is a descendant of) constructs:

```
    <items>
     <rdf:Seq>
      <rdf:li resource="http://www.newInstance.com/javaxml/techbooks" />
     </rdf:Seq>
    </items>
```

---

* This isn't a limit set by RSS 1.0, but is used for backwards compatibility with RSS 0.9 and 0.91.

Here, the `items` element is nested within the `channel` element. Then, the `li` construct, in the RDF-defined namespace, is assigned a URI through the `resource` attribute. In each item you want associated with this channel, supply the `about` attribute (again in the RDF namespace) and assign it the same URI you used in the channel's resource descriptor:

```
<item rdf:about="http://www.newInstance.com/javaxml/techbooks">
  <!-- Item content -->
</item>
```

For each item with this URI, an association can be made between that item and the channel with the same URI. In other words, you've just built a link between the channel in the RSS file and the items. The same approach applies for linking a channel to an image; you use the `image` element in the `channel` element, specifying the image URL as the value of the `rdf:resource` attribute. You should then define an `image` element, *not* within the `channel` element, supplying a URL, description, and link. Finally, use the `rdf:about` attribute (as in the `item` element) to specify the same URL as provided in the channel's `image` element. Did you follow all of that? This is all quite a bit different from RSS 0.9 and 0.91 (covered in the first edition of this book), so you'll need to be careful not to get things mixed up between the older specification and this newer one.

It is simple enough to create RSS files programmatically; the procedure is similar to how you generated the HTML for the *mytechbooks.com* web site. Half of the RSS file (the information about the channel as well as the image information) is static content; only the `item` elements must be generated dynamically. However, just as you were getting ready to open up *vi* and start creating another XSL stylesheet, another requirement was dropped into your lap: the machine that will house the RSS channel is a different server than that used in our last example, and has only very outdated versions of the Apache Xalan libraries available. Because of some of the high-availability applications that also run on that machine, such as the billing system, *mytechbooks.com* does not want to update those libraries until change control can be stepped through, a weeklong process. However, *mytechbooks.com* does have newer versions of the Xerces libraries available (as XML parsing is used in the billing system), so Java APIs for handling XML are available.* In this example,

---

*   Yes, this is a bit of a silly case, and perhaps not so likely to really occur. However, it does afford me the opportunity to look at another alternative for creating XML programmatically. Don't sneer too much at the absurdity of the example; all of the examples in this book, including the silly ones, stem from actual experiences consulting for real-world companies. Laughing at this scenario might mean your next project has the same silly requirements!

I use JDOM to convert the XML from the Foobar Public Library into an RSS channel format. Example 14-7 does just this.

Example 14-7. Java servlet to convert new book listings into an RSS channel document

```java
package com.techbooks;

import java.io.FileInputStream;
import java.io.InputStream;
import java.io.IOException;
import java.io.PrintWriter;
import java.net.URL;
import java.util.Iterator;
import java.util.List;
import javax.servlet.*;
import javax.servlet.http.*;

// JDOM
import org.jdom.Document;
import org.jdom.Element;
import org.jdom.JDOMException;
import org.jdom.input.SAXBuilder;

public class GetRSSChannelServlet extends HttpServlet {

    /** Host to connect to for books list */
    private static final String hostname = "newInstance.com";
    /** Port number to connect to for books list */
    private static final int portNumber = 80;
    /** File to request (URI path) for books list */
    private static final String file = "/cgi/supplyBooks.pl";

    public void service(HttpServletRequest req, HttpServletResponse res)
        throws ServletException, IOException {

        res.setContentType("text/plain");
        PrintWriter out = res.getWriter();

        // Connect and get XML listing of books
        URL getBooksURL = new URL("http", hostname, portNumber, file);
        InputStream in = getBooksURL.openStream();

        try {
            // Request SAX Implementation and use default parser
            SAXBuilder builder = new SAXBuilder();

            // Create the document
            Document doc = builder.build(in);
```

Example 14-7. Java servlet to convert new book listings into an RSS channel document (continued)

```java
            // Output XML
            out.println(generateRSSContent(doc));

        } catch (JDOMException e) {
            out.println("Error: " + e.getMessage());
        } finally {
            out.close();
        }
    }

    /**
     * <p>
     * This will generate an RSS XML document using the supplied
     *   JDOM <code>Document</code>.
     * </p>
     *
     * @param doc <code>Document</code> to use for input.
     * @return <code>String</code> - RSS file to output.
     * @throws <code>JDOMException</code> when errors occur.
     */
    private String generateRSSContent(Document doc) throws JDOMException {
        StringBuffer rss = new StringBuffer();

        rss.append("<?xml version=\"1.0\" encoding=\"UTF-8\"?>\n")
           .append("<rdf:RDF ")
           .append("xmlns:rdf=\"http://www.w3.org/1999/02/22-rdf-syntax-ns#\"\n")
           .append("         xmlns=\"http://purl.org/rss/1.0/\"\n")
           .append(">\n")
           .append(" <channel>\n")
           .append("  <title>mytechbooks.com New Listings</title>\n")
           .append("  <link>http://www.newInstance.com/javaxml2/techbooks")
           .append("</link>\n")
           .append("  <description>\n")
           .append("   Your online source for technical material, computers, \n")
           .append("   and computing books!\n")
           .append("  </description>\n\n")
           .append("  <image ")
           .append("rdf:resource=\"http://newInstance.com/javaxml2/logo.gif\"")
           .append(" />\n\n")
           .append("  <items>\n")
           .append("   <rdf:Seq>\n")
           .append("    <rdf:li ")
           .append("resource=\"http://www.newInstance.com/javaxml2/techbooks\"")
           .append(" />\n")
           .append("   </rdf:Seq>\n")
           .append("  </items>\n")
```

Example 14-7. Java servlet to convert new book listings into an RSS channel document (continued)

```java
    .append("  </channel>\n\n")
    .append("  <image ")
    .append("rdf:about=\"http://newInstance.com/javaxml2/logo.gif\">\n")
    .append("    <title>mytechbooks.com</title>\n")
    .append("    <url>http://newInstance.com/javaxml2/logo.gif</url>\n")
    .append("    <link>http://newInstance.com/javaxml/techbooks</link>\n")
    .append("  </image>\n\n");

// Add an item for each new title with Computers as subject
List books = doc.getRootElement().getChildren("book");
for (Iterator i = books.iterator(); i.hasNext(); ) {
    Element book = (Element)i.next();
    if (book.getAttribute("subject")
            .getValue()
             .equals("Computers")) {
        // Output an item
        rss.append("<item rdf:about=\"http://www.newInstance.com/")
            .append("javaxml/techbooks\">\n")
             // Add title
            .append("  <title>")
            .append(book.getChild("title").getContent())
            .append("</title>\n")
             // Add link to buy book
            .append("  <link>")
            .append("http://newInstance.com/javaxml2")
            .append("/techbooks/buy.xsp?isbn=")
            .append(book.getChild("saleDetails")
                        .getChild("isbn")
                        .getContent())
            .append("</link>\n")
            .append("  <description>")
             // Add description
            .append(book.getChild("description").getContent())
            .append("</description>\n")
            .append("</item>\n");

    }
}

rss. append("</rdf:RDF>");

return rss.toString();
    }
}
```

By this time, nothing in this code should be the least bit surprising to you; I've imported the JDOM and I/O classes needed, and accessed the Foobar Public Library application as in the `ListBooksServlet`. The resulting `InputStream` is used to create a JDOM `Document`, with the default parser (Apache Xerces) and the JDOM builder based on SAX doing the work.

Then, the JDOM `Document` is handed off to the `generateRSSContentMethod()`, which prints out all of the static content for the RSS channel. This method then obtains the `book` elements within the XML from the library and iterates through them, ignoring those without a `subject` attribute equal to "Computers".

NOTE   Again, I've done some rather different things simply for illustrative purposes. For example, this code directly outputs XML; you could just as easily create a JDOM tree and output it using `XMLOutputter`. Of course, you could also use DOM for the entire servlet. All these are viable and perfectly legitimate options.

Finally, each element that makes it through the comparison is added to the RSS channel. Nothing very exciting here, right? Figure 14-5 shows a sample output from accessing this servlet, saved as *GetRSSChannelServlet.java*, through a web browser.

With this RSS channel ready for use, *mytechbooks.com* has made its content available by any service provider that supports RSS! To get the ball rolling on allowing clients to use its channel, *mytechbooks.com* would like to ensure its RSS document is valid, and see a sample HTML rendering of it (as would you, I imagine).

Taking a Test Drive

At this point, let's see this thing in action. Point your browser at *http://www. redland.opensource.ac.uk/rss*. This site has a nice, online test tool called the Redland RSS viewer that will take your RSS channel and validate it, as well as render it in HTML. You'll need to ensure that the RSS feed is available online somewhere, such as through the servlet just discussed. Enter in the URL for the servlet, or RSS feed, and then select "Yes" for the "Format output as a box" option. This instructs the viewer to render your channel as an HTML box, much like it could be seen on Netscape's Netcenter or on *http://www.oreilly.com*, which has several RSS feeds running. The output from the feed we just created is shown in Figure 14-6.

You can also select several other RSS feeds from the viewer, and see how they would look formatted in HTML as well. The Meerkat channel is particularly interesting, as it contains almost all of the RSS options that are currently available for

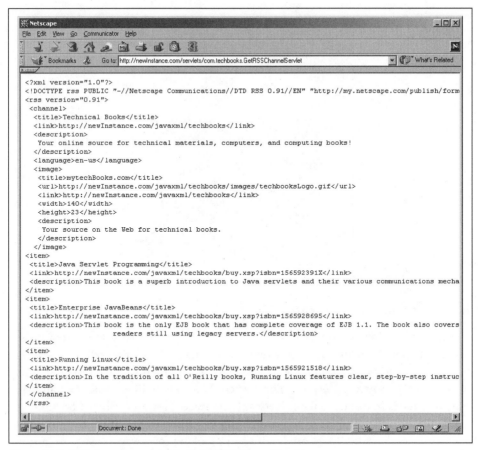

Figure 14-5. RSS channel generated by the GetRSSChannelServlet

use. Additionally, if you have any errors in your RSS, this viewer will let you know what they are, which is helpful in debugging problems before putting your RSS channel into production.

I'm not including code that parses and formats the RSS in this chapter; in addition to it being a piece of cake for you by now, each site will need to provide different formatting for RSS feeds. For some fairly diverse views of RSS channels, you should check out *http://www.servlets.com* (down at the bottom right), *http://www. oreilly.com*, and *http://www.xml.com*, all of which have some pretty different formatting going on. In reading in an RSS channel, you'll probably want to treat it like XML, and use SAX, DOM, or JDOM to read the data in and format it however you need. In other words, there's nothing that requires you to treat an RSS feed any differently from any other XML document; you just know what the formatting will look like ahead of time. With that knowledge, you're ready to use RSS feeds in your own web sites.

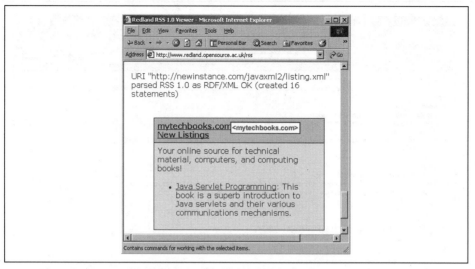

Figure 14-6. RSS formatted in HTM

What Happened to Netcenter?

Readers of the first edition may be curious as to where the section on viewing the RSS channel in Netscape Netcenter went. If you haven't seen that edition, Netscape provided a means of publishing your RSS feeds as channels capable of being added to Netscape's *my.netscape.com* site. This was cool, as you could easily format and view your RSS feeds in a slick-looking Netscape interface. However, when RSS 1.0 came out, replacing RS 0.91, Netscape removed all of its publishing links, and no longer allows this sort of thing to go on. So, if you're looking for a way to use your customized channels in your Netcenter homepage, you're out of luck.

You've gotten a good taste of RSS; most of all, you are probably realizing that like SOAP and web services, there are a ton of ways to interact with RSS feeds as well. Customize the examples and concepts in this chapter for your own applications, providing formatting and business logic specific to your business needs. Now you've got a better idea of how to do that, and will have more time for playing that guitar at night (um, that's me. . . well, you get the idea).

What's Next?

You've seen the various techniques for interoperating, such as publishing content for clients, using SOAP to talk to remote applications, and B2B communication. Now I refocus on code internals. In the next chapter, I spend some time talking about XML data binding, allowing you an easier way to work with XML documents and Java objects. I also discuss how this affects object persistence and configuration, two common tasks in enterprise programming.

15

Data Binding

I've tried to run the gamut in what I've covered so far, and even in the order that I've covered it. When I started talking about Java in Chapter 2, you had complete control. SAX provided the thinnest of veneers over XML, and basically provided a framework with which to write lots of callbacks. When I moved to DOM and JDOM, you got quite a bit more help, albeit with some loss of power. These tree-based, in-memory models were more convenient, although you had to pay a small price in terms of performance. Moving on to JAXP, you were placed higher up the chain of command, but gained another level of abstraction. At that point, you still had some control, but were working strictly in XML.

Then I shifted gears, and we looked at web publishing frameworks, XML-RPC, SOAP, and business-to-business and web services. This was a far cry from the down-and-dirty approach taken in the first half of the book. While you had immensely more convenience and specialization, you lost a lot of control over how XML was handled, and sometimes didn't see XML at all (like in XML-RPC). This may have left you (as it left me) missing getting your hands dirty a bit. You can't make the subtle tweaks in an XML document's values when working with SOAP, for example, that you could when using SAX or JDOM. However, the convenience of WSDL was nice, and had advantages over typing an element's name wrong in DOM. In short, it left me wishing for a happy medium.

Data binding provides that medium, and I want to take you through the extreme ends of the spectrum before talking about it. In this chapter, I show you a way to get most of the power of a low-level API with most of the convenience of an XML-based application framework (like SOAP). This will probably be something almost everyone can use at some point, and that many can use for a variety of tasks. First, I cover the basic principles that make data binding work. This will be a general overview, as the various data binding packages all have their own specific methodologies. Once you have some grounding, I take you on a quick tour of the two open source data binding APIs, and then Sun's emerging API, JAXB. So, buckle up and dive in.

What About Quick? What About JATO? What About...?

Some of you may be disappointed (or even upset) that I haven't covered your favorite API. However, I didn't make my decisions about which APIs to cover arbitrarily. I chose the two open source APIs that were compatible with JAXB and used the same principles. I selected open source APIs because they are free, and you can use them today; I don't expect you to shell out thousands of dollars for a product like Breeze XML Studio to run my examples.[a] And I selected Castor and Zeus because they use XML standards like XML Schema and DTDs for constraints.

If you're looking for coverage of JXQuick, you won't find it here. The schemas used by JXQuick to represent document constraints and Java classes (QIML, QJML, etc.) are not XML standards, and therefore much less useful in communicating information about your XML to other applications. For this reason, I haven't included it; you can find out more, though, online at *http://quickutil.sourceforge.net/view/Main/JXQuick*.

The same goes for JATO, located online at *http://sourceforge.net/projects/jato*, which is more of a scripting language for XML and Java mappings. Because this is less data binding, and more data mapping, it didn't fit well into this chapter or into a JAXB model of doing things. You can check both of these packages out online and make your own decisions. I always recommend you use what's best for your project.

---

a. That's not meant to be a knock on Breeze, by the way. I just generally think you should use something that's free rather than the same something you have to pay for. If you want to try a commercial offering, go for it.

First Principles

Before diving into specific packages and frameworks that handle data binding, you need to have a basic understanding of what XML data binding is. This turns out to be pretty simple, though, so you'll be coding in no time. First, take a plain old XML document, like the one shown in Example 15-1.

Example 15-1. Homespun tapes XML catalog

```
<?xml version="1.0"?>

<catalog xmlns="http://www.homespuntapes.com">
  <item id="VD-DOK-GT01" level="4">
    <title>Doc's Guitar Fingerpicking and Flatpicking</title>
```

Example 15-1. Homespun tapes XML catalog (continued)

```
    <teacher>Doc Watson</teacher>
    <guest>Pete Seeger</guest>
    <guest>Mike Seeger</guest>
    <guest>Jack Lawrence</guest>
    <guest>Kirk Sutphin</guest>
    <description>Doc Watson, a true master of traditional guitar styles, teaches,
        in detail, some of the most reuested fingerpicking and flatpicking tunes in
        his vast repertoire, for guitarists at all levels.</description>
  </item>
  <item id="VD-WLX-GT01" level="4">
    <title>The Guitar of David Wilcox</title>
    <teacher>David Wilcox</teacher>
    <description>Create fresh new guitar sounds with rich, ringing voicings! David
        even shows you how to invent your own tunings.</description>
  </item>
  <item id="VD-THI-MN01" level="3">
    <title>Essential Techniques for Mandolin</title>
    <teacher>Chris Thile</teacher>
    <description>Here's a lesson that will thrill and inspire mandolin players at
        all levels.</description>
  </item>
  <item id="CDZ-SM01" level="4">
    <title>Sam Bush Teaches Mandolin Repertoire and Techniques</title>
    <teacher>Sam Bush</teacher>
    <description>Learn complete solos to eight traditional and orignal tunes, each
        one jam-packed with licks, runs, and musical variations.</description>
  </item>
</catalog>
```

In previous chapters, you learned how to use SAX, DOM, JDOM, and JAXP to access this document. You could manipulate both its *structure* (the names and ordering of elements, attributes, and other lexical constructs) and its *content* (the actual data). However, many times you don't need access to the document's structure, and only want to work with its data.

In this latter case, it's overkill and a bit on the annoying side to have to write code that parses your document, extracts the data, and puts it into some format that you can use. It would be much nicer to run a program (or API. . . are you starting to get the picture here?) that did this for you, and produced usable Java classes. In fact, this is exactly what data binding does. With data binding, there are three distinct processes that can occur one after another, in differing order, or in completely unrelated processes. I'll cover each in turn.

Class Generation

The first process, class generation, provides a means to convert an XML document to Java. When data binding converts an XML document into a Java representation, it seeks to provide access to just the data in the document. Additionally, data binding provides some level of meaning to the information in the document. It does this by creating the Java representation with accessor and mutator* methods like `getItem()` and `setTeacher()`, instead of `getElement()` and `setAttribute()`. This makes dealing with documents like the one in Example 15-1 less about Java and more about business logic, which is obviously a good thing. However, these wonderfully Java classes must exist before an XML document can be turned into an instance of one, so I'm back to class generation.

Class generation is the process of taking a set of XML constraints and generating Java classes (and possibly interfaces) from those constraints. Think about it this way: XML constraints (like those found in a DTD or XML Schema) are equivalent to Java class definitions. They define the way that data is represented. On the other hand, an XML document is equivalent to an instance of these classes, in that it is simply a set of data that fulfills the contract defined by the document's constraints. Now, read this paragraph again, slowly, and you'll have it.

The data binding frameworks I talk about in this chapter all have a way of representing a document's constraints (usually through a DTD or an XML Schema, but there are also some other options, which I'll get to in the appropriate section). These constraints can then be run through some form of a class generation tool, and you get Java source code ready to compile. This code, once compiled, can be used to generate instance data based on an XML document. You end up with a process akin to that shown in Figure 15-1.

Note that the final product here can be concrete classes, interfaces, interfaces and implementations, or any other permutation of Java classes. In the case of Example 15-1 (assuming that the constraints are represented in some arbitrary form), you might end up with a `Catalog` interface like this:

```java
public interface Catalog {
    public List getItemList();
    public void addItem(Item item);
    public void setItemList(List items);
}
```

Further, you might have an `Item` interface like this:

```java
public interface Item {
    public String getID();
    public void setID(String id);
    public int getLevel();
    public void setLevel(int level);
```

---

* When I say "accessor," I'm referring to what most people call a "getter" method; when I say "mutator," I'm referring to what most people call a "setter" method. However, I also know that a "setter" is a dog, not a Java method, so I'm quick to tell my students not to use that term. Just an idiosyncrasy, I suppose!

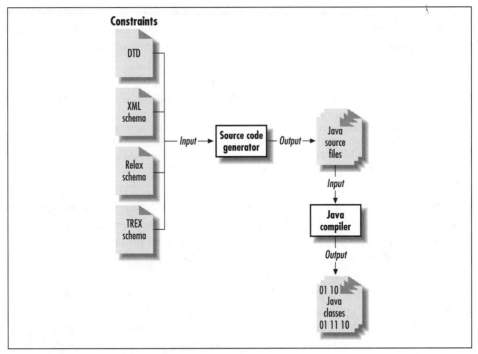

Figure 15-1. Class generation in XML data binding

```
public String getTitle();
public void setTitle(String title);
public String getTeacher();
public void setTeacher(String teacher);
public List getGuests();
public void addGuest(String guest);
public void setGuestList(List guests);
public String getDescription();
public void setDescription();
}
```

This is quite a bit more useful than writing hundreds of lines of SAX callbacks. It makes working with the document a piece of cake, instead of an exercise in your Java and XML API skills. These are just examples, and not necessarily representative of what you'll get using the APIs covered in this chapter. However, in the following sections, I'll show you exactly how to use the API and let you know what to expect.

Unmarshalling

Keep in mind that once you have a set of generated classes, you still don't have a great many uses for them. Sure, you could use an existing lower-level XML API to read in an XML document, pull out the data, create new instances of the generated classes, and populate them with the data from the XML. But data binding provides all this out of the box, so why bother with that? In fact, data binding frameworks provide for exactly that process. And in that context, *unmarshalling* is the process of converting an XML document into an instance of a Java class.

NOTE   I've seen, and even been a part of, a lot of confusion about the mar-
        shalling/unmarshalling terminology. I'm using the terminology as
        defined in Sun's latest version of the Java Architecture for Data Bind-
        ing (JAXB) specification, which is certain to become the standard-
        ized vocabulary. In that specification, marshalling is moving from
        Java to XML, and unmarshalling is moving from XML to Java. I'd
        stick with those definitions if I were you, as well.

This turns out to be a pretty simple process; you get an XML document, pass it to some tool or class instance in your data binding framework, and you get back a Java object. This is usually a class instance of the top-level Java object representing your document. So, again using Example 15-1, you would get back an instance of the `Catalog` class. You'll typically need to cast from a `java.lang.Object` to the specific class that you're expecting, since the framework won't know anything about your classes (because they were generated). But after the class cast, you're ready to work with the object as a `Catalog`, not as an XML document. You can then use the various accessor and mutator methods to work with the data, and when you are ready to send the document back to the XML from whence it came, you marshal the document.

Marshalling

Marshalling is just the opposite of unmarshalling. It is the process of converting a Java object and its dependent objects into an XML representation. In many cases, marshalling is part of a repeated cycle of transformations to and from XML, and is paired with unmarshalling. As an example, check out Figure 15-2, which is a typical application flow.

There are two distinct ways to marshal a Java object. The first is to invoke a `marshal()` method on an object; this method is usually generated along with the accessors and mutators during class generation. The method recursively calls the `marshal()` method on each of its dependent objects, until you end up with an XML document. Note that the target XML document does *not* have to be the same as the original XML; you can easily end up with a vast number of archived XML documents by supplying different filenames to the marshalling process.

A different approach to marshalling, and the one I favor, is having a standalone class that performs marshalling. Instead of invoking `marshal()` on a generated object, you invoke `marshal()` on the standalone class, and pass it the object to marshal. This is useful because it performs the same tasks as illustrated previously,

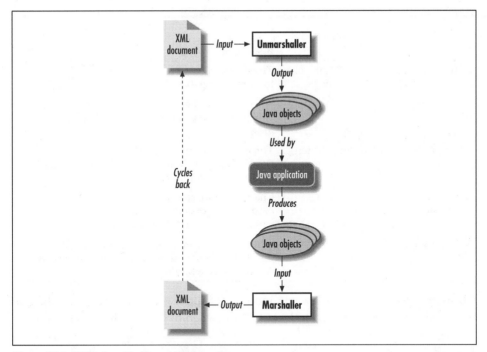

Figure 15-2. XML data binding application flow

but also allows classes that were not originally unmarshalled from XML to be converted to XML. Think about it this way: data binding, used like this, becomes a persistence framework. Any object with bean-like properties (setXXX() and getXXX()) can easily be converted to XML! You get the power of data binding with the flexibility of persistence. This is a handy combination, and supported by some of the frameworks I talk about in this chapter.

I realize that if you're new to data binding, this may sound a bit confusing and vague; sort of like talking about chemistry. I'd much rather blow some things up (err. . . you know!), so in the rest of the chapter I show you how to use some data binding frameworks. Since I'm going to cover four of these, none of the examples are immensely complex; instead I focus on how to use the class generation, marshalling, and unmarshalling capabilities of each framework. That should be more than enough to get you going.

Use Cases

As a final explanation of data binding and why it's worthwhile, I will give you a small sampling of use-cases. Some of these are best suited for the lower-level APIs like SAX or DOM, and some are perfect for data binding. In Table 15-1, I've listed a common use case, the type of API that would work well, and a short reasoning behind my decision. This should help you see how data binding fits into the XML landscape.

Table 15-1. API use cases

Use case	Well-suited API	Reasoning
XML IDE	DOM or JDOM	Tree-based viewing of XML, as in an IDE, closely follows the tree-based models of DOM and JDOM.
XML messaging server	SAX	Since speed is the most important factor, SAX allows the fastest stream-based reading of messages.
Configuration data	Data binding	The content, rather than the model, is paramount. Data binding saves time and adds convenience to reading configuration data.
XML transformations	DOM or JDOM	Changing both structure and content requires modification of content (rules out SAX) and structure (rules out data binding).
XML messaging client	Data binding	When the message format is known ahead of time, the client can benefit from easy Java objects, as created by data binding.

Obviously, these are just a few common XML applications, but they should give you an idea of when to use a low-level API and when to use a higher-level one.

Castor

The first data binding framework I will discuss is Castor, hosted online at *http:// castor.exolab.org*. This framework has been around for quite a while, and the latest release as of this writing was Version 0.92. First, it should be made clear that Castor provides quite a bit more than just XML data binding. The package provides bindings in Java for more than just XML; you can also work with LDAP objects, OQL for mapping SQL queries to objects, as well as Java Data Objects (JDO), a fairly new specification from Sun dealing with Java-to-RDBMS (relational database management system) persistence. However, this is an XML book, so I'm only going to talk about the XML bindings.

Installation

To get ready to use Castor, you'll need to download a release from the download page: *http://castor.exolab.org/download.html*. That page has links to the Exolab FTP site (or you can FTP in manually, as I did), and lists the files available. I'd recommend getting the full release (in the event you want to play with OQL or JDO later), named *castor-0.9.2.zip* or *castor-0.9.2.tgz*. Extract the *jar* files from that archive, add them to your classpath, and you're ready to go.*

---

* Actually, there are two *jar* files within the distribution: *castor-0.9.2.jar* and *castor-0.9.2-xml.jar*. The first is a superset of the second, so you only need the first; or if you want a smaller archive, you can just use the second for XML binding.

NOTE   In this and subsequent examples, I've assumed that you still have a
              SAX-compliant XML parser, like Xerces, on your classpath in addi-
              tion to the libraries discussed in this chapter. If you don't, add *xerces.*
              jar or your parser's *jar* file(s) to the classpath in addition to the data
              binding framework you are using.

Source Generation

Castor does provide for class generation, using an existing set of constraints to create Java classes. You will need to have an XML Schema that constrains your XML
to use this. Example 15-2 provides just such a schema for the document I showed
you earlier in Example 15-1.

Example 15-2. XML Schema for Example 15-1 (using Castor)

```xml
<?xml version="1.0"?>

<schema xmlns="http://www.w3.org/2000/10/XMLSchema"
        targetNamespace="http://www.homespuntapes.com">
  <element name="catalog">
    <complexType>
      <sequence>
        <element ref="item" minOccurs="1" maxOccurs="unbounded" />
      </sequence>
    </complexType>
  </element>

  <element name="item">
    <complexType>
      <sequence>
        <element name="title" type="string" />
        <element name="teacher" type="string" />
        <element name="guest" type="string" minOccurs="0" maxOccurs="unbounded" />
        <element name="description" type="string" />
      </sequence>
      <attribute name="id" type="string" />
      <attribute name="level">
        <simpleType>
          <restriction base="integer">
            <enumeration value="1" />
            <enumeration value="2" />
            <enumeration value="3" />
            <enumeration value="4" />
            <enumeration value="5" />
          </restriction>
        </simpleType>
```

Example 15-2. XML Schema for Example 15-1 (using Castor) (continued)

```
      </attribute>
    </complexType>
  </element>
</schema>
```

Obviously, you may have XML schemas of your own that you want to try out; as long as they conform to the XML Schema specification, they should work with any examples in this section.

WARNING   At least as of this writing, Castor supported only the October 2000 XML Schema Candidate Recommendation, as opposed to the final version of that specification. This could require you to make some small modifications in your existing schemas to conform to that earlier specification if you're using Castor. Hopefully that framework will have caught up by the time you are reading this; you can verify the current level of compliance for XML Schema at *http://castor. exolab.org/xmlschema.html*.

Once you have your XML Schema defined, you are ready to generate classes for the constraints. I've named my schema from Example 15-1 *catalog.xsd*, as you'll see reflected in the example instructions coming up.

Once you've got your schema, generating classes with Castor is a piece of cake. You'll need to use the `org.exolab.castor.builder.SourceGenerator` class, as shown here:

```
java org.exolab.castor.builder.SourceGenerator -i castor/catalog.xsd
    -package javaxml2.castor
```

In this example, I'm running the command with my schema in a subdirectory of the current directory, called *castor/*. I specified the schema with the "-i" flag, and the package to generate the files within through the "-package" flag. There's a whole slew of other options you can check out by simply entering the class without any options. The class will spit out the various flags and options you can supply.

Once the command executes (you'll get errors if your schema has problems), you will get a directory path correlating to the package you entered. In my example, I ended up with a *javaxml2* directory, and a *castor* directory within that. Within that directory, I ended up with a *Catalog.java* and *CatalogDescriptor.java* source file, and an *Item.java* and *ItemDescriptor.java* source file. For most situations, you'll only need to worry about working with the first of each of these pairs.

You should also get a subdirectory called *types*, with some additional files within it. These are generated because of the user-defined type in the XML Schema for the "level" attribute. The result is a class called `LevelType`. Since there are only five allowed values, Castor must create custom classes for this type to handle it. These type classes are a pain to work with, as there is no way, for example, to do this:

```
// Create a new type with a value of "1"
LevelType levelType = new LevelType(1);
```

Instead, you'll need to get the value you want to use and convert it to a String. You can then use the valueOf() method, which is static, to get an instance of LevelType with the correct value:

```
LevelType levelType = LevelType.valueOf("1");
```

Of course, once you get used to this, it's not such a big deal. If this seems a little fuzzy, you'll see how to use this class in a practical situation in the next section, so don't worry too much about it just yet. You can compile the type files, as well as the other Castor-generated sources, with this simple command:

```
javac -d . javaxml2/castor/*.java javaxml2/castor/types/*.java
```

At this point, you have classes that are ready to use. I won't show you the source for these files here, because it's quite long (and you can look at it yourself). I've listed the key methods for the Catalog class, though, so you'll get an idea of what to expect:

```
package javaxml2.castor;

public class Catalog {

    // Add a new Item
    public void addItem();
    // Get the items as an Enumeration
    public Enumeration enumerateItem();
    // Get all items
    public Item[] getItem();
    // Get number of items
    public getItemCount();
}
```

Notice that you can add items, as well as move through the items available. The names of two of these methods, enumerateItem() and getItem(), are a bit odd, so watch out for those. I did not expect getItem() to return an array, and looked for getItems() or getItemList() first, myself. Once you've got these generated classes, though, you're ready to use them in your application.

Marshalling and Unmarshalling

After you've compiled the classes Castor generates, add them to your classpath. You can then use them in your own applications. Example 15-3 shows a basic HTML form that allows a user to enter information about a new item.

Example 15-3. HTML form for adding items

```
<HTML>
 <HEAD><TITLE>Add New Item to Catalog</TITLE></HEAD>
 <BODY>
  <H2 ALIGN="CENTER">Add New Item</H2>
  <P ALIGN="CENTER">
   <FORM ACTION="/javaxml2/servlet/javaxml2.AddItemServlet" METHOD="POST">
    <TABLE WIDTH="80%" CELLSPACING="3" CELLPADDING="3" BORDER="3">
     <TR>
      <TD WIDTH="50%" ALIGN="right"><B>Item ID:</B></TD>
      <TD><INPUT TYPE="text" NAME="id" /></TD>
     </TR>
     <TR>
      <TD WIDTH="50%" ALIGN="right"><B>Item Level:</B></TD>
      <TD><INPUT TYPE="text" NAME="level" SIZE="1" MAXLENGTH="1" /></TD>
     </TR>
     <TR>
      <TD WIDTH="50%" ALIGN="right"><B>Title:</B></TD>
      <TD><INPUT TYPE="text" NAME="title" SIZE="20" /></TD>
     </TR>
     <TR>
      <TD WIDTH="50%" ALIGN="right"><B>Teacher:</B></TD>
      <TD><INPUT TYPE="text" NAME="teacher" /></TD>
     </TR>
     <TR><TD COLSPAN="2" ALIGN="CENTER"><B>Guests:</B></TD></TR>
     <TR>
      <TD COLSPAN="2" ALIGN="CENTER"><INPUT TYPE="text" NAME="guest" /></TD>
     </TR>
     <TR>
      <TD COLSPAN="2" ALIGN="CENTER"><INPUT TYPE="text" NAME="guest" /></TD>
     </TR>
     <TR>
      <TD COLSPAN="2" ALIGN="CENTER"><INPUT TYPE="text" NAME="guest" /></TD>
     </TR>
     <TR>
      <TD COLSPAN="2" ALIGN="CENTER"><INPUT TYPE="text" NAME="guest" /></TD>
     </TR>
     <TR><TD COLSPAN="2" ALIGN="CENTER"><B>Description:</B></TD></TR>
     <TR>
      <TD COLSPAN="2" ALIGN="CENTER">
       <TEXTAREA NAME="description" COLS="30" ROWS="10"></TEXTAREA>
      </TD>
     </TR>
     <TR>
      <TD COLSPAN="2" ALIGN="CENTER"><INPUT TYPE="submit" value="Add Item" /></TD>
     </TR>
    </TABLE>
```

Example 15-3. HTML form for adding items (continued)

```
    </FORM>
   </P>
  </BODY>
</HTML>
```

You should have Tomcat or another servlet engine running from some of the previous chapters, so I won't get into those details. Drop this form into one of your web applications, and then enter in and compile the servlet shown in Example 15-4.

Example 15-4. The AddItemServlet for Castor

```java
package javaxml2;

import java.io.File;
import java.io.FileReader;
import java.io.FileWriter;
import java.io.IOException;
import java.io.PrintWriter;
import javax.servlet.ServletException;
import javax.servlet.http.HttpServlet;
import javax.servlet.http.HttpServletRequest;
import javax.servlet.http.HttpServletResponse;

// Castor classes
import org.exolab.castor.xml.Marshaller;
import org.exolab.castor.xml.Unmarshaller;

// Castor generated classes
import javaxml2.castor.Catalog;
import javaxml2.castor.Item;
import javaxml2.castor.types.LevelType;

public class AddItemServlet extends HttpServlet {

    private static final String CATALOG_FILE =
        "c:\\java\\tomcat\\webapps\\javaxml2\\catalog.xml";

    public void doPost(HttpServletRequest req, HttpServletResponse res)
        throws ServletException, IOException {

        PrintWriter out = res.getWriter();
        res.setContentType("text/html");

        // Get input parameters
        String id = req.getParameterValues("id")[0];
        String levelString = req.getParameterValues("level")[0];
        String title = req.getParameterValues("title")[0];
```

Example 15-4. The AddItemServlet for Castor (continued)

```
        String teacher = req.getParameterValues("teacher")[0];
        String[] guests = req.getParameterValues("guest");
        String description = req.getParameterValues("description")[0];

        // Create new item
        Item item = new Item();
        item.setId(id);
        item.setLevel(LevelType.valueOf(levelString));
        item.setTitle(title);
        item.setTeacher(teacher);
        if (guests != null) {
            for (int i=0; i<guests.length; i++) {
                if (!guests[i].trim().equals("")) {
                    item.addGuest(guests[i]);
                }
            }
        }
        item.setDescription(description);

        try {
            // Load current catalog
            File catalogFile = new File(CATALOG_FILE);
            FileReader reader = new FileReader(catalogFile);
            Catalog catalog =
                (Catalog)Unmarshaller.unmarshal(Catalog.class, reader);

            // Add item
            catalog.addItem(item);

            // Write back out modified catalog
            FileWriter writer = new FileWriter(catalogFile);
            Marshaller.marshal(catalog, writer);

            out.println("Item added.");
        } catch (Exception e) {
            out.println("Error loading/writing catalog: " + e.getMessage());
        } finally {
            out.close();
        }
    }

    public void doGet(HttpServletRequest req, HttpServletResponse res)
        throws ServletException, IOException {

        doPost(req, res);
    }
}
```

This servlet accepts the parameters from the form shown in Example 15-3. It first reads in the XML representing the current catalog (called *catalog.xml* and also in my servlet's web application folder). At this point, the servlet needs to access the current catalog; of course, I could write a bunch of SAX code here, but why? Castor does the job nicely. I use a `FileReader` to provide read access to the XML document, and a `FileWriter` to provide write access. The rest of the work is taken care of by Castor. Once the servlet gets the form values, it creates a new `Item` instance (using Castor's generated classes) and sets the various values on this class. You'll notice that because "level" is a custom type (remember the earlier discussion?), the servlet uses the static method `LevelType.valueOf(String)` to convert the `String` value for the item level into the correct instance of the `LevelType` class. This is one of Castor's minor drawbacks; the custom classes for user-defined types are a bit unwieldy until you get used to them.

Once the servlet has a ready-to-use instance of a new `Item`, it uses the `org.exolab.castor.Unmarshaller` class to get the current catalog. This couldn't be much simpler; the servlet passes in the class to unmarshal to, and access to the file (through the `FileReader` I just mentioned). The result is a Java `Object`, which can be cast to the class type supplied. At this point, adding the item is a piece of cake! You're working in Java, rather than in XML, and can simply invoke `addItem()` and pass in the newly created `Item` instance. Then, the process is reversed. `Marshaller` (in the same package as its sister `Unmarshaller`) is used via the static `marshal()` method to write the `Catalog` instance back to XML, using a `FileWriter`. Piece of cake, isn't it? Once this process completes, you get a new entry in the XML file (you may have to stop your servlet engine to get access to it), which should look something like this:

```
<item id="CD-KAU-PV99" level="1">
  <title>Parking Lot Pickers, Vol. 3</title>
  <teacher>Steve Kaufman</teacher>
  <guest>Debbie Barbra</guest>
  <guest>Donnie Barbra</guest>
  <description>This video teaches you what to play when the
    singing stops, bluegrass style!</description>
</item>
```

And that's really it. There are quite a few more options to use with the `Marshaller` and `Unmarshaller`, so check out the API documentation. And, just to make sure you can follow along, here are the pertinent files and directories in my web application that make this all work:

```
$TOCAT_HOME/lib/xerces.jar
$TOMCAT_HOME/webapps/javaxml2/addItem.html
$TOMCAT_HOME/webapps/javaxml2/catalog.xml
$TOMCAT_HOME/webapps/javaxml2/WEB-INF/lib/castor-0.9.2.jar
$TOMCAT_HOME/webapps/javaxml2/WEB-INF/classes/javaxml2/AddItemServlet.class
```

```
$TOMCAT_HOME/webapps/javaxml2/WEB-INF/classes/javaxml2/castor/Catalog.class
$TOMCAT_HOME/webapps/javaxml2/WEB-INF/classes/javaxml2/castor/Catalog.class
$TOMCAT_HOME/webapps/javaxml2/WEB-INF/classes/javaxml2/castor/
    CatalogDescriptor.class
$TOMCAT_HOME/webapps/javaxml2/WEB-INF/classes/javaxml2/castor/
    CatalogDescriptor$1.class
$TOMCAT_HOME/webapps/javaxml2/WEB-INF/classes/javaxml2/castor/Item.class
$TOMCAT_HOME/webapps/javaxml2/WEB-INF/classes/javaxml2/castor/
    ItemDescriptor.class
$TOMCAT_HOME/webapps/javaxml2/WEB-INF/classes/javaxml2/castor/
    ItemDescriptor$1.class
$TOMCAT_HOME/webapps/javaxml2/WEB-INF/classes/javaxml2/castor/
    ItemDescriptor$2.class
$TOMCAT_HOME/webapps/javaxml2/WEB-INF/classes/javaxml2/castor/
    ItemDescriptor$3.class
$TOMCAT_HOME/webapps/javaxml2/WEB-INF/classes/javaxml2/castor/
    ItemDescriptor$4.class
$TOMCAT_HOME/webapps/javaxml2/WEB-INF/classes/javaxml2/castor/
    ItemDescriptor$5.class
$TOMCAT_HOME/webapps/javaxml2/WEB-INF/classes/javaxml2/castor/
    ItemDescriptor$6.class
$TOMCAT_HOME/webapps/javaxml2/WEB-INF/classes/javaxml2/castor/types/
    LevelType.class
$TOMCAT_HOME/webapps/javaxml2/WEB-INF/classes/javaxml2/castor/types/
    LevelTypeDescriptor.class
```

There's a lot more to Castor, as there will be to each of the packages I talk about. This short introduction should get you started, and the documentation provided will help you through the rest. Of particular interest is the ability to define mappings that allow you, for example, to convert an XML element named "item" to a Java variable named "inventory". This allows for different representations of the same data within Java and XML, and can also really help you convert between legacy Java classes. Imagine converting an old Java class to a new XML format, and then unmarshalling that new XML back into new Java classes. In two easy steps, all of your old Java code is updated to a new format! Pretty slick, huh? On the other hand, Castor's lack of support for the latest schema recommendation and generation of concrete classes instead of interfaces is a drawback. Try it out for yourself, though, and see how you like it. Each of the frameworks in this chapter has pros and cons, so pick the one that's right for you.

Zeus

Next up is the Zeus data binding framework. This is a project over at Enhydra (*http://www.enhydra.org*), and is based on a series of articles I originally wrote for the folks at IBM's Developer Works (*http://www.ibm.com/developerWorks*). It was the direct result of my need for a simple solution for data binding (at the time, Castor seemed overly complex for a fairly straightforward data binding problem). Since then, it's developed into a complete project at Enhydra, and several other folks are working on it. You can get the complete story by checking out *http://zeus.enhydra. org*. I'll touch on the same things I dealt with in Castor, so you can use either competently in your applications.

Installation

Zeus is still in the fairly early stages of functional development (it's been around a bit, but some serious architecture is still going on). As a result, I'd recommend you get the latest version from CVS instead of downloading a binary. That way, you'll be sure to get the latest and greatest in features. You can find complete instructions on getting Zeus from CVS at the web site, but in short, you'll need to get CVS (from *http://www.cvshome.org*, for example). Simply use the following command:

```
cvs -d :pserver:anoncvs@enhydra.org:/u/cvs login
```

Enter "anoncvs" as the password. Then:

```
cvs -d :pserver:anoncvs@enhydra.org:/u/cvs co toolsTech/Zeus
```

You'll get everything you need. Change into the *Zeus* directory (which is created by the CVS download), and build the binaries:

```
bmclaugh@GANDALF ~/dev/Zeus
$ ./build.sh
```

Or, on Windows:

```
c:\dev\Zeus> build.bat
```

You should also build the samples, which you can do by appending "samples" as an argument to the build command:

```
bmclaugh@GANDALF ~/dev/Zeus
$ ./build.sh samples
```

At that point, you'll end up with *zeus.jar* in the *build/* directory. Add this to your classpath, as well as *jdom.jar* and *xerces.jar*, both of which are in the *lib* directory. Finally, if you're going to use DTD generation, you should also add *dtdparser113.jar* to the classpath. And, to use the samples, add the *build/classes* directory itself, just to make things really easy. So, my classpath looks like this:

```
bmclaugh@GANDALF ~/dev/Zeus
$ echo $CLASSPATH
/dev/Zeus/lib/jdom.jar:/dev/Zeus/lib/xerces.jar:/dev/Zeus/lib/dtdparser113.jar:
/dev/Zeus/build/zeus.jar:/dev/Zeus/build/classes
```

Or, on Windows:

```
c:\dev\Zeus> echo %CLASSPATH%
c:\dev\Zeus\lib\jdom.jar;c:\dev\Zeus\lib\xerces.jar;
```

```
c:\dev\Zeus\lib\dtdparser113.jar;c:\dev\Zeus\build\zeus.jar;
c:\dev\Zeus\build\classes
```

That's it. With your classpath set, and the XML from the earlier portions of the chapter, you're ready to go.

Class Generation

The primary difference between Zeus and frameworks like Castor and even JAXB, Sun's offering, is the way that class generation is handled. Remember from Figure 15-1 that the standard means of handling class generation is taking a set of constraints, reading through them, and streaming out Java source code. While this is handy, it makes it difficult to add support for other types of constraints, like DTDs or newer schema-alternatives such as Relaxx and TREX. To accommodate this, Zeus adds an intermediary step. What occurs is that a set of constraints (in schema form, DTD form, etc.) is converted into a set of *Zeus bindings*. These bindings are not tied to any specific means of constraint representation. In other words, if you modeled a set of constraints within a DTD, and then modeled the exact set of constraints again within an XML Schema, Zeus would convert both into an identical set of bindings. These bindings are used to generate Java source code. The result is a process like that modeled in Figure 15-3.

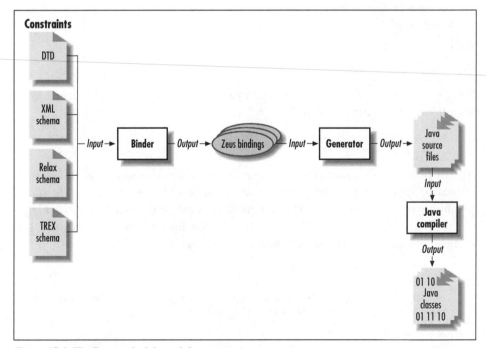

Figure 15-3. The Zeus methodology of class generation

What's nice about this, and the reasoning behind it, is that adding support for a new method of constraints like TREX becomes a very simple process. You could write a class, implementing the `org.enhydra.zeus.Binder` interface, that takes in a set of constraints and creates Zeus bindings from them. Class generation is already handled, so you don't have to deal with hundreds of annoying `out.write()` type statements. Zeus comes prepackaged with two binders, `DTDBinder` and `SchemaBinder`, both in the `org.enhydra.zeus.binder` package.

Other than that architectural change (which doesn't affect you when using existing binders), Castor and Zeus operate similarly in generating classes. Example 15-5 shows a DTD that constrains the original XML document from Example 15-1. I'll demonstrate using class generation from DTDs with this example.

Example 15-5. DTD for Example 15-1

```
<!ELEMENT catalog (item+)>
<!ATTLIST catalog
        xmlns   CDATA     #FIXED    "http://www.homespuntapes.com"
>


<!ELEMENT item (title, teacher, guest*, description)>
<!ATTLIST item
        id      CDATA     #REQUIRED
        level   CDATA     #REQUIRED
>


<!ELEMENT title (#PCDATA)>
<!ELEMENT teacher (#PCDATA)>
<!ELEMENT guest (#PCDATA)>
<!ELEMENT description (#PCDATA)>
```

Zeus is set up to allow applications to call the source generator, and therefore does not provide a static entry point for source generation within the API. Because that's a common task, though, a class within the samples (remember running the build program with the "samples" argument?) does allow easy class generation. If your classpath is set up like I showed you previously, all you need to do is create a new directory called "output". The samples program puts generated classes in there by default (programmatically, you can change that option). So, with an *output* directory in place, run the following command:

```
C:\javaxml2\build>java samples.TestDTDBinder
    -file=c:\javaxml2\ch14\xml\zeus\catalog.dtd
    -package=javaxml2.zeus
    -quiet=true
```

I have spaced things out for clarity. I've specified the file to generate source from, the package to put the source within, and that generation should occur *quietly* (without spitting out any debugging information). Generation from a schema is very similar. Since Zeus uses the final version of the XML Schema recommendation, you need to use a newer version of the XML Schema shown back in the Castor section; Example 15-6 updates that schema to a current version.

Example 15-6. Updating the Castor XML Schema

```xml
<?xml version="1.0"?>

<schema xmlns="http://www.w3.org/2001/XMLSchema"
        targetNamespace="http://www.homespuntapes.com">
  <element name="catalog">
    <complexType>
      <sequence>
        <element ref="item" minOccurs="1" maxOccurs="unbounded" />
      </sequence>
    </complexType>
  </element>

  <element name="item">
    <complexType>
      <sequence>
        <element name="title" type="string" />
        <element name="teacher" type="string" />
        <element name="guest" type="string" minOccurs="0" maxOccurs="unbounded" />
        <element name="description" type="string" />
      </sequence>
      <attribute name="id" type="string" />
      <attribute name="level">
        <simpleType>
          <restriction base="integer">
            <enumeration value="1" />
            <enumeration value="2" />
            <enumeration value="3" />
            <enumeration value="4" />
            <enumeration value="5" />
          </restriction>
        </simpleType>
      </attribute>
    </complexType>
  </element>
</schema>
```

Once you've got that, use the following command for class generation:

```
C:\javaxml2\build>java samples.TestSchemaBinder
    -file=c:\javaxml2\ch14\xml\zeus\catalog.xsd
    -package=javaxml2.zeus
    -quiet=true
```

You'll get identical output using either a DTD or a schema.

WARNING   This is a slight overstatement. Actually, you will get identical output
             if you can represent the constraints in the DTD and XML Schema
             identically. In this example, the schema defines "level" as an
             `integer`, while the DTD must define it as `PCDATA`. The result is that
             using a schema, you get a typed level (a Java `int`), and using a DTD,
             you get a `String`. I've used the DTD version throughout this sec-
             tion, to show you that option.

Within the *output* directory, you'll find a *javaxml2* directory, and then a *zeus* directory (matching up to the package hierarchy). You can take a look at the source
files generated within.

Right off, you should notice that Zeus produces an interface (for example, *Catalog.
java*) and a default implementation of that interface (for example, *CatalogImpl.
java*). The reasoning behind this, as opposed to the concrete classes that Castor
generates, is that you may want to have your own custom classes, perhaps already
in existence, that implement the `Catalog` interface. You can therefore use your
own implementation, but get the benefits of class generation. I commonly see
developers using Zeus to generate classes and then creating their own implementation of the generated interfaces as Enterprise JavaBeans (EJBs). These EJBs are
then persisted using Zeus, which is a piece of cake (as I'll show you in the next section). Without providing for user-defined implementations, this behavior would
require modifying the generated source code, which could break marshalling and
unmarshalling.

Another notable difference you should be aware of is the method names. For
example, here's the `Item` interface (trimmed down to its simplest form):

```
package javaxml2.zeus;

public interface Item {

    public Title getTitle();
    public void setTitle(Title title);

    public Teacher getTeacher();
    public void setTeacher(Teacher teacher);

    public java.util.List getGuestList();
    public void setGuestList(java.util.List guestList);
    public void addGuest(Guest guest);
    public void removeGuest(Guest guest);

    public Description getDescription();
    public void setDescription(Description description);
```

```
    public String getLevel();
    public void setLevel(String level);

    public String getId();
    public void setId(String id);
}
```

Notice that the JavaBeans naming is used, and elements that can appear multiple times are returned as Java 2 Collections classes. In any case, take a look at this source, and then compile it:

```
javac -d . output/javaxml2/zeus/*.java
```

Now you're ready to look at marshalling and unmarshalling using Zeus.

Marshalling and Unmarshalling

The process of marshalling and unmarshalling in Zeus is very similar to that in Castor. At the heart of the operations are two classes, `org.enhydra.zeus.Marshaller` and `org.enhydra.zeus.Unmarshaller`. Like Castor, the methods you will be interested in are `marshal()` and `unmarshal()`, on their respective classes. However, there are some differences. First, the `Marshaller` and `Unmarshaller` classes in Zeus don't provide static entry points. This is intentional, reminding the user to set options like the package to unmarshal XML to, and whether or not there are methods that should be ignored in marshalling. Additionally, Zeus uses the JAXP style of input and output, providing data binding flavors of the `Source` and `Result` classes I talked about in Chapter 9. Like JAXP, Zeus provides some default flavors of these in the `org.enhydra.zeus.source` and `org.enhydra.zeus.result` packages. Even with these changes, the process turns out to be very similar in both frameworks:

```
File catalogFile = new File("catalog.xml");
FileReader reader = new FileReader(catalogFile);
FileWriter writer = new FileWriter(catalogFile);

// Castor: Unmarshalling
Catalog catalog =
    (Catalog)org.exolab.castor.xml.Unmarshaller.unmarshal(Catalog.class, reader);

// Zeus: Unmarshalling
StreamSource source = new StreamSource(reader);
org.enhydra.zeus.Unmarshaller unmarshaller = new org.enhydra.zeus.Unmarshaller();
Catalog catalog = (Catalog)unmarshaller.unmarshal(source);

// Castor: Marshalling
org.exolab.castorMarshaller.marshal(catalog, writer);
```

```
// Zeus: Marshalling
StreamResult result = new StreamResult(writer);
org.enhydra.zeus.Marshaller marshaller = new org.enhydra.zeus.Marshaller();
marshaller.marshal(catalog, result);
```

While there's a bit more typing involved with using Zeus, the methodology should
seem a lot more familiar to JAXP users, which was the goal. It also allows input and
output of SAX streams and DOM trees using the appropriate Source and Result
implementations. As an example of Zeus in action, check out Example 15-7. This
program reads in the catalog supplied as the first argument on the command line,
prints out the item names and IDs, modifies an existing item, and then marshals
the catalog back to XML. There's very little user interaction here, but you should
be able to see how Zeus works.

Example 15-7. Using Zeus for catalog manipulation

```
package javaxml2;

import java.io.File;
import java.io.FileReader;
import java.io.FileWriter;
import java.io.IOException;
import java.util.Iterator;
import java.util.List;

// Zeus classes
import org.enhydra.zeus.Marshaller;
import org.enhydra.zeus.Unmarshaller;
import org.enhydra.zeus.source.StreamSource;
import org.enhydra.zeus.result.StreamResult;

// Zeus generated classes
import javaxml2.zeus.Catalog;
import javaxml2.zeus.Guest;
import javaxml2.zeus.GuestImpl;
import javaxml2.zeus.Item;
import javaxml2.zeus.ItemImpl;

public class CatalogViewer {

    public void view(File catalogFile) throws IOException {
        FileReader reader = new FileReader(catalogFile);
        StreamSource source = new StreamSource(reader);

        // Convert from XML to Java
        Unmarshaller unmarshaller = new Unmarshaller();
        unmarshaller.setJavaPackage("javaxml2.zeus");
        Catalog catalog = (Catalog)unmarshaller.unmarshal(source);
```

Example 15-7. Using Zeus for catalog manipulation (continued)

```java
        List items = catalog.getItemList();
        for (Iterator i = items.iterator(); i.hasNext(); ) {
            Item item = (Item)i.next();
            String id = item.getId();
            System.out.println("Item ID: " + id);
            String title = item.getTitle().getValue();
            System.out.println("Item Title: " + title);

            // Modify an item
            if (id.equals("CDZ-SM01")) {
                item.getTitle().setValue("Sam Bush Teaches Mandolin " +
                    "Repertoire and Technique, 2nd edition");
                Guest guest = new GuestImpl();
                guest.setValue("Bela Fleck");
                item.addGuest(guest);
            }
        }

        // Write back out
        FileWriter writer = new FileWriter(new File("newCatalog.xml"));
        StreamResult result = new StreamResult(writer);
        Marshaller marshaller = new Marshaller();
        marshaller.marshal(catalog, result);
    }

    public static void main(String[] args) {
        try {
            if (args.length != 1) {
                System.out.println("Usage: java javaxml2.CatalogViewer " +
                    "[XML Catalog Filename]");
                return;
            }

            // Get access to XML catalog
            File catalogFile = new File(args[0]);
            CatalogViewer viewer = new CatalogViewer();
            viewer.view(catalogFile);

        } catch (Exception e) {
            e.printStackTrace();
        }
    }
}
```

This reads in the file specified, and then spits out the ID and title of each item in the catalog. It also checks for a certain ID ("CDZ-SM01"), and modifies that item to reflect a second edition (and all of us around here love second editions!).

Finally, it writes the catalog back out to a new file, with the modified information. Try it out; just be sure that you already have the compiled Zeus-generated classes in your classpath.

Once you've learned how basic data binding works, you aren't in for too many surprises. You'll just need to find the framework that is most suitable for your specific application's functional needs. One thing that Zeus has going for it is the generation of interfaces and implementation classes, which allows you to use your existing classes with little modification. Additionally, Zeus provides for using DTDs, which many of you with hundreds of DTDs in older XML-based applications will love. On the other hand, Zeus is newer than Castor, and has less momentum and a smaller developer community at this point. So, check it out online, and use it if it helps you out.

JAXB

Last but not least, I want to cover JAXB, Sun's Java Architecture for Data Binding. It might surprise you that I'm dealing with JAXB last, or that I've even included coverage of other APIs. However, Sun's offering has been very slow in coming, and is still in early access as I write this book. It will probably not be in a final form when you are reading this chapter, and it has a very limited feature set. Certainly, future versions will add functionality, but for now Sun is just trying to get a stable offering out to the public. You will find features in Castor and Zeus that simply aren't available in JAXB right now; for all these reasons, I want to let you see more than just the JAXB framework. And of course, I'm generally of the opinion that open source software is just cool!

Installation

To get started, you need to download JAXB from Sun at *http://java.sun.com/xml/ jaxb/index.html*. I also recommend you get the documentation and specification.

WARNING   At the time of this writing, JAXB is in early release. Sun could easily change things before a final version, although that's not really common in EA (early access) software. Still, be warned that you may have to tweak the code shown here to work by the time you are checking JAXB out. Additionally, there are many errors in the documentation (at least in the early release). I've tried to steer clear of those here, so the examples in this section can be used as correct syntax if you run into errors using the JAXB instructions (as I did).

Once you've got the release downloaded, simply put the two included *jar* files, *jaxb-xjc-1.0-ea.jar* and *jaxb-rt-1.0-ea.jar*, in your classpath. Additionally, JAXB uses a script, *xjc*, to perform schema compilation. I have no idea why this isn't a Java class, but that's life. You can invoke the Java class manually, though, if you want to dig into the shell script. However, the early access release neglects to supply a script capable of running on Windows, as many of you may be. Example 15-8 is a Windows-compatible script to match the supplied Unix version.

Example 15-8. xjc.bat for Windows platforms

```
@echo off

echo JAXB Schema Compiler
echo --------------------

if "%JAVA_HOME%" == "" goto errorJVM
if "%JAXB_HOME%" == "" goto errorJAXB

set JAXB_LIB=%JAXB_HOME%\lib
set JAXB_CLASSES=%JAXB_HOME%\classes

echo %JAVA_HOME%\bin\java.exe -jar %JAXB_LIB%\jaxb-xjc-1.0-ea.jar %1 %2 %3 %4 %5
%JAVA_HOME%\bin\java.exe -jar %JAXB_LIB%\jaxb-xjc-1.0-ea.jar %1 %2 %3 %4 %5

goto end

:errorJVM

echo ERROR: JAVA_HOME not found in your environment.
echo Please, set the JAVA_HOME variable in your environment to match the
echo location of the Java Virtual Machine you want to use.
echo For example:
echo   set JAVA_HOME=c:\java\jdk1.3.1

goto end

:errorJAXB

echo ERROR: JAXB_HOME not found in your environment.
echo Please, set the JAXB_HOME variable in your environment to match the
echo location of the JAXB installation directory.
echo For example:
echo   set JAXB_HOME=c:\java\jaxb-1.0-ea

:end
```

Place this in your JAXB installation's *bin* directory, along with *xjc*; as you can see, I called mine *xjc.bat*. Finally, add an environment entry for both JAVA_HOME and JAXB_HOME (you only need JAVA_HOME if you are on Unix platforms). On my Windows system, I did this:

```
set JAVA_HOME=c:\java\jdk1.3.1
set JAXB_HOME=c:\javaxml2\jaxb-1.0-ea
```

Then you are ready to proceed.

Class Generation

While Castor supports only XML Schema, JAXB supports only DTDs. So, I'll use the DTD from Example 15-5 for class generation here. However, JAXB also requires a *binding schema* for class generation. A binding schema tells JAXB the specifics of how to convert the constraints in a DTD to a Java class (or classes). At its simplest, you need to specify the root element in the DTD (or multiple root elements, if your DTD defines them). Example 15-9 is the simplest possible binding schema for the *catalog.xml* document used in this chapter.

Example 15-9. Binding schema for the catalog document

```
<?xml version="1.0"?>

<xml-java-binding-schema version="1.0ea">
  <element name="catalog" type="class" root="true" />
</xml-java-binding-schema>
```

This specifies the document as a binding schema, and defines the root element. Save this file as *catalog.xjc*.

With a DTD (*catalog.dtd* from the last section on Zeus) and a binding schema, you're ready to generate Java classes. Execute the following command:

```
xjc c:\javaxml2\ch14\xml\jaxb\catalog.dtd c:\javaxml2\ch14\xml\jaxb\catalog.xjc
```

Or, on Unix or Cygwin:

```
xjc /javaxml2/ch14/xml/jaxb/catalog.dtd /javaxml2/ch14/xml/jaxb/catalog.xjc
```

Once that command completes, you get two classes in your current directory, *Catalog.java* and *Item.java*. These have the typical set of methods you would expect:

```
public class Item {
    public String getLevel();
    public void setLevel();

    public String getId();
    public void setId(String id);

    public List getGuest();
    public void deleteGuest();
    public void emptyGuest();

    // And so on...
}
```

Note how JAXB deals with lists. It's a step up from Castor (in my opinion), as it does provide access to the `List` of guests. However (also my opinion), it lacks the convenience of an `addGuest()` method that Zeus provides. You'll need to handle all list manipulation by getting the list and working on it directly:

```
// The Zeus way
item.addGuest(new Guest("Bela Bleck"));

// The JAXB way
List guests = item.getGuest();
guests.add("Bela Fleck");
```

The generated classes are also all concrete classes, much like the model that Castor uses.

The binding schema does provide some nifty options (even if it's not XML). First, you can specify the package that generated classes should be in; this is done using the `options` element, with the `package` attribute. Add this line to your binding schema:

```
<?xml version="1.0"?>

<xml-java-binding-schema version="1.0ea">
  <options package="javaxml2.jaxb" />
  <element name="catalog" type="class" root="true" />
</xml-java-binding-schema>
```

Now, generated source will be placed in the *javaxml2/jaxb* directory with the same structure as the package hierarchy. Next, let's specify that the `level` attribute on the `item` element should be a number (instead of the default, a `String`):

```
<?xml version="1.0"?>

<xml-java-binding-schema version="1.0ea">
  <options package="javaxml2.jaxb" />
  <element name="catalog" type="class" root="true" />
  <element name="item" type="class">
    <attribute name="level" convert="int" />
  </element>
</xml-java-binding-schema>
```

As you can see, I first added an element declaration for the `item` element. This allows me to reference its `level` attribute using the `attribute` construct. To handle the datatype, I specified the type I wanted (`int`) with the `convert` attribute.

Continuing with the options that a binding schema supplies, here's a really nice feature. You can actually change the name of a property from what it is in the DTD. For example, I hate methods like `getId()`. Instead, I really prefer `getID()`, which looks much better. So, what I really want is to name the `id` property from my DTD as `ID` in Java. This turns out to be simple with JAXB:

```
<?xml version="1.0"?>

<xml-java-binding-schema version="1.0ea">
  <options package="javaxml2.jaxb" />
  <element name="catalog" type="class" root="true" />
  <element name="item" type="class">
    <attribute name="level" convert="int" />
    <attribute name="id" property="ID" />
  </element>
</xml-java-binding-schema>
```

Once you've made all of these various changes, run the schema compiler (*xjc*) again. You'll get the modified classes I've been talking about, and now can compile those:

```
javac -d . javaxml2/jaxb/*.java
```

If you have any problems, ensure that you still have *jaxb-rt-1.0-ea.jar* in your classpath.

There are quite a few more options for the binding schema than those discussed here; in fact, many of these were undocumented, and I found them by looking at the *xjc.dtd* included with JAXB. I suggest you do the same, in addition to reading the supplied documentation. Once you've got your classes generated, it's on to marshalling and unmarshalling.

Marshalling and Unmarshalling

The process of marshalling and unmarshalling turns out to be the same song, third verse, for this chapter. Since that is the case, I will get right to some code, shown in Example 15-10.

Example 15-10. The Categorizer class

```
package javaxml2;

import java.io.File;
import java.io.FileInputStream;
import java.io.FileOutputStream;
import java.io.IOException;
import java.util.Iterator;
import java.util.LinkedList;
import java.util.List;

// JAXB Classes
import javax.xml.bind.UnmarshalException;
```

Example 15-10. The Categorizer class (continued)

```java
// JAXB Generated Classes
import javaxml2.jaxb.Catalog;
import javaxml2.jaxb.Item;

public class Categorizer {

    public void categorize(File catalogFile) throws IOException,
        UnmarshalException {

        // Convert from XML to Java
        FileInputStream fis = new FileInputStream(catalogFile);
        Catalog catalog = new Catalog();
        try {
            catalog = Catalog.unmarshal(fis);
        } finally {
            fis.close();
        }

        // Create new catalogs for the different categories
        Catalog fingerpickingCatalog = new Catalog();
        Catalog flatpickingCatalog = new Catalog();
        Catalog mandolinCatalog = new Catalog();

        List items = catalog.getItem();
        for (Iterator i = items.iterator(); i.hasNext(); ) {
            Item item = (Item)i.next();
            String teacher = item.getTeacher();
            if ((teacher.equals("Doc Watson")) ||
                (teacher.equals("Steve Kaufman"))) {
                flatpickingCatalog.getItem().add(item);
            } else if (teacher.equals("David Wilcox")) {
                fingerpickingCatalog.getItem().add(item);
            } else if ((teacher.equals("Sam Bush")) ||
                    (teacher.equals("Chris Thile"))) {
                mandolinCatalog.getItem().add(item);
            }
        }

        // Write back out to XML
        FileOutputStream fingerOutput =
            new FileOutputStream(new File("fingerpickingCatalog.xml"));
        FileOutputStream flatpickOutput =
            new FileOutputStream(new File("flatpickingCatalog.xml"));
        FileOutputStream mandolinOutput =
            new FileOutputStream(new File("mandolinCatalog.xml"));
        try {
            // Validate the catalogs
            fingerpickingCatalog.validate();
```

Example 15-10. The Categorizer class (continued)

```
            flatpickingCatalog.validate();
            mandolinCatalog.validate();

            // Output the catalogs
            fingerpickingCatalog.marshal(fingerOutput);
            flatpickingCatalog.marshal(flatpickOutput);
            mandolinCatalog.marshal(mandolinOutput);
        } finally {
            fingerOutput.close();
            flatpickOutput.close();
            mandolinOutput.close();
        }
    }

    public static void main(String[] args) {
        try {
            if (args.length != 1) {
                System.out.println("Usage: java javaxml2.Categorizer " +
                    "[XML Catalog Filename]");
                return;
            }

            // Get access to XML catalog
            File catalogFile = new File(args[0]);
            Categorizer categorizer = new Categorizer();
            categorizer.categorize(catalogFile);

        } catch (Exception e) {
            e.printStackTrace();
        }
    }

}
```

There is not a whole lot of interest here; you've seen this several times. However, JAXB does do a few things differently. First, the `marshal()` and `unmarshal()` methods are on the generated classes themselves, rather than on static `Marshaller` and `Unmarshaller` classes:

```
// Convert from XML to Java
FileInputStream fis = new FileInputStream(catalogFile);
Catalog catalog = new Catalog();
try {
    catalog = Catalog.unmarshal(fis);
} finally {
    fis.close();
}
```

The generated classes provide static methods that allow for marshalling and unmarshalling. These static methods return an instance of the class with the data from the supplied file filled in. However, *you must be sure to assign this return value to an instance variable!* An extremely frustrating mistake to make is this:

```
// Convert from XML to Java
FileInputStream fis = new FileInputStream(catalogFile);
Catalog catalog = new Catalog();
try {
    catalog.unmarshal(fis);
} finally {
    fis.close();
}
```

Notice the bolded line: if you try to access the instance variables of the `catalog` instance after this code snippet, you will get no data, regardless of what's in the supplied XML file. That's because the `unmarshal()` method is static, and returns a live instance of the `Catalog` class; since that value is never assigned here, it's lost. This can be quite annoying, so watch out! That very issue is actually a case for the external `Marshaller` and `Unmarshaller` classes, as used in Castor and Zeus.

In the example, once I have an instance of the XML catalog, I iterate through it. Depending on the teacher, the code adds the item to one of three new catalogs: a flat picking one, a finger picking one, or a mandolin one. Then, each of these new catalogs is marshalled back out to a new XML document. As an example, here's what I got for my *mandolinCatalog.xml* document:

```
<?xml version="1.0" encoding="UTF-8"?>

<catalog>
  <item level="3" id="VD-THI-MN01">
    <title>Essential Techniques for Mandolin</title>
    <teacher>Chris Thile</teacher>
    <description>Here's a lesson that will thrill and inspire mandolin players at
    all levels.</description></item>
  <item level="4" id="CDZ-SM01">
    <title>Sam Bush Teaches Mandolin Repertoire and Techniques</title>
    <teacher>Sam Bush</teacher>
    <description>Learn complete solos to eight traditional and orignal tunes,
    each one jam-packed with licks, runs, and musical variations.</description>
</item></catalog>
```

The spacing is, as always, added in production, so your line feeds may not match up. However, JAXB's marshalling and unmarshalling is that simple to use. Once you get past the static method issue I just mentioned, it's almost identical to the other two frameworks.

While I encourage you to check out JAXB today, be leery of using it in production until a final release becomes available. There are several undocumented features still floating around that could easily be changed before a final release. Additionally, JAXB does not yet support taking arbitrary objects (ones not generated by JAXB) and marshalling them; this is something the other frameworks do allow for, and might be a drawback for your applications. JAXB also, as mentioned, has no XML Schema support, as well as no namespace support. On the upside, Sun will obviously put a lot of resources into JAXB, so expect it to shape up in the coming months.

In any case, you should have a pretty good taste of what data binding provides by now. The ins and outs of a particular framework are left for you to discover, but with these basics you could pick up any one (or all) of the projects mentioned here and put them to work. Be sure to let whichever project you choose to work with know about what works and what doesn't; it can really affect future development, particularly the open source ones.

What's Next?

We're getting to the latter pages of this book, so it should be no surprise to you that I'm beginning to wrap things up. In the next chapter, I'm going to do a little hocus-pocus and let you know what I think is worth watching out for over the next year or so. Chapter 16 is my "Looking Forward" chapter, included for two reasons. The first is the obvious one: I want you to be ahead of the curve. The second, more interesting reason is to point out how quickly things change. This is particularly true in Java and XML, and I anticipate you and I will laugh at a few of the suggestions in the next chapter just a short year from now. In any case, it will help you think about what might be coming on the horizon, and give you some preparation for those important new technologies when they surface.

16

In this chapter:
- *XLink*
- *XPointer*
- *XML Schema Bindings*
- *And the Rest. . .*
- *What's Next?*

Looking Forward

It's almost time to wrap up the journey through Java and XML. I hope you've had fun. Before I leave you to mull over all the possibilities, I want to finish up with a little crystal-ball gazing. Like any good programmer, I always try and outguess the technology space and be ahead of the curve. This usually involves knowing more than just cursory information about a whole lot of technologies, so I can easily get up to speed when something breaks. In this chapter, I'm going to point out some of the interesting things coming up over the horizon, and let you in on some extra knowledge on each. I'll be the first to admit that some of these guesses may be completely off; others may be the next big thing. Take a look at each, and then be ready to react when you see where they might fit into your applications.*

XLink

First on my list of up-and-coming stars in the XML world is XLink. XLink defines an XML linking mechanism for referring to other documents. For those of you who are HTML authors, this may sound like the "a" element you are used to:

```
<a href="http://www.nickelcreek.com">Check out Nickel Creek!</a>.
```

However, XLink offers much more than simply unidirectional (one-way) linking. Using XLink, you can create bidirectional links, define how links are processed, and most importantly, allow linking from any XML element (instead of just the "a" element). For all these reasons, it's worth getting into here.

Example 16-1 is a small XML document, representing a few of my guitars.

---

* Many of the sections within this chapter are based in whole or in part on articles and tips I have written for the IBM DeveloperWorks online publication, located at *http://www.ibm.com/developer*. Thanks to Nancy Dunn and the kind folks at IBM for letting me update and reprint parts of those articles.

Example 16-1. XML document using XLink

```
<?xml version="1.0"?>

<guitars xmlns="http://www.newInstance.com/about/guitars"
         xmlns:xlink="http://www.w3.org/1999/xlink">
 <guitar luthier="Bourgeois"
          xlink:type="simple"
          xlink:href="http://www.newInstance.com/about/guitars/bourgeoisOM">
  <descripton xlink:type="simple"
              xlink:href="http://www.newinstance.com/pics/bougOM_front_full.jpg"
              xlink:actuate="onLoad" xlink:show="embed">
  This is a real beauty in a small body. Although this is an OM, I use it for
  flatpicking bluegrass as well as for producing some beautiful fingerstyle sounds.
  </description>
 </guitar>
 <guitar luthier="Bourgeois"
          xlink:type="simple"
          xlink:href="http://www.newInstance.com/about/guitars/bourgeoisD150">
  <descripton xlink:type="simple"
              xlink:href="http://www.newinstance.com/pics/bougd150_con_rim2.jpg"
              xlink:actuate="onLoad" xlink:show="embed">
   Here's the holy grail in process. Dana Bourgeois is building this Brazilian
  rosewood and adirondack bluegrass monster right now... you'll know it's
  finished when you hear a run and your windows shatter!
  </description>
 </guitar>
</guitars>
```

First, you'll notice that I reference the XLink namespace, so that the document has access to the XLink attributes and features. Second, I'm going to cover only XLinks of the "simple" type, specified by the `xlink:type` attribute. That's because browser support for XLinks is minimal, found only in Mozilla and Netscape 6 (I haven't been able to test IE 6.0, but 5.5 has no support for them), so keeping to the basic aspects will serve you well.

Once the formalities are out of the way, XLinking just requires using some attributes on the elements that have links. Take my document's guitar element. It specifies a luthier for each guitar (that's a guitar maker for those of you who are missing out on guitar playing!). I already mentioned the use of the `xlink:type` attribute, which is set to the value "simple". It then specifies a URL to link to using XLink. To specify this URL, it uses the `xlink:href` attribute. So far, this looks a lot like HTML. No big deal, right? By default (assuming browser support, of course), this will set the link up to replace the current window when clicked upon. If you want the target of the link to open in a new window, you can add the `xlink:show` attribute, and give it a value of "new"; the default is "replace", which is normal HTML behavior.

Of course, this only covers basic linking. Things get more interesting when you want to access remote locations as resources, such as linking in images. Look at the description element; this sets the value of the xlink:show attribute to "embed". The resource, in this case an image file showing the guitar being described, should be processed inline within the page. This instructs an XLink-aware browser to insert the specified document inline within the XML. It becomes really interesting when you consider this could be *another XML document*, and not just an image.

Taking things even further, you can specify *when* the resource should be shown. This is handled by the xlink:actuate attribute. It defines when the resource is read and shown. When the value is "onLoad", as it is in Example 16-1, the resource should be loaded when the initial document is loaded. You could also specify the value "onRequest", which means that until the link is clicked, the resource is not shown. This is handy for keeping bandwidth low, allowing the user to view only the resources that they want to see.

XLink could definitely have major impact on the next generation of XML documents. For the complete specification, check out *http://www.w3.org/TR/xlink*. I'd also keep an eye on the latest browsers and versions to see when complete XLink support shows up.

XPointer

XPointer is another XML linking technology, and in fact builds on XLink's capabilities. XLink, while useful in and of itself, only allows you to refer to another document. However, there are many times when you may want to refer to a specific *part* of another document. This is a very common task, and is somewhat analogous to using named anchors in HTML. It is made possible by using XPointer on top of XLink; the specs build very naturally on each other, and are intended to work together. First, you want to take a look at the target document you are going to link to. If you can, ensure that this document uses id attributes in it. This will make the linking and pointing much easier. Example 16-2 shows the listing of some of the guitars that luthier Dana Bourgeois makes, and has IDs for each type.

Example 16-2. A listing of Bourgeois guitars

```
<?xml version="1.0"?>

<guitarTypes xmlns="http://www.bourgeoisguitars.com">
 <type model="OM" ID="OM">
  <picture url="http://www.bourgeoisguitars.com/images/vvOM.jpg"/>
  <description>Small bodied orchestra model.</description>
 </type>
 <type model="D" ID="D">
  <picture
```

Example 16-2. A listing of Bourgeois guitars (continued)

```
    url="http://www.bourgeoisguitars.com/images/ricky%20skaggs%20model.jpg"/>
   <description>Bluegrass powerhouse in a standard dreadnought shape.</description>
  </type>
  <type model="slopeD" ID="slopeD">
   <picture
    url="http://www.bourgeoisguitars.com/images/slope%20d,%20custom%20version.jpg"/>
   <description>
     Slope shouldered dreadnought, perfect for vocal accompaniment.
   </description>
  </type>
</guitarTypes>
```

For the sake of discussion, assume that this document is available at *http://www. bourgeoisguitars.com/guitars.xml*. Instead of just referencing the entire document, which doesn't help a whole lot, XPointer allows for linking to specific parts of the document. Remember the `xlink:href` attribute? The value supplied to that attribute was the target of an XLink. But you can add a pound sign (#), and then an XPointer expression to these URLs. For example, the expression `xpointer(id("slopeD"))` refers to an element in a document with the ID "slopeD". So, to refer to the XML shown in Example 16-2, and then to the Slope D model guitar described in that document, the URL *http://www.bourgeoisguitars.com/ guitars.xml#xpointer(id("slopeD"))* would be used. Easy enough. Let me show you a modified version of the XML document I introduced in the XLink section (Example 16-1), which describes my guitars, using some XPointer references. (Forgive the awkward formatting; I had a lot to fit on some lines.) Take a look at Example 16-3.

Example 16-3. My guitars in XML using XPointer

```
<?xml version="1.0"?>

<guitars xmlns="http://www.newInstance.com/about/guitars"
         xmlns:xlink="http://www.w3.org/1999/xlink">
 <guitar luthier="Bourgeois"
         xlink:type="simple"
         xlink:href=
         "http://www.bourgeoisguitars.com/guitars.xml#xpointer(id(&apos;OM&apos;))">
  <descripton xlink:type="simple"
              xlink:href="http://www.newinstance.com/pics/bougOM_front_full.jpg"
              xlink:actuate="onLoad" xlink:show="embed">
   This is a real beauty in a small body. Although this is an OM, I use it for
   flatpicking bluegrass as well as for producing some beautiful
   fingerstyle sounds.
  </description>
 </guitar>
```

Example 16-3. My guitars in XML using XPointer (continued)

```
<guitar luthier="Bourgeois"
        xlink:type="simple"
        xlink:href=
          "http://www.bourgeoisguitars.com/guitars.xml#xpointer(id(&apos;D&apos;))">
  <descripton xlink:type="simple"
              xlink:href="http://www.newinstance.com/pics/bougd150_con_rim2.jpg"
              xlink:actuate="onLoad" xlink:show="embed">
  Here's the holy grail in process. Dana Bourgeois is building this Brazilian
  rosewood and adirondack bluegrass monster right now... you'll know it's
  finished when you hear a run and your windows shatter!
  </description>
 </guitar>
</guitars>
```

Now my document can reference the XML content that Dana Bourgeois keeps about his guitars. If he changes this information, I don't have to worry; my document stays current because it simply links to his information. Notice that I had to "escape" the quotation marks within the XPointer expression by using `&amp;` instead of an ampersand (&). However, this makes for a rather long URL to link to. Long URLs, in my experience, lead to annoying typos (and annoying formatting in a book!). Luckily, XPointer allows a handy shorthand form when linking to an element with an ID tag. Instead of using the `xpointer(id("D"))` form, you can simply use the value of the ID to target. In this case, that would simply be "D". I can simply combine the document in Example 16-3 to that shown in Example 16-4. Makes for a much cleaner link syntax.

Example 16-4. Using XPointer shorthand to simplify Example 16-3

```
<?xml version="1.0"?>

<guitars xmlns="http://www.newInstance.com/about/guitars"
         xmlns:xlink="http://www.w3.org/1999/xlink">
 <guitar luthier="Bourgeois"
         xlink:type="simple"
         xlink:href="http://www.bourgeoisguitars.com/guitars.xml#OM" >
  <descripton xlink:type="simple"
              xlink:href="http://www.newinstance.com/pics/bougOM_front_full.jpg"
              xlink:actuate="onLoad" xlink:show="embed">
  This is a real beauty in a small body. Although this is an OM, I use it for
  flatpicking bluegrass as well as for producing some beautiful
  fingerstyle sounds.
  </description>
 </guitar>
 <guitar luthier="Bourgeois"
         xlink:type="simple"
         xlink:href="http://www.bourgeoisguitars.com/guitars.xml#D" >
```

Example 16-4. Using XPointer shorthand to simplify Example 16-3 (continued)

```
  <descripton xlink:type="simple"
              xlink:href="http://www.newinstance.com/pics/bougd150_con_rim2.jpg"
              xlink:actuate="onLoad" xlink:show="embed">
   Here's the holy grail in process. Dana Bourgeois is building this Brazilian
   rosewood and adirondack bluegrass monster right now... you'll know it's
   finished when you hear a run and your windows shatter!
  </description>
 </guitar>
</guitars>
```

In addition to this direct listing, you can point to elements *relative* to other elements. As an example of this, my `description` elements in Example 16-5 have been changed to point to the image specified in the *bourgeois.xml* file from Example 16-2.

NOTE   For the sake of getting this lengthy URL into the code space of an O'Reilly book, I've abbreviated the URL *http://www.bourgeoisguitars.com* as simply *http://bg.com*. This isn't a valid URL, but it works for the example.

Example 16-5. Using relative links

```
<?xml version="1.0"?>

<guitars xmlns="http://www.newInstance.com/about/guitars"
         xmlns:xlink="http://www.w3.org/1999/xlink">
 <guitar luthier="Bourgeois"
         xlink:type="simple"
         xlink:href=
 "http://bg.com/guitars.xml#xpointer(id(&apos;OM&apos;))/descendant::picture[@url]">
  <descripton xlink:type="simple"
              xlink:href="http://www.newinstance.com/pics/bougOM_front_full.jpg"
              xlink:actuate="onLoad" xlink:show="embed">
   This is a real beauty in a small body. Although this is an OM, I use it for
   flatpicking bluegrass as well as for producing some beautiful
   fingerstyle sounds.
  </description>
 </guitar>
 <guitar luthier="Bourgeois"
         xlink:type="simple"
         xlink:href=
 "http://bg.com/guitars.xml#xpointer(id(&apos;D&apos;))/descendant::picture[@url]" >
  <descripton xlink:type="simple"
              xlink:href="http://www.newinstance.com/pics/bougd150_con_rim2.jpg"
              xlink:actuate="onLoad" xlink:show="embed">
   Here's the holy grail in process. Dana Bourgeois is building this Brazilian
```

Example 16-5. Using relative links (continued)

```
  rosewood and adirondack bluegrass monster right now... you'll know it's
  finished when you hear a run and your windows shatter!
  </description>
 </guitar>
</guitars>
```

Here, you can see that once the element referred to by the ID is found, the descendant of that element (specified by the `descendant` keyword) named "picture" is found. Then, the value of the attribute of that element named "url" is the final target of the link. I know that's a mouthful, but if you take it step by step, it turns out to be fairly straightforward. For more information on the huge variety of options that XPointer offers, check out the XPointer specification online at *http://www.w3.org/TR/xptr*.

NOTE   Notice that I did not use the shorthand form of ID links I talked
            about in the last section. That's because using that form of ID link-
            ing allows for only a direct link; no further linking (such as the child-
            traversing reference in Listing 4) is allowed without the longer form
            of ID linking.

XLink and XPointer stand to change how XML is linked and authored in major ways. I expect to see a variety of support in Java APIs for this once the specifications are fully supported by browsers as well, so keep an eye out.

XML Schema Bindings

Moving more into the Java side of things, one major aspect of XML programming I expect to see is a set of datatypes defined in Java that represent XML Schema constructs. This is somewhat similar to the DOM Level 2 HTML bindings I talked about in Chapter 6. I consider these infinitely more useful. Because an XML Schema is itself an XML document, it can be parsed and dealt with like any other XML document. However, trying to work with an XML Schema as just any old XML document turns out to be a bit of a pain. You can't, for example, query an element definition and determine if it is a complex type. Instead, you have to get the element, see if it has any children, determine if one of those children is named `complexType`, and so on. This gets even worse when things like sequencing are used; suddenly the complex type definition appears nested *two* levels deep.

What I expect to see (and in fact, already hear rumblings of) is a grammar and set of Java objects built to specifically match up with XML Schema datatypes. This would presumably be built on an existing object-based API, like DOM or JDOM.

So, for the sake of example, assume that DOM Level 4 or JDOM 1.1 define such objects. You might see code like this:

```
// THIS CODE IS PURELY HYPOTHETICAL
XSDDocumentParser schemaParser =
    new org.apache.xerces.parsers.XSDParser();
parser.parse(mySchema);
XSDDocument doc = parser.getXSDDocument();
```

Now, instead of working with root elements and attributes in XML, you would deal with this document (where all the classes are prefixed by XSD, for *XML Schema Datatypes*) using schema concepts, as shown here:

```
// Get "root" element
XSDSchema schema = doc.getXSDSchema();

// Get target namespace for this document
String targetNamespaceURI = schema.getTargetNamespace().getURI();

// Get some named element definition
XSDElementDef def = schema.getElementDef("movie");
if (def.isComplexType()) {
    List attributeDefs = def.getAttributeDefs();
    List nestedElementDefs = def.getElementDefs();
} else {
    XSDType elementType = def.getType();
}
```

Obviously this is a bit contrived, because I'm making up syntax as I go. However, it's clear that my Java code is working on an XML Schema, and taking advantage of schema semantics. I'm not working with basic XML semantics (although if these classes extended basic DOM or JDOM classes, you could also work in that medium), but using what the XML Schema specification says about legal schemas to work a bit smarter. Hopefully the third edition of this book will have details about this API, because it would be very useful.

And the Rest. . .

There's a lot more that I want to see, and that I could talk about. However, this book would take another six months to complete if I put them all in, and then it would be time for another revision! Instead, I'll give you a quick rundown of hits. These are blurbs of information that may be helpful or may bore you, but will almost certainly have an impact on Java and XML in the next few years:

- Scalable Vector Graphics (SVG) and Apache Batik (*http://xml.apache.org*)
- MathML (the Math Markup Language, an extension of XML)
- Specifications related to and built upon ebXML (*http://www.ebXML.org*)

- Xerces 2.0 (*http://xml.apache.org*)

- JAXM, the Java API for XML Messaging (*http://java.sun.com/xml/xml_jaxm.html*)

- JAXRPC, the Java API for XML-based RPC (*http://java.sun.com/xml/xml_jaxrpc.html*)

There they are, my quick picks for what will be important a year from now (if not sooner). I'll probably be recanting a few in the next edition, but that's life in the fast lane, and XML is definitely the fast lane.

What's Next?

Appendixes. The index. Then some information about me, and a colophon. And probably some advertising for other great O'Reilly books.

Seriously, I've covered quite a bit of information at this point. Taking a few days to let the material sink in, and then applying your new XML skills on a project for work or something personal should help you polish your XML knowledge. Soon you'll be an XML wizard, and find your applications' values increasing as they are more flexible, configurable, and productive. Finally, you'll see your value to your boss (and potential bosses at other companies) rise dramatically as you code maintainable and performance-driven applications. Have fun, and stay extensible. I'll see you online.

A

API Reference

This appendix is an API reference for the four lower-level Java and XML APIs covered in this book, SAX, DOM, JDOM, and JAXP. It is broken down into sections based on the API being documented.

SAX 2.0

SAX 2.0 provides a sequential look into an XML document. Detailed in Chapters 3 and 4, SAX defines a set of interfaces that can be implemented and will be invoked as callbacks during the XML parsing process. The SAX packages are detailed here, with the classes and interfaces listed alphabetically. In the org.xml.sax.helpers package, most of the methods in the helper classes are implementations of interfaces already defined in the core SAX package (org.xml.sax).

Package: org.xml.sax

This package contains the core interfaces and classes for SAX 2.0. Most of the interfaces defined are intended to be implemented by you, the Java developer, with the exception of the actual XMLReader and Attributes implementation. These interfaces should be implemented by your vendor's XML parsing software. In addition, several exceptions that SAX methods are allowed to throw are defined. Several of the interfaces defined here are part of the SAX 1.0 and 2.0 alpha distributions, and are now deprecated.

AttributeList [deprecated]

This interface was defined in SAX 1.0, and is now deprecated. The Attributes interface should be used instead of AttributeList for SAX 2.0 implementations.

```
public interface AttributeList {
    public abstract int getLength();
    public abstract String getName(int i);
    public abstract String getType(int i);
    public abstract String getValue(int i);
    public abstract String getType(String name);
    public abstract String getValue(String name);
}
```

Attributes

This interface represents a listing of XML attributes. It is reported to the callbacks associated with the start of element (`startElement()` in `ContentHandler`), and is somewhat analogous to a Java `Vector`. The number of attributes represented can be obtained, as well as various views of the attributes' names (local, namespace prefix and URI, and raw) and values. Additionally, methods are available for locating the index of an attribute given its name. The primary difference between this interface and its predecessor, `AttributeList`, is that this interface is namespace-aware.

```
public interface Attributes {
    public abstract int getLength();
    public abstract String getURI(int index);
    public abstract String getLocalName(int index);
    public abstract String getQName(int index);
    public abstract String getType(int index);
    public abstract String getValue(int index);
    public int getIndex(String uri, String localName);
    public int getIndex(String qName);
    public abstract String getType(String uri, String localName);
    public abstract String getType(String qName);
    public abstract String getValue(String uri, String localName);
    public abstract String getValue(String qName);
}
```

ContentHandler

This interface defines the callback methods available to an application that deal with the content of the XML document being parsed. These include notification of the start and end of parsing (which precede and follow all other handler callbacks, respectively), processing instructions, and entities that may be skipped by nonvalidating parsers. Element callbacks, complete with namespace mappings, are also made available.

```
public interface ContentHandler {
    public void setDocumentLocator(Locator locator);
    public void startDocument() throws SAXException;
    public void endDocument() throws SAXException;
```

```
        public void startPrefixMapping(String prefix, String uri)
            throws SAXException;
        public void endPrefixMapping(String prefix)
            throws SAXException;
        public void startElement(String namespaceURI, String localName,
                                 String qName, Attributes atts)
            throws SAXException;
        public void endElement(String namespaceURI, String localName,
                               String qName)
            throws SAXException;
        public void characters(char ch[], int start, int length)
            throws SAXException;
        public void ignorableWhitespace(char ch[], int start, int length)
            throws SAXException;
        public void processingInstruction(String target, String data)
            throws SAXException;
        public void skippedEntity(String name)
            throws SAXException;
    }
```

DocumentHandler

This interface was defined in SAX 1.0, and is now deprecated. The
ContentHandler interface should be used instead of DocumentHandler for SAX
2.0 implementations.

```
    public interface DocumentHandler {
        public abstract void setDocumentLocator(Locator locator);
        public abstract void startDocument() throws SAXException;
        public abstract void endDocument() throws SAXException;
        public abstract void startElement(String name, AttributeList atts)
                throws SAXException;
        public abstract void endElement(String name)
                throws SAXException;
        public abstract void characters(char ch[], int start, int length)
                throws SAXException;
        public abstract void ignorableWhitespace(char ch[], int start, int length)
                throws SAXException;
        public abstract void processingInstruction (String target, String data)
                throws SAXException;
    }
```

DTDHandler

This interface defines callbacks that are invoked in the process of parsing a DTD.
Note that this interface does not provide information about the constraints within
the DTD, but instead about references to unparsed entities and NOTATION declarations, indicating items that are generally unparsed data.

```
public interface DTDHandler {
    public abstract void notationDecl(String name, String publicId,
                                      String systemId)
            throws SAXException;
    public abstract void unparsedEntityDecl(String name, String publicId,
                                      String systemId,
                                      String notationName)
            throws SAXException;
}
```

EntityResolver

This interface allows applications to intervene in the process of referencing external entities, such as an XML document that references a DTD or stylesheet. By implementing this interface, a modified or even completely different SAX InputSource can be returned to the calling program. Additionally, null can be returned to indicate that a normal URI connection should be opened to the specified system ID.

```
public interface EntityResolver {
    public abstract InputSource resolveEntity(String publicId,
                                      String systemId)
            throws SAXException, IOException;
}
```

ErrorHandler

This interface allows custom behavior to be attached to the three types of problem conditions that can occur within the lifecycle of XML parsing. Each receives the SAXParseException indicating what problem initiated the callback. The SAXException is provided to allow a means of throwing an exception that could stop parsing altogether.

```
public interface ErrorHandler {
    public abstract void warning(SAXParseException exception)
            throws SAXException;
    public abstract void error(SAXParseException exception)
            throws SAXException;
    public abstract void fatalError(SAXParseException exception)
            throws SAXException;
}
```

HandlerBase

This helper class provides empty implementations of all the SAX 1.0 core handler interfaces, and can be extended to allow the quick addition of handlers by overriding methods with application-defined behavior. This class was defined in SAX 1.0, and is now deprecated. The `org.xml.sax.helpers.DefaultHandler` class should be used instead of **HandlerBase** for SAX 2.0 implementations.

```
public class HandlerBase implements EntityResolver, DTDHandler,
                                    DocumentHandler, ErrorHandler {

        // EntityResolver implementation
        public InputSource resolveEntity(String publicId, String systemId);

        // DTDHandler implementation
        public void notationDecl(String name, String publicId,
                                 String systemId);
    public void unparsedEntityDecl(String name, String publicId,
                                   String systemId, String notationName);

        // DocumentHandler implementation
        public void setDocumentLocator(Locator locator);
    public abstract void startDocument() throws SAXException;
    public abstract void endDocument() throws SAXException;
    public abstract void startElement(String name, AttributeList atts)
            throws SAXException;
    public abstract void endElement(String name)
            throws SAXException;
    public abstract void characters(char ch[], int start, int length)
            throws SAXException;
    public abstract void ignorableWhitespace(char ch[], int start,
                                                           int length)
            throws SAXException;
    public abstract void processingInstruction(String target,
                                               String data)
            throws SAXException;

        // ErrorHandler implementation
    public abstract void warning(SAXParseException exception)
            throws SAXException;
    public abstract void error(SAXParseException exception)
            throws SAXException;
    public abstract void fatalError(SAXParseException exception)
            throws SAXException;
}
```

InputSource

This class encapsulates all information about a resource used in XML processing. This can be as little as a **String** or **InputStream** used for locating input, or as complex as an entity with a public ID and system ID as well as a URI reference (such as a DTD publicly defined). This class is the preferred wrapper for passing input into a SAX parser.

```
public class InputSource {
    public InputSource();
    public InputSource(String systemId);
    public InputSource(InputStream byteStream);
    public InputSource(Reader characterStream);
    public void setPublicId(String publicId);
    public String getPublicId();
    public void setSystemId(String systemId);
    public String getSystemId();
    public void setByteStream(InputStream byteStream);
    public InputStream getByteStream();
    public void setEncoding(String encoding);
    public String getEncoding();
    public void setCharacterStream(Reader characterStream);
    public Reader getCharacterStream();
}
```

Locator

This class is a complement to an XML document or other parsed construct, as it provides the document's system ID and public ID as well as information about the location within the file being processed. This is particularly helpful for use in IDE applications and for identifying where errors occur in parsing.

```
public interface Locator {
    public abstract String getPublicId();
    public abstract String getSystemId();
    public abstract int getLineNumber();
    public abstract int getColumnNumber();
}
```

Parser

This interface was defined in SAX 1.0, and is now deprecated. The XMLReader interface should be used instead for SAX 2.0 implementations.

```
public interface Parser {
    public abstract void setLocale(Locale locale) throws SAXException;
    public abstract void setEntityResolver(EntityResolver resolver);
    public abstract void setDTDHandler(DTDHandler handler);
    public abstract void setDocumentHandler(DocumentHandler handler);
    public abstract void setErrorHandler(ErrorHandler handler);
    public abstract void parse(InputSource source)
            throws SAXException, IOException;
    public abstract void parse(String systemId)
            throws SAXException, IOException;
}
```

SAXException

This is the core exception thrown by SAX callbacks and parser implementations. Because it is often thrown as a result of other exceptions, it has a constructor that allows the passing in of a lower-level Exception as well as an accessor method to retrieve the originating Exception. It is also the base class for all other SAX Exception classes.

```
public class SAXException extends Exception {
    public SAXException(String message);
    public SAXException(Exception e);
    public SAXException(String message, Exception e);
    public String getMessage();
    public Exception getException();
    public String toString();
}
```

SAXNotRecognizedException

This class provides a means for an XMLReader implementation to throw an error when an unrecognized identifier is received. This is most common in the setProperty() and setFeature() methods (as well as their accessor counterparts) when a URI is supplied about which the parser has no information.

```
public class SAXNotRecognizedException extends SAXException {
    public SAXNotRecognizedException(String message);
}
```

SAXNotSupportedException

This class provides a means for an XMLReader implementation to throw an error when an unsupported (but recognized) identifier is received. This is most common in the setProperty() and setFeature() methods (as well as their accessor counterparts) when a URI is supplied for which the parser has no supporting code.

```
public class SAXNotSupportedException extends SAXException {
    public SAXNotSupportedException(String message)
}
```

SAXParseException

This class represents exceptions that can occur during the parsing process. Information about the location of the error within the XML document is available through this class's accessor methods. The preferred means of supplying this information to the class is through a Locator, but the line and column number where problems occurred can be supplied directly through overloaded constructors. The system ID and public ID of the document with the problem are also made available to the class through various means in the constructors.

```
public class SAXParseException extends SAXException {
    public SAXParseException(String message, Locator locator);
    public SAXParseException(String message, Locator locator,
                             Exception e);
      public SAXParseException(String message, String publicId,
                               String systemId, int lineNumber,
                                   int columnNumber);
    public SAXParseException(String message, String publicId,
                             String systemId, int lineNumber,
                                 int columnNumber, Exception e);
    public String getPublicId();
    public String getSystemId();
    public int getColumnNumber();
}
```

XMLFilter

This class is analogous to an XMLReader, but it obtains its events from another XMLReader rather than a static document or network resource. These filters can also be chained on each other. Their primary use is in modifying the output from a lower-level XMLReader in the chain, providing filtering of the data reported to callback methods before the final application receives notification of the data.

```
public interface XMLFilter extends XMLReader {
    public abstract void setParent(XMLReader parent);
    public abstract XMLReader getParent();
}
```

XMLReader

This is the core interface that defines parsing behavior in SAX 2.0. Each vendor's XML parsing software package must include at least one implementation of this interface. It replaces the SAX 1.0 Parser interface by adding support for namespaces in a document's elements and attributes. In addition to providing an entry into parsing (with either a system ID or InputSource as input), it allows registering of the various handler interfaces that SAX 2.0 provides. The features and properties available to a SAX parser implementation are also set through this interface. A complete list of SAX core features and properties is contained in Appendix B.

```
public interface XMLReader {
    public boolean getFeature(String name)
        throws SAXNotRecognizedException, SAXNotSupportedException;
    public void setFeature(String name, boolean value)
            throws SAXNotRecognizedException, SAXNotSupportedException;
```

```
        public Object getProperty(String name)
                throws SAXNotRecognizedException, SAXNotSupportedException;
        public void setProperty(String name, Object value)
                throws SAXNotRecognizedException, SAXNotSupportedException;
        public void setEntityResolver(EntityResolver resolver);
        public EntityResolver getEntityResolver();
        public void setDTDHandler(DTDHandler handler);
        public DTDHandler getDTDHandler();
        public void setContentHandler(ContentHandler handler);
        public ContentHandler getContentHandler();
        public void setErrorHandler(ErrorHandler handler);
        public ErrorHandler getErrorHandler();
        public void parse(InputSource input)
                throws IOException, SAXException;
        public void parse(String systemId)
                throws IOException, SAXException;
    }
```

Package: org.xml.sax.ext

This package provides extensions to the SAX core classes and interfaces. Specifically, additional handlers are defined for less common processing within the SAX
parsing process. XMLReader implementations are not required to support these
extension handlers.

DeclHandler

This interface defines callbacks that give specific information about DTD declarations. Element and attribute definitions invoke the appropriate callback with their
names (and the element names for attributes) as well as constraint information.
While this is a fairly rigid set of data for attributes, elements only receive a String
with the constrained model as pure text. Additionally, internal and external entity
reference notifications are defined.

```
    public interface DeclHandler {
        public abstract void elementDecl(String name, String model)
                throws SAXException;
        public abstract void attributeDecl(String eName, String aName,
                                           String type, String valueDefault,
                                           String value)
                throws SAXException;
        public abstract void internalEntityDecl(String name, String value)
                throws SAXException;
        public abstract void externalEntityDecl(String name, String publicId,
                                                String systemId)
                throws SAXException;
    }
```

LexicalHandler

This interface defines callbacks for various events that are at a document level in terms of processing, but do not affect the resulting data within the XML document. For example, the handling of a DTD declaration, comments, and entity references would invoke callbacks in implementations of this interface. Additionally, a callback is defined to signal when a CDATA section is started and ended (although the reported data will always remain the same).

```
public interface LexicalHandler {
    public abstract void startDTD(String name, String publicId,
                                  String systemId)
            throws SAXException;
    public abstract void endDTD()
            throws SAXException;
    public abstract void startEntity(String name)
            throws SAXException;
    public abstract void endEntity(String name)
            throws SAXException;
    public abstract void startCDATA()
            throws SAXException;
    public abstract void endCDATA()
            throws SAXException;
    public abstract void comment(char ch[], int start, int length)
            throws SAXException;
}
```

Package: org.xml.sax.helpers

This package provides extensions to the SAX core classes and interfaces. Specifically, additional handlers are defined for less common processing within the SAX parsing process. XMLReader implementations are not required to support these extension handlers.

NOTE   In the classes in this package that are default implementations of core org.xml.sax interfaces, I have left out the repeated methods for brevity. Instead, I've simply added a comment indicating what interface's methods are implemented.

AttributeListImpl

This class provides a default implementation of the org.xml.sax. AttributeList interface, and is deprecated in SAX 2.0. It allows addition and removal of attributes as well as a clearing of the list.

```
public class AttributeListImpl implements AttributeList {
      public AttributeListImpl();
      public AttributeListImpl(AttributeList atts);

      // Implementation of AttributeList interface

      // Additional methods
      public void setAttributeList(AttributeList atts);
      public void addAttribute(String name, String type, String value);
      public void removeAttribute(String name);
      public void clear();

}
```

AttributesImpl

This class provides a default implementation of the `org.xml.sax.Attributes` interface. It allows addition and removal of attributes as well as a clearing of the list.

```
public class AttributesImpl implements Attributes {
      public AttributesImpl();
      public AttributesImpl(Attributes atts);

      // Implementation of Attributes interface

      // Additional methods
   public void addAttribute(String uri, String localName,
                            String qName, String type, String value);
   public void setAttribute(int index, String uri, String localName,
                            String qName, String type, String value);
      public void clear();
}
```

DefaultHandler

This helper class provides empty implementations of all the SAX 2.0 core handler interfaces, and can be extended to allow for quick addition of handlers by only overriding methods with application-defined behavior. This replaces the SAX 1.0 `org.xml.sax.HandlerBase` class.

```
public class DefaultHandler implements EntityResolver, DTDHandler,
                                ContentHandler, ErrorHandler {

      // (Empty) Implementation of EntityResolver interface

      // (Empty) Implementation of DTDHandler interface

      // (Empty) Implementation of ContentHandler interface
```

```
                    // (Empty) Implementation of ErrorHandler interface
    }
```

LocatorImpl

This class provides a default implementation of the `org.xml.sax.Locator` interface. It also provides a means of directly setting the line and column numbers.

```
public class LocatorImpl implements Locator {
        public LocatorImpl();
        public LocatorImpl(Locator locator);

        // Implementation of Locator interface

        // Additional methods
        public void setPublicId(String publicId);
        public void setSystemId(String systemId);
        public void setLineNumber(int lineNumber);
        public void setColumnNumber(int columnNumber);
    }
```

NamespaceSupport

This encapsulates namespace behavior, allowing applications to not have to implement the behavior on their own (unless desired for performance reasons). It allows handling of namespace contexts in a stack fashion, and also provides the ability to process XML 1.0 names, retrieving their "namespace-aware" counterparts.

```
public class NamespaceSupport {
        public NamespaceSuport();
        public void reset();
    public void pushContext();
    public void popContext();
    public boolean declarePrefix(String prefix, String uri);
    public String [] processName(String qName, String parts[],
                                 boolean isAttribute);
    public String getURI(String prefix);
    public Enumeration getPrefixes();
    public Enumeration getDeclaredPrefixes();
    }
```

ParserAdapter

This helper class wraps a SAX 1.0 `Parser` implementation and makes it behave like a 2.0 `XMLReader` implementation (making namespace support available). The only callback that does not behave normally is `skippedEntity()` in the `ContentHandler` interface; it is never invoked.

```
public class ParserAdapter implements XMLReader, DocumentHandler {
    public ParserAdapter() throws SAXException;
    public ParserAdapter(Parser parser);

    // Implementation of XMLReader interface

    // Implementation of DocumentHandler interface
}
```

ParserFactory

This class contains methods that dynamically create an instance of a `Parser` implementation from a specified class name, or if none is supplied, from a system property named "org.xml.sax.driver".

```
public class ParserFactory {
    public static Parser makeParser() throws ClassNotFoundException,
                IllegalAccessException, InstantiationException,
                NullPointerException, ClassCastException;
    public static Parser makeParser(String className)
                throws ClassNotFoundException, IllegalAccessException,
                InstantiationException, ClassCastException;
}
```

XMLFilterImpl

This class provides a default implementation of the `org.xml.sax.XMLFilter` interface.

```
public class XMLFilterImpl implements XMLFilter, EntityResolver,
                                      DTDHandler, ContentHandler,
                                      ErrorHandler {
    public XMLFilterImpl();
    public XMLFilterImpl(XMLReader parent);

    // Implementation of XMLFilter interface

    // Implementation of XMLReader interface

    // Implementation of EntityResolver interface

    // Implementation of DTDHandler interface

    // Implementation of ContentHandler interface

    // Implementation of ErrorHandler interface
}
```

XMLReaderAdapter

This helper class wraps a SAX 2.0 `XMLReader` implementation and makes it behave like a 1.0 `Parser` implementation (making namespace support unavailable). The namespaces feature (*http://xml.org/sax/features/namespaces*) must be supported, or errors in parsing will occur.

```
public class XMLReaderAdapter implements Parser, ContentHandler {
        public XMLReaderAdapter () throws SAXException;
        public XMLReaderAdapter (XMLReader xmlReader);

    // Implementation of Parser interface

        // Implementation of ContentHandler interface
}
```

XMLReaderFactory

This class contains methods that dynamically create an instance of an `XMLReader` implementation from a specified class name, or if none is supplied, from a system property named "org.xml.sax.driver".

```
final public class XMLReaderFactory {
    public static XMLReader createXMLReader() throws SAXException;
    public static XMLReader createXMLReader(String className)
            throws SAXException;
}
```

DOM Level 2

DOM provides a complete, in-memory representation of an XML document. Developed by the W3C, DOM provides detail about the structure of a document *after* it has been completely parsed. While DOM Level 3 will specify an API for getting the DOM `Document` object, there is currently nothing in DOM that defines this behavior. Like SAX, most of the core DOM package is made up of interfaces that define structures within an XML document, and map those structures to the Java language (these same mappings apply to CORBA, JavaScript, and other languages as well).

Package: org.w3c.dom

This package contains the core interfaces and classes for DOM Level 2. Typically a vendor's parsing software provides an implementation of those interfaces that are implicitly used by your application software.

Attr

This interface represents an XML attribute (on an element) within Java. It provides access to the name and value of the attribute, and allows the setting of the value (for mutability).* The `getSpecified()` method indicates if the attribute (and its value) was explicitly noted in the XML document, or if a value was not specified but the document's DTD assigned a default value to the attribute. Finally, the "owning" element can be obtained from this interface.

```
public interface Attr extends Node {
    public String getName();
    public boolean getSpecified();
    public String getValue();
    public void setValue(String value) throws DOMException;
    public Element getOwnerElement();
}
```

CDATASection

This interface does not define any methods of its own; instead it inherits all of the Text interface's methods. However, by having its own interface (and thus its own node type), a distinction can be drawn between text within XML CDATA sections and simple text (not in a CDATA section) within an element.

```
public interface CDATASection extends Text {
}
```

CharacterData

This interface is the "super" interface for all textual Node types in DOM (Text, Comment, and indirectly CDATASection). It defines methods for accessing and setting the data within a textual node, as well as a set of methods for dealing with the textual data directly as characters: obtaining the length, appending, inserting, and deleting data, and replacing all or part of the data. All of these methods throw DOMExceptions when the node is read-only.

```
public interface CharacterData extends Node {
    public String getData() throws DOMException;
    public void setData(String data) throws DOMException;
    public int getLength();
    public String substringData(int offset, int count)
        throws DOMException;
    public void appendData(String arg) throws DOMException;
    public void insertData(int offset, String arg) throws DOMException;
    public void deleteData(int offset, int count) throws DOMException;
```

---

* In this and other setXXX() methods in DOM, a DOMException results when a modification is attempted on a node that is read-only.

```
        public void replaceData(int offset, int count, String arg)
            throws DOMException;
    }
```

Comment

This interface provides a Java representation for an XML comment. Similar to
CDATASection, it adds no methods of its own but does allow a distinction (based
on the type of the interface) to distinguish between text and comments in an XML
document.

```
    public interface Comment extends CharacterData {
    }
```

Document

This interface is the DOM representation of a complete XML document. It is also
the key for creating new XML elements, attributes, PIs, and other constructs. In
addition to allowing retrieval of the DTD declaration (getDocType()) and root
element (getDocumentElement()), this allows searching through the tree in a
pre-order fashion for a specific element (getElementsByTagName()). Because
the DOM model requires that all Node implementations be tied to a DOM
Document object, this provides methods for creating the various types of DOM
Nodes. Each createXXX() method has a complement that supports namespaces
through createXXXNS(). Additionally, Nodes can be imported into this Document
through importNode(); the boolean value indicates if the children of the
imported Node should be recursively imported as well.

```
    public interface Document extends Node {
        public DocumentType getDoctype();
        public DOMImplementation getImplementation();
        public Element getDocumentElement();
        public Element createElement(String tagName) throws DOMException;
        public DocumentFragment createDocumentFragment();
        public Text createTextNode(String data);
        public Comment createComment(String data);
        public CDATASection createCDATASection(String data)
            throws DOMException;
        public ProcessingInstruction
            createProcessingInstruction(String target, String data)
            throws DOMException;
        public Attr createAttribute(String name) throws DOMException;
        public EntityReference createEntityReference(String name)
            throws DOMException;
        public NodeList getElementsByTagName(String tagname);
        public Node importNode(Node importedNode, boolean deep)
            throws DOMException;
        public Element createElementNS(String namespaceURI,
                                        String qualifiedName)
            throws DOMException;
```

```
       public Attr createAttributeNS(String namespaceURI,
                                      String qualifiedName)
           throws DOMException;
       public NodeList getElementsByTagNameNS(String namespaceURI,
                                              String localName);
       public Element getElementById(String elementId);
   }
```

DocumentFragment

This interface provides for dealing with only a portion of a complete Document object at one time. It is useful for manipulating portions of a DOM tree without having to store the entire tree in memory.

```
   public interface DocumentFragment extends Node {
   }
```

DocumentType

This interface represents an XML document's DOCTYPE declaration. The name is the element name immediately following <!DOCTYPE, and the system ID and public ID of any referenced DTD are available as well. Additionally, if any inline entities or notations are present, they can be obtained through the appropriate getXXX() methods.

```
   public interface DocumentType extends Node {
       public String getName();
       public NamedNodeMap getEntities();
       public NamedNodeMap getNotations();
       public String getPublicId();
       public String getSystemId();
       public String getInternalSubset();
   }
```

DOMException

This class provides an Exception for DOM interfaces to throw when problems occur. It also provides a set of error codes that represent the various problems that occur using DOM and might result in the Exception being thrown.

```
   public class DOMException extends RuntimeException {
       public DOMException(short code, String message);

       // Exception codes
       public static final short INDEX_SIZE_ERR;
       public static final short DOMSTRING_SIZE_ERR;
       public static final short HIERARCHY_REQUEST_ERR;
       public static final short WRONG_DOCUMENT_ERR;
       public static final short INVALID_CHARACTER_ERR;
```

```
    public static final short NO_DATA_ALLOWED_ERR;
    public static final short NO_MODIFICATION_ALLOWED_ERR;
    public static final short NOT_FOUND_ERR;
    public static final short NOT_SUPPORTED_ERR;
    public static final short INUSE_ATTRIBUTE_ERR;
    public static final short INVALID_STATE_ERR;
    public static final short SYNTAX_ERR;
    public static final short INVALID_MODIFICATION_ERR;
    public static final short NAMESPACE_ERR;
    public static final short INVALID_ACCESS_ERR;
}
```

DOMImplementation

This interface attempts to provide a standard entry point for accessing vendor-specific DOM implementations, and allowing the creation of a DocumentType and Document within those vendor implementations.* It also provides a method (hasFeature()) for querying the implementation for a specific feature support, like the DOM Level 2 Traversal or Range modules.

```
    public interface DOMImplementation {
        public boolean hasFeature(String feature, String version);
        public DocumentType createDocumentType(String qualifiedName,
                                               String publicId,
                                               String systemId)
            throws DOMException;
        public Document createDocument(String namespaceURI,
                                       String qualifiedName,
                                       DocumentType doctype)
            throws DOMException;
    }
```

Element

This interface provides a Java representation of an XML element. It provides methods to get its name and attributes, as well as to set these values. It also supplies several flavors of access to the XML attributes, including namespace-aware versions of the getXXX() and setXXX() methods.

```
    public interface Element extends Node {
        public String getTagName();
        public String getAttribute(String name);
        public void setAttribute(String name, String value)
            throws DOMException;
```

---

* Unfortunately, to obtain an instance of a DOMImplementation, you must have a Document object and use getDOMImplementation(), or directly load the vendor's classes. This tends to result in a chicken-and-egg scenario; see Chapters 5 and 6 for more details.

```
    public void removeAttribute(String name) throws DOMException;
    public Attr getAttributeNode(String name);
    public Attr setAttributeNode(Attr newAttr) throws DOMException;
    public Attr removeAttributeNode(Attr oldAttr) throws DOMException;
    public NodeList getElementsByTagName(String name);
    public String getAttributeNS(String namespaceURI, String localName);
    public void setAttributeNS(String namespaceURI, String qualifiedName,
                            String value)
        throws DOMException;
    public void removeAttributeNS(String namespaceURI, String localName)
                            throws DOMException;
    public Attr getAttributeNodeNS(String namespaceURI, String localName);
    public Attr setAttributeNodeNS(Attr newAttr) throws DOMException;
    public NodeList getElementsByTagNameNS(String namespaceURI,
                                    String localName);
    public boolean hasAttribute(String name);
    public boolean hasAttributeNS(String namespaceURI, String localName);
}
```

Entity

This provides a Java representation of an entity (parsed or unparsed) in an XML document. Access to the system ID and public ID as well as the notation for the entity (from the DTD) is provided through accessor methods.

```
public interface Entity extends Node {
    public String getPublicId();
    public String getSystemId();
    public String getNotationName();
}
```

EntityReference

This interface represents the resulting value from an entity reference once the entity has been resolved. This interface assumes that character and predefined entity references have already occurred when this interface is exposed to the application client.

```
public interface EntityReference extends Node {
}
```

NamedNodeMap

This interface defines a list, much like NodeList, but requires that each Node in the list be a named Node (such as an Element or Attr). Because of this requirement, methods can be provided to access members of the list by their names (with or without namespace support). The list also provides for removal and modification of its members. These methods all throw DOMExceptions when the referenced Node is read-only.

```
public interface NamedNodeMap {
    public Node getNamedItem(String name);
    public Node setNamedItem(Node arg) throws DOMException;
    public Node removeNamedItem(String name) throws DOMException;
    public Node item(int index);
    public int getLength();
    public Node getNamedItemNS(String namespaceURI, String localName);
    public Node setNamedItemNS(Node arg) throws DOMException;
    public Node removeNamedItemNS(String namespaceURI, String localName)
        throws DOMException;
}
```

Node

This is the central interface for all DOM objects. It provides a robust set of methods for accessing information about a Node in the DOM tree. It also allows for
handling of a Node's children (if they exist). While most of the methods are self-
explanatory, there are several methods worth noting: getAttributes() only
returns non-null data if the Node is an Element; cloneNode() provides for a
shallow or deep copy of a Node; normalize() moves all text into non-adjacent
Text nodes (no two Text nodes are adjacent, and all resolved textual entity references are consolidated into Text nodes); and isSupported() provides information about the feature set of the Node. Namespace-aware methods are also
provided (getNamespaceURI(), getPrefix(), and getLocalName()). Finally, a
set of constants is provided for identifying the type of a Node by comparing the
constants against the result of getNodeType().

```
public interface Node {
    public String getNodeName();
    public String getNodeValue() throws DOMException;
    public void setNodeValue(String nodeValue) throws DOMException;
    public short getNodeType();
    public Node getParentNode();
    public NodeList getChildNodes();
    public Node getFirstChild();
    public Node getLastChild();
    public Node getPreviousSibling();
    public Node getNextSibling();
    public NamedNodeMap getAttributes();
    public Document getOwnerDocument();
    public Node insertBefore(Node newChild,  Node refChild)
        throws DOMException;
    public Node replaceChild(Node newChild, Node oldChild)
                        throws DOMException;
    public Node removeChild(Node oldChild) throws DOMException;
    public Node appendChild(Node newChild) throws DOMException;
```

```
    public boolean hasChildNodes();
    public Node cloneNode(boolean deep);
    public void normalize();
    public boolean isSupported(String feature, String version);
    public String getNamespaceURI();
    public String getPrefix();
    public void setPrefix(String prefix) throws DOMException;
    public String getLocalName();
    public boolean hasAttributes();

    // Node Type Constants
    public static final short ELEMENT_NODE;
    public static final short ATTRIBUTE_NODE;
    public static final short TEXT_NODE;
    public static final short CDATA_SECTION_NODE;
    public static final short ENTITY_REFERENCE_NODE;
    public static final short ENTITY_NODE;
    public static final short PROCESSING_INSTRUCTION_NODE;
    public static final short COMMENT_NODE;
    public static final short DOCUMENT_NODE;
    public static final short DOCUMENT_TYPE_NODE;
    public static final short DOCUMENT_FRAGMENT_NODE;
    public static final short NOTATION_NODE;
}
```

NodeList

This interface is a DOM structure analogous to a Java `Vector` or `List`. It is the
return value of any method that supports multiple `Node` implementations as a
result. This allows iteration through the items as well as providing the ability to get
a `Node` at a specific index.

```
public interface NodeList {
    public Node item(int index);
    public int getLength();
}
```

Notation

This interface represents a `NOTATION` construct in a DTD, used to declare the format of an unparsed entity or for declaration of PIs. This provides access to both
the system ID and public ID within the declaration. Both return `null` if they are
not present.

```
public interface Notation extends Node {
    public String getPublicId();
    public String getSystemId();
}
```

ProcessingInstruction

This interface represents an XML processing instruction (PI). It provides methods for getting the target and the data of the PI. Note that there is no means of accessing the "name/value" pairs within the PI individually. The data can also be set for the PI.

```
public interface ProcessingInstruction extends Node {
    public String getTarget();
    public String getData();
    public void setData(String data) throws DOMException;
}
```

Text

This interface provides a Java representation of an XML element's textual data. The only method it adds to those defined in CharacterData is one that will split the node into two nodes. The original Text node contains text up to the specified offset, and the method returns a new Text node with the text after the offset. Like other mutability methods, a DOMException is thrown when the node is read-only.

```
public interface Text extends CharacterData {
    public Text splitText(int offset) throws DOMException;
}
```

JAXP 1.1

JAXP provides an abstraction layer over the process of getting a vendor's implementation of a SAX or DOM parser, as well as providing transformations in a vendor-neutral way.

Package: javax.xml.parsers

This is the single package used in JAXP, and details the classes needed for the JAXP abstraction and pluggability layer over XML parsing.

DocumentBuilder

This class is the wrapper over an underlying parser implementation class. It allows parsing to occur in a vendor-neutral way.

```
public abstract class DocumentBuilder {
    public Document parse(InputStream stream)
        throws SAXException, IOException, IllegalArgumentException;
    public Document parse(InputStream stream, String systemID)
        throws SAXException, IOException, IllegalArgumentException;
    public Document parse(String uri)
        throws SAXException, IOException, IllegalArgumentException;
```

```
    public Document parse(File file)
        throws SAXException, IOException, IllegalArgumentException;
    public abstract Document parse(InputSource source)
        throws SAXException, IOException, IllegalArgumentException;

    public abstract Document newDocument();
    public abstract boolean isNamespaceAware();
    public abstract boolean isValidating();
    public abstract void setEntityResolver(EntityResolver er);
    public abstract void setErrorHandler(ErrorHandler eh);
    public DOMmplementation getDOMImplementation();
}
```

DocumentBuilderFactory

This class is the factory used to create instances of the DocumentBuilder class,
and allows namespace and validation features to be set for the production of those
instances.

```
public abstract class DocumentBuilderFactory {
    public static DocumentBuilderFactory newInstance();
    public abstract DocumentBuilder newDocumentBuilder()
        throws ParserConfigurationException;

    public void setAttribute(String name, Object value);
    public void setCoalescing(boolean coalescing);
    public void setExpandEntityReferences(boolean expand);
    public void setIgnoringComments(boolean ignoreComments);
    public void setIgnoringElementContentWhitespace(boolean ignoreWhitespace);
    public void setNamespaceAware(boolean aware);
    public void setValidating(boolean validating);

    public boolean isCoalescing();
    public boolean isExapandEntityReferences();
    public boolean isIgnoringComments();
    public boolean isIgnoreingElementContentWhitespace();
    public boolean isNamespaceAware();
    public boolean isValidating();
    public Object getAttribute(String name);
}
```

FactoryConfigurationError

This defines an Error that is thrown if a factory instance cannot be created.

```
public class FactoryConfigurationException extends Error {
    public FactoryConfigurationError();
    public FactoryConfigurationError(String msg);
    public FactoryConfigurationError(Exception e);
    public FactoryConfigurationError(Exception e, String msg);
}
```

ParserConfigurationException

This defines an `Exception` that is thrown if a parser is requested but cannot be constructed with the specified validation and namespace-awareness settings.

```
public class ParserConfigurationException extends Exception {
    public ParserConfigurationException();
    public ParserConfigurationException(String msg);
}
```

SAXParser

This class is the wrapper over an underlying SAX 1.0/2.0 parser implementation class, and allows parsing to occur in a vendor-neutral way. It essentially has a pair of each method: one for SAX 1.0, and one for SAX 2.0.

```
public abstract class SAXParser {
    public void parse(InputStream stream, HandlerBase base)
        throws SAXException, IOException, IllegalArgumentException;
    public void parse(InputStream stream, HandlerBase base, String systemID)
        throws SAXException, IOException, IllegalArgumentException;
    public void parse(String uri, HandlerBase base)
        throws SAXException, IOException, IllegalArgumentException;
    public void parse(File file, HandlerBase base)
        throws SAXException, IOException, IllegalArgumentException;
    public void parse(InputSource source, HandlerBase base)
        throws SAXException, IOException, IllegalArgumentException;

    public void parse(InputStream stream, DefaultHandler dh)
        throws SAXException, IOException, IllegalArgumentException;
    public void parse(InputStream stream, DefaultHandler dh, String systemID)
        throws SAXException, IOException, IllegalArgumentException;
    public void parse(String uri, DefaultHandler dh)
        throws SAXException, IOException, IllegalArgumentException;
    public void parse(File file, DefaultHandler dh)
        throws SAXException, IOException, IllegalArgumentException;
    public void parse(InputSource source, DefaultHandler dh)
        throws SAXException, IOException, IllegalArgumentException;

    public Parser getParser() throws SAXException;
    public XMLReader getXMLReader() throws SAXException;

    public Object getProperty(String name);
    public void setProperty(String name, Object value);
    public boolean isNamespaceAware();
    public boolean isValidating();
}
```

SAXParserFactory

This class is the factory used to create instances of the SAXParser class, and allows namespace and validation features to be set for the production of those instances.

```
public abstract class SAXParserFactory {
    public static SAXParserFactory newInstance();
    public SAXParser newSAXParser()
        throws ParserConfigurationException, SAXException;

    public void setNamespaceAware(boolean aware);
    public void setValidating(boolean validating);
    public void setFeature(String name, boolean value);
    public boolean isNamespaceAware();
    public boolean isValidating();
    public boolean getFeature(String name);
}
```

Package: javax.xml.transform

This is the package used in JAXP for transforming XML documents. It allows these transformations to be pluggable and vendor-neutral, provided they use the TrAX (Transformations API for XML) interfaces defined here.

ErrorListener

This interface is analogous to ErrorHandler in SAX, and provides error notification for transformations. Implement it in your own applications using TrAX.

```
public interface ErrorListener {
    public void warning(TransformerException exception);
    public void error(TransformerException exception);
    public void fatalError(TransformerException exception);
}
```

OutputKeys

This class is just a holder for several static constants used in the rest of the TrAX API.

```
public class OutputKeys {
    public static final String CDATA_SECTION_ELEMENTS;
    public static final String DOCTYPE_PUBLIC;
    public static final String DOCTYPE_SYSTEM;
    public static final String ENCODING;
    public static final String INDENT;
    public static final String MEDIA_TYPE;
    public static final String METHOD;
    public static final String OMIT_XML_DECLARATION;
```

```
        public static final String STANDALONE;
        public static final String VERSION;
    }
```

Result

This interface provides for output of XML transformations. Default implementations of this interface are provided in the JAXP javax.xml.transform.* packages.

```
    public interface Result {
        public static final String PI_DISABLE_OUTPUT_ESCAPING;
        public static final String PI_ENABLE_OUTPUT_ESCAPING;

        public String getSystemId();
        public void setSystemId();
    }
```

Source

This interface provides for input of XML transformations. Default implementations of this interface are provided in the JAXP javax.xml.transform.* packages.

```
    public interface Source {
        public String getSystemId();
        public void setSystemId();
    }
```

SourceLocator

This interface is analogous to the SAX Locator interface, and details location information about an input to TrAX. Like ErrorListener, it's most useful in error handling and reporting.

```
    public interface SourceLocator {
        public int getColumnNumber();
        public int getLineNumber();
        public String getPublicId();
        public String getSystemId();
    }
```

Templates

This interface is provided to perform a means of optimal transformations using the same stylesheet. Its only methods allow for generation of Transformer instances, and viewing its current set of output properties.

```
    public interface Tempaltes {
        public Properties getOutputProperties();
        public Transformer newTransformer();
    }
```

Transformer

This is the core (abstract) class for providing XML transformation facilities through TrAX and JAXP. In addition to setting the various properties and objects on the interface, you can perform the actual transformation with the `transform()` method.

```
public class Transformer {
    public void setErrorListener(ErrorListener errorListener);
    public ErrorListener getErrorListener();
    public void setURIResolver(URIResolver resolver);
    public URIResolver getURIResolver();

    public void setOutputProperties(Properties properties);
    public Properties getOutputProperties();
    public void setOutputProperty(String name, String value);
    public String getOutputProperty(String name);
    public void clearParmaters();
    public void setParameter(String name, String value);
    public Object getParameter(String name);

    public void transform(Source xmlSource, Result outputTarget);
}
```

TransformerFactory

This is the other "half" of the transformation engine in JAXP. You can specify the stylesheet to use for transformation, and then obtain new instances of a `Transformer` instance. You can also use this to generate a new `Templates` object for multiple transformations using the same stylesheet.

```
public class TransformerFactory {
    public TransformerFactory newInstance();
    public Transformer newTemplates(Source stylesheet);
    public Transformer newTransformer(Source stylesheet);
    public Transformer newTransformer();

    public Source getAssociatedStylesheet(Source source, String media,
                                          String title, String charset);
    public ErrorListener getErrorListener();
    public void setErrorListener(ErrorListener errorListener);
    public URIResolver getURIResolver();
    public void setURIResolver(URIResolver uriResolver);
    public Object getAttribute(String name);
    public void setAttribute(String name, String value);
    public boolean getFeature(String name);
}
```

URIResolver

This is the interface responsible for URI resolution, and is analogous to the SAX `EntityResolver` interface.

```
public interface URIResolver {
    public Source resolve(String href, String base);
}
```

Package: javax.xml.transform.dom

This package provides two classes: `DOMResult` and `DOMSource`. These are implementations of the `Result` and `Source` interfaces, and are used when DOM trees should be the input and output of a transformation. Because these are simple implementation classes, their methods are not detailed here; however, their usage is covered in detail in Chapter 9.

Package: javax.xml.transform.sax

This package provides two classes: `SAXResult` and `SAXSource`. These are implementations of the `Result` and `Source` interfaces, and are used when SAX events should be the input and output of a transformation. Because these are simple implementation classes, their methods are not detailed here; however, their usage is covered in detail in Chapter 9.

Package: javax.xml.transform.stream

This package provides two classes: `StreamResult` and `StreamSource`. These are implementations of the `Result` and `Source` interfaces, and are used when I/O streams should be the input and output of a transformation. Because these are simple implementation classes, their methods are not detailed here; however, their usage is covered in detail in Chapter 9.

JDOM 1.0 (Beta 7)

JDOM 1.0 (beta 7), detailed in Chapters 7 and 8, provides a complete view of an XML document within a tree model. Although this model is similar to DOM, it is not as rigid a representation; this allows the content of an `Element`, for example, to be set directly, instead of setting the value of the child of that `Element`. Additionally, JDOM provides concrete classes rather than interfaces, allowing instantiation of objects directly rather than through the use of a factory. SAX and DOM are only used in JDOM for the construction of a JDOM `Document` object from existing XML data, and are detailed in the `org.jdom.input` package.

Package: org.jdom

This package contains the core classes for JDOM 1.0.* These consist of XML objects modeled in Java and a set of Exceptions that can be thrown when errors occur.†

Attribute

Attribute defines behavior for an XML attribute, modeled in Java. Methods allow the user to obtain the value of the attribute as well as namespace information about the attribute. An instance can be created with the name of the attribute and its value, or the Namespace and local name, as well as the value, of the attribute. Several convenience methods are also provided for automatic data conversion of the attribute's value.

```
public class Attribute {
    public Attribute(String name, String value);
    public Attribute(String name, String value, Namespace ns);

    public Element getParent();
    public String getName();
    public Namespace getNamespace();
    public void setNamespace(Namespace ns);
    public String getQualifiedName();
    public String getNamespacePrefix();
    public String getNamespaceURI();
    public String getValue();
    public void setValue(String value);

    public Object clone();
    public boolean equals(Object obj);
    public int hashCode();
    public String toString();

    // Convenience Methods for Data Conversion
    public String get StringValue(String default Value);
    public int getIntValue() throws DataConversionException;
    public long getLongValue() throws DataConversionException;
    public float getFloatValue() throws DataConversionException;
    public double getDoubleValue() throws DataConversionException;
    public boolean getBooleanValue() throws DataConversionException;
}
```

---

* Please note that while the JDOM API is fairly stable, it is still in beta. Minor changes may occur after the publication of this book. Please consult *http://www.jdom.org* for the latest JDOM classes.

† To avoid complete boredom in this section, I've left out all the JDOM exceptions aside from the core one, JDOMException. I'd rather focus on the classes rather than the odd exceptional condition.

CDATA

The CDATA class defines behavior for XML CDATA sections.

```
public class CDATA {
    public CDATA(String text);

    public String getText();

    public Object clone();
    public boolean equals(Object obj);
    public int hashCode();
    public String toString();
}
```

Comment

Comment is a simple representation of an XML comment, and contains the text within the XML comment.

```
public class Comment {
    public Comment(String text);

    public Document getDocument();
    public Element getParent();
    public String getText();
    public void setText(String text);

    public Object clone();
    public boolean equals(Object obj);
    public int hashCode();
    public String toString();
}
```

DocType

DocType represents a DOCTYPE declaration within an XML document. It includes information about the element name being constrained, as well as the public ID and system ID of the external DTD reference, if one is present.

```
public class DocType {
    public DocType(String elementName, String publicID, String systemID);
    public DocType(String elementName, String systemID);
    public DocType(String elementName);

    public Document getDocument();
    public String getElementName();
    public String getPublicID();
    public DocType setPublicID(String publicID);
    public String getSystemID();
    public DocType setSystemID(String systemID);
```

```
        public Object clone();
        public boolean equals(Object obj);
        public int hashCode();
        public String toString();
    }
```

Document

Document models an XML document in Java. Document requires that it be created with a root Element, although that Element can be replaced with setRootElement(). The getContent() method returns all the content of the Document, which includes the root Element and any Comments that may exist at the document level in the XML document.

```
    public class Document {
        public Document(Element rootElement, DocType docType);
        public Document(Element rootElement);
        public Document(List content);
        public Document(List content, DocType docType);

        public Document addContent(Comment comment);
        public Document removeContent(Comment comment);
        public Document addContent(ProcessingInstruction pi);
        public Document removeContent(ProcessingInstruction pi);
        public Element getRootElement() throws NoSuchElementException;
        public Document setRootElement(Element rootElement);
        public DocType getDocType();
        public Document setDocType(DocType docType);
        public List getContent();
        public void setMixedContent(List content);

        public Object clone();
        public boolean equals(Object obj);
        public int hashCode();
        public String toString();
    }
```

Element

Element is a Java representation of an XML element. It is completely namespace-aware, so all methods take in a single element name as an argument, as well as optional namespace information. The result of calls to getText() is always a String, either the textual content of the XML element or an empty String. An Element is considered to have mixed content when it has a combination of textual data and nested elements, as well as optional comments, entities, and processing instructions. This complete List of content can be obtained with getContent(), and the results in the List evaluated through instanceof against a String, Element, or Comment.

The addXXX() methods are designed to be chained together, and therefore return the modified Element:

```
Element element = new Element("root");
element.addChild(new Element("child")
    .addChild(new Element("grandchild")
        .addAttribute("name", "value")
        .setContent("Hello World!"))
    .addChild(new Element("anotherChild"))
);
```

This would result in the following XML document fragment:

```
<root>
  <child>
    <grandchild name="value">
      Hello World!
    </grandchild>
  </child>
  <anotherChild />
</root>
```

Here's the API listing:

```
public class Element {
    public Element(String name);
    public Element(String name, String uri);
    public Element(String name, String prefix, String uri);
    public Element(String name, Namespace ns);

    public Document getDocument();
    public Element getParent();
    public Element detach();
    public String getName();
    public void setName(String name);
    public Namespace getNamespace();
    public Namespace getNamespace(String prefix);
    public void setNamespace(Namespace ns);
    public String getNamespacePrefix();
    public String getNamespaceURI();
    public String getQualifiedName();
    public void addNamespaceDeclaration(Namespace additionalNS);
    public void removeNamespaceDeclaration(Namespace additionalNS);
    public List getAdditionalNamespaces();

    public List getContent();
    public Element setMixedContent(List mixedContent);
    public Element addContent(CDATA cdata);
    public Element addContent(Comment comment);
    public Element addContent(Element element);
    public Element addContent(EntityRef entityRef);
```

```
public Element addContent(ProcessingInstruction pi);
public Element addContent(String text);
public boolean removeContent(CDATA cdata);
public boolean removeContent(Comment comment);
public boolean removeContent(Element element);
public boolean removeContent(EntityRef entityRef);
public boolean removeContent(ProcessingInstruction pi);

public boolean hasChildren();
public Element getChild(String name);
public Element getChild(String name, Namespace ns);
public List getChildren();
public List getChildren(String name);
public List getChildren(String name, Namespace ns);
public boolean removeChild(String name);
public boolean removeChild(String name, Namespace ns);
public boolean removeChildren();
public boolean removeChildren(String name);
public boolean removeChildren(String name, Namespace ns);
public Element setChildren(List children);

public Attribute getAttribute(String name);
public Attribute getAttribute(String name, Namespace ns);
public List getAttributes();
public String getAttributeValue(String name);
public String getAttributeValue(String name, Namespace ns);
public boolean removeAttribute(String name);
public boolean removeAttribute(String name, Namespace ns);
public Element setAttribute(Attribute attribute);
public Element setAttributes(List attributes);

public String getChildText(String name);
public String getChildText(String name, Namespace ns);
public String getChildTextTrim(String name);
public String getChildTextTrim(String name, Namespace ns);
public String getText();
public String getTextNormalize();
public String getTextTrim();
public Element setText(String text);

public boolean isRootElement();

public Object clone();
public boolean equals(Object obj);
public int hashCode();
public String toString();
}
```

EntityRef

This class defines a JDOM model for entity references in XML documents. It allows for setting and accessing of the reference's name, public ID, and system ID.

```
public class EntityRef {
    public EntityRef(String name);
    public EntityRef(String name, String publicID, String systemID);

    public Document getDocument();
    public Element getParent();
    public String getName();
    public EntityRef setName(String name);
    public String getPublicID();
    public void setPublicID(String publicID);
    public String getSystemID();
    public void setSystemID(String systemID);
    public EntityRef detach();

    public Object clone();
    public boolean equals(Object obj);
    public int hashCode();
    public String toString();
}
```

JDOMException

This is the core JDOM Exception that other JDOM Exception classes subclass. It provides for error messages as well as the wrapping of a root cause Exception, in the case that a JDOMException needs to wrap a lower-level Exception.

```
public class JDOMException extends Exception {
    public JDOMException();
    public JDOMException(String message);
    public JDOMException(String message, Throwable rootCause);

    public Throwable getCause();
    public String getMessage();
}
```

Namespace

The Namespace class handles namespace mappings used in JDOM objects.

```
public class Namespace {
    public static Namespace getNamespace(String uri);
    public static Namespace getNamespace(String prefix, String uri);

    public String getPrefix();
    public String getURI();
```

```
        public boolean equals(Object obj);
        public int hashCode();
        public String toString();
    }
```

ProcessingInstruction

ProcessingInstruction defines behavior for an XML processing instruction, modeled in Java. It allows specific handling for the target as well as the raw data for the target. Additionally, as many PIs use data in the form of name-value pairs (much like attributes), this allows retrieval and addition of name-value pairs. For example, in the <?cocoon-process type="xslt"?> processing instruction, invoking getValue("type") on the ProcessingInstruction representing that XML PI would return "xslt".

```
    public class ProcessingInstruction {
        public ProcessingInstruction(String target, Map data);
        public ProcessingInstruction(String target, String data);

        public ProcessingInstruction detach();
        public Document getDocument();
        public Element getParent();
        public String getTarget();
        public String getData();
        public ProcessingInstruction setData(String data);
        public ProcessingInstruction setData(Map data);
        public String getValue(String name);
        public ProcessingInstruction setValue(String name, String value);
        public boolean removeValue(String name);

        public Object clone();
        public boolean equals(Object obj);
        public int hashCode();
        public String toString();
    }
```

Text

This class represents character data "owned" by a JDOM Element. It is generally invisible to the user, as the Element class converts this class to a simple String when the value is requested. It is only exposed through an Element's getContent() method.

```
    public class Text {
        public Text(String stringValue);

        public Element getParent();
        public void append(String stringValue);
```

```
    public String getValue();
    public void setValue(String stringValue);

    public Object clone();
    public boolean equals(Object obj);
    public int hashCode();
    public String toString();
}
```

Package: org.jdom.adapters

This package contains adapters that allow a standard interface for obtaining a
DOM Document object from any DOM parser (including DOM Level 1 parsers).
Adapters can be easily added for any parser that desires to have JDOM support.

AbstractDOMAdapter

This class provides default behavior for the version of getDocument() that takes
in a filename by wrapping the file in a FileOutputStream and delegating invocation to getDocument(InputStream).

```
    public abstract class AbstractDOMAdapter implements DOMAdapter {
        public abstract Document getDocument(InputStream in, boolean validate)
            throws IOException;
        public abstract Document getDocument(File filename, boolean validate)
            throws IOException;
        public abstract Document createDocument(DocType docType)
            throws IOException;
    }
```

DOMAdapter

This class defines the interface that adapters must implement. This includes a
means to produce a DOM Document from a filename or an InputStream, as well
as a means of obtaining a new, empty DOM Document object.

```
    public interface DOMAdapter {
        public abstract Document getDocument(InputStream in, boolean validate)
            throws IOException;
        public abstract Document getDocument(File filename, boolean validate)
            throws IOException;
        public abstract Document createDocument(DocType docType)
            throws IOException;
    }
```

Specific adapter classes are not detailed here, as additions and modifications may
be made during publication of the book. As of this writing, functional adapters are
provided for the following parsers:

- Oracle Version 1 XML Parser

- Oracle Version 2 XML Parser

- Sun Project X Parser

- Sun/Apache Crimson Parser

- Apache Xerces Parser

- IBM XML4J Parser

Package: org.jdom.input

This package defines the classes for building a JDOM `Document` object from various input sources, such as SAX streams and existing DOM trees. It also provides an interface for using customized versions of the JDOM classes, like user-defined subclasses of `Element` and `Attribute`.

BuilderErrorHandler

This is the default error handler used for JDOM document construction.

```
public class BuilderErrorHandler
    implements org.xml.sax.ErrorHandler {

    public void warning(SAXParserException exception);
    public void error(SAXParserException exception);
    public void fatalError(SAXParserException exception);
}
```

DOMBuilder

This class provides the ability to create a JDOM `Document` object from an XML input source using a parser that supports DOM, the Document Object Model. It uses the various adapters in `org.jdom.adapters`, so if a parser is requested for which there is no adapter, errors occur. Additionally, a method is provided for building a JDOM `Document` object from an existing DOM tree (`org.w3c.dom.Document`). When the `DOMBuilder` is constructed, validation can be requested, as can the class name of the adapter to use. If neither is supplied, the default behavior occurs: no validation takes place and the Apache Xerces parser is used.

You can also set the factory to use (see the `JDOMFactory` entry) for generating JDOM classes in the build process.

```
public class DOMBuilder {
    public DOMBuilder(String adapterClass, boolean validate);
    public DOMBuilder(String adapterClass);
    public DOMBuilder(boolean validate);
    public DOMBuilder();
```

```
public Document build(InputStream in);
public Document build(File file);
public Document build(URL url);
public Document build(org.w3c.dom.Document domDocument);
public Element build(org.w3c.dom.Element domElement);

public void setValidation(boolean validate);
public void setFactory(JDOMFactory factory);
}
```

JDOMFactory

This interface allows users to provide their own factories that produce JDOM constructs (`Element`, `Attribute`, etc.). When a factory implementation is passed to a builder using the `setFactory()` method, this is used for creating new JDOM constructs. It allows complete customization of the JDOM object creation process.

For the sake of brevity and clarity, I'm not going to include the very extensive list of methods available to this factory, but instead refer you to the Javadoc. Every possible construction of every JDOM class is included in this class, and all these methods return the type of object being constructed.

SAXBuilder

This class provides the ability to create a JDOM `Document` object from an XML input source using a parser that supports SAX, the Simple API for XML. It can use any SAX parser implementation that is SAX 2.0–compliant. When the `SAXBuilder` is constructed, validation can be requested, as well as the class name of the SAX driver to use. If neither is supplied, the default behavior occurs: no validation takes place and the Apache Xerces parser is used.

You can also set the factory to use (see the `JDOMFactory` entry) for generating JDOM classes in the build process.

```
public class SAXBuilder {
    public SAXBuilder(String saxDriverClass, boolean validate);
    public SAXBuilder(String saxDriverClass);
    public SAXBuilder(boolean validate);
    public SAXBuilder();

    public Document build(InputStream in);
    public Document build(InputStream in, String systemID);
    public Document build(InputSource inputSource);
    public Document build(Reader characterStream);
    public Document build(Reader characterStream, String systemID);
    public Document build(File file);
    public Document build(URL url);
```

```
        public Document build(org.w3c.dom.Document domDocument);
        public Element build(org.w3c.dom.Element domElement);

        public void setDTDHandler(DTDHandler dtdHandler);
        public void setEntityResolver(EntityResolver entityResolver);
        public void setErrorHandler(ErrorHandler errorHandler);
        public void setExpandEntities(boolean expandEntities);
        public void setXMLFilter(XMLFilter xmlFilter);
        public void setIgnoringElementContentWhitespace(boolean ignore);
        public void setValidation(boolean validate);
        public void setFactory(JDOMFactory factory);
    }
```

Package: org.jdom.output

This package defines behavior for output of JDOM Document objects. Of particular note is the SAXOutputter class, which allows a JDOM Document to fire SAX events off to an application expecting SAX behavior, and DOMOutputter, which converts from JDOM to DOM structures. And, of course, XMLOutputter is by far the most common output class for JDOM objects. Like some of the classes in the org.jdom.input package, these three classes have, literally, hundreds of methods between them. Rather than fill ten pages with this rather boring information, I'll again refer you to the Javadoc online at *http://www.jdom.org*. That will have the most current options for using any of the JDOM outputter classes.

B

SAX 2.0 Features and Properties

This appendix describes the SAX 2.0 standard features and properties. Although a vendor's parsing software can add additional features and properties for vendor-specific functionality, this list represents the core set of functionality that any SAX 2.0–compliant parser implementation should support.

Core Features

The core set of features supported by SAX 2.0 XMLReader implementations is listed here. These features can be set through setFeature(), and the value of a feature can be obtained through getFeature(). Any feature can be read-only or read/write; features also may be modifiable only when parsing is occurring, or only when parsing is not occurring. For more information on SAX features and properties, refer to Chapters 2 and 3.

Namespace Processing

This feature instructs a parser to perform namespace processing, which causes namespace prefixes, namespace URIs, and element local names to be available through the SAX namespace callbacks (startPrefixMapping() and endPrefixMapping(), as well as certain parameters supplied to startElement() and endElement()). When this feature is true, the processing will occur. When false, namespace processing will not occur (this implies that the namespace prefix reporting feature is on). The default in most parsers is true.

> URI: *http://xml.org/sax/features/namespaces*
> Access: Read-only when parsing, read/write when not parsing

Namespace Prefix Reporting

This feature instructs a parser to report the attributes used in namespace declarations, such as the xmlns:[namespace URI] attributes. When this feature is not on (false), namespace-related attributes are not reported, as the parser consumes them in order to discover a namespace prefix to URI mappings, and they are generally not of value to the wrapping application in that context. In addition, when namespace processing is turned on, generally namespace prefix mapping is turned off. The default in most parsers is false.

> URI: *http://xml.org/sax/features/namespace-prefixes*
> Access: Read-only when parsing, read/write when not parsing

String Interning

This feature dictates that all element raw and local names, namespace prefixes, and namespace URIs are interned using java.lang.String.intern(). When not on (false), all XML components are left as is. Newer, high-performance parsers usually have this set to false by default, so they can perform their own optimizations for dealing with character data.

> URI: *http://xml.org/sax/features/string-interning*
> Access: Read-only when parsing, read/write when not parsing

Validation

This feature requests that validation occur and that any errors as a result of broken constraints be reported through the SAX ErrorHandler interface (if an implementation is registered). When set to false, no validation occurs, which is generally the default setting. You'll need to check your parser vendor's documentation to determine if this feature applies to both DTD and XML Schema validation.

> URI: *http://xml.org/sax/features/validation*
> Access: Read-only when parsing, read/write when not parsing

Process External Entities (General)

This feature requests that all general (textual) entities be processed within an XML document. Generally set to true in most parsers by default.

> URI: *http://xml.org/sax/features/external-general-entities*
> Access: Read-only when parsing, read/write when not parsing

Process External Entities (Parameter)

This feature requests that all external parameters be parsed, including those in any external DTD's subset. By default, this is also usually true in most parsers.

> URI: *http://xml.org/sax/features/external-parameter-entities*
> Access: Read-only when parsing, read/write when not parsing

Core Properties

Properties provide a way to deal with objects used in the parsing process, particularly when dealing with handlers such as `LexicalHandler` and `DeclHandler` that are not in the core set of SAX 2.0 handlers (`EntityResolver`, `DTDHandler`, `ContentHandler`, and `ErrorHandler`). Any property can be read-only or read/write; features also may be modifiable only when parsing is occurring, or only when parsing is not occurring.

Lexical Handler

This property allows the setting and retrieval of a `LexicalHandler` implementation to be used for handling of comments and DTD references within an XML document.

> URI: *http://xml.org/sax/properties/lexical-handler*
> Datatype: `org.xml.sax.ext.LexicalHandler`
> Access: Read/write when parsing, read/write when not parsing

Declaration Handler

This property allows the setting and retrieval of a `DeclHandler` implementation to be used for handling of constraints within a DTD.

> URI: *http://xml.org/sax/properties/declaration-handler*
> Datatype: `org.xml.sax.ext.DeclHandler`
> Access: Read/write when parsing, read/write when not parsing

DOM Node

When parsing is occurring, this property retrieves the current DOM node (if a DOM iterator is being used). When parsing is not occurring, it retrieves the root DOM node. Most of the parsers I used in testing for this book did not support this property except in very special cases; I wouldn't rely on it providing useful information in the general case.

URI: *http://xml.org/sax/properties/dom-node*
Datatype: `org.w3c.dom.Node`
Access: Read-only when parsing, read/write when not parsing

Literal (XML) String

This retrieves the literal characters in the XML document that triggered the event in process when this property is used. Like the DOM node feature, I found little use and little support for this property. Don't depend on it, particularly across parsers.

URI: *http://xml.org/sax/properties/xml-string*
Datatype: `java.lang.String`
Access: Read-only when parsing, read-only when not parsing

Index

We'd like to hear your suggestions for improving our indexes. Send email to *index@oreilly.com.*

About the Author

Brett McLaughlin is one of the leading authorities on Java, XML, enterprise applications, and open source software. He works as the Enhydra strategist at Lutris Technologies and is responsible for the direction and strategy for the Enhydra application server. In addition, he is the founder or co-founder of numerous other open source projects, such as JDOM (currently in JSR at Sun), ApacheTurbine (a servlet-based web applications framework), and Enhydra Zeus (an XML data binding framework). He is a committer on OpenEJB, jBoss, and Apache Cocoon as well, placing him in the middle of Java and XML innovation.

In addition to his technology contributions, Brett is a prolific writer; he is the author of *Java & XML, First Edition* (O'Reilly), the moderator of IBM's Java and XML tools and technologies newgroup, *flashline.com*'s biweekly component columnist, and has written dozens of articles for *IBM Developer Works, JavaWorld,* and *oreilly.com.*

Colophon

Our look is the result of reader comments, our own experimentation, and feedback from distribution channels. Distinctive covers complement our distinctive approach to technical topics, breathing personality and life into potentially dry subjects.

The animals on the cover of *Java & XML, Second Edition* are lions (*Panthera leo*). These great cats differ from other solitary felines in that they form family groups, called prides. Prides consist of as many as 30 to 40 lions, most of which are females and their offspring. The lifespan of a lion is approximately 3–4 years. Full grown males can grow up to 10 feet in length; the only cat larger is the tiger. The lion's eye is particularly sensitive to movement, and it can detect the movement of its prey from a great distance. Special receptor cells in the cat's eye give it exceptional night vision.

Lions live in eastern and southern Africa, although some subspecies of the African lion are endangered. The Asiatic lion (*P.l. persica*) once lived throughout India, the Middle East, and Southern Asia. Today, its population has been reduced to approximately 290 animals, which can be found in the Gir Forest National Park in Gujarat, western India. The Barbary and Cape lions are extinct.

Lions are carnivores and prey on large herd animals. They are at the top of the food chain, the apex predator of their environment. The females are the hunters, while the males' role is to protect the pride from other aggressive males. Lions are not as fast as other big cats, such as the cheetah. As a result, they concentrate on heavier, less agile animals, and hunt from ambush by driving prey toward concealed members of the hunting group. They use coordinated, cooperative techniques that enable the group to hunt with more success than an individual could. African lions eat wildebeest, zebra, antelope, gazelle, impala, and giraffe.

Colleen Gorman was the production editor and copyeditor for *Java & XML, Second Edition*. Emily Quill was the proofreader, and Catherine Morris and Jane Ellin provided quality control. John Bickelhaupt wrote the index.

Ellie Volckhausen designed the cover of this book, based on a series design by Edie Freedman. The cover image is a 19th-century engraving from Grosvenor Prints in London. Emma Colby produced the cover layout with QuarkXPress 4.1 using Adobe's ITC Garamond font.

Melanie Wang designed the interior layout, based on a series design by Nancy Priest. The heading font is Bitstream Bodoni, the text font is ITC New Baskerville, and the code font is Constant Willison. Neil Walls and Anne-Marie Vaduva converted the files from Microsoft Word to FrameMaker 5.5.6 using tools created by Mike Sierra. The illustrations that appear in the book were produced by Jessamyn Read and Rob Romano using Macromedia FreeHand 9 and Adobe Photoshop 6.

Whenever possible, our books use a durable and flexible lay-flat binding. If the page count exceeds the lay-flat binding limit, perfect binding is used.